THE
ORIENTAL INSTITUTE
2006–2007
ANNUAL REPORT

Cover and title page illustration: Mirror image of Sennacherib and attendant reliefs. Khorsabad, Iraq. A7368. Sennacherib raises his hand in greeting to his father, Sargon, pictured in a relief not shown. An attendant, thought to be a eunuch, follows. The façade of the throneroom at Khorsabad was 85 m (92 yds) long. It was decorated with monumental carved reliefs showing processions of human figures. The doorways, like many of the other palace portals, were guarded by human-headed winged bulls known as lamassu. Oriental Institute archaeologists excavated the throneroom courtyard in 1928–1929 and were given a lamassu and the reliefs as part of the division of finds from that season. Photo by Sarah Sapperstein

The pages that divide the sections of this year's report feature "Portraits of the Past," photographs of Oriental Institute Museum gallery objects representing human faces across the different cultures and eras of the ancient Near East.

Editor: Gil J. Stein

Production Editor: Sarah Sapperstein

Printed by United Graphics Incorporated, Mattoon, Illinois

The Oriental Institute, Chicago

Copyright 2007 by The University of Chicago. All rights reserved.
Published 2007. Printed in the United States of America.

CONTENTS

INTRODUCTION 5
   INTRODUCTION. *Gil J. Stein* 7
   IN MEMORIAM 11

RESEARCH 13
   PROJECT REPORTS 15
      ARCHAEOLOGY OF ISLAMIC CITIES. *Donald Whitcomb* 15
      ÇADIR HÖYÜK. *Ronald L. Gorny* 18
      CENTER FOR ANCIENT MIDDLE EASTERN LANDSCAPES (CAMEL). *Scott Branting* 33
      CHICAGO ASSYRIAN DICTIONARY (CAD). *Martha T. Roth* 37
      CHICAGO DEMOTIC DICTIONARY (CDD). *François Gaudard and Janet H. Johnson* ... 38
      CHICAGO HITTITE DICTIONARY (CHD) *Theo van den Hout* 41
      DIYALA PROJECT. *Clemens D. Reichel* 43
      THE EPIGRAPHIC SURVEY. *W. Raymond Johnson* 49
      HAMOUKAR. *Clemens D. Reichel* 59
      KERKENES DAĞ PROJECT. *Scott Branting* 68
      MODELING ANCIENT SETTLEMENT SYSTEMS (MASS). *Benjamin Studevent-Hickman* ... 73
      NIPPUR. *McGuire Gibson* 76
      NUBIAN EXPEDITION. *Geoff Emberling and Bruce Williams* 78
      PERSEPOLIS FORTIFICATION ARCHIVE PROJECT. *Matthew W. Stolper* 92
      RELIGION AND POWER: DIVINE KINGSHIP IN ANCIENT MESOPOTAMIA AND BEYOND. *Nicole Brisch* 103
      SYRIAC MANUSCRIPT PROJECT. *Stuart Creason* 107
      ZINCIRLI EXPEDITION. *J. David Schloen and Amir S. Fink* 109
   INDIVIDUAL RESEARCH 115
   RESEARCH SUPPORT 139
      COMPUTER LABORATORY. *John C. Sanders* 139
      ELECTRONIC RESOURCES. *John C. Sanders* 142
      PUBLICATIONS OFFICE. *Thomas G. Urban* 145
      RESEARCH ARCHIVES. *Magnus Widell* 147
      THE TABLET COLLECTION. *Walter Farber* 148

MUSEUM 149
   MUSEUM. *Geoff Emberling* 151
      SPECIAL EXHIBITS. *Emily Teeter* 153
      PUBLICITY. *Emily Teeter* 156
      REGISTRATION. *Helen McDonald* 158
      ARCHIVES. *John A. Larson* 160
      CONSERVATION. *Laura D'Alessandro* 161
      PREP SHOP. *Erik Lindahl* 163
      SUQ. *Denise Browning* 164
      MUSEUM EDUCATION. *Carole Krucoff* 165
      VOLUNTEER PROGRAM. *Catherine Dueñas and Terry Friedman* 182

MEMBERSHIP AND DEVELOPMENT 193
   MEMBERSHIP AND DEVELOPMENT 195
      MEMBERSHIP. *Sarah Sapperstein* 195
      DEVELOPMENT. *Monica Witczak* 200
      HONOR ROLL OF DONORS AND MEMBERS 205

CONTENTS

VISITING COMMITTEE TO THE ORIENTAL INSTITUTE 239

FACULTY AND STAFF OF THE ORIENTAL INSTITUTE 241

INFORMATION 248

INTRODUCTION

Overleaf. Ba Bird Statue. Sandstone. Ballana Cemetery B. Meroitic Phase IIIB–IV (A.D. 225–300). OIM 22487. In later periods of Nubian history, the soul of the deceased was represented in the form of a bird with a human head and feet. These statues stood in niches in pyramid-shaped private tombs, or in offering chapels to the east of the tomb where they were the focus of an offering cult.

INTRODUCTION

Gil J. Stein

The 2006–2007 academic year has seen major developments in virtually every aspect of the Oriental Institute. The scale and scope of the work presented in this *Annual Report* are so broad that I can only call your attention to a few highlights.

Oriental Institute archaeologists have launched two important new field projects. David Schloen has begun what we hope will be a long-term program of excavations at Zincirli, near the Syrian border in southeast Turkey. Zincirli can be identified from inscriptions as ancient Sam'al, one of the most important Neo-Hittite and Neo-Assyrian cities. Zincirli boasts not only extraordinary monumental architecture and carved basalt reliefs, but more importantly provides the rare opportunity to make broad horizontal clearances that we need in order to understand the workings of this important Iron Age center. When compared with the results of Scott Branting's ongoing excavations at Kerkenes on the plateau (also presented in this *Annual Report*), we have the chance to do serious comparative studies of first-millennium urbanization in highland versus lowland Anatolia.

The second new Oriental Institute excavation begun in the past year is Geoff Emberling and Bruce Williams' program of rescue archaeology in Nubia, modern Sudan. Construction of the Merowe Dam along the Fourth Cataract of the Nile will flood a large, and so-far poorly known, area of ancient Nubia. We have only two years to learn as much as possible about this area before its ancient sites disappear beneath the rising waters of the dam reservoir. Our excavations at el-Widay and at Hosh al-Guruf provide a fascinating look at the rural economic foundations of the Kerma state. Most notably, at Hosh al-Guruf, Geoff and Bruce's team has recovered a small rural gold processing center. By tracking the production and exchange of gold — probably the most important export of Nubia — we can begin to understand the economic underpinnings of Kerma, the earliest known powerful indigenous state to emerge in this part of the Nile Valley.

In tandem with our archaeological projects, two new text-based projects have started to make vital contributions to both scholarship and the protection of cultural heritage.

The Syriac Manuscript Project, co-directed by Oriental Institute Research Associates Stuart Creason and Abdul Masih Sa'adi, is scanning and cataloging thousands of images from the Vööbus photographic archive — about 70,000 images of the texts from almost 700 manuscripts in Syriac — a dialect of Aramaic once widely spoken across the Near East. These manuscripts, recorded from twenty-three different monasteries and other locations, cover a time span of almost 1,500 years and provide a priceless record of Syriac Christian culture from Byzantine times up to the late nineteenth century. By making digital scans of the images on the decaying emulsion film of the photographic archive, we will be able to preserve this extraordinary heritage and make it available to both scholars and to modern Syriac-speaking communities around the world.

The Persepolis Fortification Texts are a second priceless archive under grave threat of destruction. Excavated by the Oriental Institute in the 1930s and brought to Chicago on a long-term loan from Iran for purposes of translation and study, the Persepolis texts are a unique, irreplaceable

INTRODUCTION

record of the inner administrative workings of the Persian empire in the time of Darius, ca. 500 B.C. This archive is currently the subject of a lawsuit seeking damages from the state of Iran; if successful, the suit could result in the confiscation, sale, and dispersal of these texts, which have both extraordinary scholarly importance, and the highest value as the cultural heritage of the Iranian people. To counter this threat, Prof. Matt Stolper has successfully organized the Persepolis Fortification Archive Project to make high resolution digital scans of as many of the texts as possible. Matt has been working in partnership with Prof. Bruce Zuckerman and his team from the University of Southern California to apply the most advanced imaging technologies to this important material.

In addition to these new initiatives, ongoing Oriental Institute projects continue to make major contributions to archaeology, philology, and cultural heritage preservation. Clemens Reichel's excavations at Hamoukar in Syria are reshaping our ideas about the roles of warfare, trade, and geography in the origins of ancient Near Eastern cities. In Egypt, under the able direction of Ray Johnson, the Epigraphic Survey is documenting the reliefs at Medinet Habu, while stabilizing and reconstructing the architecture and carvings at Luxor. The Epigraphic Survey has also been instrumental in preserving the site of Luxor through its work with USAID on a large-scale project to lower the water table around the site as a way to protect the fragile sandstone architecture from decay and collapse.

Our three dictionary projects continue their work of generating the fundamental research tools for scholarship on the ancient Near East. The final U/W volume of the Chicago Assyrian Dictionary (CAD) is on the verge of going to press. At the same time, CAD editor-in-chief Martha Roth has taken on major new duties as the new Dean of the Humanities at the University of Chicago. The Demotic Dictionary, under Jan Johnson's able direction, has made major progress with the infusion of new staff and new computer systems. We estimate that the Demotic Dictionary will be completed within five years. Under the co-directorship of Harry Hoffner and Theo van den Hout, the Chicago Hittite Dictionary has now moved into the third floor space formerly occupied by the CAD. By doing so, the entire research team and its indispensable files are finally all in one work area, greatly facilitating the work of this ongoing project.

In parallel with our research programs, the museum has implemented and regularized our new program of presenting two new special exhibits every year. Museum Director Geoff Emberling and Special Exhibits coordinator Emily Teeter have done a wonderful job in planning these exhibits and in turning them into a physical reality. This year's exhibits — Embroidering Identities: A Century of Palestinian Clothing (guest curator Iman Saca) and Daily Life Ornamented: The Medieval Persian City of Rayy (guest curators Tanya Treptow and Donald Whitcomb) have given us all fascinating windows into the material culture of the ancient and modern Near East.

The Oriental Institute has made significant progress in information technology as well. John Sanders played in instrumental role in coordinating with the University to completely redesign the Oriental Institute's Web site, which was successfully launched in February 2007. The new site is beautiful to look at, easily navigated, and a remarkably rich source of information about the ancient Near East. At the same time, under Scott Branting's direction, our CAMEL laboratory continues to grow as one of the world's leading digital archives of maps, aerial photographs, and satellite imagery of the fertile crescent. The CAMEL lab has rapidly become an indispensable resource for virtually all of the archaeologists here at the Institute. Our Research Archives (library) has made great progress in expanding its electronic catalog as a vital research tool, thanks to the efforts of Magnus Widell. Magnus will be leaving Chicago to take up a new position in Assyriology at the University of Liverpool, but he leaves the Research Archives in wonderful shape.

One final noteworthy aspect of information technology at the Oriental Institute is that of publications. For the last few years, the Institute has been committed to the simultaneous publication of our research in both print and electronic form, with the latter freely available to any interested researcher as a downloadable PDF file on our Web site. The many letters we have received from scholars all over the world are a wonderful testimony to the value of this commitment. We are now extending the availability of this resource to include our earlier publications as well. Publications Department editor-in-chief Thomas Urban, working in tandem with Leslie Schramer, has now made an additional forty-six previously published Oriental Institute publications available online. In doing this, our highest priority has been to scan publications on Mesopotamian archaeology and philology, as a way to help our Iraqi colleagues, whose research is greatly hampered by the catastrophic destruction of libraries and archives in Iraq.

In order to insure our continuing ability to carry out our work of exploration and discovery, in this last year we launched the Research Endowment Campaign — a five year initiative aimed at raising three million dollars to double the size of those endowments at the Oriental Institute that specifically support research. We have targeted five areas: Archaeological Fieldwork, Ancient Languages, Technology, Research Archives, and the Museum as key areas of research infrastructure. The campaign is ambitious in the sense that we have made the commitment to build future capacity, while at the same time continuing to raise funds to support our existing projects. Development Director Monica Witczak has been working tirelessly to insure that both areas of fundraising proceed apace. Oriental Institute Executive Director Steve Camp has played a key role in the planning and implementation of this campaign. I especially want to single out for thanks the members of the Oriental Institute's Visiting Committee. These devoted friends and supporters have collectively committed to raise one million of the three million dollars needed for the Research Endowments Campaign. Their gifts to date and pledges have brought us extremely close to fulfilling that part of the campaign at the end of our first year. All of us here at the Oriental Institute deeply appreciate this enthusiasm and support. This brief overview of the past year's work and of the Research Endowments Campaign points the way toward our next steps.

What challenges face the Oriental Institute, and what directions should we follow over the next decade?

I see several areas where we can and must move if we are to maintain our position as one of the world's leading centers of research on the civilizations of the ancient Near East. If we rest on our laurels, we will be left behind. First and foremost — we must rebuild our excavation and fieldwork programs in Israel, Iran, and Iraq. We can do so quickly in Israel, but will obviously have to wait until political conditions in Iraq and Iran improve to the point where we can resume our work in those countries. In the meantime, we will work consistently to maintain ties with scholars in Iraq and Iran while retaining our own expertise in these core research areas.

Our second challenge is that of resources. The Research Endowments Campaign is an important first step toward insuring that we will have the resources we need to develop and carry out important new research throughout the Near East. However, even after the successful conclusion of this five year initiative, we will need to plan carefully and continue to build our own endowment resources much further as the costs of excavations, digital technology, and skilled expertise continue to rise.

A third challenge is that of people. We must develop the next generation of Oriental Institute members and supporters through education programs, outreach, public presentations of Oriental Institute research through the media and our membership program, and through innovative special exhibits in the museum. We must wholeheartedly embrace the expansion of Web-based resources for both teachers and students, and through our publication program.

INTRODUCTION

If we can meet these three challenges successfully, then the Oriental Institute will flourish in the coming decades and will continue to enrich our understanding of ancient civilizations.

The Oriental Institute is a uniquely valuable center for scholarship and it is a precious cultural resource for the general public. The work presented in the pages of this *Annual Report* is a tribute to this talented group of researchers, staff, membership, and supporters.

————————

IN MEMORIAM
Larry Scheff

Presented on Tuesday, May 29, 2007, at Larry Scheff's Memorial Service, held at the Oriental Institute, Breasted Hall, by Terry Friedman and Catherine Dueñas, Volunteer Coordinators.

We are honored to share with you our memories of an exceptional person, a true Renaissance man, Dr. Lawrence Scheff, who sadly lost his valiant battle with cancer in May of this year. Larry, as his colleagues and friends knew him, distinguished himself in his professional life as a dentist and in his volunteer service at both the Oriental Institute and The Field Museum.

It will be hard to imagine a Volunteer Day without Larry Scheff in the second row aisle seat listening attentively to the guest speaker. Larry came to these monthly programs to listen, to learn, and to spend time with old friends in a place he truly held dear to his heart, the Oriental Institute. Despite his frail health in recent years, he continued to remain involved with the Oriental Institute and the Volunteer Program. With great pride and enthusiasm, he continued to bring friends, guests, and out of town visitors to view the collection with him.

Larry's thirst for knowledge and intellectual curiosity never took a back seat. He was an exemplary life-long learner with an inquisitive mind, insightful perspectives, and a thorough mastery of numerous subjects including archaeology, classical music, Shakespeare, and opera to name a few.

Larry began his volunteer service at the Institute in 1987 as a Tuesday afternoon museum docent, and quickly became a Docent Captain. He was an excellent teacher and mentor to not only the Tuesday afternoon docents, but to the entire Volunteer Program as a whole. He enjoyed sharing his wealth of knowledge with everyone. Over the past twenty years, Larry donated scores of interesting articles as well as hundreds of books to our Docent Library's permanent collection.

He was an avid supporter of the program and always on the lookout to recruit new volunteers and to make them feel welcome.

In the mid-nineties, when the museum closed for renovation and climate control, Larry continued to forge ahead with his docent activities through the Outreach Program. With his trusty slide projector in hand, Larry would give amazing slide presentations about the Oriental Institute's collection. He especially enjoyed discussing ancient Egypt. Larry would come alive in front of an audience. He exuded enthusiasm and people would hang on his every word. Larry continued the tradition of sharing his love of learning throughout the remainder of his life.

We would be remiss if we did not share with you some personal memories of Larry,

Larry Scheff

IN MEMORIAM

not in the context of the Oriental Institute, but as a prominent dentist in the Chicago area community. Larry made a visit to the dentist "a pain-free-experience" and there was always an interesting educational component added to the mix with good music and interesting current event topics that peaked his interest.

Dr. Scheff was also an upstanding role model throughout the civil rights movement, extending his practice to people of all backgrounds, and refusing to recommend patients to practitioners who did not serve everyone equally. His professionalism, personal empathy, and social justice ethic resonated throughout not only his practice, but also the Chicago area communities he served.

Larry's enthusiasm to continue learning and teaching never stopped. When he and his wife, Dorothy, moved to the retirement community at Montgomery Place, Larry took charge of the Speakers' Bureau. He would line up fascinating speakers such as professors and scholars from the University of Chicago, the Oriental Institute, and The Field Museum. In this way both he and Dorothy and the Montgomery Place residents were continuing their education and expanding their horizons by hearing great lectures on a wide variety of topics.

Then there was the archaeologist in the dentist, who decided to go on a dig to Ashkelon, Israel, with Professor Larry Stager from Harvard. It was at Ashkelon that Larry discovered his dental training and his dental tools were a valuable asset in getting at brittle and delicate artifacts on the excavation. He would collect and donate old dental tools, which would be used to extract tiny things like the bones of a dog fetus. However, Larry did not limit his dental training to working on people and on dogs. He went on to something even bigger. He would use his dental skills on the dinosaur remains at The Field Museum. He would work on cleaning their teeth and bones with the same care and dexterity that he used on his human patients.

But there was much more to Dr. Lawrence Scheff according to Bob Cantu, Docent Coordinator / Human Resources at The Field Museum. Larry's delightful sense of humor and wit could make the Egyptian exhibition come to life for the visitor, making you feel as though you were there at the time the pyramids were being built. Bob enjoyed when Larry would stop by his office to see him whenever he was at The Field Museum. Even when he was in a wheel chair, Larry would say to Bob: "Don't worry I'll be back when I get better." This was the beauty of Larry; he was an eternal optimist with a positive attitude about everything.

These recent years have not always been easy for Dorothy and Larry. Despite many health set backs, they never took "NO" for an answer. Larry was a fighter until the end. He would often say, "I'm not giving up. I'm coming back to the Oriental Institute and The Field Museum to give tours as long as I can." And he did! We will always remember Larry as a dynamic docent with an ironclad will to survive and a heart of pure gold.

RESEARCH

Overleaf. Persian Human-headed Bull. Limestone, restored. Persepolis, Iran. Achaemenid period. Reign of Xerxes (486–465 B.C.). OIM A24066. The members of the Persepolis Expedition discovered fragments of stone capitals topped by pairs of composite creatures that combine features of both men and bulls. The capitals originally supported the roof beams of the Tripylon Hall, which rested on the backs of the human-headed bulls. Photo by Sarah Sapperstein

PROJECT REPORTS

ARCHAEOLOGY OF ISLAMIC CITIES

Donald Whitcomb

As mentioned in last year's *Annual Report*, research on the archaeology of Islamic cities at the Oriental Institute began with the subject of Sasanian and Islamic cities in Iran. While active fieldwork in Iran continues to be postponed, the author was able to participate in the Siraf Congress and revisit that port site (see *News & Notes,* Fall 2004, #183).

Rayy

The discussion of Islamic cities in last year's *Annual Report* concluded with some notes on the medieval city of Rayy, also known as Rhages in ancient times and the predecessor of modern Tehran. There is a connection to the Oriental Institute in the archaeologist Erich Schmidt, who before he excavated Persepolis, worked for Breasted at Alishar Höyük in Turkey. By 1932 he had established his own project in Iran on the fertile plain south of Tehran. This was the Rayy expedition, which included the prehistoric site of Cheshmeh Ali and Sasanian palaces with their great stucco decorations. My student, Tanya Treptow, and I went to Philadelphia to see their objects from Rayy, but in the end decided to rely on the records and many potsherds in the Oriental Institute collections for an exhibition entitled Daily Life Ornamented (May 14–October 14, 2007). While the exhibit is intended to convey a broad sense of Islamic cultural history and the process of archaeology, the specific urban history of Rayy was the main subject.

The tenth-century geographer Muqaddasi epitomized the city of Rayy as one of the glories of Islam and a great metropolis (390). He proceeds to give details on the nature of the population and structure of the city. Thus he states "… the markets are spacious, the hostels attractive, the baths good … and further that there is a castle and an inner city, [as well as] suburbs with the markets" (391). This description fits the expected model for medieval Persian cities which were often divided into a citadel, and inner city, and suburbs. Further as he describes Rayy, mature and prosperous cities tended to find migration of urban functions into the suburbs (not unlike the modern phenomenon of American cities).

The urban focus of the Islamic city continued to be the Congregational (or Friday) mosque. This structure was located in the inner or oldest part of the city and may be that built by al-Mansur and completed in A.D. 775, where no doubt the future caliph Harun al-Rashid worshipped as a youth. Muqaddasi adds an interesting detail, stating that "the watermelon building is beside the mosque" and comments on "the amazing courtyard of the water melon" (391). In Arabic the names *maidan*

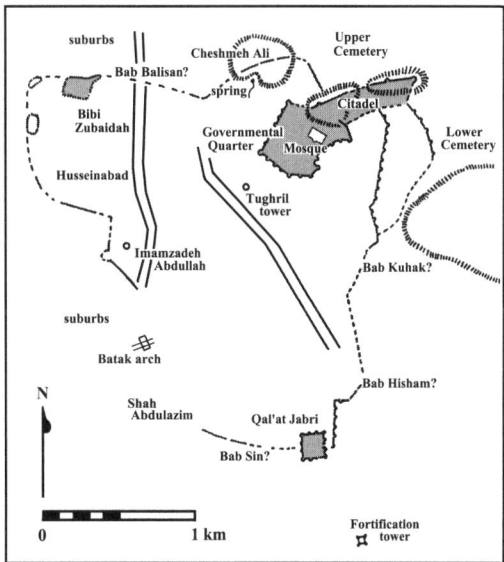

Figure 1. Plan of Rayy (after Kleiss, W. Qal'eh Gabri, Naqarah Khaneh, und Bordj-e Yazid bei Reyy, Archäologische Mitteilungen aus Iran 15 (1982), fig. 2)

ARCHAEOLOGY OF ISLAMIC CITIES

Figure 2. Molded ware juglet from the Rayy excavations (OIM 115148)

al-Batikh and *dar al-Batikh* may have been nicknames (*laqabs*?) and not a central produce market. There are interesting parallels from other early Islamic cities: the *dar al-imara* on the *qibla* side of the great mosque in Damascus was named the Dar al-Khayl, the "house of horses" (stables); likewise, next to the mosque of Ramla was the Dar al-Sabbaghin, the "house of dyers," a profession of noxious smoke and odors. No doubt there were other examples which may bear references to colors or decorative elements for administrative centers.

Another feature of Rayy which attracted Muqaddasi's attention was the library. Here he claims to have examined a manuscript of al-Balkhi, presumably the now-lost world geography which formed the basis of the school followed by Istakhri, Ibn Hauqal, and indeed Muqaddasi himself. Apparently this was but one of its "remarkable books" and would later be used by the philosopher Ibn Sina (known as Avicenna in the West). The library was in the Rudha quarter, near the Surkani canal, and "… in a caravanserai" (391). This may be another clue to one of the myriad uses for this architectural form and a caution to archaeologists when interpreting the discovery of such buildings. One may further imagine the library set among other buildings in a garden area, such as one finds depicted on molded juglets from the Rayy collection (fig. 2).

We know from preliminary reports that Schmidt found the Congregational mosque in the excavations of the inner city. He also excavated in the suburbs now known as Huseinabad, as reported by Keall who examined the excavation records at the Oriental Institute. More recently there have been renewed excavations by Fazeli, the present director of ICAR. What is clear from reading Muqaddasi, and indeed other geographers and historians, is that they may inspire archaeologists with concepts and interpretations and lead to definitive publications of this great city. Appreciation of medieval Iranian culture may be facilitated by these archaeological materials, just as the humble (and often beautiful) potsherds in the Oriental Institute Museum reveal details of lives within Islamic cities.

Baalbek

"A farsakh from Istakhr is the theater of Sulayman, to which one ascends by handsome stairs cut in the rock. Here are black pillars, and statues in niches, and remarkable constructions like other theaters of al-Sham …. When a man sits in this stadium, the villages and the farms are all before him, as far as the eye can see" (Muqaddasi 444).

Muqaddasi's visit to Persepolis seems to have sparked a nostalgia, a memory of "other theaters of al-Sham (greater

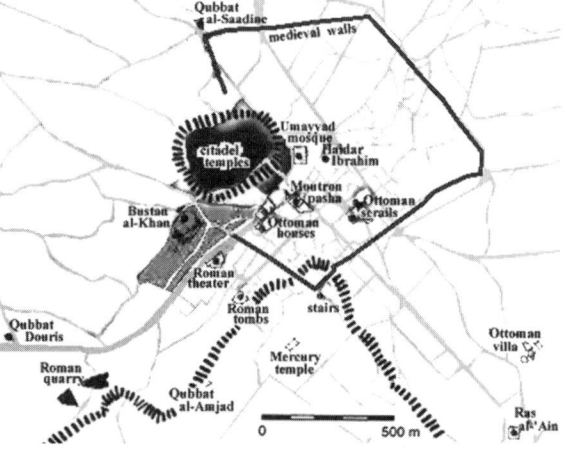

Figure 3. Plan of Baalbek (after Lebanonatlas.com/sriArcheological/map)

Syria)," which was his homeland. In his mind, he would sit amidst the great ruins of Solomon and look out on the beauty of vast villages and farmlands. Muqaddasi mentions Baalbek as "... an ancient city of Sulayman ibn Da'ud, with remarkable ruins" (160). This year I was able to visit for the first time the great monuments of Baalbek in the Biqa' Valley of Lebanon with my student, Rana Mikati, as my cicerone (as recounted in *News & Notes*, Fall 2006, #191). These ruins have completely changed their character since the Crusades (and after al-Muqaddasi's time). The great hill of classical temples was enclosed in medieval fortifications, not unlike Crusader castles, in the early twelfth century. Saladin appointed his father, Najm al-din Ayyub, its governor and inaugurated a Middle Islamic prosperity, reflected by new archaeological surveys of the Baalbek region.

The archaeology of Baalbek demonstrates a continuing prosperity during the early Islamic period when it had a mint of regional importance (as the excavations in Beirut are testifying). The archaeological remains have been investigated by German archaeologists, included Friedrich Sarre who in 1898 may have been the first Islamicist included in a classical excavation; renewed research by the Deutsches Archäologisches Institut presents sophisticated reconstructions as well as a welcome interest in the Ottoman remains. Unlike the city of Rayy, Baalbek does not seem to have hit an apogee during the Abbasid period and had to endure the violence of the Crusades. Baalbek was renewed under the Zangids and Ayyubids with fortification of the classical buildings, as mentioned above, and walling of the lower town. This prosperity of the twelfth and thirteenth centuries is, somewhat ironically, exactly contemporary with the wonderful artifacts displayed in the Rayy exhibition at the Oriental Institute Museum.

The later encrustation of medieval facade, towers, and walls recalls later occupations at the Temple of Bel in Palmyra (the medieval Tadmor). Before these fortifications, the temple was almost certainly the *qasr* mentioned by al-Muqaddasi and said to have been built by Sulayman ibn Da'ud. Indeed the classical remains in Amman, Jordan, were yet another example of "... a stadium of Sulayman" (Muqaddasi 175). Some years after al-Muqaddasi, the great geographer al-Yaqut commented that "when people wondered at buildings and did not know who erected them, they always attributed them to Solomon and the Jinns ...." This cynicism was anticipated by the Arabian geographer al-Hamdani, a contemporary of Muqaddasi, who states, "Just as the Arabs ascribe all ancient [remains] to 'Ad, so do they attribute all colossal buildings to Solomon" (135).

The wonders of antiquity were only curiosities and the geographer al-Muqaddasi was clearly not an archaeologist; rather his interests were focused on contemporary people and products, and above all, the locational structures of their settlements, particularly the contemporary cities.

Happily his account is chronologically situated between the glories of the Abbasid caliphate (he notes the decline of the vast capital of Samarra in Iraq) and the revivals from the twelfth century onwards. For Islamic archaeologists this is a fortunate guide to the crucial understanding of urbanism and indeed settlement history in the Middle East. Comparison of Rayy and Baalbek is more than intriguing, beyond the common references in Muqaddasi. The search for patterns of cultural development is fundamental to the advance in understanding of medieval Islamic civilization pursued through the under-utilized evidence of archaeology.

Figure 4. A glazed sherd of the twelfth/thirteenth century from the Rayy excavations, similar to those recovered from Baalbek. See Verena Daiber, "Islamic Fine Wares from Baalbek," BAAL *7 (2003): 135–38.*

ÇADIR HÖYÜK
Ronald L. Gorny

Introduction

The 2006 season at Çadır Höyük continued to illuminate the story of this important mound near the village of Peyniryemez in Yozgat Province, central Turkey (fig. 1). A staff of sixteen individuals worked in four different areas of the site and helped bring to light important materials from Çadır's various periods of occupation.[1] We were ably served in our efforts by our representative from the Turkish Department of Culture and Tourism, Mr. Mehmet Doğan and we are indebted to him for his many contributions.

A success of some note involved the beginnings of a new depot. The small converted building we have been using as a depot has become totally insufficient for the burgeoning amount of cultural materials excavated at Çadır Höyük. The new 18 × 6 m, two-story building will be large enough to hold all the materials excavated in recent years, plus whatever we uncover for years to come. It also features lab space for analyzing materials, as well as work rooms and a comfortable porch overlooking the excavation house complex (figs. 2–3). Other projects are also in the works, giving the Çadır team even more flexibility in dealing with the many aspects of excavation. We take heart in this because, as the excavation complex continues to expand, the need for documenting and preserving the splendid history of this critical mound increases dramatically.[2] The new depot will provide added dividends for everyone interested in the ancient history of central Anatolia.

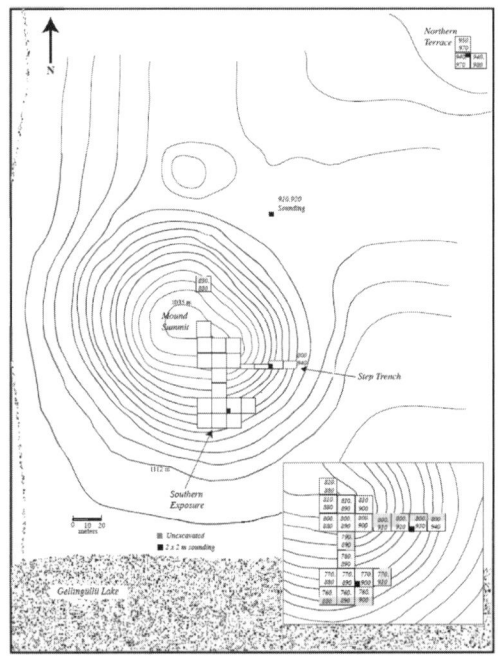

Figure 1. Topographic map of Çadır Höyük

Another piece of good news came to us over the winter. The Turkish National Railroad had been considering building a spur line past our village. The spur line would have run directly between the mound (Zippalanda) and Çaltepe to the south (Mt. Daha), perhaps destroying important evidence of the sites' histories. Fortunately, after several letters and discussions, the railroad

Figure 2. Clearing a place for the new depot

Figure 3. Preparations for the new depot

was convinced not to lay its new line through the valley, and whatever materials lie in the valley remain untouched and await excavation in future years.

In terms of excavation, our goals for the 2006 season included the following: 1) further exposure of the wide Byzantine settlement on the terrace, 2) further exposure of the Iron Age wall overlying the Hittite Empire period monumental gate, 3) further exposure of the "Dark Age" level and the preceding Hittite level on the South Slope, 4) clarification of the settlement sequence on the complicated East Slope, and 5) mapping of the structures on top of nearby Çaltepe. Each of these goals was met and progress was made that will ultimately bear fruit in coming seasons. Details of the 2006 season follow below.

Area 1 (The East Trench)

Work continued in the East Trench defining both the vertical cultural sequence and exploring horizontally the second millennium levels (fig. 4). Current excavations are enhancing our understanding of the areas explored during the previous two seasons, including the Old Hittite exposure in square 800.920, as well as a Hittite Empire period wall in square 800.910. Several significant adjustments to the chronology should be noted in the comments below.

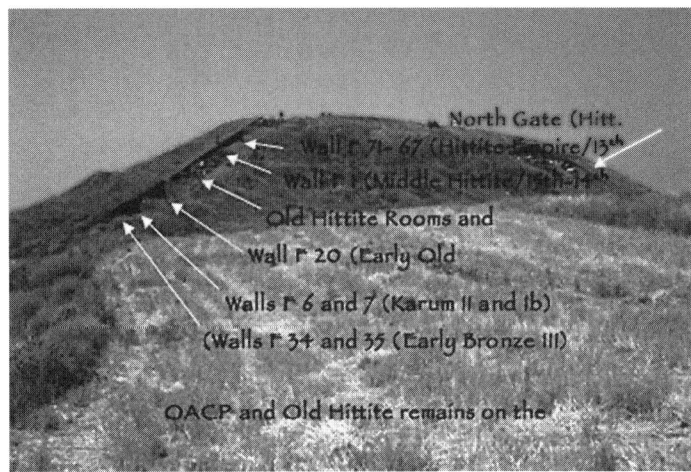

Figure 4. Second-millennium sequence in East Trench

Work in the East Trench progressed along several areas of the slope and touched on materials from the Early Karum period through the end of the Hittite Empire and into the transitional "Dark Age" period. One phase of the work was undertaken in an area we believe to be a courtyard in the Old Hittite manifestation of the Stormgod's temple. This is an area in square 800.920 that had revealed two contiguous rooms in 2005, one of which contained pit F 41 (Gorny 2006a: 17; 2006b: 49, fig. 7). A variety of interesting materials were found inside, but the pit was left unfinished due to a lack of time. Our investigation continued there in 2006, but provided no additional small finds. Pottery analyses, however, indicated that the two rooms date from the Early Old Hittite period and seem to be chronologically contemporary with wall F 20, though the rooms are stratigraphically later. The precise architectural relationship between wall F 20 and the two rooms has not yet been firmly established and was the focus of a project designed to evaluate that relationship.

That project took place below the two rooms, but on top of the area where we presumed the superstructure of wall F 20 to have been located. Wall 20 has been a puzzle of sorts since its discovery in 2001 (Gorny et al. 2002: 110–11, fig 3). What we found in the initial excavation of wall F 20 was a 1.35 m wide structure situated directly above the sliced off mudbrick superstructure of wall F 6. Although the stones that made up the wall were larger than those of any of the other walls we found on the slope, it still seemed an oddly small wall for the citadel, especially considering the 6 m width of Kārum Ib period wall F 6 (1850–1700) that preceded it. We considered the possibility that F 20 represented a newer and poorer settlement. The apparent importance of

Figure 5. Overview of second-millennium levels in East Trench

the site as seen in the archaeological remains, however, casts doubt on this theory. As we suspected, new excavations in 2006 located what appears to be the extant portion of a large mudbrick structure and suggests that wall F 20 was, indeed, just the exterior foundation of a larger undiscovered casemate wall with its interior side presumably set somewhat higher up on the slope, just beneath the two rooms of the early Old Hittite period. Wall F 20 itself rested on approximately 1.5 m of extant mudbrick from the F 6 casemate wall which was also constructed on the east slope of the mound.

We had already determined that wall F 20 had been destroyed in a conflagration, most likely at the end of the Kārum Ia or Old Hittite period (1700–1500 B.C.). A question, however, remained to be explored. If F 20 represented only the front facing of a much larger structure, had the entire wall been destroyed or could a portion of the wall have been left standing? It now appears from the sloping line of the section that while the front part of the superstructure burned and collapsed, a portion of the interior section remained intact. This theory accounts for the large amount of burned mudbrick we dug through in 1994, as well as the massive mudbrick structure becoming evident in squares 800.920 and 800.910.[3]

After the destruction of wall F 20 and the two rooms, their remains were leveled to accommodate the construction of wall F 1 directly above the nearly 2 m of extant remains from Wall F 20 (fig. 5). This Middle Hittite wall was built immediately after the destruction of the Old Hittite settlement, presumably around 1500 B.C. If the ^{14}C sample from the base of wall F 20 (dated to ca. 1730 B.C.) is an indicator of the structure's date of construction, we could surmise that this predecessor to the Middle Hittite wall was in use for about 230 years. Using those dates as an anchor, it seems reasonable to assume that wall F 1 would have continued to exist until a Hittite Empire period wall was built still higher on the mound in squares 800.920 and 800.910, probably around 1350 B.C.

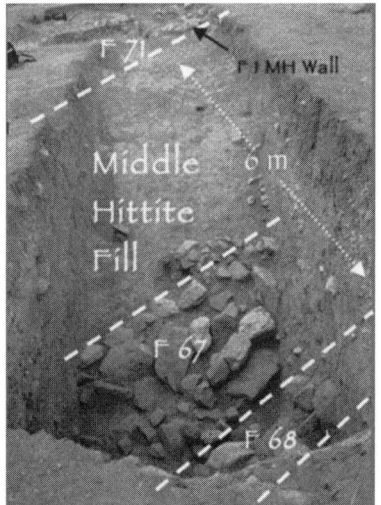

Figure 6. Walls F 67 and F 71, interior and exterior facing walls of the Hittite Empire period citadel wall

The protective function of wall F 1 was not readily apparent to us early on, once again because it appeared to be a single small wall. In 2006, however, it became clear that wall F 1 was simply the exterior face of another casemate wall, this one belonging to the Middle Hittite period. This frontal casing is 1.20 m thick, which seems to be close to a standard width for the casemate walls of the second millennium.[4] The interior section of this Middle Hittite casemate wall remains buried under the later Hittite Empire period wall, but we can postulate from analogy to the other walls that it too must have been at least 6 m in width.

When we initiated work in square 800.920 during the 2005 season, the narrowness of the trench made the interpretation of its contents difficult. Most of the trench was composed of earthen fill which conveyed a sense that we had come down on what was probably the core of a large casemate wall foundation. The extent of the wall, however, was hard to determine. The area was better defined in 2006 and consequently shown to be part of a larger complex that appeared to be focused on Çaltepe across the valley (fig. 6). It's now apparent that we are in the middle of another 6 m wide wall of casemate rubble-filled construction with a 1.20 m interior wall foundation (F 67) and a 1.20 m exterior wall foundation (F 71). The core of the casemate is filled with the rubbly brown fill we observed in 2005 and was topped by mudbricks. Ceramics from the fill of this level compare well with ceramic materials from both Boğazköy and Kuşaklı - Sarissa and appear to be produced in the early part of the Hittite Empire period or what is now referred to as the Middle Hittite period (ca. 1500–1350 B.C.; see Shoop 2006: 215). Among the types of pottery found in the fill were examples of Goldglimmer ware, Red Lustrous wheel-made ware, platters, a trough-shaped sieved-pitcher, and other pieces consistent with the Middle Hittite period level defined by F 1 in 800.920 (fig. 7). This all suggests that the Hittite Empire period wall was build right after the destruction of its Middle Hittite predecessor and made use of the abundantly available remains from the Middle Hittite structure in the empire period wall's construction.

Figure 7. Goldglimmer ware vessel (MH) from 800.910

We can also see that once the Hittite Empire period citadel wall was built, it was immediately abutted in the southeast corner of the trench by a slightly higher and parallel wall foundation (F 68) that served as the base of a building that probably stood taller than the citadel wall itself. In this case, the citadel wall would have served as a retaining wall for the taller building. Wall F 68 is bisected in the corner of the trench by a perpendicular wall (F 69) which separates an internal building with a thick succession of plaster floors (F 72) from what may have been an unpaved exterior courtyard. Surfaces on both sides of this wall can be seen lipping up to the bisecting wall. The building would have been at least two stories high, and depending on how it was constructed, may have been as high as three stories. The building and court would appear to be oriented toward Çaltepe (Mt. Daha) and are presumed to be part of the Hittite Empire period temple complex.[5]

Settlement on the East Slope did not end with the fall of the Hittite empire, but continued through several more periods of occupation. A still higher wall observed in the west section probably dates to the Iron Age and would be contemporary with walls observed on both the north and south slopes. In addition, another wall, resting just above the Iron Age wall, has the appearance of a Hellenistic wall. Both underlie the three periods of Byzantine settlement. We will need further excavation, however, in order to confirm these chronological assignments, though they fit well in terms of our historical understanding of the region's history.

With our new understanding of building developments in the East Trench, we are able to propose a solid "second-millennium" sequence on the East Slope that runs (with approximate dates) as follows:

ÇADIR HÖYÜK

LB I	Hittite empire	F 71 and F 67 (800.910)	citadel casemate wall	1350–1185 B.C.
LB IIa	Middle Hittite	F 1 (800.920)	citadel casemate wall	1500–1350 B.C.
LB IIb	Old Hittite	Rooms 1 and 2	2 rooms + pit (temple?)	1600–1500 B.C.
MB Ia	Kārum Ia	F 20 (800.930)	citadel casemate wall	1730–1600 B.C.
MB Ib	Kārum Ib	F 6 (800.930)	citadel casemate wall	1850–1730 B.C.
MB II	Kārum II	F 7, F 40 (800.940)	citadel "gateway" system	2100–1850 B.C.
EB III	Kārum IV–III	F 34–35	citadel wall	2500–2100 B.C.

Of further note is the fact that the Kārum period is becoming increasingly important in the overall development of settlement on the mound and this story will almost certainly be played out in greater detail during the proposed excavation of the terrace where we know from soundings that a significant Middle Bronze Age settlement once existed. Whether it takes the form of a *kārum* or a *wabartum* remains to be seen. What appears certain is that there was a significant pre-Hittite settlement at Çadır Höyük and that this settlement will greatly influence our understanding of the long-term development of culture on the central Anatolian plateau.

Area 2 (The Northeast Terrace)

Efforts to understand the Byzantine settlement sequence continued on the Northeast terrace with the opening of two new 10 × 10 m squares, 930.970 and 930.980. The efforts in these squares once again produced evidence of a three phase Byzantine occupation. As in previous exposures, the last phase is rather weak and decrepit in nature. The middle phase once again makes use of the earliest phase 1 walls while adding new partition walls in various places. The first or earliest phase is again the best built of the three phases.

Figure 8. Large stone piller base (left) reused in Byzantine construction

The continued exposure of the settlement area revealed interesting new aspects of the Byzantine town. One of these was a large column base, apparently fitted for a square wooden pillar (fig. 8), that had been situated in a street or passage. This seems to be a secondary placement of a Hittite era pillar base and is set across from a building with multiple entrances that was originally constructed in phase 1 but reused with one entrance blocked in phase 2. Other examples of blocks reused in the second phase construction are readily apparent, including one with multiple depressions that may have come from the Hittite monumental gate just up the slope (fig. 9).

The newly excavated area includes a building with rooms that appear to have been used for storage. A larger original room was subdivided into three small rooms to create separate storage units. Multiple pieces of metal were found in one of the store rooms, including an adz/scraper, a hook that may have been used for pulling rocks, and a broken pick. My assumption is that these tools were used for building purposes and not for agricultural production. Taken together, it appears that these tools were used to work with the stone building materials during the process of rebuilding the site in phase 2, and then discarded. We must also take into account, however, two in situ ovens of unknown function that occupy a corner of the excavation area. The two ovens were situated curiously at the end of the street where the pillar base had been found (fig. 10). Their relationship to the overall function of the area will be investigated in coming seasons. A final feature of note is what seems to be a platform construction which is facing the mound itself, just outside of the storerooms.

Figure 9. Stone with multiple depressions reused in Byzantine second phase

In general, we have good stratigraphic data for the Byzantine period remains, though the past season provided only a few new hints at the site's chronology. The best was a single coin impressed with the image of Justin II (ca. 520–578) and his wife Sophia (fig. 11a–b). Justin II was the nephew of Justinian I and ruled as Eastern Roman emperor after Justinian (565–578). Sophia was the niece of the late empress Theodora, and therefore a member of the Justinian dynasty. This coin, which was found in the middle level of the terrace, probably originated in Çadır's earliest sixth-century level. This is significant in that it strengthens the argument for an early date that was first based on the ceramic inventory collected in the original Çadır survey (Gorny et al. 1995: 72). The coin, which is one of some sixteen coins being

Figure 10. Two ovens from Byzantine level

a

b

Figure 11a–b. Byzantine coin from Çadır Höyük's earliest Byzantine level showing Justin II (ca. 520–578) and his wife Sophia

used for dating purposes, is consistent with our overall understanding of the Byzantine occupation (Gorny 2004).[6]

Our results make it interesting to think of how future excavations on the terrace may play out. Our goal on the terrace remains to reach the second-millennium levels here as soon as possible, but we already know from a sounding done in the 2001 and 2002 seasons (Gorny 2006: 35) that there are Iron Age remains preceding the Hittite and Middle Bronze levels. One has to wonder how much of the Iron Age sequence will present itself in that locale and how widely spread the Iron Age settlement was. Questions concerning the presence of a *kārum* or *wabartum* also come into play in this area. There is clearly much to learn about this intriguing site.

Area 3 (The Lower South Exposure)

Test excavations in the Lower South Trench brought together the efforts of several years in a fitting way. Previous work had revealed a rather sophisticated settlement in this area complete with a circuit wall (F 22) and gated entryway. We now surmise that this wall once continued around the nascent mound and was even documented in the lower portion of square 800.940 during the 1994 excavations as wall F 5 (Gorny et al. 1995: 75, fig. 16a). The circuit wall, however, had been cut on both its eastern and western extent (Gorny et al. 1999: 151, fig. 8). Work in 2004 uncovered part of the reason for the disappearance of the wall on the east side of the trench. Investigations that year provided evidence that the "enclosure wall" had been severed by the mound's Early Bronze inhabitants in the process of constructing their own dwellings on the spot.

Efforts during the 2006 season continued to address the issue of the "enclosure wall" and ultimately uncovered what appears to be the continuation of the wall's foundation (F 29). This discovery supports the idea that there is a wide declivity between the two wall segments in which at least two sublevels of buildings are nestled inside the cut. The earlier of the two, a transitional Late Chalcolithic–Early Bronze Age structure that supersedes the wall is topped by what we presume to be a later Early Bronze level construction.

The earlier transitional period house is the better preserved of the two structures and was partially excavated in 2004. It was this construction that originally cut through the "enclosure wall," an indication that the "enclosure wall" (ca. 3600–3200) had gone out of use at that time and that the houses nested in that cut were inaugurating a new era. The transitional house had two rooms that were composed of mudbrick wall foundations and earthen floors and contained what appears to be a plaster covered bench (fig. 12). The eastern wall of the dwelling seems to have been built against the remains of the "enclosure" wall, perhaps using it for support. The structure is only partially exposed and the southern half appears to have been lost to erosional processes taking place along the south slope. Considering the date of the "enclosure wall and associated ruins, the

Figure 12. Foundations of Transitional Chalcolithic–Early Bronze I House, ca. 3000 B.C.

stratigraphically later house must date to the very late fourth or very early third millennium. That places it around the 3200 B.C. date of other nearby "Late Chalcolithic" remains.[7]

The higher and later of the two structures is much smaller than the structure that preceded it and less well preserved. Excavation provided only the barest evidence of a date. Some organic remains were identified, but the house had been burned and collapsed inward. The remarkable scarcity of cultural remains in the buildings meant that dating is mostly circumstantial and based primarily on the relative relationship of the house to nearby remains with established dates (cf. Gorny et al. 2002: 127; see table 2). An important ceramic indicator, however, is the presence of Incised-Punctated pottery in this later structure. The ware is found commonly in the Oriental Institute excavations at nearby Alişar Höyük and has been established as the primary indicator of the Early Bronze I period in this area of central Anatolia. It would be worth noting that various Early Bronze Age pithos burials found in 1994, 1998, and 2000 (Gorny et al. 1999: 152–03, 165, figs 5, 7; 2002: 115), as well as the courtyard containing multiple fire pits found in 1998 (Gorny et al. 1999: 156) must have been connected with this dwelling. An oven (F 50) found in 2001 had been cut into the "burned house" of 770.900 and was "packed" with Incised-Punctuated ware (Gorny et al. 2002, fig. 7), apparently linking it to the later of the two houses which also produced pieces of Incised-Punctated ware. The structure, which appears to be too small for a dwelling, may have served as a storage facility that was associated with the fire pits and ovens in the courtyard. The organic materials found within its walls may bear witness to that function.

Finally, I would add that the location of the earliest settlement at Çadır Höyük is important in understanding the mound's physical development. The original settlement formed along a limestone ridge overlooking the Eğri Su river basin. Because of the ridge and the river basin, expansion could not proceed in that direction so it is not surprising that evidence of the Chalcolithic and Early Bronze periods indicate that, in the earliest stages of the mound's expansion, settlement was already climbing the natural slope towards the northeast. The destruction of structures located higher up the slope accounts, in part, for the thin layers of soil that flowed down the slope, covering both the Chalcolithic and Early Bronze Age constructions. This phenomenon preserved the early materials near the surface of the south slope while, at the same time, encouraging the expansion of the settlement back towards the northeast where the lower terrace began to take shape.

Area 4 (The Citadel)

No excavations were undertaken on the citadel proper in 2006 as we prepared to remove and delve beneath the Byzantine building level.

Area 5 (The Upper South Slope)

Excavations in Area 5 have gained in significance as the trench expands. Originally a 5 m wide test trench (Gorny et al. 2002: 120), the Upper South Slope trench has been expanded to become a 10 × 20 m area encompassing everything from Early Bronze II to the Byzantine period. Current work has been focused on the upper 10 × 10 m portion of the trench and especially the area where we are tracing the transition from the Hittite Empire period to the Iron Age, including the enigmatic "Dark Age" (Gorny 2006: 15–16).

The western 5 × 10 m half of the trench has already been taken down to the Early Iron Age/ Hittite Empire period transition. The goal for the 2006 season was to bring the whole eastern side of the trench down into phase with the western half. To that end we expended a good amount of time and energy without actually completing our goal. We began the season with three Late Iron Age steps stretching down the south slope. This was a complicated task in that the whole unit

Figure 13. Upper South Trench stratigraphy

displayed a myriad of stratified floors and walls that take on a simple beauty in the section (fig. 13), but which resulted in a very complex process of excavation, along with an equally challenging process of interpretation

The highest step on the western side of the trench produced a series of surfaces with interesting bits of architecture but was limited by both the size of the trench and the slope of the mound. Of particular note is a partial room from the Late Iron Age that was framed by perpendicular walls and a hearth. Several lapis lazuli(?) beads found in the area of the hearth may be indicators of long-distance trade during the Iron Age. Below the level of the hearth was discovered a sequence of floors with deposits of what appear to be an in situ slab of wood. Around it were three (of a possible four?) postholes (fig. 14). This seems to have been some sort of installation, perhaps religious in character.

East of the installation was a large pit (L. 88) that had been dug through the floor and which had cut an associated mudbrick wall (F 63). The pit was presumably for the disposition of ash, a large quantity of which was found

Figure 14. Installation near Phrygian "gate" on Upper South Slope

inside it. The date and reason for ash deposit is unclear. In this light, however, it may be of some significance that it is directly above the ash pits from the second millennium and one has to wonder if any connection or continuity of function is involved. In any case, the wall that this oblong pit was cut into is a substantial stone wall with an associated pavement (F 73). The function of the assemblage is unclear, but I have conjectured that we are looking at the eastern side of a gate (fig. 15). If we take into account the gate found in the western half of the trench in 2001 (cf. Gorny 2006: 15), we might understand a continuity of function in this area with this structure being an earlier precursor to the gate found in 2001.

Figure 15. Remains of Late Iron Age "gate" on Upper South Slope

The above noted installation sat near to or inside this "gate." By way of explanation, the wood slab may have once served as the base for a statue of some deity that had graced the gate's entryway, perhaps with some sort of covering stretching between the poles to cover or shield the statue. This would not be unlike the Kubaba/Kybele statue from the same Late Iron Age period that stood at the entry to the Phrygian city at Boğazköy (Bittel 1970: 150–54).

The most intriguing project in this area took place in a sounding opened beneath the building found in 2005 that we speculated had something to do with a weaving or dying industry. This idea was based on the large number of spindle whorls associated with several plaster surfaces situated in close proximity to the building (Gorny 2006: 15–16). In 2006 we opened a small 2 × 5 m test trench across the front of the square that was intended to give us a chance to examine the second millennium–Early Iron Age transition more closely while we brought the rest of the square down into phase with the level of the "weaving" building. This square had been disturbed on the west side by a pit from the Middle Iron Age and in the middle by the remains of the tumulus we excavated in 2001. The remains of these intrusions were cleared until we had an undisturbed view of the soil below.

The pottery from the Early Iron Age building found in 2005 was unique. It looked very Hittite in general, but with various new Iron Age elements. Decoration began to appear in the form of painted vessels with crosshatching, loops, and parallel lines that anticipate the coming Middle Iron Age decoration. Traditional Hittite forms appear alongside newer Iron Age forms. Once we hit the Hittite level in 2006, however, the pottery corpus became very Hittite in its composition, leaving no doubt as to which level we were excavating.

Architecturally, the most interesting discovery in this sounding was the presence of two side-by-side "pits" that are seen in section to contain many lenses of ash, charcoal, and bone (fig. 16). To call these features pits may not be totally correct as there is a clear wall stub between the two declivities, perhaps indicating that the "pits" are really only the fill of a room, though the many clear layers of charcoal and ash seem to suggest otherwise. In addition, I would note that all the buildings and wall stubs in this area are oriented directly towards Çaltepe, as are the side-by-side pits. Associated with these pits is a mudbrick construction of some sort. While the "pits" have yet to be fully excavated, they must be somehow connected with the cult of the storm-god and may contain remnants of the sacrificial activities connected with the cult, perhaps for the deposition of sacrificial trash within a ritual purity context. Not surprisingly, the most interesting item discovered in the clearing of these pits was the lower right leg of what is presumed to be a lion figurine. The fur of the lion is indicated by triangular impressions as is common in other Hittite animal figures. The head of what seems to be a separate "lioness" was found in the same deposit, along with numerous spindle whorls.

As Hittite laws §50–51 show, the priests and weavers of Zippalanda were given a special dispensation by the Hittite king and are presumably part of this whole cultic equation. It is hoped that these pits will provide further evidence of the two occupations' interconnectedness. I also suspect that once we make further progress, it will become clear that the Iron Age building exhibits a continu-

Figure 16. Hittite period "pits" in section. Early Iron Age building to top and right

ity of function with the "pits" just below that we will be able to trace back to, at least, the early second millennium.

Taking into account this "Dark Age" transitional level, we can now propose an Iron Age sequence for Çadır Höyük that segues from the second millennium into the first with a sequence that tentatively runs as follows:

Late Iron Age	ca. 500–300 B.C.
Middle Iron Age	ca. 800–500 B.C.
Early Iron Age	ca. 1100–800 B.C.
"Dark Age"	ca. 1185–1100 B.C.

It should be noted that the same Iron Age sequence, though less well documented, is evident on the mound's North Slope, an indication that the settlements of each period covered the entire upper mound. In addition, just like in the East Trench, a very strong representative sample of Early Bronze III, Early Bronze II, and Chalcolithic sherds were found and they make it abundantly clear that the settlement in those periods also climbed the slopes at Çadır in their own day. Theses earlier remains are almost certainly situated just beneath us, soon to make their own debut.

Area 6 (The North Slope)

A limited operation was performed on the North Slope in 2006 and produced some interesting results. It continues to be clear that the area holds evidence that will illuminate the history of several periods, but especially that of the Hittite period when the monumental gateway was presumably built.

We noted in our report on the 2005 season that a (presumably Late) Iron Age wall had been uncovered high on the hill that seemed to block the entry of the original second-millennium Hittite gate (Gorny et al. 2006: 38–39, fig. 15). That gate had been destroyed and burned at the end of the Hittite Empire period (ca. 1185 B.C.). The Iron Age wall apparently butted up to large surviving stones of the gateway's eastern superstructure that have since fallen down the slope.

In 2006 we picked up where we left off in 2005 and began to clear what we assumed would be the western extent of wall F 5. This operation was successfully completed but with unexpected results. Once the western extremity of the wall was reached, it became apparent that it was joined to another perpendicular wall (F 10) that extended north from F 5 (fig. 17). It was not clear if this was just an Iron Age appendage of wall F 5 or something different. First appearances suggested it was Iron Age in date, though pottery from just west of the wall was Hittite, suggesting that it could have been part of the second-millennium gate's superstructure. A tantalizing mudbrick wall popping up in the lower section of the trench may be the first evidence of the gate's western extremity.

We also noted in our earlier report that two rooms were exposed in the eastern part of the trench. Inside the higher of the two

Figure 17. Remains of second-millennium (left) and Iron Age walls (right) on the North Slope

rooms were found materials from the Hittite Empire period. Along with one piece of "Dark Age" pottery with a crescent-shaped plastic design that came from the upper portion of the room (cf. Genz 2001: 160, figs. 10–11, for similar examples). This piece suggested that the room may have been reused in the "Dark Age" or since it was at the top of the level, it may have just been an artifact of the Dark Age that came to rest on top of the Hittite ruins. The orientation of the room suggests the location of the gate's entryway and the small stones just west of it appear to be part of a cobbled path leading into the gate itself.

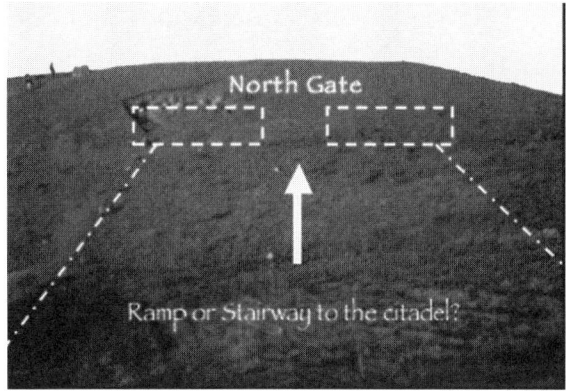

Figure 18. Possible location of stairs or ramp leading into the citadel

An arched stone at the base of the proposed entryway is reminiscent of the parabolic arches that graced the entrance of gates found at Boğazköy-Hattuša. An earthen ramp in front of the gate may hold evidence of how the citadel gate was approached (fig. 18)

In 2006 we discovered that what we thought was a second room slightly down the slope from the first room was actually part of a curtain wall from the Hittite period. It now appears that the room is really part of a buttress or tower similar to those found encircling Boğazköy (Seeher 2006: 200). This structure may well be a continuation of the wall 20 complex known from the East Trench as there is an abundance of burned mudbrick littering the slope below it, just as we observed in the case of wall F 20. If so, this would make the north curtain wall Old Hittite in date. Unfortunately, so little of this complex has been excavated and we will have to wait for results from another season of work in order to gain a fuller explanation of its construction. With any kind of luck, it may be possible to eventually date the wall based on the construction scheme of the tower as suggested by Seeher. For now, only a corner of the tower is exposed making it impossible to tell which of the two styles is represented in this construction.

Area 7 (Çaltepe)

Çaltepe lies less than a kilometer across the Eğri Su valley from Çadır Höyük. We have identified the height with one known in the Hittite texts as Mt. Daha, a mountain associated with Zippalanda, Katapa, and Ankuwa. After a survey of the mountain in 2005, we began mapping the slopes of Çaltepe during the 2006 season and in anticipation of test excavations during the 2007 season. The main building at the summit of Çaltepe measures approximately 40 × 80 m and appears to be a type of open-air worship area. It consists of one entrance on the north side of the construction and what appear to be storerooms on the west side. The large open interior area would have contained the actual worship site. A lower area within the so-called storerooms may be a pool or basin set in the central portion of the storerooms and not unlike the basin found in Building C on Büyükkale (Bittel 1970: 85; Neve 1982: 113–15), perhaps the location of the Ishtar *luliya* (PÚ) mentioned in Hittite texts as being located within the cult area on the mountain (see KBo 16 78; cf. Popko 1994: 147). Trial excavation in coming seasons will clarify this interesting anomaly.

Final Comments, Observations, and Conclusions

The 2006 season was successful on many fronts. In general, we have proceeded slowly in order to carefully excavate and thoroughly document Çadır's material remains. This is of particular importance because of the inherent difficulty of excavating a mound where multiple civilizations have successively made use of the mound's steep slope. This past season, however, we not only were able to delineate more levels of the second millennium, add more examples to the ceramic corpus, and document the transition from Hittite Empire into the so-called "Dark Age"), but we also made strides towards gaining a better understanding of the Byzantine, Iron Age, and Chalcolithic settlements. Çadır Höyük continues to express its amazingly complicated and culturally fertile personality.

Among the areas where progress can be seen is in the already mentioned construction of a new depot. Beyond that, articles were published in the 2005–2006 Oriental Institute *Annual Report* and the journal *Anatolica* while a major publication on the Chalcolithic period is forthcoming in the journal *Anatolian Studies*. Of particular importance is the progress made by Ben Arbuckle in analyzing the backlog of faunal materials that have accumulated in the project depot. Of some note in this respect was his observation that the remains of animals in the Byzantine pen on the citadel almost certainly represented a catastrophic death event, much as had been projected in our earlier analysis (Gorny et al. 2004: 20). This would also buttress our contention that the animals had been brought there for protection and give added credence to our suggestion that the Byzantine period settlement was actually a *kastron* (Gorny 2006: 14). Jeff Geyer also made significant progress in cataloging and understanding Çadır Höyük's lithic inventory. Additionally, more students were introduced to the discipline of archaeological fieldwork and our Turkish workers gained new experience in the subtleties of archaeological field excavation. All these advances bode well for the future and help guarantee successes in coming seasons at the site of Çadır Höyük-Zippalanda.

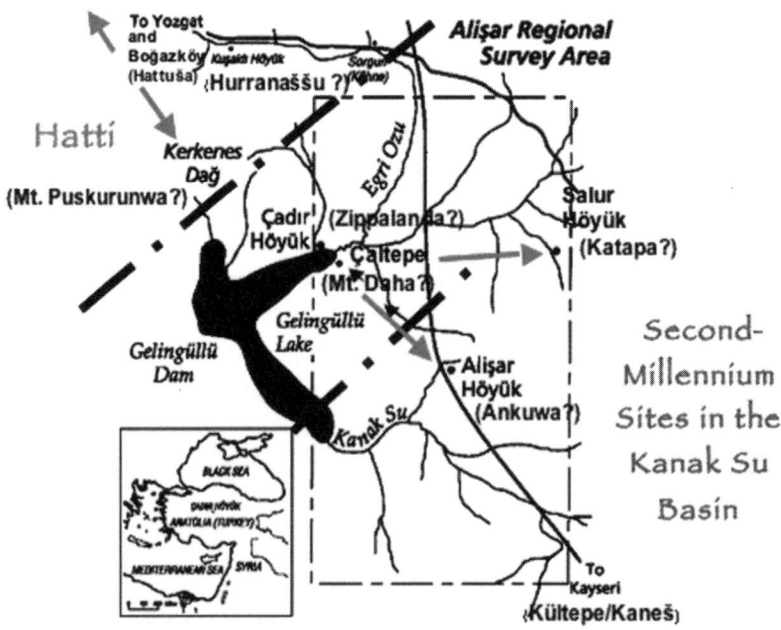

Figure 19. Proposed identifications for sites in the Kanak Su Basin

In summary, the dominating nature of the second-millennium materials at Çadır Höyük continue to impress us with a strong sense of the importance this mound must have had during the second millennium. The remains are consistent with what we know of the Hittite era Zippalanda, though they do inspire new questions about the pre-Zippalanda existence of the site. Nonetheless, the probability that Çadır Höyük is to be equated with Zippalanda increases with every shovelful of dirt taken from the site. It also provides a better sense of the region's geography and allows for the identification of other sites throughout the region (fig. 19). With this in mind, coming seasons will focus increasing amounts of time, money, and energy on documenting and explaining the second-millennium remains. It is hoped the literary evidence confirming our hypothesis will come to light in ensuing seasons of work. In the meantime, however, we continue to explore the diachronic impact of this amazing site on the social, political, and religious development of central Anatolia.

Notes

[1] The staff included Benjaman Arbuckle, Carolyn Armstrong, Remi Berthon, Robert Cochran, Jeffery Geyer, Ronald Gorny, Carola Manzano, Juliana McKittrick, Gregory McMahon, Megan McMahon, Samuel Paley, Jennifer Ross, Sharon Steadman, Carol Schneider, Bruce Verhaaren, and Vannessa Weinert.

[2] The chronological terms used in this paper derive from U.-D. Schoop and J. Seeher (2006). In their analysis, Shoop and Seeher suggest that the "early" period may be equated with the Old Hittite (ca. seventeenth–sixteenth centuries B.C.), "middle" with the Middle Hittite (ca. fifteenth and first half of fourteenth century), and "late" with the empire period (ca. second half of fourteenth and thirteenth century). To this table we can also add the subsequent "Dark Age" period (ca. first half of the twelfth century). Older dates are based on the findings of Newton and Kuniholm 2004: 165–76, suggesting Karum II dates from ca. 2100 to 1850 and Karum Ib from ca. 1850 to 1700.

[3] Surprisingly, there are no mudbricks visible in the structure, though the material is very brick-like in character. It is possible that the brick has just "melted" and is now indiscernible to the eye, or it may be that the actual brick is yet to come, being topped by a layer of mud or plaster to seal the top of the wall or to create a smooth surface, perhaps a *chemin de ronde* or even as a cap over the destroyed wall.

[4] One item of note in the excavation of the East Slope fortification walls is the uniformity of construction methods. The casemates are constructed 6.0 m wide with 1.20–1.35 m front and back facing walls. The style is also very similar to other known Hittite fortification walls across the central plateau and closely approximates the width of most casemate walls known from other Hittite sites such as Boğazköy-Hattuša and Kuşaklı-Sarissa. The continual rebuilding of these citadel fortification walls is not insignificant and surely provides further evidence of the settlement's importance to the Hittites during the second millennium.

[5] Of some significance is the fact that we also opened an exposure of the so-called "Dark Age" level on the South Slope, with a Hittite Empire period level situated directly beneath it. This is providing us with a good look at the important Late Bronze–Iron Age transition period of which so little is known. The 2006 investigations suggested that the exposure just below the "Dark Age" level is part of the Hittite Empire period temple compound, perhaps an area where sacrifices were made to the storm-god of Zippalanda in a structure nearly three hundred years later than the one we are excavating on the East Slope. The area is clearly associated with the temple on Çaltepe (Mt. Daha) and is already beginning to show a strong sense of continuity between the "Dark Age" and the Late Hittite Empire period. These efforts, combined with work on the north slope's monumental gateway, are helping to link the entirety of Çadır's second-millennium discoveries into a more coherent understanding of the settlement as a whole, as well as its role in the political and religious life of the Hittite empire.

[6] Analysis of the coins is being done by Ken Harl and will appear in a later publication.

[7] A newly returned ^{14}C date from F 23 in the earlier transitional house provides a date of 3520–3350 B.C. (Cal 5470–5300 B.P.) which is somewhat problematic in that it seems a little earlier than we had expected for this building. This date may, because of the samples proximity to the Late Chalcolithic "Burned House," actually reference that building as it is in keeping with previous samples taken from that complex.

References

Gorny, Ronald L.

2006a   "The Alişar Regional Project: Excavations at Çadır Höyük." *The Oriental Institute 2005–2006 Annual Report*, edited by Gil J. Stein, pp. 13–22. Chicago: The Oriental Institute.

2006b   "The 2002–2005 Excavations at Çadır Höyük in Central Turkey." *Anatolica* 32 (2006): 29–54.

2006c   "Of Mounds and Mountains: Is Çadır Höyük and Çaltepe actually the Hittite City of Zippalanda and the Holy Mt. Daha?" *Oriental Institute News & Notes* 188: 22–25.

2005   "Çadır Höyük: Zippalanda Reborn?" *Oriental Institute News & Notes* 184: 9–12 and 29–30.

2004   "Alishar Regional Project: Excavations at Çadır Höyük." *Oriental Institute 2003–2004 Annual Report*, edited by Gil J. Stein, pp. 13–24. Chicago: The Oriental Institute.

Gorny, Ronald L.; Gregory McMahon; Sam Paley; and Lisa Kealhofer

1995   "The Alishar Regional Project: 1994 Season." *Anatolica* 21: 68–100.

Gorny, Ronald L.; Gregory McMahon; Samuel Paley; Sharon Steadman; and Bruce Verhaaren

1999   "The 1998 Season at Çadır Höyük in Central Turkey." *Anatolica* 25: 149–83.

Gorny, Ronald L.; Gregory McMahon; Samuel Paley; Sharon Steadman; and Bruce Verhaaren

2002   "The 2000 and 2001 Seasons at Çadır Höyük in Central Turkey." *Anatolica* 28: 109–36.

Neve, P.

1982   *Büyükkale: Die Bauwerk. Grabungen 1954–1966*. Berlin: Gebr. Mann.

Newton, M., and P. Kuniholm

2004   "A Dendrochronological Framework for the Assyrian Colony Period in Asia Minor." *TUBA-AR* VII: 165–76.

Popko, M.

1997   Review of *Zippalanda: Ein Kultzentrum in hethitischen Kleinasien*. Texte der Hethiter 21. Heidelberg: Universitätsverlag C. Winter, 1994. (Reviewed by R. L. Gorny, "Zippalanda and Ankuwa: The Geography of Central Anatolia in the Second Millennium B.C." *JAOS* 117 [1997]: 549–57.)

Schoop, U.-D.

2006   "Dating the Hittites with Statistics: Ten Pottery Assemblages from Boğazköy-Hattuša." In *Structuring and Dating in Hittite Archaeology*, edited by D. P. Mielke, U.-D. Schoop, and J. Seeher. BYZAS 4. Istanbul: Ege Yayınları.

Schoop, U.-D., and J. Seeher, eds.

2006   "Absolute Chronologie in Boğazköy-Hattuša: Das Potential der Radiokarbondaten." *Structuring and Dating in Hittite Archaeology*, edited by D. P. Mielke, U.-D. Schoop, and J. Seeher. BYZAS 4. Istanbul: Ege Yayınları.

Seeher, J.

2006 "Chronology in Hattuša: New Approaches to an Old Problem." *Structuring and Dating in Hittite Archaeology*, edited by D. P. Mielke, U.-D. Schoop, and J. Seeher, pp. 197–213. BYZAS 4. Istanbul: Ege Yayınları.

CENTER FOR ANCIENT MIDDLE EASTERN LANDSCAPES

http://oi.uchicago.edu/research/camel

Scott Branting

Following its major reorganization, CAMEL entered its second year with a number of important tasks to complete. These included growing the collection of digital maps, aerial photos, and satellite images, finding ways to manage and quickly retrieve items from this rapidly expanding digital collection, continuing to support projects and teaching with data and expertise, and expanding the knowledge of what CAMEL is and what it offers. All four of these tasks were accomplished during the course of the year.

The new large format scanner and plotter that were acquired last summer as a part of the Provost's Program for Academic Technology Innovation (ATI) grant saw nearly constant use throughout the year. Volunteers and students spent countless hours toiling on the scanner in order to create digital versions of over half of the 3,700 maps held in the Research Archives collections (fig. 1). Many of these maps are extremely hard to find these days, and this important work will make them much more available. Having a large format scanner that can handle an entire map all at once is critical to processing them (fig. 2), though some of the older and more fragile maps still are done by hand, with small portions of the whole map scanned a bit at a time using a special scanner and then digitally pieced together (fig. 3). With over half of this important collection of maps now scanned,

Figure 1. A scan of the Research Archives copy of a British Survey of India map from 1918 showing portions of Persia south of the Caspian Sea

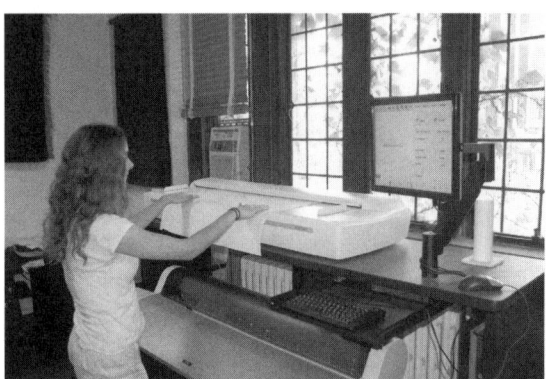
Figure 2. A student assistant in CAMEL scans a map from the Research Archive's map collection on the wide-format scanner (a Context Crystal XL 42")

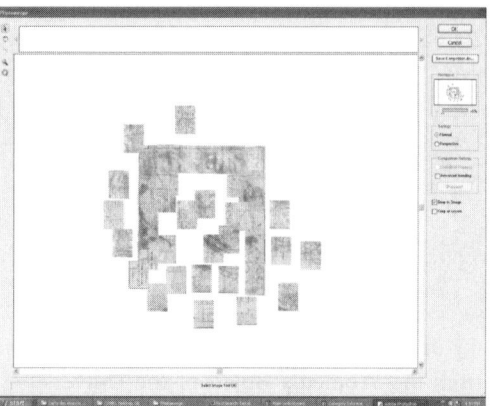
Figure 3. Some maps are too fragile to be fed through the wide-format scanner so they must be scanned piece by piece. The scanned pieces must then be sorted through like puzzle pieces and assembled back into the entire map

next year should see the completion of the scanning portion and the start of the georectification portion of this long-term project.

The large and invaluable collection of aerial photos and other types of spatial data in the Museum Archives is another treasure trove of spatial data acquired by the Institute over the years. Over 5,600 aerial photos collected from 1920 onward by various researchers in the Institute provide an unparalleled view of how the Middle East has changed over roughly a century (fig. 4). Thousands of ancient cities and villages that have been destroyed or covered over by the sprawl of modern cities or agricultural practices can still be seen in these photographs. This makes them an invaluable tool for researchers trying to find and understand the settlements that remain. CAMEL has begun to work with the Museum Archives to scan a number of these images and georectify them. Georectification is a process of digitally shifting these scanned images to their real-world position on the surface of the earth for use with various forms of mapping software. This will make these images much more accessible and useful to researchers around the world. It is hoped that most of this unparalleled collection of images will be digitized over the next two years.

Figure 4. This image, taken from the air by Erich Schmidt in May 1937, captures the complete terrace at Persepolis as it stood seventy years ago

A third important source of new data acquired this year were over seven hundred declassified U.S. Spy Satellite images purchased from the United States Geological Service (USGS). This imagery, much of it from the CORONA series of satellites, dates from the 1960s to the 1980s and greatly complements the Institute's important collection of in-house imagery showing how broad regions of the Middle East have changed over the decades (fig. 5). With a significant grant from the Women's Board of the University of Chicago, CAMEL's collection of this imagery increased this year to 1,111 images, one of the largest collections in the world. Work continues on the georectification of all of this imagery.

Figure 5. A declassified Corona image recently acquired from the USGS. Taken June 8, 1970, it shows the ancient tell of Ashkelon in Israel

Finally, data continued to be acquired from high-resolution, commercial satellites on behalf of numerous projects. This data, collected over the past eight years, provides a present-day look at the landscape of the Middle East that is very useful both for projects that will soon be in the field or for projects that cannot immediately travel to the place in the world in which they are interested. As with the image of Samarra last year, CAMEL once again had the opportunity to task Digital Globe's Quickbird satellite and direct it, this time to central Turkey, to acquire a real-time image of the area around Amasya for a researcher (fig. 6). Receiving imagery taken by the satellite only a few days before is always an exciting event and provides an unparalleled, current resource that can readily be coupled and compared with our georectified, historical archive.

With this influx of new imagery on top of considerable existing collections an additional investment of labor was needed by CAMEL staff to design a database to manage and support queries of this collection (fig. 7). The Oriental Institute's terabyte storage system, which was set up last year, continues to do an excellent job of providing huge amounts of reliable and secure storage space for all the digital collections of the Oriental Institute including CAMEL. However, finding a particular image for a researcher among the thousands — soon to be tens of thousands — in CAMEL's collections can be a daunting task. This new database will allow CAMEL to do just that smoothly and efficiently for years to come.

The numbers of requests that CAMEL receives has also increased markedly in the past year. Over fifty requests for data and expertise from over forty different researchers and individuals in North America, Europe, the Middle East, and Australia were received and completed during 2006/2007. The data requested came from

Figure 6. Part of the image taken by the CAMEL-tasked Digital Globe Quickbird 2 satellite on July 10, 2007. It shows an as-yet unexcavated site near Amasya in Turkey

CAMEL

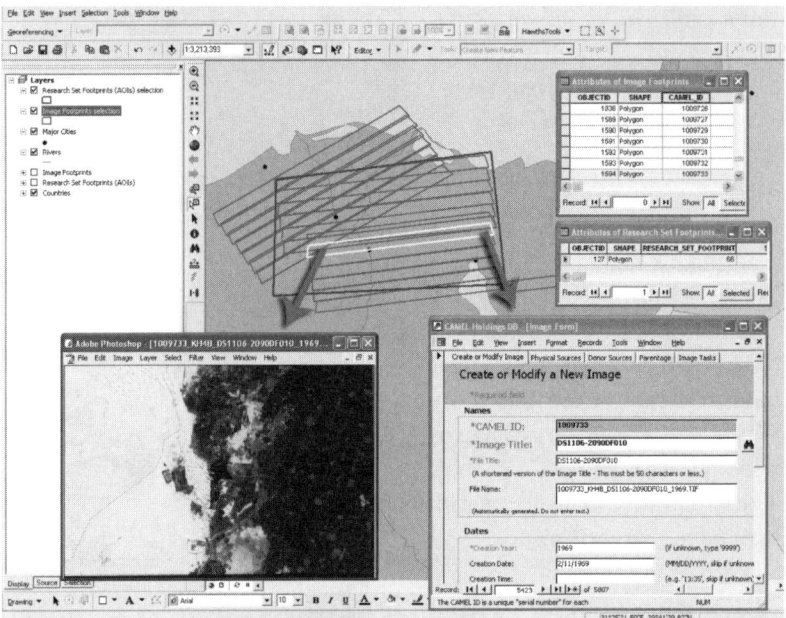

Figure 7. The CAMEL Holdings ArcGIS/Access database tracks the metadata of each of its archived images — where it came from, who created it, what distribution rights it has — and links this information to a geographical "footprint." Using the ArcGIS interface, one can easily define an area of interest, find the footprints of images within it, and view the original satellite image or map

all corners of CAMEL's collection area and even a bit beyond. These requests are on top of the dozens and dozens of people that each year make use of the CAMEL laboratory facilities within the Institute. With the installation of the large format plotter purchased by the ATI grant CAMEL was also able to expand its support abilities further this year. The plotter allows the printing of large-sized maps, posters, and plans in support of the Institute's numerous research projects, education programs, and outreach opportunities.

CAMEL has also remained very active in the teaching and training of students and has contributed to two temporary exhibits in the museum. Several classes made use of the CAMEL facilities and expertise, and a number of masters and doctoral students made extensive use of them in their research, including two students awarded Master's degrees within the Department of Near Eastern Languages and Civilizations. Aerial photos from the Museum Archives scanned by CAMEL also appeared in the temporary exhibit, Daily Life Ornamented: The Medieval Persian City of Rayy, and posters produced by CAMEL appeared in the Through Young Eyes: Ancient Nubian Art Recreated exhibit.

The past two years have been instrumental in undertaking the foundational work that allows CAMEL to acquire, manage, and effectively disseminate spatial data pertaining to the Middle East along with expertise in how to use that data. With an increasing number of researchers inside and outside of the Oriental Institute benefiting from these labors CAMEL can only continue to grow in the years ahead. Talks continue with NASA on formalizing a Space Act Agreement to expand the range of data at CAMEL's disposal and partnerships are being formed with other institutions. These efforts will continue in the years ahead. The work of CAMEL is even starting to stir up interest in broader circles as was witnessed in the Sun-Times article on CAMEL in January 2007.

No project can exist without supporters and workers. I would like to personally thank all those who have donated data or financial means to CAMEL. I would also like to thank all those who have donated their time and effort to CAMEL this year. Joshua Trampier continued to serve exceptionally well in his new role of Associate Director, while Robert Tate was promoted to the duties of Assistant Director. Elise MacArthur served as Senior Supervisor, while Caitlin Flanagan, Joseph Phillips, and Brian Brown all served as Student Assistants. Susan Penacho coordinated our wonderful volunteers for the year, who were Ronald Wideman, Alex Elwyn, Gaby Cohen, and Alex Muir. Thank you all for your excellent efforts.

CHICAGO ASSYRIAN DICTIONARY (CAD)
Martha T. Roth

In 2006/2007 we truly entered the final phase of the Chicago Assyrian Dictionary Project. In December, two volumes, T and Ṭ, were published. Both volumes are dedicated to the memory of Erica Reiner, who died one year earlier, on December 31, 2005.

The resident staff continued preparing the final volume, U/W, for press. The crucial task of "checking" a volume provides two benefits. First, the accuracy of all entries is secured by confirming the Dictionary citation against the original publication. Second, as the checkers examine texts by genre, often concentrating on their own areas of expertise, the entire volume is viewed through a series of unique cross-sections, quite different from that seen by the draft writer or by the editor who works on one article at a time. For example, in checking all the medical texts, or all the Neo-Assyrian letters, or all the Old Babylonian real estate contracts, the checker often rectifies inconsistencies across the articles or discovers new correlations between texts. Checking was accomplished by Jacob Lauinger and John Nielsen, graduate students in the Department of Near Eastern Languages and Civilizations, along with Robert D. Biggs, Gertrud Farber, and Martha Roth. Jake checked texts from Mari, Alalakh, and Old Babylonian letters and legal texts; John concentrated on historical texts and Neo-Babylonian and Neo-Assyrian letters and administrative texts; Gertrud checked all the lexical and bilingual texts; Bob checked medical texts, omens, and literary texts; and Martha checked Nuzi, Old Assyrian, and peripheral texts. Then Bob, Jake, and Martha combed through the binders of manuscript pages verifying every remaining or problematic citation.

Simultaneously, we received comments, corrections, and additions from our outside consultants: Professors Wilfred G. Lambert (Birmingham, England), Simo Parpola (Helsinki, Finland), and Klaas R. Veenhof (Leiden, The Netherlands). In the past these consultants' input was primarily at the galley stage. For this final volume, we decided to ask for their input at the manuscript stage, better utilizing the available staff and making the intensive work of incorporating their suggestions at an earlier moment more economical. After making all corrections in the electronic manuscript, including all cross-references, and verifying all headings and discussions, the final manuscript was printed out and prepared for the compositor. We mailed off more than 1,200 marked manuscript pages for typesetting to Eisenbrauns, Inc., by the end of June 2007 and will mail the remaining 1,400 pages by the end of July.

While preparing this final volume for press, we also finished the last stage of space consolidation of the CAD files and materials. At one time, the CAD staff occupied several offices on the third floor. In addition to the several faculty members' offices, there has been a room for CAD research associates (320), a room for the CAD books and manuscripts (315 and then 324), a supply closet for CAD back files and stored manuscripts of published volumes (321), and — most notably — the "dictionary room" for the CAD card files and the manuscript editors. This last room (323), the largest in the Oriental Institute, was constructed with the CAD in mind when the Oriental Institute was built in 1931, with a floor specially reinforced to hold the weight of the millions of file cards that form the primary resource for writing the dictionary articles. Over the last twelve years, we consolidated materials and people in order to free up valuable space for other projects. Now, by the end of June 2007, all the CAD files and manuscripts are in the storeroom (321) and a corner of 323. This Herculean task — sorting, discarding, and consolidating more than eighty years of accumulated matter, was accomplished thanks primarily to the labor and organizing skill of Jake Lauinger, assisted by Erin Guinn-Villareal, Joseph Rosner, and Lillian Rosner, and thanks to the good will and facilitation of Steve Camp.

But room 323 is still distinguished in the building as a "dictionary room" — now, however, it is the new home of the Hittite Dictionary project (CHD), headed by Prof. Theo van den Hout. Theo and his CHD team, eagerly anticipating the move to their new and more spacious quarters, were ever graceful and patient. The CHD project and staff are worthy successors to the space and are now welcome neighbors on the third floor.

With the project's end truly in sight, the amazing support team that has helped us get to this point has begun to find new interests and employment. Linda McLarnan, the manuscript editor since 1986 and a valued colleague and friend, accepted a position in the office of the President. Linda is not abandoning us, however; she will continue overseeing the final stages of publication of the last volume. Jake Lauinger finished his Ph.D. dissertation, defended his thesis in June, and accepted an assistant professorship at Roanoke College. John Nielsen decided to devote all his energy to completing his Ph.D. by the end of 2007. And I, after three years half-time in the Provost's office, have accepted the deanship of the Humanities Division beginning July 1st. The responsibilities of that position will keep me occupied while I await the arrival of galleys for the last volume of the CAD.

During the year we were aided by graduate student Katie L. Johnson, whose keen proofreading and inputting skills have been of immense assistance to us, and by college students Elliott Goodman and Erin Guinn-Villareal, who willingly and eagerly have undertaken all manner of tasks. Additionally, volunteer Brittany Piovesan has been working to complete a full bibliography for works cited in the CAD.

CHICAGO DEMOTIC DICTIONARY (CDD)
François Gaudard and Janet H. Johnson

The Chicago Demotic Dictionary was happy this year to welcome back François Gaudard, who returned to us as Research Associate after a year with the Epigraphic Survey in Luxor. The rest of the staff includes Jackie Jay (who will be leaving us after this year because she has received a fellowship to finish her dissertation on narrative strategies in Egyptian literature), Foy Scalf,

Mary Szabady (who began working this year and will replace Jackie), and Janelle Pisarik (an undergraduate who is doing volunteer work for us), all under the general direction of Janet Johnson. In addition to our ongoing work checking and correcting drafts (we are currently working on the letters W, Š, and Ḥ), one of our major tasks this year has been to convert all our data, including our fonts, to the new Macintosh "system 10" operating system. Clement Robinson (an undergraduate computer specialist) is undertaking the task of modifying our fonts and converting our files. We would also like to thank John Sanders and Lec Maj for their invaluable help throughout this process. As we write, we are making good progress. Jan also had the opportunity this spring to participate in a panel entitled "Online Dictionaries for Historic and Lesser Known Languages: An Update," for the annual meeting of the Dictionary Society of North America, held here at the Oriental Institute in June. She presented a short paper providing an overview of the goals, methods, and current status of the CDD to quite an interested audience.

Lexicography is a challenging discipline which, in addition to requiring a wide knowledge of the language being recorded, demands various skills in several fields plus a great deal of patience and perseverance. Many obstacles stand in the way of the lexicographer, some of which have been discussed in earlier *Annual Reports*. Here we discuss a few more, starting first with ghost words. According to *The Random House Dictionary of the English Language*, a ghost word is "a word that has come into existence by error rather than by normal linguistic transmission, as through the mistaken reading of a manuscript, a scribal error, or a misprint." Ghost words are then non-existent words. Although the idea of having such words "haunting" a dictionary may sound very romantic to some readers, ghost words can be a source of major misinterpretations and therefore a lexicographer's nightmare. Indeed, once such a word has been created, it is not unusual that scholars, trusting their colleagues, should repeat the same error again and again, citing it as a real word in grammars, dictionaries, or other scholarly works, giving it each time a little more credibility.

As a first example, let us consider the Demotic word w^c ⟨⟩ which appears in a "notification of payment" dating from the Ptolemaic period (namely Papyrus Rylands 31, line 1). This word was correctly read w^c by Sethe in 1920, but he mistakenly read a definite article (pʒ) in front of it (following Griffith who had made the same error when he first published this text in 1909) and translated it "*Schriftstück*" ("document"). His translation was accepted by Erichsen, who incorporated it, with the same meaning, first in his *Demotische Lesestücke* in 1940 and then in his *Demotisches Glossar*, published in 1954, with a reference to the publication by Sethe and Partsch. Erichsen also cited the same word as occurring in what he considered to be the compounds w^c (n) *mkmk*, w^c (n) *smy*, and w^c *bʒk*, which he translated respectively "*Eingabe*" ("petition"), "*Klageschrift*" ("complaint"), and "*Original-dokument*(?)" ("original document(?)"). But in 1958, Hughes demonstrated that, in all these cases, we are simply dealing with the well-known indefinite article w^c. In 1980, discussing a note from an article by Reymond, who thought Sethe's theory was admissible, he pointed out again that "There is no such demotic word as w^c ... meaning a document of some kind. ... It is always and only the indefinite article, and P. Rylands D. 31, 1 is the only instance in which it appeared that there was such a word because Griffith and Sethe misread *ḫ.t* (n) w^c *sḫ gyd*, 'Copy of a *cheirographon* [a document written in (a person's) own handwriting],' as *ḫ.t* (n) pʒ w^c *sḫ gyd*."[1]

A more comical example of a ghost word stems from a misreading of a word in Papyrus Bibliothèque Nationale 215, better known as, although improperly called, *The Demotic Chronicle*. This rather enigmatic text, dating from the Ptolemaic period, deals with the political history of Egypt during the Twenty-eighth through Thirtieth Dynasties. It consists of a series of oracular statements referring to kings ranging from Amyrtaios (404–399 B.C.) to the last native Egyptian pharaoh Nectanebo II (360–343 B.C.) and mentions various calendrical dates, rituals, and festivals, as well as various divinities and cities. Each statement is followed by an interpretation usually also quite obscure. The text presents a description of legitimate kingship, illustrating both good and bad kings and showing how their fates are dependent on the manner in which they governed. In one passage (column 4, line 16), the original editor of the text, Wilhelm Spiegelberg, left out one word in his translation, here translated into English: "The measuring tool of the builder. Day 1. It means: The one who is upon the ...?, his father built." The word ⟨𓃱⟩ was left unread by Spiegelberg, who preferred a question mark. But in a footnote and in his glossary, he proposed the reading *mỉmỉ.t* "female giraffe(?),"[2] by comparison with the word 𓃱 *mmy* "giraffe," occurring, for example, in the famous Middle Egyptian hieratic tale *The Shipwrecked Sailor*. It should be noted, however, that Spiegelberg wondered what the meaning of this passage could be. In addition to being hilarious, the image of a pharaoh riding a giraffe is quite surrealistic. Nevertheless, this word was later included in Erichsen's *Demotisches Glossar*, although with the comment "*Ob richtig?*" ("Is this correct?"). When Jan was working on *The Demotic Chronicle*, she realized that this word is actually a writing of *mỉ.t* "road," and it has been so read by recent editors of *The Demotic Chronicle* and by the CDD.

An example from a different time and different culture, namely the Byzantine world, shows us another type of misinterpretation that was at the origin of what could be called a "ghost author." This involves Suidas, the presumed author of a colossal Byzantine encyclopedia of Greek literature and history compiled at the end of the tenth century A.D. The title of this compilation, Suda, is subject to several interpretations. It has been suggested that it derives from the Byzantine Greek word σοῦδα (*souda*) meaning "fence, palisade," referring to this work as being a stronghold against ignorance, or that it is an acronym, ΣΟΥΔΑ, from Συναγωγὴ Ὀνομαστικῆς Ὕλης Δι᾽ Ἀλφαβήτου, a Greek title meaning *Collection of Lexical Matter in Alphabetical Order*. Eustathios, an erudite of the twelfth century A.D. and archbishop of Thessalonika, mistook the title Σοῦδα (*Souda*) for the name of the author, whom he called Σουίδας (*Souidas*), in consequence of which, for centuries, generations of classicists took the fictitious Suidas to be the author of this encyclopedia.

Another category of problematic words are the so-called *hapax legomena*. This expression, from a Greek phrase "said once," refers to "a lexical unit found only once in the surviving records of a language."[3] The fact that a word is known from a single attestation can render its meaning quite difficult to establish. One of the most famous examples of *hapax legomena* in Demotic occurs in the first tale of Setna Khaemwas (= Papyrus Cairo 30646, in column 5, line 30), from the Ptolemaic period. The beginning of the story is lost, but it is clear that Setna, a son of Ramesses II and the hero of the story, having learned that a book of magic writings composed by Thoth himself was buried with the magician Naneferkaptah in Memphis, forced his way into the tomb. There, the ghost of Ihweret, Naneferkaptah's wife, told Setna how she, her husband, and their son Merib lost their lives for having stolen the magical book. Setna was so eager to possess the book that he accepted Naneferkaptah's challenge to play a game of drafts for it. Setna lost three games in a row but, thanks to his magical amulets and scrolls, he eventually succeeded in stealing the book and leaving the tomb with it. Shortly after this episode, Setna met a beautiful woman named Tabubu and was mesmerized by her. Before allowing him to get close to her, she required him to turn over to her all his belongings and to kill all his children. When Setna was finally about to have sex with her, Tabubu cried out and Setna awoke, realizing that all of this was nothing but a nightmare caused by Naneferkaptah. He understood he had to return the book to Naneferkaptah.

The passage we are interested in describes Setna when emerging from his nightmare. It reads as follows: "Setna awoke in a state of heat, with his penis inside a *šḥy*ꜣ and without any clothes on him at all." The *hapax legomenon* ⟨glyphs⟩ *šḥyꜣ* has been translated by various scholars in many different ways: "jar," "mudpuddle," "vaginal secretions," "limp, halt," "tuyère" of a (blast) furnace, or "chamber pot." Others simply did not translate it at all (all these suggestions are referenced in the entry for *šḥyꜣ* in the file for the letter Š). As noted by Robert Ritner, "The uncertain word, attested uniquely here, is determined by two signs indicating dung, and either water or a pot." Although the exact meaning of the word is still unknown to us, the determinatives clearly indicate that we are not dealing with a body part.

These are only a sample of the range of problematic types of words with which we deal as we strive to identify Demotic vocabulary, its earlier and later Egyptian relatives, and, especially with foreign words, its etymology and usage within Egyptian. Some words are "cut and dried" and one completes the entry quickly and moves along, feeling progress has been made. But in other cases, like these, there is more challenge and, when we do sort it out, a real sense of accomplishment.

Notes

[1] G. Hughes, *Journal of Near Eastern Studies* 17 (1958): 7, n. a; idem, *Serapis* 6 (1980): 63, n. a.

[2] W. Spiegelberg, *Die sogenannte Demotische Chronik des Pap. 215 der Bibliothèque Nationale zu Paris nebst den auf der Rückseite des Papyrus stehenden Texten.* Demotische Studien 7 (Leipzig, 1914), p. 18, n. 14, and p. 56, #101.

[3] P. H. Matthews, *The Concise Oxford Dictionary of Linguistics* (Oxford and New York, 1997), p. 157.

CHICAGO HITTITE DICTIONARY (CHD)

Theo van den Hout

The high point of the past year was the move late in May to the former space of the Chicago Assyrian Dictionary (CAD). This means that all CHD offices are now on the third floor which makes for more efficient work in many ways. The move was a collaborative effort in all respects, but especially the cooperation of Martha Roth, Editor-in-Chief of the CAD, and the Oriental Institute's Executive Director Steve Camp made it all run very smoothly. With everybody's consent the room was painted a bright light blue, and with its newly waxed floor it has a fresh new look that is a pleasure to work in.

The work on the third and final installment of the letter Š has now reached its last part with words starting in *šu-*. In the past year co-editor Harry Hoffner and executive editor Theo van den Hout worked on words in *ši-* with among them such large entries as *šipand-* "to offer, bring an offering to" (which the Hittites apparently took very seriously) and *šiu-* "deity, god(dess)." Being the proverbial "thousand gods" of the Hittites, they get mentioned a lot and so make for another very long

Harry Hoffner in the Chicago Hittite Dictionary Office

and interesting dictionary article. Our new Assistant Professor, Petra Goedegebuure, who came to Chicago in October, helped us in transforming first drafts into pre-final drafts, wrote some herself, and started work on the difficult local adverb *šer* "on top, over, above," which turned out not to have been finished.

Our Research Associates Richard Beal and Oğuz Soysal continued their work ahead of us on words in *t*-; while Beal is dealing with long everyday words such as *dai*- "to put, place" and *da*- "to take," Soysal has made the transition into the words starting with *te-/ti-*.

Staff member Kathleen Mineck and undergraduate student Anna Maccourt were responsible for the upkeep of the files. Anna completely got rid of our backlog and both Kathleen and Anna undertook the task of reorganizing our file cabinets now that we finally could order some new ones because of our enlarged working space.

Programmer Sandy Schloen and graduate students Dennis Campbell and Seunghee Yie made significant progress in several key areas of the electronic version of the CHD (*eCHD*) over the past year thanks in part to the wonderful grant from the Provost's Program for Academic Technology Innovation and another generous gift from Mr. Howard Hallengren of New York. Dennis, by the way, successfully defended his dissertation in January and is now officially Dr. Campbell. Fortunately for us, Dennis will continue to work for us until he will have found a job.

With the permission of colleagues in Mainz, Germany (see last year's *Annual Report*), who produce the *Konkordanz der hethitischen Keilschrifttafeln,* we were able to extract and compile a master list of Hittite texts, from which the dictionary content is derived, and import this information in a way that integrates it with our existing dictionary data. Information describing over 25,000 source texts was entered, including the text date, script used, genre categorization, and even, if known, the findspot of every clay tablet fragment. This provides an enormous increase in information to the *e*CHD users regarding the source of the textual material. Citations within a dictionary article can now be linked to the source text and be traced back to the archaeological context in which a tablet was found. This is also the first step in establishing links between our electronic version and other relevant electronic data sources like the *Konkordanz*.

Over the past year the process of proofreading and polishing the newly available electronic material, letters L, M, and N, was completed. This means that with the P words that had already been done, the electronic version has, in effect, caught up with the printed version in terms of availability. In addition, improvements have been made in the following areas:

- Bibliographic information has been expanded and linked into the core dictionary material.

- A look up-and-link feature has been added which allows an online writer of a dictionary article to look up existing information about a text as part of a citation, and automatically drop that information into the article.

- The development of a hierarchical "taxonomy" to explicitly describe the grammatical characteristics of various forms of the dictionary words is well underway. This is a comprehensive tagging scheme that will allow scholars and students to do in-depth morphological analysis.

Finally, as the depth and scope of the material integrated within the *e*CHD increases, it has become a significant challenge to provide the means by which a researcher can enter a wide variety of complex query criteria and be presented with meaningful results. Our current focus is on developing a new model for querying the *e*CHD that will guide the user through several intuitive stages to compose the questions that he or she wishes to ask of the data. Much work remains to be done here, but we are optimistic that significant improvements can be made to the query facility to allow easier access to the electronic content. As we enhance the query facility we will also be making a concerted effort to document its effective use more clearly for users of all kinds.

Exciting was the visit of Dr. Andreas Schachner, the director of the German excavations in Boğazköy, the former capital of the Hittite empire Hattuša, who gave two lectures. We also talked about possible ways of future cooperation, especially in light of the *e*CHD. It has always been our aim to present where relevant in the dictionary as much archaeological evidence as possible. For instance, in treating the word *šeppikkušta-* "needle, pin" we, of course, refer to the existing excavation reports that publish all known pins and needles found, but the *e*CHD would give us the possibility of actually showing them and linking to the publications. This is something that we will have to explore in the coming years.

DIYALA PROJECT

Clemens D. Reichel

> Started work after lunch with 12 men from Shergat [=Assur, modern Qala'at Shergat]. Dug trench at north and south end of deeper pit (g), in order to find out: 1) whether that long low lying stretch of ground could be used anywhere for dumping; 2) with what the pit hangs together; 3) to get a baked brick building so that the men could be trained first on easy work. Soon baked bricks turn up with the name of Ur-nin-giš-zi-da, patesi [= governor, modern reading: ensí] of Ashnunnak [= Ešnunna]. All the stamps are in his name. To the south of the pit they seem to be laid in bitumen. To the north nothing is found.

Thus, on a cloudy Sunday morning on November 17, 1930, began work at the site of Tell Asmar some 50 km northeast of Baghdad (fig. 1). The events were noted by Henri Frankfort, Director of the Oriental Institute's Diyala Expedition in his field diary (fig. 2). On that day no one could have foreseen the impact that these excavations were going to have for the field of Mesopotamian archaeology. A field photograph (fig. 3) indicates that, by the end of day two, things indeed did not yet look too promising, a fact also recorded by Frankfort in an entry dating to November 18:

> At the end of this day the situation is entirely altered. It appeared at once that the baked bricks at the southend formed a drain with bitumen inside, which ran between a double layer of tapouk [baked brick]. Between this and the pit is mud brick. At the north end it appears that we cut through a brick wall yesterday. It makes an angle. There are many angles.

More "angles" and further complications showed up — the workmen were untrained, there were strikes among them, and sandstorms, rainfalls, and the occasional holdup took their toll on excavators and excavations likewise. Things, however, gradually improved, and by the end of the first season it had long become

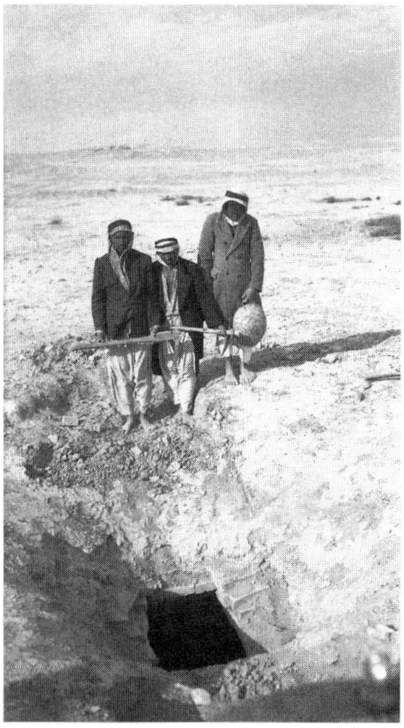

Figure 1. Tell Asmar: first day of excavation (November 17, 1930; described by Henri Frankfort in field diary, see figure 2)

DIYALA PROJECT

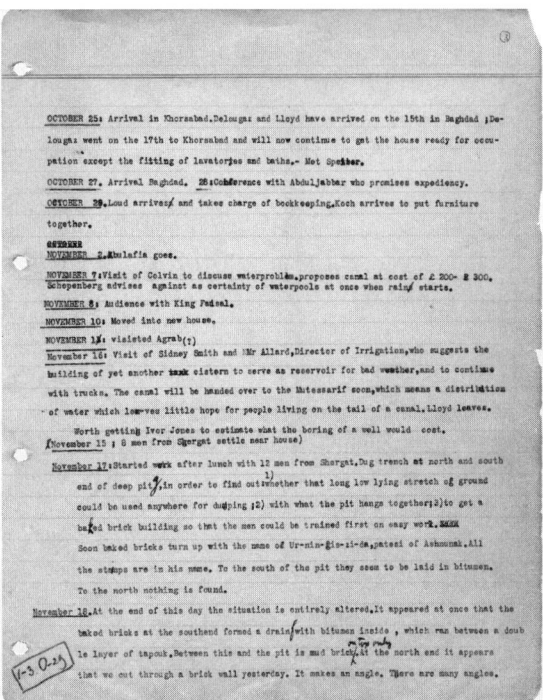

Figure 2. Page from Henri Frankfort's field diary (1930). Oriental Institute Museum Archives

clear that the walls discovered (or missed) on the first day of the excavation were part of the Palace of the Rulers, a large complex that housed Ešnunna's governor for over 300 years (between 2070 and 1750 B.C.). Over the next few years excavations expanded. Between 1930 and 1938 palaces, temples, domestic quarters, and industrial/manufacturing installations were excavated systematically layer by layer at Tell Asmar, Khafaje, Tell Agrab, and Ishchali — four major sites in the Diyala region — covering a time period of 3000-1750 B.C. This was a crucial time in Mesopotamian history, covering the end of the Uruk period, the time of competing Early Dynastic city states, the empires of Akkade and Ur III, and Ešnunna's time as a powerful independent state.

What Frankfort probably would not have imagined in his wildest dreams is that, seventy-seven years after the first shovel of dirt was moved in the first controlled excavation in this area of Iraq, the publication of his work would still be the main focus of a large number of scholars. After all, following the end of the excavations the Diyala excavators initiated an ambitious publication project in which most of the architecture and many of the key artifacts — including major pieces of sculpture, seals, and pottery — were published in nine volumes of the Oriental Institute Publication series. The last of them, called *Old Babylonian Public Buildings in the Diyala Region*, was published in 1988. Much of the work, however, remained undone. Most of the "miscellaneous findspots" (buildings located in search trenches) remain unpublished. More significantly, over 12,000 items recovered during excavations have remained unpublished. This is unfortunate, since to the present day the Diyala cultural and chronological sequence has remained the backbone of early Mesopotamian chronology and history.

The current Diyala Project, begun by McGuire Gibson in 1994 and aimed at completing the Oriental Institute's mandate to fully publish this vital excavation, has been described in detail in previous *Annual Reports* (comprehensive summaries are found in the 2002, 2003, and 2005 reports), and I will abstain from repeating the various challenges and shifts that transformed our final objective from a book publication to an online searchable database. I am pleased to report that our initial objective, the creation of an online database of all

Figure 3. Tell Asmar: second day of excavation (November 18, 1930; described by Henri Frankfort in field diary, see figure 2)

DIYALA PROJECT

objects found during excavation, is nearing completion. Our efforts have been helped greatly by the National Endowment for the Humanities (NEH), which in 2004 gave us a $100,000 grant in their Iraq Initiative and which made it possible for us to process our data systematically and efficiently with the help of new computers, data storage devices, and new software. George Sundell, who joined us in 2000 as a data architect for the Oracle-based back-end database, has been instrumental in the project's success.

In this report, let me focus on some of the new challenges that we have been facing and our responses to them. As I indicated before, the Diyala excavations ended some seventy years ago. With the death of Mary Chubb, the object registrar of the Diyala Expedition in 2003, the last eye witness of this work disappeared. What was left for us to consult was their archival records — notebooks, plans, locus and object cards, field registers, and letters from the field. During my own Ph.D. research on the Palace of the Rulers between 1996 and 2001, I realized the great "filter" imposed by final publication on the comprehensive dissemination of information. Book publications are expensive — every word published has to be weighted for its significance. Dissenting viewpoints and ongoing discussion among the excavators — a common phenomenon on excavations — are barely reflected and often left aside. Information deemed "insignificant" is left away, making a re-evaluation of the excavators' own interpretations difficult if not impossible. Publishing photographs in a volumes drives up the cost of publication even further, reducing the number of photographs eventually published to a fraction of what had been taken in the field.

Figure 4. Tell Asmar: page from Henri Frankfort's field diary, showing photograph of "Urningishzida Pit" with handwritten annotations to photograph below

This, however, leaves the end user with much less of an impression of how an excavated context looked like or how an object might have appeared when photographed from a different angle. This situation is in stark contrast to the wealth of data contained in the excavation's archive, now housed at the Oriental Institute's Museum Archive. The information contained in it is more subjective, repetitive, than the published accounts and quite often ambiguous; moreover, gathering it from various sources such as notebook pages, catalog cards, sketches, negatives, and plane table sheets can be laborious and cumbersome. It is this "undigested" state of affairs, however, that gives a scholar an unbiased look at the data as it was retrieved without the filter of what the excavators themselves had deemed "significant" or "insignificant." Seventy years after the end of the excavations and following numerous other post-World War II excavations at Mesopotamian sites such as Nippur, Uruk, Abu Salabikh, and the sites in the Hamrin basin, many of the Diyala excavators' conclusions on the archaeological history and cultural sequence of early Mesopotamia are in need of revision. Only full access to the excavated data, however, will allow a researcher to fully re-evaluate their interpretations.

To illustrate my point, let me return to the example quoted at the outset of this summary. As mentioned earlier, the area in which excavations at Tell Asmar began was part of the so-called Palace of the Rulers. More precisely, it turned out to be part of a large baked brick structure (fig. 4). As indicated earlier, these bricks were stamped with the name of Urningišzida, a governor (ensí) of Eshnunna around 1920 B.C. In the final publication this structure was published as "Urningišzida Pit." Three more of these "pits" were found in roughly the same area, all built of baked bricks and all of them stamped with the names of different rulers (Azuzum, Urninmarki, Ipiqadad I). Their function, however, remained unexplained in the final publication. None of them had contained any finds that were published. When I went through the field notebooks, however, I noted that the excavators recorded the retrieval of buttons, garment pins, and, most significantly, fragments of bones that had been scattered all over the floor — clear indications of robbed tombs. What these "pits" appear to be, therefore, are the burial grounds of several of Ešnunna's rulers. Since the information crucial to this interpretation had not been published, however, this interpretation would have been impossible to achieve without access to the field notes.

Figure 5. Tell Asmar: plan of Shusin Temple (black) and Palace of the Rulers (gray)

DIYALA PROJECT

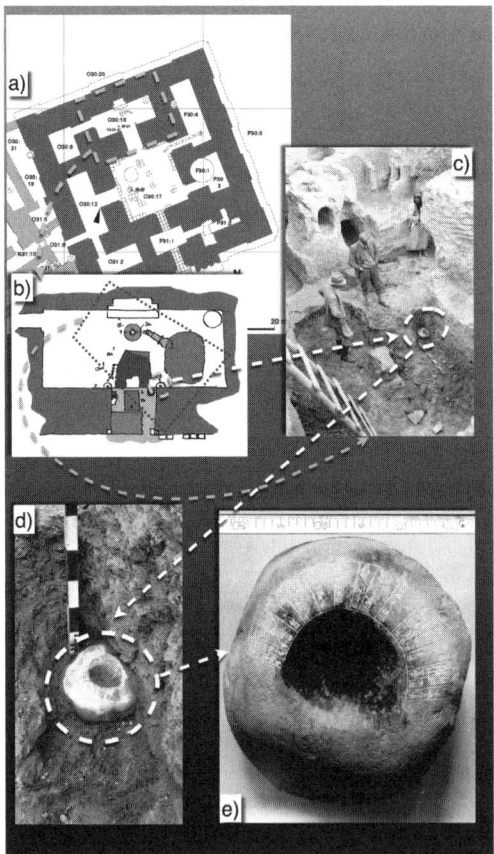

Figure 6. Cella of Shusin Temple (ca. 2030 B.C.): a) Plan; b) sketch of cella from Seton Lloyd's field notebook; c) photograph of cella (from northwest) during excavation; d) door socket with inscription of Ituria, governor of Eshnunna, in situ; e) door socket after excavation

In many cases consulting the original field notes allows a data resolution that is remarkable for a seventy year-old excavation, occasionally allowing archaeological contexts to be dated to a narrow range of absolute year dates. An example for that can be found in a temple dedicated to king Shusin, the divine overlord of the Ur III state between 2037 and 2028 B.C., of which Eshnunna was part (fig. 5). This temple, which had been attached to the Palace of the Rulers, only served its original owner for a few years. With Eshnunna's independence from Ur after 2026 B.C. the temple soon was put to a different use. The entrance to its cella was blocked off and soon afterwards two kilns installed in it, making it abundantly clear that the cult to the divine overlord had been terminated. While the desecration of the temple was mentioned in the final publication, its description did not match the archaeological evidence as presented, and numerous details remained unexplained. A combined re-examination of plans, excavation photographs, and field notes allowed me to refine and redate the archaeological sequence and to come to a somewhat different reconstruction:

Figure 6 shows the plan of the cella (a), a sketch plan from the excavator's notebook (b), and a photograph of the ongoing excavations (c), taken from the northwest of the cella. As the sketch plan indicates two door sockets associated with the earliest floor were found next to the cella's entrance, of which one (e) is visible in the photographs (c and d). An inscription on the door socket relates that the temple was built by a governor named Ituria to his divine overlord Shusin. Shusin's reign lasted from 2037 to 2028 B.C.; the door socket and the earliest floor of the temple therefore probably date to the middle of his reign, i.e., somewhere between 2035 and 2030 B.C.

Remains of a slightly higher floor in the cella with heavy traces of burning, shown in figure 7, are visible in a photograph taken after the removal of the door socket (c, marked in photograph). Embedded in this floor right before the cult niche were two drains (c) — most likely to receive libations for the deity worshipped in the temple. Within the fill below the floor, right up against the neck of one of the larger drain (marked in d), was a clay sealing (e) impressed with the seal of a cupbearer of Nurahum, a later city ruler of Eshnunna dating to approximately 2010 B.C. The drains suggest that the cella was actually refurbished, not destroyed. The sealing dates this refurbishment to about 2010 B.C. — more than fifteen years after the end of the Ur III overlordship over Eshnunna. This is surprising, for wouldn't one have assumed that the desecration of a temple to the foreign (and presumably now reviled) overlord took place immediately or at least soon after the city gained independence?

DIYALA PROJECT

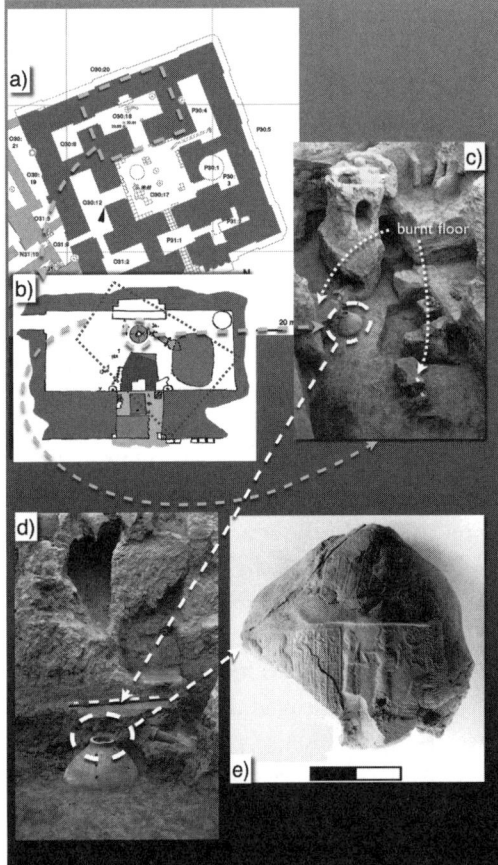

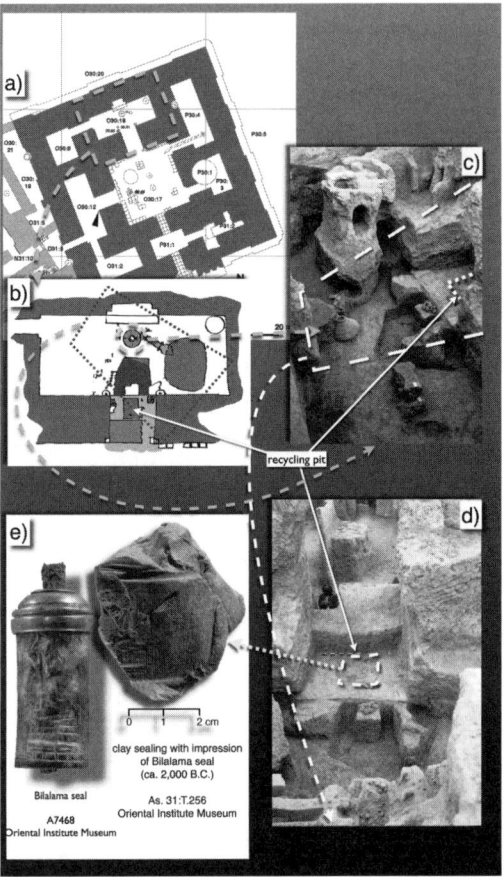

Figure 7. Cella of Shusin Temple (ca. 2010 B.C.): a) Plan; b) sketch of cella from Seton Lloyd's field notebook; c) photograph of cella (from northwest) during excavation, showing location of burnt floor and of drains; d) close-up of larger drain, showing findspot of clay sealing, e) clay sealing with impression of seal of cup-bearer of Nurahum, city ruler of Eshnunna

Figure 8. Cella of Shusin Temple (ca. 2005 B.C.): a) Plan; b) sketch of cella from Seton Lloyd's field notebook; c) photograph of cella (from northwest) during excavation, showing location of recycling pit; d) view of blocked cella doorway and recycling pit, e) clay sealing with impression of Bilalama seal, Bilalama seal (Oriental Institute Museum)

The desecration, which included the blocking of the cella's doorway, in fact, was associated with yet a higher floor (fig. 8). The blocking of the doorway (visible in photo 8d) left a niche, in which a rectangular clay slab was found embedded (fig. 8b, c, d). What the excavators took as a "foundation deposit" is actually a pit that contained sealing clay. Within this clay a sealing impressed with the deal of Bilalama, crown prince and son of the ruler Kirikiri, was recovered (fig. 8e). Visitors familiar with the Mesopotamian gallery will easily recognize the seal — made of lapis lazuli and with one gold cap still in place — it is one of the Oriental Institute's most beautiful seals, exhibited in a separate case. Finding an ancient impression of a seal is a rare coincidence, so the fact that no less than three impressions of the Bilalama seal have been found in the cella and its adjacent rooms is indeed remarkable. Kirikiri, whose name denoted foreign (Elamite?) origin, succeeded Nurahum as a ruler around 2005 B.C. under less than smooth terms, most likely in a coup d'état.

It would go too far to fully discuss the implication of this reanalysis in this context — notably who was actually worshipped in this temple after the end of the Ur III period. The potential for a refined archaeological chronology, however, should be apparent from this example. With the help of the excavators' notes and field photographs we are able to date floors (and hence their pottery and artifact assemblage) within the range of a few years. The earliest floor of the temple hence dates somewhere between 2035 and 2010 B.C., the second one (the refurbishment floor with the drains embedded in it) to about 2010–2005 B.C., and the third one (the one associated with the desecration of the temple) to about 2005 B.C. This kind of chronological resolution — in a context that is over 4,000 years old — is remarkable especially in an excavation that happened over seventy years ago. It is to the credit of the excavators and their meticulous record-keeping that this kind of reanalysis is possible.

But how does one make this data available to the scholarly community? A scholar at the Oriental Institute can visit the Museum Archives and study it, but an outside scholar might not even be aware of the existence of these records. As elaborated in previous years we had hoped to publish all Diyala archival records in an online "Virtual Archive," but this is a time-consuming, laborious, and ultimately expensive procedure. Scanning all the plans, cards, and notebooks requires enormous amounts of storage capabilities, which we could not meet under the previous circumstances. This March, however, we received excellent news: the National Endowment of the Humanities awarded us a grant over $337,000 for 2007–2009 to complete our work on the virtual archive. Once our work is accomplished, the Diyala Expedition will be one of the few truly comprehensively published excavations, providing equal access to all data to any scholar (or interested lay person) anywhere on the globe.

Plenty of work remains to be done, but with our well-trained student assistants and volunteers we hope to accomplish this final step in the publication of all Diyala data in the next two years. Alexandra (Ali) Witsell, who joined our team in 2005 as a student assistant and since 2006 has been working on a dissertation on the Temple Oval at Khafaje, recently was joined by Michael Fisher. So far Ali and Michael have been editing literally thousands of object photographs scanned between 2004 and 2005, but soon they will take upon the challenge of indexing the archival materials for keywords, a vital step to make the vast amount of data searchable. I also want to thank Robert Wagner for his tireless efforts in getting the Diyala field negatives scanned — with some 4,000 scans (each at about 150 megabytes) a truly monumental undertaking that was successfully accomplished. I am delighted that Karen Terras, who continued to work on an index of the Diyala archival material off-site and who already has started to transcribe several of the excavators' notebooks, has agreed to rejoin the Diyala Project — her enthusiasm and organization skills have been a key in making this project a success. We are confident that, more than seventy years after its humble beginnings described at the outset of this summary, the Diyala excavators' magnificent work finally will get the full and well-deserved recognition in the world of Near Eastern archaeology.

———

THE EPIGRAPHIC SURVEY

W. Raymond Johnson

On April 15, 2007, the Epigraphic Survey, in cooperation with the Egyptian Supreme Council of Antiquities (SCA), completed its eighty-third field season in Luxor, one of its most memorable ever. For more than a year now Luxor has been the focus of an urban renewal project designed to address recent dramatic increases in tourism and a growing population. Luxor is no stranger

EPIGRAPHIC SURVEY

Margaret penciling the facade of the Small Amun Temple. Photo by Ray Johnson

to ambitious building programs, from the founding of the Amun-Re cult in Thebes at the beginning of the Middle Kingdom four thousand years ago. But the speed at which this current program is being implemented has not been seen since Akhenaten threw up his enormous Aten complex at Karnak (or when Horemheb took it down again almost as quickly) in the late Eighteenth Dynasty. In an effort to assist the city and our SCA friends in coping with the enormous challenges to the antiquities sites of Luxor during this time, more than 50% of the Epigraphic Survey's program this past season was outside of and in addition to its scheduled activities. What follows is the report on Chicago House's activities in Luxor, scheduled and unscheduled, particularly at Medinet Habu Temple and Luxor Temple, during the last six months.

Medinet Habu Small Amun Temple

Epigraphic Documentation

The epigraphic team supervised by senior epigrapher Brett McClain continued the drawing and collation for the second, third, and fourth volumes of the small Amun temple series in the Eighteenth Dynasty temple ambulatory and bark sanctuary, and the Twenty-fifth Dynasty Kushite additions. The first volume in the series, *Medinet Habu* IX, The small Amun Temple: The Sanctuary, dedicated to the innermost six-painted sanctuaries, is in production now in Chicago and scheduled to be published this winter. The team was made up of epigraphers Brett, Jen Kimpton, and Ginger Emery, and artists Margaret De Jong, Susan Osgood, Krisztian Vertes, and Christian Greco. Tina Di Cerbo and Richard Jasnow continued the systematic mapping, documentation, and translation of the graffiti in the small Amun temple, on the rooftop of the Ramesses III mortuary temple, and in the Treasury and Slaughterhouse rooms below.

A special focus this season in the small Amun temple was the four Twenty-ninth Dynasty Akoris columns and northeastern gateway in the ambulatory as well as the inscribed window blocking on the facade which appears to have been part of his building program. Photographer Yarko Kobylecky assisted by Ellie Smith produced new negatives of the western two Akoris columns in the bark sanctuary ambulatory for drawing enlargements, and artist Sue Osgood and Krisztian Vertes made major inroads with the penciling and inking of these and the eastern pair. While they are inscribed by Akoris and dedicated to the memory and monument of Thutmose III, they are actually reused, faceted columns from the Twenty-fifth Dynasty God's Wives funerary chapels across the way with numerous traces of the original inscriptions, which must also be carefully documented. Epigrapher Jen Kimpton is doing an in-depth analysis of each of the four columns to determine exactly where each of them originated.

Another focus of the epigraphic team this season was the painting history of the Eighteenth Dynasty temple proper, where in some areas — but not all — the Thutmoside reliefs were repainted in later periods of restoration, repair, and embellishment. The evidence suggests that there were at least two major periods of repainting in selected areas, one Ptolemaic in date, which may have corresponded to episodes of major structural repair to that part of the temple. The contrast in style, detail, and palette between the Eighteenth Dynasty and Ptolemaic period (more than a thousand years later) is quite pronounced, and clearly representing the sequence in our drawings has presented some interesting challenges. A breakdown of drawing progress for this season follows:

>Penciling completed: sixteen drawing enlargements
>Inking completed: fifteen drawing enlargements
>Collation completed: seven drawings
>Transfer Check completed: thirteen drawings
>Director Check completed: seven drawings
>Awaiting Director Check: eight drawings

Conservation

Lotfi Hassan, Adel Azziz, and the conservation team (including four local Egyptian conservation students this season) extended the consolidation of the deteriorating exterior walls of the Eighteenth Dynasty sanctuary along the northern, western, and southern sides, where the decay due to groundwater salts was found to be extreme. Old mortar infill was removed and replaced with new breathable lime mortar, and in some cases radically decaying stone was reinforced with Wacker OH 100 silicate. In the case of the northeastern outer wall section, three sandstone slabs (96 × 86 × 21 cm; 80 × 86 × 21 cm [in two sections]; and 98.5 × 86.0 × 21.0 cm [in two sections]) were inserted to replace the totally decayed stone by mason Frank Helmholz working closely with Lotfi. Photographer Yarko took pre-conservation photographs of the decaying walls and the bark sanctuary ambulatory and bark sanctuary exterior eastern and western faces prior to cleaning, and then again afterward. A meter and a half of debris around the southern and northern exterior walls of the sanctuary was removed to the depth of about a meter to allow the decaying stone walls to breathe, and poulticing with Sepiolite clay was applied on all sides to dissolve and eliminate the surface salts. The dirt trenches around the sanctuary were lined with brick to prevent erosion, and to prevent the local dogs and other animals from burrowing into them. We missed Adel's wife Nahed Samir at the temple this season. She was on maternity leave taking care of the newest member of their family, little Joia, but will be back with us in the autumn.

Thutmose III greeted by Amun, east pillar face from facade of the Small Amun Temple. Drawing by Will Schenck and Susan Osgood

Restoration

Master mason and new team member Frank Helmholz completed the sandstone floor and footing for the granite naos of Ptolemy IX (started by stonecutter Dany Roy) to the original floor level of the room and moved the naos

Frank and Saber inserting patch stones into the northern outer wall of the Small Amun Temple sanctuary. Photo by Ray Johnson

EPIGRAPHIC SURVEY

Restored naos back in position. Photo by Yarko Kobylecky

back into place in December. He then raised the eastern floor of that sanctuary in front of the naos to its original level as well, and with our workmen moved the naos back into its original position in March, no mean feat. The missing floor section of the naos (which we found at the bottom of the foundation pit several seasons ago) was reinserted into its original position, and except for a few corner pieces, the naos is now 95% complete, and looking good. Kudos must go to Dany and Frank for a truly remarkable achievement, a fitting endpoint to the ten-year program funded by ARCE and EAP for the conservation and restoration of the small Amun temple sanctuary.

Rescue Efforts: The Southern Well of Ramesses III and the Blockyard

In response to an emergency appeal from the SCA, the Epigraphic Survey added to its program the restoration of the collapsing Ramesses III southern well, which the Epigraphic Survey began dismantling in late March. Lotfi and the conservation team consolidated the crumbling reliefs of Ramesses III inside the well prior to dismantling, and covered the shattered surfaces with gauze impregnated with acrylic resin — Paraloid B 44 diluted in 15% acetone designed to hold the surface together during the moving. Frank made detailed plans and drawings of all the faces of the well and numbered each block. Then Frank and our workmen erected strong, I-beam scaffolding all around the well for the dismantling process. They carefully removed and winched up the largest blocks in the well: the two broken roof blocks and the great broken door lintel, and moved each piece (on rollers) off a specially-built ramp to the south of the well onto protected platforms for restoration next season. The conservators then protected the blocks for the summer with cotton sheeting lashed to the blocks to prevent wind erosion. Next season Chicago House will dismantle the well to its foundations and do whatever consolidation, damp-coursing, and restoration is necessary, including replacing at least two whole decayed blocks with new stone. Chicago House also collaborated in the planning and construction of a new Medinet Habu blockyard against the southern interior wall of the Medinet Habu precinct. It was decided by the SCA that the blockyard should be moved to a drier and less obtrusive area for the protection of the material, which comes from all over (and outside of) the Medinet Habu precinct. This season Hourig Sourouzian moved five objects originally from the Amenhotep III mortuary temple back to the Amenhotep III mortuary temple complex blockyard where she is working, the first — but not the last — material at Medinet Habu to be returned to its original site. Next season we will assist with the moving, inventory, organization, and protected storage of the material presently in the old blockyard.

Lotfi and Frank consulting at the collapsing Ramesses III well. Photo by Ray Johnson

Luxor Temple

Roman Vestibule Frescos

Cleaning and stabilization of the late third century A.D. Roman painted frescos in the Roman Vestibule by the American Research Center in Egypt (ARCE) and Chicago House resumed under the direction of Michael Jones, Director of ARCE's Egyptian Antiquities Conservation project (EAC), funded by the United States Agency for International Development (USAID). The conservation work this season focused on the frescos of the southern wall, eastern end; and the eastern wall southern end, and was supervised by conservators Luigi De Cesaris, Alberto Sucato, and Maria Cristina Tomassetti. The work involved manual cleaning of the painted wall surfaces, infilling of losses, stabilizing the edges of the plaster, and consolidating the surfaces. The work for this season finished on December 15th, and the scaffolding was taken down and rebuilt farther away from the wall for post-conservation photography by photographer Yarko assisted by Ellie. The crew will return next November to complete the cleaning of the southern wall including the painted apse in the blocked-up central doorway of the chamber.

The Medinet Habu blockyards

Luxor Temple Blockyard Conservation and Protection Project

Conservator Hiroko Kariya continued the condition surveying and consolidation of the fragmentary inscribed wall material in the blockyard and began preparing seventy-six fragments for restoration to the eastern wall of the Amenhotep III solar court, northern end. She processed and treated 350 new inscribed blocks and block fragments recovered by the SCA in the groundwater lowering trenching to the east of the temple last season. Ted Brock, working this season with Chicago House, continued the process of cataloging and numbering all the fragmentary material from the dewatering trenching with an "EG" designation, standing for "Eastern Garden" to distinguish the fragmentary material from the other fragments in the blockyard, mostly found over the Sphinx Road in front of the temple between 1958 and 1962. Hiroko also helped consolidate new fragmentary material recovered in the clearing and restoration of the Roman east gate and tetrastyle (four monumental columns) area to the east of the temple, before and after moving, totaling 950 more blocks (see next section). About 150 feet of new, three-tiered shelving was constructed along the inside of the new Luxor Temple eastern enclosure wall at the southern end for the protected storage of smaller fragments, many from the Roman area; more will be constructed next season along the northern extent of the wall. The shelves are designed to be covered with canvas fabric covers which can them be tied down securely for additional protection.

The Luxor Temple blockyard database entries for 2006/2007 season were carried out once again by volunteer (and Oriental Institute Visiting Committee member) Nan Ray, and included the triennial condition survey of the original collection (approximately 1,700 fragments); the annual survey of approximately 370 fragments carried out during this season; and tracking locations of all fragments. Nan is very kindly continuing the data entry, a crucial component of the treatment process, this summer as well.

Conservator Cristina cleaning Roman frescos. Photo by Ray Johnson

EPIGRAPHIC SURVEY

Moving fragmentary material from the east Roman gate area into the Luxor Temple blockyard. Photo by Ray Johnson

A five-year plan (three years for the first phase and two years for the second phase) of an open-air museum for the Luxor Temple blockyard was developed by Hiroko and Nan this winter, part of which will be supported by the World Monuments Fund (WMF) starting in the 2007/2008 season. The museum will be constructed with sandstone walkways that will direct visitors along the eastern side of Luxor Temple from the sanctuary to the Colonnade Hall. Using blocks and reassembled fragment groups from the blockyard, it will feature a chronological, art historical, and stylistic chain of examples from the Middle Kingdom through the Islamic period. Informative, permanent signage is being designed, and a brochure will be written for the general public. The museum will also include displays showing artistic techniques, conservation methods, and ancient sculptures and marks an exciting, educational phase of our operations in the blockyard.

Fragmentary Material from the Roman Eastern Gateway/Tetrastyle Area

Tina, Hiroko, Ted, and the Chicago House workmen assisted the SCA this season in the recovery and moving into the blockyard of fragmentary inscribed material from the area of the Roman gateway and tetrastyle east of Luxor Temple. Under Ted's supervision our workmen carefully dismantled the old retaining walls made of reused blocks that surrounded the old excavation area demarcating the Roman gateway. All inscribed pieces were then moved into the blockyard while the SCA built new retaining walls. Tina, Ted, and Hiroko also recorded and dismantled a set of medieval foundations built around the northern bastion in front of the eastern Roman gate; many were in a fragile condition and had to be consolidated by Hiroko before they could be moved. The eastern side of this medieval foundation was exposed when the Governor of Luxor Dr. Samir Farag kindly allowed the moving of the eastern garden wall several meters to the east to accommodate the two brick bastion towers in front of the eastern stone gate. The reused material from the Roman area totals approximately 950 blocks and fragments (400 from the retaining walls and around the Roman precinct, and 550 from the medieval foundations around the bastion). The material from the medieval foundation around the north bastion is mostly broken up sphinxes from the four-kilometer Sphinx Road linking Karnak and Luxor Temples, and Nectanebo II portal blocks. All these fragments appear to be reconstructible and are being given separate "ET," "Eastern Tetrastyle," numbers. Stay tuned for future analysis and reconstruction!

Demolition of the eastern garden wall to expose Roman bastions. Photo by Ray Johnson

EPIGRAPHIC SURVEY

Restoration of the Brick Bastions of the Roman Eastern Stone Gate

SCA Director Mansour Boraik, Ray, and Ted used plans of the Roman Luxor gateways drawn up by former Karnak Franco-Egyptian Center Director Jean-Claude Golvin in the 1980s as a guide for the restoration of the missing sections of the two brick bastions which abutted the stone gateway. This reconstruction was started on April 11, 2007. Ted Brock laid out the outlines of the restoration in string for the restorers and supervised the initial reconstruction work in new baked and mud brick. The restoration was continued by the SCA and was in its final stages as of July 2007.

Hiroko consolidating fragments before moving. Photo by Ray Johnson

Luxor Temple Structural Condition Study

Structural Engineer Conor Power, P.E., was with us from February 19th to the 25th to continue his annual monitoring of the Luxor Temple structure, especially important this season since the activation of the dewatering system for Luxor and Karnak Temples in late November. He noted no structural changes in Luxor Temple as a whole, or in the Colonnade Hall in particular, and no new cracks or signs of instability elsewhere in the temple. It should be noted here that in the spring ARCE initiated a comprehensive post-dewatering monitoring program for both Karnak and Luxor Temples, and a conservation and conservation training program for Egyptian conservators at both sites. This project is funded by a special grant from USAID and was envisioned from the beginning as a follow-up phase of the dewatering program.

Chicago House

Marie Bryan completed her third season as Chicago House librarian, and accessioned ninety-nine new monographs, seventy-three new journals, and twenty-six new series, totaling 198 accessions; twenty-eight of the new acquisitions were gifts. This year Marie was assisted by Anait Helmholz who proved quite adept at helping supervise the library and its Egyptian and foreign patrons and is now indispensable. Marie, Anait, and library assistant Louis Elia Louis inventoried and cataloged all the books from Dr. Henri Riad's library given to us by Henri's family. Part of the library, which has been designated as the Henri Riad Memorial Library, is being rebound now and will be set up in the library alcove where Henri worked for so many years with us, with a framed portrait of him opposite the framed portrait of Labib Habachi. Duplicate publications from Henri's library were given bookplates with his name and were distributed to the Luxor Museum library and the new Mubarak Library which has an Egyptology section. In this way Henri will continue to be a part of our community in Luxor, forever. Photo Archives registrar Ellie Smith registered forty-seven rolls of 35-mm negatives and contact sheets (1,167 images); sixty-four large-format images take at Luxor Temple; and fifty large-format images taken at Medinet Habu. She also labeled 280 CDs of scanned images coordinated by photo archivist Sue Lezon. Ellie, Sue, and Tina did a considerable amount of work on illustrations, both photographic and drawing, for Lotfi Hassan's final EAP report of the small Amun temple cleaning and conservation program; the digital images Tina prepared that show the various treatments on all the wall surfaces will be the model for all future publications of this kind. This season the digital scanning continued to be supported by a grant from ARCE's Egyptian Antiquities Fund (AEF) and was made possible through the digital scanning facility of the Franco-Egyptian Center at Karnak, for which we once again extend our sincerest thanks to Karnak Center Director Emmanuel Laroze. The scanning of the Habachi and Jacquet negative archives is now almost finished, leaving miscellaneous prints and slides in both archives to be scanned, a major milestone. Sue has also been kept extremely busy joining the scanned, digital black-and-white and color photographs for *Medinet Habu* IX, The Small Amun Temple: The Sanctuary. She has also assisted Brett who has been doing the painstaking digital joining of the facsimile drawings for that publication, with extraordinary results.

We were pleased to welcome colleagues Alain and Emmanuelle Arnaudiès who this season inaugurated a Digital Archive Project for Chicago House, similar to one they designed for the site of Karnak at the Franco-Egyptian Center. This ambitious project includes the creation of digital archive database of all the documentation generated by Chicago House in Luxor, site by site, since its creation in 1924, utilizing document retrieval software for electronic record management (4th Dimension Program software) to make the data available for staff members and all scholars. The ultimate goal is for the data eventually to be Internet accessible. For the next four years the work will focus on the large-format photographic database and the documentation of Medinet Habu temple. During this first season Alain worked on the development of the main database and the importing of the old data from the FileMaker program and Emmanuelle, as egyptologist, worked on the acquisition and the input of new data. They were assisted by Egyptian architect Louis Elia Louis, who has been redrawing all of Harold Nelson's Key Plans of the Luxor monument in Autocad to enhance their usefulness in the database. We are extremely pleased to be moving into this next phase of our documentation program with its new levels of accessibility, something James Henry Breasted would have appreciated very much. This project and much of our operating expenses in Luxor this past year were supported by a grant from USAID.

Finance manager Safi Ouri assisted by administrator Samir Guindy continued to maintain the financial and administrative support without which our preservation work would not be possible. We are particularly grateful to Safi for all her tireless work administering the grants which support our expanding activities, most recently the USAID grant; she is a godsend. Helen and Jean Jacquet joined us in November and continued to work on their publications, lend us their expertise, and inspire us. Jean finished an article on the hermitage called "Kom 4" at Kellia excavated by him for the French Archaeological Institute in 1964. Helen finished volumes 2 and 3 of *Karnak North* X, which brings the pottery publications up through the New Kingdom into the Roman period. Special thanks must go as always to Tina Di Cerbo for arriving early in Luxor to open and prepare the house for the resumption of our work in mid-October and to coordinate the laying of another section of new driveway, and for staying late in April to close the facility after work was finished. Chicago House is very, very lucky to have her.

Visitors this season were nonstop and varied. We were very pleased to welcome Oriental Institute Professor Matt Stolper and his family at Thanksgiving; Steve Camp and his family at New Years; and in April Andrea Dudek who cashed in her "week at Chicago House" (auctioned at the Oriental Institute Gala in October) with cousin Michaelene Hojnicki. In February we hosted the wedding reception for photographer Yarko Kobylecky and Pia Nicolai which was quite joyous (and perhaps a first for Chicago House). In March we hosted a dinner for U.S. Ambassador to Egypt, the Honorable Francis Ricciardone and Dr. Marie Ricciardone. Of special note were a series of visits from descendants of our founders: Barbara Breasted Whitesides, her husband George and their family; Ernesta Kraczkiewicz — another descendant of Breasted — and her family; Ann Wilson — granddaughter of John Wilson — her husband Dan Coster and their family; and Uvo Holscher the 13th and 14th and their families, all passed through our doors this season, some for the first time. Other visitors of note were the present Lord and Lady Carnarvon who were

EPIGRAPHIC SURVEY

Chicago House staff, 2006/2007

traveling with Audrey Carter, a distant cousin of Howard Carter; and U.S. Secretary of State Condoleeza Rice in Luxor for meetings with Mubarak. She was not able to come by Luxor Temple as originally planned, but I had a pleasant meeting with her at the Old Winter Palace with SCA Luxor director Mansour Boraik at the conclusion of her meetings. The Oriental Institute tour to Egypt in March led by Robert Ritner is always great fun; this year assistant to the director Carlotta Maher's time in Luxor coincided with the tour, which made the visit even more pleasurable. I should also mention that Carlotta represented Chicago House while I was in Cairo when the CEO of Coca-Cola, E. Neville Isdell, visited Luxor, and she accepted an award from him in honor of our preservation work in Luxor. Carlotta continues to lovingly maintain the Friends of Chicago House donor program, for which we are enormously grateful!

Finally, it should be mentioned that in an attempt to preserve through documentation the many areas of historic Luxor that are being removed or modified in the city's urban renewal program, Chicago House expanded its documentation program this year to include those parts of Luxor which are being directly affected. Yarko Kobylecky, Sue Lezon, and Ted Brock were sent out into Luxor this season on both sides of the river to photograph the buildings scheduled for demolition in the city's road-widening program and those covering the Sphinx Road between Karnak and Luxor temples. Yarko also photographed the towns of Dira Abu El Naga and Gurna on the west bank before they were demolished, and recorded the demolition process and its aftermath. These buildings may not represent ancient history, but they represent a major period of Luxor's

EPIGRAPHIC SURVEY

more recent history which is now past, and now part of the historical record, in part through our documentation. We will continue this program over the next few seasons and dedicate a new part of our archives to this important and fast-disappearing period of historic Luxor.

****

The Epigraphic Survey professional staff this season, besides the field director, consisted of J. Brett McClain, Jen Kimpton, Christina Di Cerbo, and Ginger Emery as epigraphers; Richard Jasnow as epigrapher consultant; Margaret De Jong, Susan Osgood, Krisztian Vertes, and Christian Greco as artists; Yarko Kobylecky as staff photographer; Susan Lezon as photo archivist and photographer; Elinor Smith as photo archives registrar and photography assistant; Carlotta Maher as assistant to the director; Safinaz Ouri as finance manager; Samir El-Guindy as administrator; Marie Bryan as librarian; Anait Helmholz as librarian assistant; Dany Roy as stonecutter; Frank Helmholz as master mason; Lotfi Hassan, Adel Aziz Andraws, Mohamed Abou El-Makarem, Hanem Ahmed El-Tayib Ahmed, Nehal Mahmoud Yassin, and Hala Aly Handaka as conservators at Medinet Habu; Hiroko Kariya as field conservator at Luxor Temple; and David and Nan Ray as blockyard supervisors. Ted Brock kindly assisted us this season in the Luxor Temple blockyard. Alain and Emmanuelle Arnaudiès designed and developed the new CH Digital Archives database; Louis Elia Louis Hanna worked as database architect and library assistant; Conor Power worked as structural engineer; Helen Jacquet-Gordon and Jean Jacquet continued to consult with us in the library and photo archives; and Girgis Samwell worked with us as chief engineer.

To the Egyptian Supreme Council of Antiquities we owe a special debt of thanks for an especially productive collaboration this season: especially to Dr. Zahi Hawass, Secretary General of the SCA; Mr. Magdy El-Ghandour, General Director of Foreign Missions; Dr. Sabry Abdel Aziz, General Director of Antiquities for Upper and Lower Egypt; Dr. Mansour Boraik, General Director of Luxor; Dr. Ali Asfar, General Director for the West Bank of Luxor; Dr. Mohamed Assem, Deputy Director of Luxor; Mr. Ibrahim Suleiman, Director of Karnak and Luxor Temples; Mr. Taha, Director of Luxor Temple; and Mme. Sanaa, Director of the Luxor Museum. Special thanks must go to our inspectors this season, at Medinet Habu temple: Abdel-Fatah Abdel Kader Hamed (Oct. 15–Dec. 15), Ezat Abou Bakr Saber (Dec. 15–Feb. 15), and Omar Yousef Mohamed (Feb. 15–April 15); and at Luxor Temple: Mme. Sanaa Yousef El-Taher (Oct. 15–Dec. 15), Ms. Hanem Seddiq Kenawi (Dec. 15–Feb. 15), and Hassan Mahmoud Hussein (Feb. 15–April 15). Many, many thanks to all.

It is always a pleasure to acknowledge and extend thanks to the many friends of the Oriental Institute whose loyal, tireless support allows us to continue our preservation work in Luxor. Special thanks must go to the American Ambassador to Egypt, the Honorable Frank Ricciardone and Dr. Marie Ricciardone; the former Ambassador to Egypt (now Undersecretary of State for the Middle East) the Honorable David Welch; Helen Lovejoy, Cultural Affairs Officer of the US Embassy; Ken Ellis, Director of the United States Agency for International Development in Egypt; Ahmed Ezz, EZZ Group, Cairo; David and Carlotta Maher; David and Nan Ray; Mark Rudkin; Dr. Barbara Mertz; Daniel Lindley and Lucia Woods Lindley; Dr. Marjorie M. Fisher; Eric and Andrea Colombel; Piers Litherland; Dr. Fred Giles; Marjorie B. Kiewit; Nancy Lassalle; Tom and Linda Heagy; Judge and Mrs. Warren Siegel; Barbara Breasted Whitesides and George Whitesides; Miriam Reitz Baer; Mary Grimshaw; Andrea Dudek; Laura and George Estes in honor of Bill Roberts; Khalil and Beth Noujaim; James Lichtenstein; Jack Josephson and Magda Saleh; The Secchia Family; Roger and Jane Hildebrand; Kenneth and Theresa Williams; Louise Grunwald; Lowri Lee Sprung; Andrew Nourse and Patty Hardy, Kate Pitcairn; Drs. Francis and Lorna Straus; Donald Oster; Dr. William Kelly Simpson; Dr. Ben Harer; Dr. Roxie Walker; Tony and Lawrie Dean; Dr. Gerry Scott, Kathleen Scott, Mary Sadek, Amir Abdel Hamid, and Amira Khattab of the American Research Center in Egypt; Dr. Chip Vincent, Dr. Jarek Dobrolowski, and Janie Azziz of the Egyptian Antiquities Project; Dr. Michael Jones of the Egyptian Antiquities Conservation Project; and all our friends and colleagues at the Oriental Institute. I must also express special gratitude to British Petroleum, the Getty Grant Program of the J. Paul Getty Trust, LaSalle National Bank, Mobil Oil, Coca-Cola Egypt, Vodafone Egypt, and the World Monuments Fund for their invaluable support of our work. Thank you all!

HAMOUKAR

Clemens D. Reichel

The cell phone rang as I was working in the photo studio. Somewhat unwillingly — I am still not used to this new medium of on-site communication, in spite of its advantages — I finally picked it up. It was Ali (Alexandra Witsell) — the excitement in her voice cut through the static caused by the generally poor reception on-site: "Come quickly — I have something to show you — you'll love it…." No time to wait for the car to return from its shopping run. I walked — although the closest excavation area to the house still a ten minute walk at a brisk page. Ali was waiting for me at the top of Area B, the southern spur of Hamoukar's high mound that yielded the remains of our burnt buildings, remains of the city destroyed by a violent conflagration around 3500 B.C., described in the 2005 *Annual Report*. "Have a look," she said, pointing toward a rectangular room, which had walls preserved up to 1.70 m and which had been the focus of her excavation for the last two weeks. In it I found Ula Abu Rashid, a talented Syrian student who had been working with Ali on the excavation, carefully clearing away the last remains of collapse from the floor. Right away I saw what had caused the excitement. It was a round, shallow depression in the floor — a basin (fig. 1). Embedded in the basin was a jar in a way that its rim was level with the bottom of the basin. The basin also contained remains of clay. Its function was beyond any question — it was a recycling bin, a "paper shredder" dating to a time when writing had not been invented, in which discarded clay sealings were soaked and recycled. Not a surprise to find such an installation, considering the vast quantities of clay sealings that we had already recovered. What caught our attention, however, was a row of roughly ovoid clay lumps lined up against the edge of the basin. Sling bullets!

Figure 1. LAST STAND: Basin in floor of room, containing sealing clay and row of sling bullets

My throat tightened. Sometimes it is hard even for a seasoned archaeologist to retain a distance to what he encounters. Over the past weeks we had found more evidence of intense destruction — massive amount of burnt debris, collapsed walls, and vast numbers of sling bullets that rained down on these buildings. For weeks the intensity of the fight that had raged there on a fateful day some 5,500 years ago had literally been "in the

Figure 2. NOAH'S ARK: sheep surrounding Hamoukar dig house during rainfall and floods (late October 2006)

air" in the form of ash stirred up by the excavation. The bullets from the recycling bin added another vivid image — the despair of the defenders. Even this little recycling bin, less than 50 cm in diameter, was used in a "last stand" to make weapons. Weapons that never were used, for the roof came down on them before they had a chance to dry out.

Following the 2005 season, when we first reported the violent end to this early city by warfare, a barrage of reports appeared in the media on our findings. A Google search shows that Hamoukar has almost turned into a household name (recently even an item on *Jeopardy!*), intrinsically connected to "early warfare." Our discoveries, however, also found some highly critical responses in the scientific community. Some colleagues went as far as doubting our identification of those ovoid clay lumps as "sling bullets" and, in fact, doubted our warfare "scenario" altogether. An article published in *Science Magazine* on our findings in June 2006 took a neutral stance on this dispute, but nonetheless labeled our interpretation as "controversial." It was clear that more evidence was needed to prove our point.

By the first week of September 2006 we were back in Damascus. The Syrian Department of Antiquities had extended our permit to work at Hamoukar (which, considering Hamoukar's location close to the border with Iraq, should never be taken for granted for an American team). Following the completion of formalities, we headed out to Hamoukar on September 11 and started work on September 16. As a joint Syrian-American project, this season saw the second year of co-directorship between myself and Salaam al-Kuntar, who works for the Syrian Department of Antiquities and is also finishing her Ph.D. at Cambridge University. The team included six students from Chicago — three of them (Dan Mahoney, Tate Paulette, Ali Witsell) had already worked there in 2005, while three of them (Michael Fisher, Kate Grossmann, Katharyn Hanson) joined us for the first time. The architecture was mapped by Carlo Colantoni (Cambridge University), who had worked at Hamoukar in 2000 and 2001. Lamya Khalidi, who had worked at Hamoukar in 2001 and 2006, rejoined the team as excavator and obsidian specialist. Torsten Muehl (Chicago) joined us as object draft person. On the Syrian side, Ibrahim al-Aliya (Aleppo University), Khalid Abu Jayyab, and Dina Kallas (Damascus University) had been present in 2005, while Ula Abu Rashid (Damascus University), Fahd Shabi (Aleppo University), and Ahmed Sleivi (Damascus University) joined us for the first time. Three more Syrian students joined us for shorter periods of time. Ghasan Abdel-Aziz from the Syrian Department of Antiquities, who had worked with us in 2001 and 2005, once more worked as site con-

Figure 3. Plan of Hamoukar's Main Mound, showing 2006 excavation areas (Southern Extension not included)

Figure 4. BURNT CITY: View of Area B from north (composite photograph). New excavation areas are indicated with dashed lines

servator. I was more than pleased that Mahmoud al-Kittab (Raqqa Museum), who had built and (in 2004) rebuilt the expedition house, could join us again as housekeeper and chauffeur.

The season started most successfully but almost ended in disaster in late October, when heavy rainfalls and flash floods inundated Syria. Several people drowned at Hassake, and even Palmyra experienced flooding. For days we were confined to the house. The site turned into a gigantic pile of mud, making it impassable. Over a week of digging time was lost, and mapping was difficult if not impossible. With frequent power outages, even work in the house, such as pottery analysis and object photography, was largely impeded for days. The area around our house had turned into a major refuge for sheep herds, which took an extra toll on our nerves — the constant sounds of

Figure 5. BUREAUCRATIC WEIGHT. Area B: (left) Torsten Muehl and Ali Witsell excavate some of the hundreds of clay sealings retreived in small room west of TpB-B; (right) paper tags marking the findspots of sealings for subsequent mapping

Figure 6. Clay sealing with geometric seal design. Area B; date: ca. 3500 B.C.

Figure 7. Clay sealing with impression of crescent-shaped seal depicting six lions. Over 160 impressions of this seal were found during the excavation of one room. Area B; date: ca. 3500 B.C.

sheep mixed in with the rain made us feel as if we had boarded Noah's Ark (fig. 2). The fact that the season still came to a successful conclusion is largely due to an exceptionally disciplined team that went out of its way to use those precious rain-free and electrified moments to get the work done.

Following the large-scale work of 2005, I had planned on a smaller season in 2006 — completing the picture, rounding off corners, and answering questions. In my wildest dreams I never would have anticipated that we were going to both excavate and find more than we did in 2005. Work plans have to be adjusted in the field. In most cases it is a matter of scaling down. Hamoukar, with its remote and politically "delicate" location, however, offers special challenges, including getting to the site, setting up the house, and getting provisions. In a nutshell, once you are there you try to do what you can do (even if it means closing your eyes on your budget…).

Figure 8. Clay sealing with seal depicting two dancers. Area B; date: ca. 3500 B.C.

Figure 9. Clay sealing with seal depicting scorpion. Area B; date: ca. 3500 B.C.

This certainly held true for Area B, the area of the burnt buildings, which had been the center of our excavations in the past (fig. 3). In 2001 and 2005, we had partially excavated two large complexes (C-A and C-B) of the same type. They both consisted of rooms surrounding a square courtyard and tripartite building at their northern sides. The general layout of these units had become clear to us in 2005, yet we didn't reach the outer perimeter of either one of them. In the east, the area of C-A, the proximity of the topsoil prevented a full recovery of the architectural layout, but it seemed possible to get the full layout of C-B by adding a 5 × 10 m trench to the south, and two 5 × 10 m trenches to the west (fig. 4). Since the

Figure 10. Seal, bone, in shape of crouching bear. Reverse shows seal design with human facing animal (gecko?). Area B; date: ca. 3500 B.C.

Figure 11. Area B: burial from post-destruction floor

mound sloped downwards in both directions, all I could hope for is that erosion had left enough of the architecture to retrieve the layout of the buildings. I was wrong — at least in parts. To the west, the level of preservation actually increased to a degree that walls were preserved up to an unprecedented height of 1.80 m. Once more we encountered massive destruction, vast numbers of sling bullets, and even more clay sealings (ca. 900) than in 2005. The closure for the complex in the west, however, that we had been looking for remained elusive. The western edge of the courtyard excavated in 2005 was indeed formed by three rooms, but two of these rooms opened to another large room to the west — the one with the recycling pit described above (marked a in fig. 4) — and this room had another doorway in the west opening to a space beyond the limits of our excavation. Farther to the north, along the western side of the tripartite building (TpB-B) excavated in 2005, we found a long narrow room, similar to a room excavated along the western side of the other tripartite building (TpB-A) in 2005. The latter one, however, could be accessed through a small room from within TpB-A, hence was an add-on to that building. The new long room, by contrast, had no connection to TpB-B to its east, making an association with it impossible for the moment. It was in this room, however, that work almost came to a grinding halt, for in it we found the largest deposit of clay sealings so far discovered at Hamoukar (fig. 5, marked b in fig. 4). Our own stringent mapping procedures — nothing gets removed without it being recorded three-dimensionally — made work very difficult, but it became clear that we had encountered a large dump of clay sealings with several repetitive designs. Some of them showed

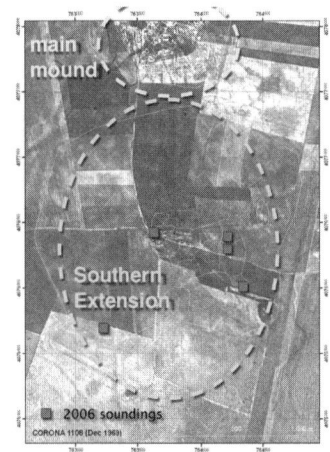

Figure 12. Satellite image showing Southern Extension in relation to Hamoukar Main Mound. 2006 excavation areas are marked

HAMOUKAR

Figure 13. Lithic core, grooved line indicate blades that have been knapped off. Southern Extension; date: 4500–4000 B.C.

a large seal with a geometric pattern (fig. 6); another one, a crescent-shaped seal showing six lions, showed up on no less than 160 sealings from this room (fig. 7). Even if we account for gradual accumulation such a number has to mean something — quite clearly we are dealing with large-scale accounting for one particular commodity. The latter impressions were found on jar sealings, so we have to assume the storage and possible redistribution of a liquid (oil?) at a fairly large scale.

The repertoire of seal motives encountered in 2005 was augmented substantially in 2006. Highlights include several impressions of seals with two dancers (fig. 8), a complex seal with lions and a seal showing a scorpion (fig. 9). An actual seal in the shape of a crouching bear (fig. 10), showing a human facing an animal (gecko?) as seal design, complements the picture.

To the south the level of preservation was not as good as in the west, but we managed to answer a number of important questions. A narrow alleyway (marked c in fig. 4) provided the closure of C-B that we had looked for. The complex was entered through an entrance room that opened to its central courtyard. The relatively poor level of architectural preservation in this area became understandable once we realized that post-destruction surfaces ran across some of the walls. These surfaces were covered with remains of coarse pottery and animal bones — evidence of extensive on-site cooking. Several graves were found in association with these surfaces, some of them truncating the walls below (fig. 11). These discoveries allowed us to modify our

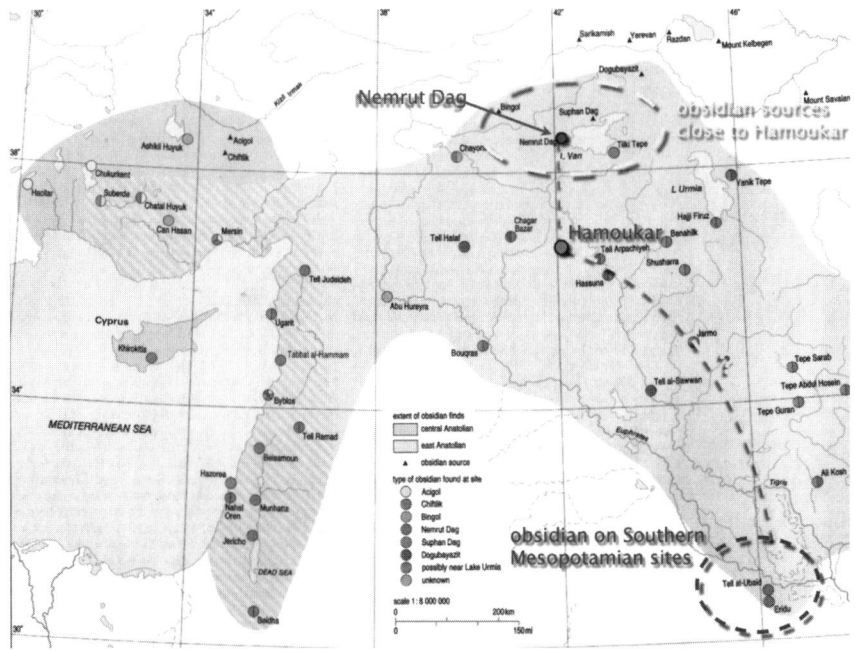

Figure 14. Map showing location of Hamoukar in relation to obsidian sources an possible trade connections with Southern Mesopotamia

reconstruction of the post-destruction events. In 2005 we had encountered numerous pits dug from a higher level of architecture, which itself had fallen victim to soil erosion. These pits were full of southern Mesopotamian Uruk pottery — hence, we concluded, the city was destroyed by southerners and almost immediately colonized by them. Our new discoveries indicate that the situation was not as clear-cut as it first appeared to be; following the destruction of the city, this area appears to have been occupied by squatters (most likely of the survivors of the attack) who leveled out the area for temporary housing. Casualties of war or victims of subsequent diseases or famine were buried in the ruins of the buildings. Once more, we encountered plenty of sling bullets — over 2,300 so far in 2005 and 2006 combined, including several hundred more of the squashed ones (the ones we nicknamed "Hershey's Kisses" in 2005). One bullet was found stuck in a chunk of wall plaster.

The evidence suggests that Uruk culture attacked and destroyed Hamoukar — the question remains why. The answer to that may be found in a vast extension of the main mound to its south (fig. 12), an area of about 280 hectares (almost three times the size of Hamoukar at its later apex as a city around 2200 B.C.). Surveys in 2000 and 2001 had encountered vast amounts of obsidian fragments in association with early Late Chalcolithic pottery (ca. 4300–4000 B.C.). We had already dropped two large soundings in this area in 2005, but in 2006 we expanded work by opening six large trenches in several areas (marked in fig. 12). In all these trenches we encountered early Late Chalcolithic architecture, pottery, and — most significantly — vast amounts of lithic material. In addition to tools, such as blades and spearheads, we found production debris such as lithic cores (fig. 13). Their discovery is almost more significant than the retrieval of tools, for they ascertain that obsidian tools were not only used at Hamoukar in the late fifth and early fourth millennium B.C., they were also made there.

Figure 15. Stamp seal, stone, showing two dancers. Southern Extension; date: 4500–4000 B.C.

The discovery of a 280 hectares obsidian-producing facility at Hamoukar dating to the fifth millennium B.C. gives reason to pause and ponder. Uruk, the largest known city in the fifth and fourth millennium B.C., is a mere 100 hectares around 4000 B.C. Around 3500 B.C., the city of Hamoukar extends for about sixteen hectares. The only logical way to explain the size of our Southern Extension is as a shifting settlement. Even though it is abundantly clear that a production facility of this magnitude extended far beyond the needs of Hamoukar itself, its main purpose had to be export. This raises two important questions — what were the sources of the obsidian, and where were the markets for the tools made from it?

The next source of obsidian from Hamoukar is about 70 miles to the north at the Nemrud Dagh volcano to the west of Lake Van (not to be mixed up with the famous archaeological site with the same name, close to Adiyaman) (fig. 14). Scientific analyses have matched the chemical fingerprint of Nemrud Dagh obsidian in blades from Ur and Eridu from the sixth and fifth millennia B.C. Even if a chemical analysis of the Hamoukar obsidian is still lacking, the fact that Hamoukar is in direct line between the Nemrud Dagh and Southern Mesopotamia seems to be more than a coincidence. A large-scale obsidian-producing facility at Hamoukar could also answer another important question raised in connection with Hamoukar's early urban adventure — why did people move into the confines of a city in an area that by its geographic and climatic conditions

Figure 16. Late third-millennium ware from Area C; date: ca. 2200 B.C.

Figure 17. Clay sealing with impression of cylinder seal showing banquet scene. Area C; date: ca. 2200 B.C.

allows rain-fed agriculture, hence favoring a village and subsistence-based lifestyle? A large-scale export of obsidian tools to the south would have required a significant surplus production and resulted in an accumulation of wealth that had to be protected by a wall — such as the Late Chalcolithic city wall of Hamoukar discovered in 1999. Such a powerful position in the obsidian trade could also have contributed to Hamoukar's ultimate doom — before the widespread use of copper in the later fourth millennium B.C., lithics not only were used for household tools but also for weaponry. If Hamoukar attempted to monopolize access to the Nemrud Dagh obsidian sources and the manufacture of tools from it, then it may have been seen as threat to vital interests of the Uruk state and hence had to be eliminated. The whole operation could have been part of a larger push to the west — Tell Brak, some 100 km to the west, shows a similar destruction layer that roughly dates to the same period. Both sites are situated along an ancient trade route that ran across the Tigris River at Nineveh, and ran west to the Mediterranean or up into Anatolia. Since this route led towards southern Turkey's major copper ore sources (Ergani Maden), we should also consider the possibility that securing access to this vital new raw material could have played part in the decision to attack and destroy Hamoukar.

Even though the Southern Extension itself cannot be called a "city" — perhaps the term "industrial suburb" would be more appropriate — it contained certain pieces of evidence usually associated with urbanism. This included several stamp seals, two of them showing two dancers (fig. 15), and several clay sealings. Significantly, the occurrence of Late Ubaid pottery and even of Late Halaf Ware in at least two of the trenches suggests a chronological overlap of these periods with the Late Chalcolithic period, which had not been attested before.

The excitement over evidence for early urbanism at Hamoukar occasionally makes us forget that the main site is mainly occupied by a late third-millennium city. Thus it was also part of the second blooming of urbanism in the Upper Khabur region, a phenomenon also found at Tell Mozan, Tell Brak, Tell Leilan, Tell Khuera, and Tell Beydar — though at about 100 hectares, Hamoukar was one of the largest cities. Excavations at the northern slope of the High Mound (Area A) in 1999 (the step trench) and in 2005 have revealed large-scale architecture dating to the post-Ninevite V period (i.e., after 2500 B.C.). I have little doubt that these remains, which had yielded walls over one meter wide, were either part of, or directly associated with, the city's palace. Unfortunately, most of the rooms found were empty; a rapid sequence of rebuildings was noted, and in some cases it remained unclear as to whether we had found rising walls or a substantial mudbrick foundation. A much better situation had already been noted to the northeast of the High

Mound (Area C). A sounding dropped in this area of the lower town in 1999 revealed the remains of a niched building. During excavations in 2000 and 2001, the remains of what appeared to be two substantial buildings separated by an alley were found. Both of them showed extensive traces of burning; a violent end to this occupation was also suggested by vast amounts of pottery that had been thrown into open spaces, possibly indicating widespread looting. Both pottery and ^{14}C dates suggest a date somewhere between 2300 and 2200 B.C. Several enigmatic sealings (long, thin clay slabs) had been retrieved from one room. The seals found on them suggested a date into the early Akkadian period. The exact architectural layout in this area, however, had remained highly elusive, so we put Tate Paulette to work there who in 2005 had gained experience with excavating third-millennium B.C. mudbrick (which at Hamoukar contains no visible straw as temper, hence is hard as cement and often indistinguishable from the adjacent debris that essentially consists of exactly the same material). Tate managed to excavate several rooms down to floor level. As it turned out, almost all of them had baked brick floors — clearly a sign of wealth in an area that is generally devoid of large quantities of fuel. The floors were covered with third-millennium B.C. pottery — often very fine wares (fig. 16) including stone ware vessels known from Tell Brak and other northern Syrian sites. More sealings of the same type as retrieved in 2001 were found. One sealing (fig. 17), however, was clearly earlier, showing a banquet scene similar to those found in the Diyala region during the Early Dynastic III period (i.e., roughly 2400 B.C.). Sadly, Tate's work could not be finished due to extensive flooding at the end of the season (Area C literally had turned into a lake then), but it is clear that we are dealing with a major administrative structure in this area. Whether or not this is a palace built off the main mound will hopefully become clear in the future.

At this point we are getting ready to head out again to Hamoukar. We are planning a two-month study season to prepare the publication of our finds; in addition, we have invited a group of geophysicists from the University of Akron (Ohio) to join our work. Geophysical surveys have been undertaken with great success on other third-millennium B.C. cities, and we hope to be able to retrieve at least part of the ground plan of Hamoukar's Lower Town this year.

Numerous individuals and institutions once more supported the Hamoukar expedition in 2006. On the Syrian side I must thank the Department of Antiquities, notably Dr. Bassam Jamous (Director of Antiquities and Museums) and Dr. Michel Maqdissi (Director of Excavations) for their help and generosity, which also included a financial contribution to the season. The Syrian Embassy once more has been exceptionally helpful in providing us with visas from the U.S., and also aided us in obtaining Syrian visas in countries where visas to U.S. citizens normally are not issued. Numerous individuals in the U.S. have contributed to the 2006 season: Mr. Howard Hallengren (New York), who renewed his generous financial support for both 2006 and 2007; Mr. Alan Brodie (Chicago); and Dr. Ronald Michael (Chicago). Mrs. Carlotta Maher literally went out of her way to help us raise the necessary funds — her continued enthusiasm for our work is most gratefully acknowledged here. As mentioned in last year's report, in June 2006 the Syrian community in Chicago met for a fund-raiser in support of our work — here I would like to thank Dr. Antoun and Sonja Koht for their extraordinary dedication in organizing this meeting, which raised almost 25% of last year's budget, and for their continued support. The geophysical work this upcoming season is possible thanks to a generous grant from the University of Chicago Women's Board. More recently, a meeting of West Monroe Partners (www.westmonroepartners.com) held at the Oriental Institute on June 29, raised $3,000 towards this year's season — thanks to Mrs. Sandra Felker and Paulette McKissic for making this event possible. Last, but of course by no means least, I want to thank the Oriental Institute, notably Director Gil Stein, for continued logistical and financial support of the Hamoukar Expedition.

The Hamoukar Expedition was revived despite what was then a highly adverse political climate. With political relations between Syria and the U.S. having thawed to some degree one could say it was the right step at the right time. I am convinced that the cooperation with our Syrian friends and colleagues at this highly important site will continue to be successful and help to rewrite a significant chapter in the early development of Near Eastern cities.

KERKENES DAĞ PROJECT

Scott Branting

http://www.kerkenes.metu.edu.tr/

Study seasons usually provide many fewer surprises than a season of active digging. That was certainly not the case during the 2006 season at Kerkenes Dağ in central Turkey. The bulk of the season was devoted to the continued study and conservation of the incredible stonework uncovered in the monumental entryway to the Palatial Complex over the past four years. However, several weeks in May were dedicated primarily to the ongoing geophysical survey that proved to yield very exciting results. Conservation and survey work on-site also continued throughout June and July, as did the activities of the parallel Kerkenes Eco-Center project focused on environmental sustainability and rural development initiatives within the village of Şahmuratlı.

Geophysical Investigations

Over three weeks during the month of May the resistivity survey, which uses electrical pulses to map walls and features buried under the surface of the ground, continued to reveal impressive details of the plan of the late Iron Age city at Kerkenes Dağ (fig. 1). From its start in 2001 to 2005 the resistivity survey had focused primarily on the central portion of the lower city. This portion of the city is found at its lowest elevations and therefore possesses more natural moisture within the soil which is a key necessity for attaining successful readings with the resistivity meter. The results achieved over the past years provided an excellent map of the buried buildings and urban blocks in this limited area of the much larger city. It was unknown though how well the resistivity survey would work elsewhere within the one square mile area contained by the city walls.

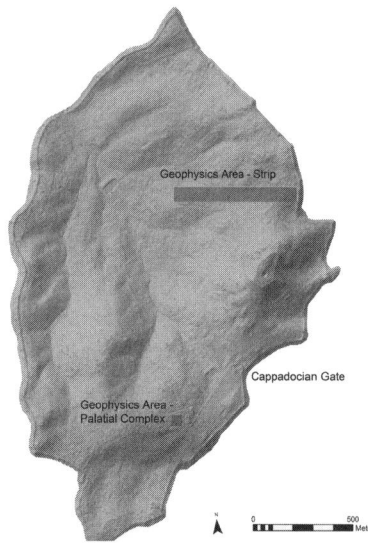

Figure 1. Locations of the resistivity survey at Kerkenes Dağ in 2006

The focus then of this year's survey was to expand the use of the resistivity meter across a wide range of the often dryer slopes and higher areas in the city. To accomplish this task two areas of work were selected. The first was a lengthy 60 m × 660 m strip running from the eastern city wall all the way down the slopes along that side and into the center of the city (fig. 2). The second was a 4,000 sq m test area in the Palatial Complex itself,

KERKENES DAĞ

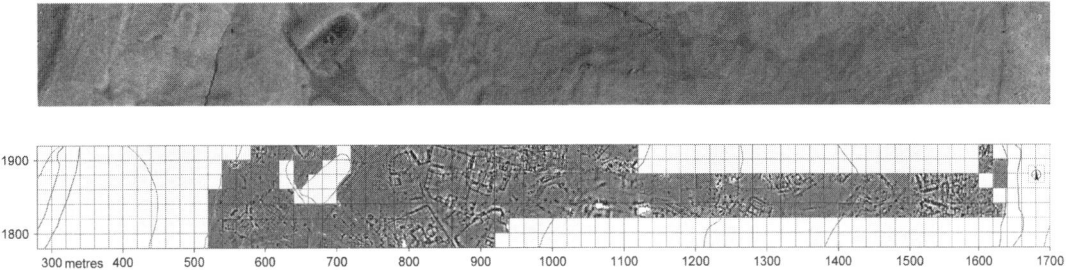

Figure 2. The results of the resistivity survey along the 60 m wide strip from the eastern city wall down into the lower city can be seen in the lower half of this figure. Portions of over a hundred buried buildings are visible in the data. Above the resistivity image is an aerial photograph of this same area showing what is visible on the surface of the ground

high up on the top of the ridge running through the southern portion of the city (fig. 3). Although portions of both areas had significantly less soil moisture than the lowest areas of the city, the results attained were extremely good. Along the 60 m wide strip portions of forty-three different urban blocks were surveyed and 132 unique building footprints from the buried city were identified in whole or in part (fig. 4). In the Palatial Complex the results were so impressive that next year a primary focus of the survey will be the complete coverage of this important complex. This will provide a better understanding of its inner workings and will complement what has already been learned through limited excavation. Of course the best result of all was the knowledge that the resistance survey can be successfully used to map out nearly the entire city in astonishing detail.

Complementing the collection of this data was the testing of several new ways to productively put it to use within geographic information system (GIS) computer software. This included the numeric combination of the growing amounts of resistivity data with that of the magnetometry survey data conducted from 1995 to 2002. When combined these complementary data sources can reveal more information about features such as floor surfaces or even the level of burning in the final destruction of the city around 547 B.C. One practical application of the GIS work conducted this summer was the preliminary modeling (fig. 5) of points at which the final fire was intentionally set by its destroyers within the city as well as the spread of the flames from building to building across entire neighborhoods on that fateful day of destruction.

Significant work was also undertaken on ground-truthing the map of the urban blocks and streets of the ancient city that had been

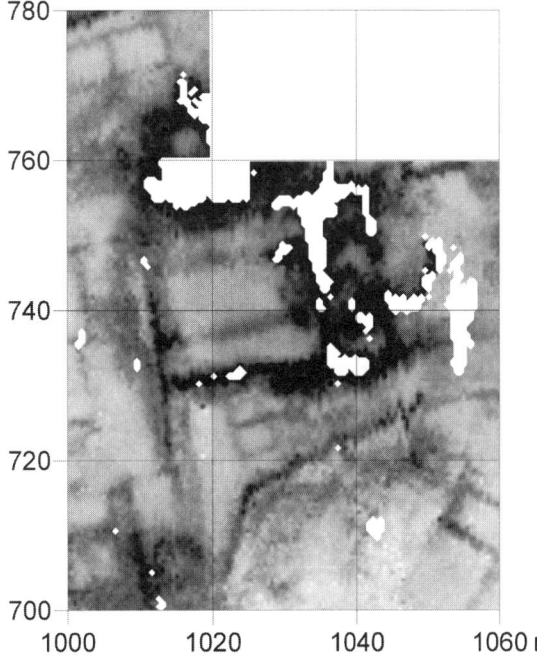

Figure 3. Results of the resistivity survey test area in the Palatial Complex. Most of the extended areas of white within the image are places where excavations occurred in past years. The large building in the center is a partially excavated columned hall that may have served as an audience hall in which the ruler would have received visitors

 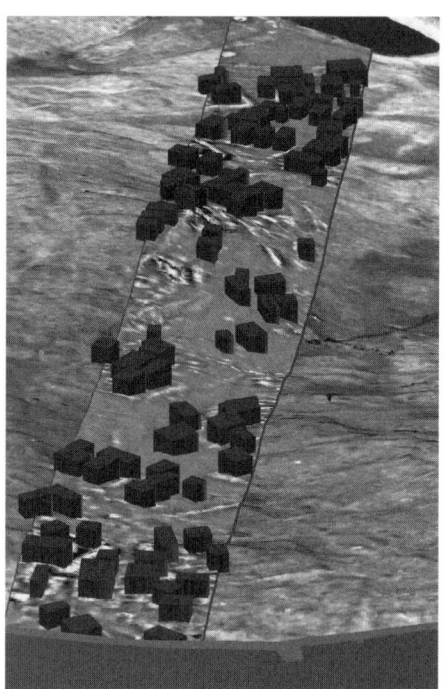

Figure 4. Part of a three-dimensional model of the locations of the numerous buildings seen in the resistivity survey data from the end of the 60 x 660 m long strip. (left) Looking up from the lower city to the eastern city wall, showing the slopes over which the survey was conducted this year, while (right) looks back down these same slopes. The resistivity data upon which this reconstruction is based can be seen on top of the aerial photo between the two parallel dark gray lines

created from a combination of aerial photographs, highly detailed maps of the terrain, and the various forms of geophysical data. It is this map of the urban blocks that the ongoing resistivity survey is able to fill in so wonderfully with detailed data on the locations of so many buildings. Using a handheld computer with a global positioning system (GPS) receiver the team was able to walk around on the surface of the ground and see in real-time where they were in relation to the buried walls and structures (fig. 6). This is extremely useful in figuring out which walls are walls that are partially visible on the surface in order to check them against the plan and where necessary to correct details on the map. The entire southern quarter of the city was checked in this manner during the 2006 season and several relatively minor updates were made to the plan of the city.

Conservation and Restoration

The key focus of this season's campaign, however, was to continue to piece together and conserve the thousands of shattered fragments of burnt stone architectural elements that work between 2002 and 2005 had uncovered in the monumental entryway to the Palatial Complex. Here the walls of the flanking towers and façades had come crashing down in the final fiery destruction of the city. The pieces of the wall's constituent architectural blocks and adornments mixing with those of the already smashed and scattered monuments, statuary, and inscriptions that had once stood proudly in the entryway prior to its looting. To add to this complicated stratigraphy robbers for centuries thereafter had dug through this massive pile of jumbled stone in a search for objects of value, thereby mixing and scattering pieces farther from those to which they once adjoined.

KERKENES DAĞ

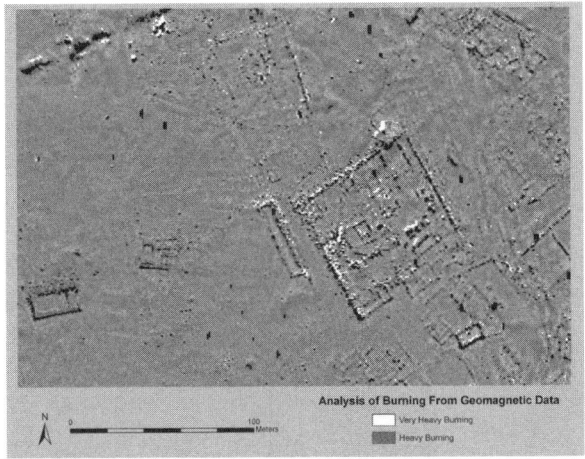

Figure 5. Some of the output from the preliminary modeling of the final burning of the city. This analysis can be used to better understand where the fires were intentionally set and how they spread across the city

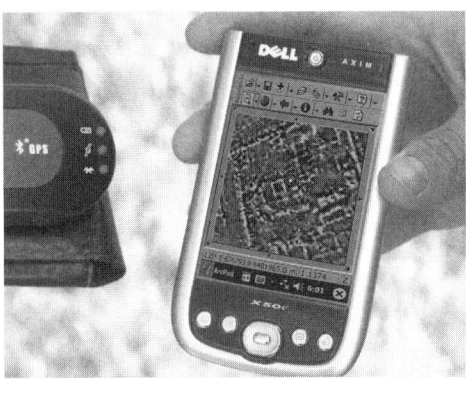

Figure 6. Using a Dell Axim Pocket PC computer and connected Mobile Crossing GPS receiver team members can now walk around the site and see what lies buried directly beneath their feet

Against this seemingly inscrutable jigsaw puzzle the diligent work of conservator Noël Siver and the rest of the team produced remarkable results. By patiently finding and joining together piece after piece some amazing architectural elements have emerged. Foremost among these were at least nine different examples of sandstone blocks carved in a shape reminiscent of the letter Ω. Each stands approximately a meter in height with a roughly equally sized diameter in the upper circular top. Raised bands, varying in width from block to block, run around the circumference of the circular top and end on either side not in a line but in a closed circle with a raised boss in the center (fig. 7). These semi-aniconic representations, with the raised bands representing hair running around an empty face and curling at the shoulders, are found on both the inside and outside faces of each block demonstrating that they were freestanding. This as well as the position in which they were found strongly suggests that they were originally positioned on the top of the short towers, forming iconographic crenellations running around its edge. One can imagine how this would have looked to a traveler entering the Palatial Complex, passing down beneath the faces of the crenellations as they gleamed in the rays of the sun.

Other architectural elements that emerged from this mass of stone were bolsters and a stepped block that may have served as a base for the inscription. Still other forms are just beginning to emerge and will take more time and piecing together in future seasons in order to reveal what they actually are. In addition to what was found through diligent work in the laboratory, an exciting chance discovery was also made on-site within the Cappadocian Gate. This was a large curving piece of carved stone that proved to be a portion of the head of the semi-aniconic stele that had been uncovered in the inner court of the gate in

Figure 7. On the right is a reconstruction of one of the semi-aniconic crenellations being pieced together from the architectural fragments recovered in the monumental entranceway to the Palatial Complex. On the left, Pamela and Natalie Summers are flanking one of the partially reconstructed crenellations and demonstrate with their own curls of hair what is likely represented on these unique pieces

KERKENES DAĞ

Figure 8. A photograph of the stele from the Cappadocian Gate showing the newly found large piece of the head in place on the top of the stele

2003. This large fragment joined directly to the body of the stele and provides a much better idea of what the whole would have looked like (fig. 8).

In addition to conserving and assembling the various architectural elements, each was photographed and drawn for full publication alongside the remaining fragments of the sculpture and inscription. A monograph dealing specifically with the sculpture and inscription was reviewed and accepted for publication through the Oriental Institute Publications Office. Two additional final report volumes on the excavations in the Cappadocian Gate and the Palatial Complex will appear in the next few years.

Limited conservation work was also undertaken on-site along the glacis in front of the Cappadocian Gate and in the monumental entryway to the Palatial Complex. In the monumental entryway the heavily burnt walls of the flanking towers and freestanding column bases weathered very badly over the winter. To prevent collapse and help insulate the stone from the elements a stabilizing layer of earth-filled tires were placed alongside the standing architecture and covered with earth and stone. Meanwhile in front of the East Tower at the Cappadocian Gate a breach in the glacis, started by the removal by vandals of the large glacis stones restored in 2003, was buttressed with large timbers and encased within a sloping ramp of stone. This will provide temporary support to the glacis while preventing further slippage that might undermine the entire glacis. Both measures were undertaken to ensure the safety of visitors and to preserve the standing architecture as well as possible until more permanent measures can be taken.

Figure 9. Using solar energy to prepare part of a meal in Şahmuratlı. These solar cookers were a major initiative of the Kerkenes Eco-Center Project this year and many have been distributed throughout the village

Kerkenes Eco-Center Project

Solar cooking and drip irrigation were two of the many projects undertaken jointly by the Eco-Center and the Şahmuratlı village cooperative this year. The limited availability of water in the village has always been a major problem. By pioneering and facilitating the use of drip irrigation in several fields within the village the project has helped to reduce the strain on this limited resource and provided a model that can be replicated throughout the region. A second primary focus was on designing solar cookers, large parabolic reflectors that focus the heat of the sun on pots or kettles held above, and training numerous families in the village how to use them to reduce their dependence on natural gas or other fuels (fig. 9). The training program proved extremely popular and by the end of the year solar cookers were scattered throughout the village being used on a daily basis for ubiquitous tasks like the making of tea or cooking meals.

Acknowledgments

The Kerkenes Dağ Project is a joint project between the Oriental Institute and the British Institute of Archaeology in Ankara co-directed by Dr. Geoffrey Summers of Middle Eastern Technical University (METU) in Ankara and myself. The Kerkenes Eco-Center Project is directed by Françoise Summers of METU. Our thanks go to the Director and staff of the General Directorate of Cultural Assets and Museums, our official representative Nurettin Özkan from the Konya Museum, and the Director, Mustafa Akkaya, and staff of the Yozgat Museum. Our principal financial sponsors for this season were the Oriental Institute, the British Institute of Archaeology at Ankara, Middle East Technical University, the Archeocommunity Foundation, the Joukowsky Family Foundation, the Charlotte Bonham Carter Trust, Adante Travel, Toreador Turkey, John Kelly Consulting Inc., Yibitaş/Lafarge, Yenigün and anonymous donors. A full list of all participants and sponsors can be found on our Web site.

———————

MODELING ANCIENT SETTLEMENT SYSTEMS (MASS)
Benjamin Studevent-Hickman

The year 2006/2007 marked the fifth year of the Oriental Institute's Modeling Ancient Settlement Systems (MASS) project. In collaboration with Argonne National Laboratory, members of the Oriental Institute and the University of Chicago create agent-based computer models of settlements (and groups of settlements) in Bronze Age Mesopotamia — all toward analyzing their reactions to and development under prescribed conditions. One specific goal of the project is to compare the rise and fall of cities and states in northern and southern Mesopotamia in light of the regions' distinct landscapes; to that end, the models incorporate the fullest possible range of social, economic, and ecological data available from texts, archaeological remains, satellite imagery, geomorphological analyses, and ethnographic studies. A final monograph, entitled *Modeling Mesopotamia: Exploring the Dynamics of Ancient Society* (University of Chicago Press), will present the project's framework and results. MASS is funded by the "Biocomplexity in the Environment" program of the National Science Foundation.

General Project Developments and the MASS Team

MASS saw several significant changes in 2006/2007. First, the project received a no cost time extension of one year, allowing the team to continue its work through July 2008. Second, McGuire Gibson became the Principal Investigator (PI) of the project in May 2007, replacing Tony Wilkinson, who now teaches at Durham University (Professor Wilkinson remains a Co-PI on the project, along with John Christiansen of Argonne). Third, Tate Paulette, a graduate student in Mesopotamian Archaeology at the University of Chicago and a long-standing member of the project, became the principal liaison between the Oriental Institute and Argonne. His primary task now is to oversee the development and implementation of the GUI (pronounced "gooey," for "Graphical User Interface"), the means by which a user will interact with the model. Finally, MASS hired two new computer programmers, Robert Law II and Nolan Frausto — undergraduate students at the University of Chicago. Their mission is to facilitate the transfer of the model to the Oriental Institute itself so other team members (and, ultimately, the general public) can manipulate the input parameters and run the model on terminals in the building. Members of Argonne will, of course, remain involved in the project, helping the new programmers develop a more comprehensive model of civilization in Bronze Age Mesopotamia.

As of June 2007, the members of the MASS team are as follows:

Principal Investigators:
>McGuire Gibson, The Oriental Institute, University of Chicago (PI)
>Tony Wilkinson, Durham University (Co-PI)
>John Christiansen, Argonne National Laboratory (Co-PI)

Senior Members:
>Scott Branting, The Oriental Institute, University of Chicago
>David Schloen, The Oriental Institute, University of Chicago
>Christopher Woods, The Oriental Institute, University of Chicago

Computer Modeling:
>Mark Altaweel, Argonne National Laboratory
>Robert Law II, University of Chicago
>Nolan Frausto, University of Chicago

Research Associate/Post-doctoral Fellow:
>Benjamin Studevent-Hickman, The Oriental Institute, University of Chicago

Graduate Students:
>Tate Paulette, University of Chicago
>Dan Mahoney, University of Chicago

Consultants:
>John Sanders, The Oriental Institute, University of Chicago
>Hermann Gasche, University of Ghent

Active Members:
>Carrie Hritz, Washington University, St. Louis (previously Research Associate/Post-doctoral fellow)
>Jason Ur, Harvard University
>Magnus Widell, The Oriental Institute, University of Chicago (previously Research Associate/Post-doctoral fellow)

Model Developments (with John Christiansen)

Much of the programming this past year was devoted to the model framework for social and economic structure. MASS is well along in the development of a prototype modeling approach for automatically synthesizing regional-scale ground movement networks and surface cover patchworks (including settlement field mosaics) from digital maps of settlement layouts, elevations, watercourses, and agricultural land partitions. With the modeling of larger settlements and settlement clusters, considerable attention has also been given to the emergence of ruling elites, leadership contention and succession, distribution of temple resources, and the onset and perpetuation of social stratification — including the establishment of patron-client relationships among households. Nomads and exchange networks incorporating agents outside the settlement continue to be integral features of the model. Other research has focused on climate stress.

Northern Mesopotamia

Much of the work in the north has been devoted to regional analysis of settlement clusters; now, the basic framework for a system of some thirty settlements is in place. The MASS team is designing improved context-sensitive mechanisms for efficiently distributing the computational load for the heterogeneous, multi-model simulations across the nodes of a processor cluster/network. With this, the MASS team has also developed a ground-movement model for both internal, socioecological, process representation and animation graphics to display the flow of workers and materiel through and among villages and to and from work sites. Future work in this area includes the possibility of incorporating "Shulgi," a new pedestrian simulator developed by the Center for Ancient Middle Eastern Landscapes of the Oriental Institute, into the model.

Southern Mesopotamia

To support agricultural simulations in irrigated southern Mesopotamia, the MASS team has researched and constructed a comprehensive, fine-scale simulation representation of the dynamics of irrigated agriculture. This was a major challenge, including, as it did, the requirement to represent strongly interlinked cultivation and irrigation activities and water balance processes in the same landscape partitions (e.g., crop fields). As a critical part of this activity, members of Argonne designed and implemented enhancements to the USDA's SWAT model to accommodate the increased complexity and subtlety of irrigation management operations. Later elements to be incorporated into the southern model include date cultivation and fishing.

Education, Outreach, and Other Developments
(with John Christiansen and Tony Wilkinson)

Several efforts were devoted to educational outreach and related developments this past year. At the initiative of M. Altaweel, the team introduced a possible curriculum for teaching modeling methods (e.g., system dynamics, agent-based and process-oriented modeling, etc.) to a larger audience. This is currently being developed at Argonne and will include a toolkit for model-building similar to those toolkits already available in other contexts. Along these lines, the team is also looking at the possibility of making the model freely available with open-source software.

In October 2007, MASS members based at Argonne participated in the Argonne Open House, an all-day event open to the general public and attended by over 18,000 people. MASS members continuously ran simulations with projected animation displays and discussed both the NSF-supported ancient Mesopotamian project and a recent spin-off pilot project that focuses on modern Southeast Asian micro-agroeconomics. The MASS Bronze Age simulation project and its modern-day Southeast Asian spin-off project were later featured in Argonne's "Introduce a Girl to Engineering Day," February 22, 2007. There, MASS members demonstrated and described this work and engaged in spirited discussions with groups of middle school girls and their schools' faculty mentors. At both events, the MASS work was selected as one of a handful of research efforts upon which to direct the public's attention, from among the hundreds of diverse and worthy ongoing R&D activities at Argonne. Along with this outreach, MASS has spawned several projects through the University of Chicago/Argonne National Laboratory Joint Theory Institute, including more refined simulations of specific issues such as human movement and the formation and evolution of language. Through these related projects, the MASS model itself grows more refined.

During his tenure as PI, Tony Wilkinson was particularly active in communicating MASS work to other researchers within the field of social modeling and in promoting general outreach activities to inform fellow academics about the advantages of modeling complex systems. He was awarded $2,800 to organize a seminar on "Modeling Behavior" at Durham University, with an additional £1,000 ($1,900) made available for a lecture series on the subject of "Modeling Being Human" to follow in 2008 (with Professor Michael Goldstein; Durham, Dept. of Mathematics). Through Professor Wilkinson's efforts, MASS representatives have participated in sessions on modeling complex systems organized by Doug White (Oxford), Tim Kohler (Santa Fe Institute and the Society for American Archaeology), and others. More general communications are being presented at meetings such as the Theoretical Archaeology Group conference, (Exeter, UK), the Hewlett Packard Centre's eGrid Seminars (Birmingham, UK) and at the University of Durham Institute of Advanced Studies (the last named has as its theme "Modeling," for 2007/2008).

The list of talks and publications given by individual members of the MASS team is far too lengthy to present in full here. Two noteworthy publications, representing collaborations by several team members, appeared this past year: "Modeling Settlement Systems in a Dynamic Environment: Case Studies from Mesopotamia" (in *The Model-Based Archaeology of Socionatural Systems*, edited by T. A. Kohler and S. E. van der Leeuw, pp. 175–208 [Sante Fe: School for Advanced Research Press]) and "Urbanization within a Dynamic Environment: Modeling Bronze Age Communities in Upper Mesopotamia" (*American Anthropologist* 109: 52–68).

Work for the Coming Year

In 2007/2008 the MASS project enters its final year under the present NSF grant. The team has begun initial planning for a MASS symposium to be held at the Oriental Institute in January 2008 (immediately following the annual meeting of the American Institute of Archaeology, which takes place in Chicago next year). A draft of the final monograph will be presented to the University of Chicago Press by August 2008.

NIPPUR

McGuire Gibson

As far as anyone can tell from this distance, Nippur is relatively safe from looting. Our guards report to our representative in Baghdad that the site is fine and that they wish we would come back to dig. Besides our guards, there are supposed to be a number of special antiquities guards housed in a new building near our expedition house. These new guards are responsible not only for Nippur but also for the other sites in the area. A fairly recent satellite image showed that there was no new illegal digging at Nippur. The damage done in 2003 was restricted to the northern part of the West Mound, and the holes were relatively shallow. A couple of small outlying mounds of Sasanian and Islamic date were also dug on, but they probably did not give the diggers much, unless they found some glass bottles, for which there is a very active market.

The looting of sites is still going on all over southern Iraq. Again, satellite images show dramatic increases in the areas of mounds that are being destroyed. The images shown here are of the site of Isin, which is only about 30 km south of Nippur. It was already being dug on in the 1990s, when the embargo was creating economic problems in Iraq, which resulted in the laying off of many government employees, including antiquities inspectors. At the same time, because the government had very little control over the south of Iraq, looters could dig with impunity. The first photo is from 2002, and you can see a lot of holes in one part of the site. The second photo is from 2006, and you can see the great increase in the digging. Isin, as one of the important capitals in Babylonia in two different periods (2017–1794 and 1157–1026 B.C.), has drawn the interest of scholars for a century, and a German expedition worked there from the 1970s until 1990. Whether anyone will be willing to work there in the future will depend on how much of the site is left intact. Although the antiquities organization is currently trying to stop looting at some sites in the south, it is not certain that it can have much effect, especially at places like Isin, which is miles from a town, and therefore hard to police. Nippur, being only five miles from the town of Afak, is more easily brought within the orbit of whatever government presence there is.

Map of Mesopotamia

Here in Chicago, we continue to work on publication of our excavation reports, and there is slow progress. The recent death of Donald P. Hansen, longtime professor of art history and archaeology at New York University's Institute of Fine Arts, adds greater urgency to the need for publishing previous work at Nippur. Don was an excavator of extraordinary skill, and a great

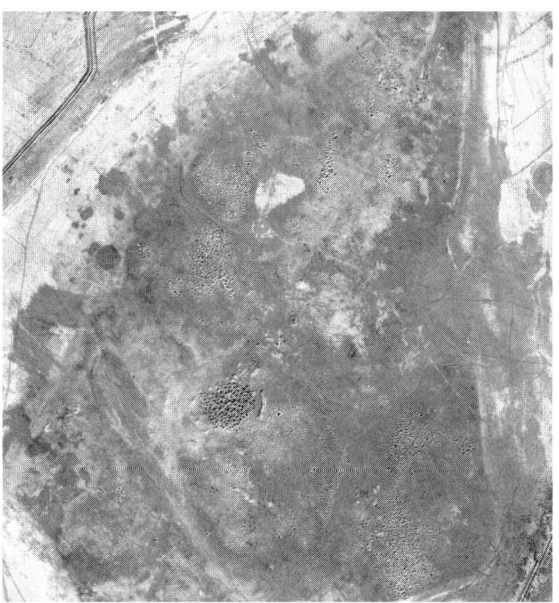
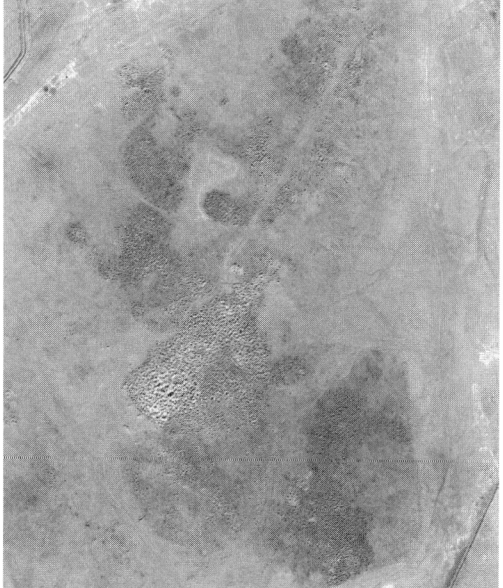

Isin: (left) 12/27/02 and (right) 12/25/06

synthesizer of material. Working as a Research Associate of the Oriental Institute under Carl Haines, the director of the Nippur excavations in the early 1960s, he was the person responsible for the detailed excavation of the Inanna Temple, with its dozens of fine statues, seals, and other objects of the Early Dynastic period (ca. 3000–2450 B.C.). That sequence of temples gave the evidence for a new organization of the pottery and other objects of the period, with Hansen eventually coming to the conclusion that instead of dividing the era into three parts, it would be better divided into two. His arguments were given in a series of brilliant articles, and in a dissertation by one of his students, Jean Evans. But even with all this work, the manuscript of the final report that Hansen was doing with Richard L. Zettler, professor at Pennsylvania, is not yet finished. We now need to assemble all the persons with an interest in the Inanna Temple and in the two seasons that he conducted for the Oriental Institute at Abu Salabikh and decide how best to parcel out the effort to see all his work to publication. At the same time, I need to gather together all the pieces from different team members to get my own excavations at Nippur finished. This will take up a lot of time in the next year, and I expect it to lead to real results.

James A. Armstrong, former team member at Nippur and now the Curator of the Semitic Museum at Harvard, received a grant to work with Hermann Gasche in Paris with the aim of finishing the Corpus of Second Millennium Pottery that the University of Ghent and the Oriental Institute have been cooperating on for more than twenty-five years. Steven Cole hosted Gasche for a week in Chicago in order to proceed with the analysis of the southern end of the Iraqi/Iranian alluvial plain, another aspect of the cooperation that the Ghent and Nippur expeditions have fostered.

Augusta McMahon's *The Early Dynastic to Akkadian Transition*, volume five in the *Nippur* series, for which I wrote an introduction and did the initial editing, appeared this year. It is a very handsome book, reflective of the care and precision that has been McMahon's hallmark. During the year, I wrote a long article on the history of excavation at Nippur, listing all the operations and the important findings. I delivered a digested form of this article at the British Association for Near Eastern Archaeology meetings in Edinburgh. The article was supposed to go into a volume being published in Britain. As it happens, most of the other contributors did not meet the deadline, and the volume was canceled. I am looking into an alternative for publication, probably a journal. If I could find the time, I would like to expand it into a book about the site, its significance, and the history of investigations there.

NUBIAN EXPEDITION

Geoff Emberling and Bruce Williams, with Contributions by Justine James

The Oriental Institute Nubian Expedition (OINE) was revived in 2007, with a season of excavation in the Merowe Dam salvage project in northern Sudan, co-directed by Geoff Emberling and Bruce Williams. The last fieldwork of the OINE ended thirty-nine years ago in 1968.

The Merowe Dam, located just upstream of royal Kushite pyramids at Nuri and Jebel Barkal, will form a lake one hundred miles long and two miles wide when it is finished in the summer of 2008. It will flood virtually all of the Fourth Cataract (fig. 1), a region in which virtually no archaeological research had been conducted before the dam project began. That alone is a

NUBIAN EXPEDITION

remarkable fact — there are few such blank spots on the archaeological map of the Near East and its margins. It is even more remarkable considering that the Fourth Cataract is within the heartland of the Napatan dynasty, which eventually conquered Egypt and ruled as its Twenty-fifth Dynasty in 750–650 B.C.

Surveys of each bank and the many islands in this stretch of the Nile Valley suggest that as many as 2,500 archaeological sites will be flooded by the new lake. Work in previous years by as many as eleven international teams recovered evidence of abundant occupation of the Neolithic, Kerma, post-Meroitic, and Christian periods in particular. The archaeological remains have included abundant rock drawings, burial sites, a very few settlements, the foundations of a small Napatan pyramid, and a number of Medieval fortresses (fig. 2).

Among the most surprising results was the extensive occupation of the later Kerma period (Middle to Classic Kerma, ca. 2000–1500 B.C.). The polity centered at Kerma, known as Kush in antiquity, has long been known to have posed a military threat to Egypt during the Second Intermediate Period (1650–1550 B.C.). Settlement throughout the Fourth Cataract of the Middle Kerma period, however, raised the possibility that Kush was far more extensive (and powerful), over a longer period of time, than previously recognized.

With the support of Oriental Institute Director Gil Stein, we began to investigate the possibility of an Oriental Institute project in this region that would aim to contribute broadly to the salvage effort while also focusing to the extent possible on the Kerma period.

We made a reconnaissance trip in spring 2006, accompanied by the journalist Andrew Lawler who wrote an excellent story for *Archaeology* about the dam salvage project. It was immediately clear that the crisis in Darfur presented no practical obstacles to our work — Darfur begins about 400 miles across the Sahara from the Nile Valley, and in an area with very few roads, this represents a significant barrier to travel and communication.

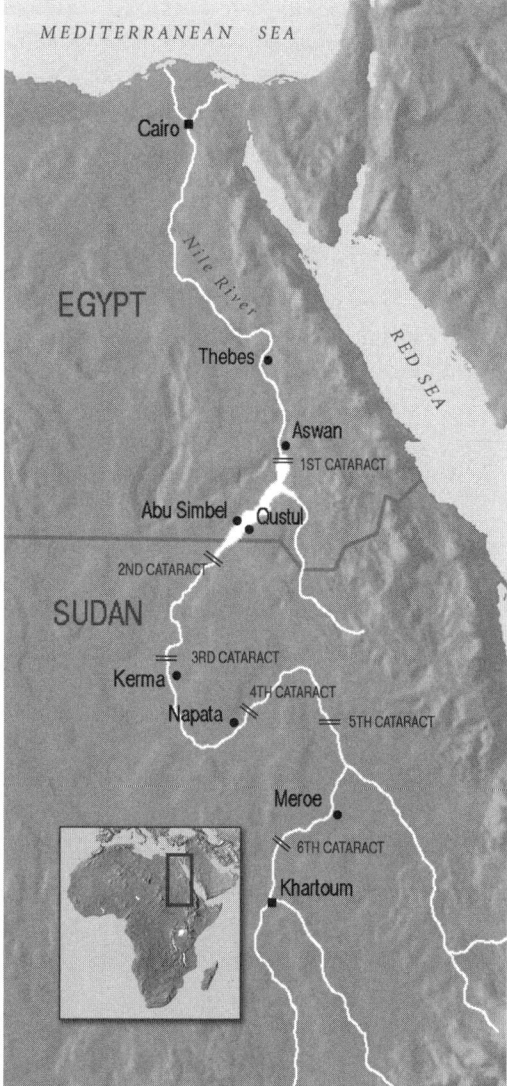

Figure 1. *Map of the Nile Valley*

Figure 2. *Tom James looks for rock art on the island of Umm Gebeir, Fourth Cataract*

We found that there were other local issues, however. The construction of the dam will displace approximately 50,000 people from their homes. The government of Sudan is compensating them for the loss of their houses, fields, and palm trees and has also constructed new settlements for displaced people. The new settlements are not located on the Nile, however, and there is considerable tension between the government and one of the local tribes in particular — the Manasir — that has resulted in a Manasir ban on archaeological work in their territory.

2007 Season

The National Corporation for Antiquities and Museums (NCAM) offered us a concession area in the middle of the Fourth Cataract that consisted of Shirri Island and a stretch of the west bank opposite the island. Although Shirri was in the center of Manasir territory, we made plans for a survey of both areas along with limited excavation of Kerma period sites. We recognized that it was very possible that we would not be able to work in this area, so we contacted several other teams to see if we could help out in other concession areas as a backup plan.

We were fortunate that the Packard Humanities Institute contacted us, along with the other projects working in the Fourth Cataract, to offer their generous financial support. The National Geographic Society also supported our plans.

Another hurdle was obtaining permission from the American government to travel to Sudan at all. Because of current American sanctions, we needed to apply for a permit to work in Sudan from the Office of Foreign Assets Control (OFAC), which we obtained just one week before we were scheduled to travel.

As it turned out, when we arrived in Khartoum on January 26, the Manasir were in active talks with the Governor of Nile Province. We had to wait a few extra days in Khartoum before we could hear the results of these talks, which was that we could not work on Shirri. Fortunately, the team from the Gdansk Archaeological Museum, headed by Henryk Paner, had just arrived in Khartoum and was willing to let us work on Kerma sites in their concession.

The Gdansk team offered us a chance to excavate a Kerma-period settlement site known as Hosh el-Guruf, located at the edge of Manasir territory, and we were eventually able to find a house in a nearby village that we could rent. The following day, we loaded a truck with all our equipment and set out for the house, which was in a Manasir village. Our truck got a flat tire on the desert track, and we decided to send half the team ahead to begin preparing the house. The team that went to the house found that the Manasir village elders had decided to overrule the owner of the house we had rented, but the Gdansk team again kindly intervened, providing a house, food, and beds for the night. Those of us that stayed with the truck were stranded in the desert for about twelve hours and arrived at the Gdansk team's house in Abu Haraz village near midnight. With the help of the local Omda (a local leader), we located another house in al-Widay village and moved there the next day. We were finally able to begin excavations on the following day, February 7.

Excavation Results: Hosh el-Guruf

The Gdansk team had identified a site near the modern village of Hosh el-Guruf as a possible Kerma settlement site (figs. 3–4). It is located in a rocky area that is not well suited to agriculture, but nevertheless next to the river. It is a large site by local standards, with the ceramic scatter covering an area of 9.5 hectares, but concentrated on a single low mound of 1.5 hectares.

The surface of the site was covered with large and small stones in addition to ceramics of the Neolithic, Kerma, and Napatan periods. The concentration of stones, in contrast to the sand and

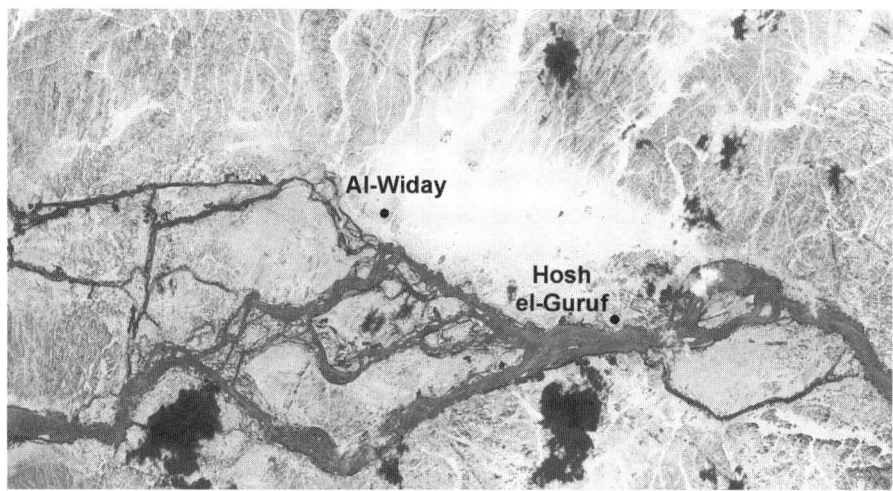

Figure 3. Corona satellite image showing location of Hosh el-Guruf and Al-Widay

Figure 4. Hosh el-Guruf (looking south; the Nile is to the left)

gravel surfaces that are more typical of the area, suggests that the site was once covered with structures built of stone and mud.

Our initial investigation involved a topographic survey (fig. 5) and controlled surface collection in thirty-three collection units each with a radius of 3 m. In addition to ceramic finds, a single partial inscribed seal impression (fig. 6) was discovered in the course of surface collection.

Following the controlled surface collection and using the preliminary analysis of the collection as a guide we opened a series of twenty-one excavation units throughout the site in an attempt to locate in situ architectural remains. Unfortunately, we found that the entire site had been disturbed; only one trench provided possible evidence for architecture, and that was not well preserved (fig. 7). The reason for this disturbance only became clear through further investigation (see below).

Further surface survey revealed that there were fifty-five large grindstones or mills made of gneiss (a metamorphic rock composed, in this case, of granite) on the surface of the site (figs. 8–9). None was in its original position and almost all were broken. Some were re-used, and some had received such heavy wear that they had worn through. Up to 60 cm long, they were significantly larger than the domestic grindstones used to grind grain, and there were many more of them than would have been required for domestic use on a site of that size. A more systematic survey showed that there were also large numbers of stone hammers and grinding stones on the surface of the site, some in concentrations that suggested that they were in situ (fig. 10). We

NUBIAN EXPEDITION

Hosh el-Guruf
Excavation Units and Surface Collection Points

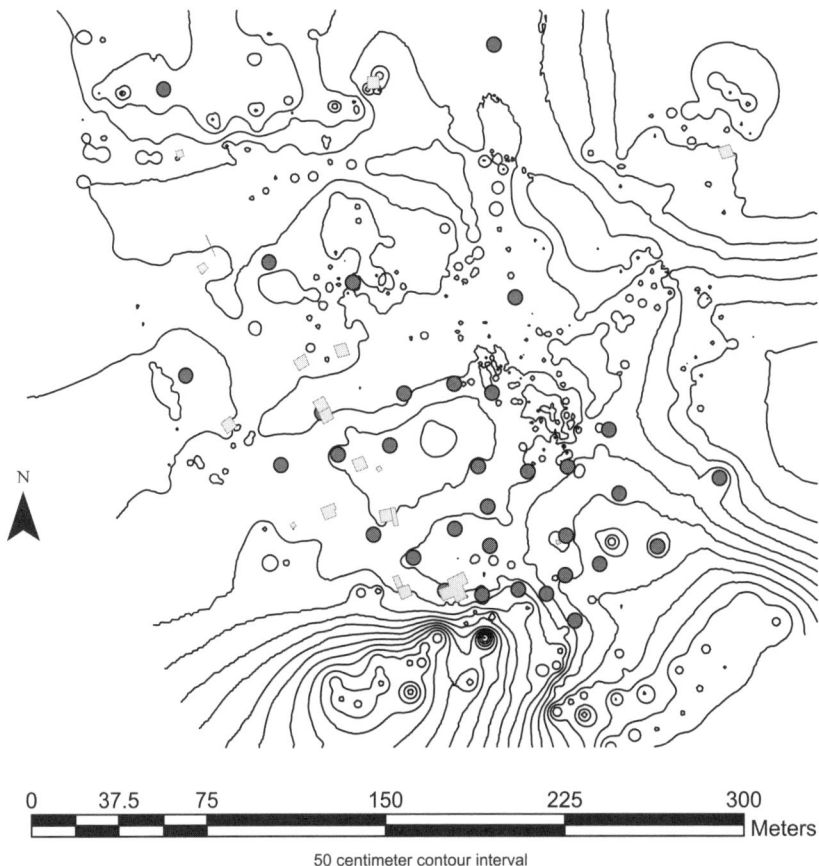

Figure 5. Topographic survey, surface collection units, and excavation squares at Hosh el-Guruf

Figure 6. Impression of an inscribed seal of the Napatan(?) period found on the surface at Hosh el-Guruf

Figure 7. Possible remains of a stone structure, Hosh el-Guruf

Hosh el-Guruf - Grinding Stones

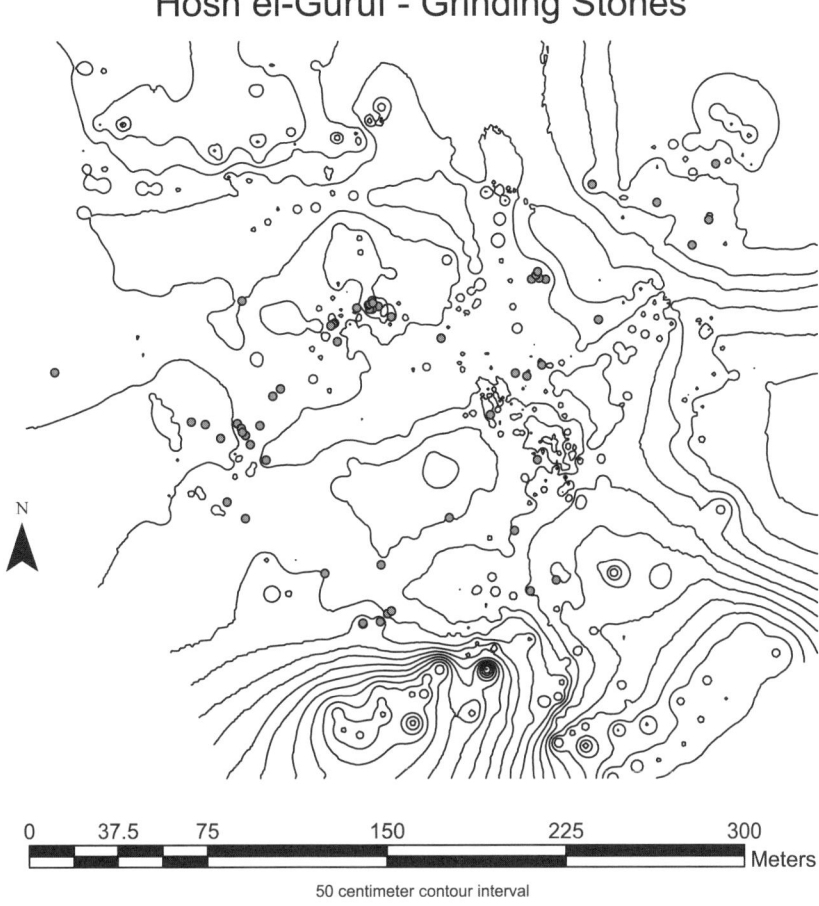

Figure 8. Topographic map showing location of large grindstones at Hosh el-Guruf

propose that the most likely explanation for this concentration of grinding technology is that it was used in gold extraction.

There are two possible sources of gold at the site. One is veins of quartz that are part of the bedrock at the site (fig. 11). In this case, the grindstones or mills, grinding stones, and hammers would have been used to crush the quartz into dust which would then have been "washed" or panned to extract gold. We took samples of quartz and intend to analyze them for gold content when they arrive in the U.S.

It is also possible that the alluvial sediment of the site itself, whether washed in from the Nile or by wadis from the Eastern Desert, may also have contained gold. In this case, the grindstones would have been used to crush gravel and the alluvial deposits themselves in order to increase the yield from washing the sediment.

Ancient authors support this latter possibility. Diodorus of Sicily (*History*

Figure 9. Concentration of five large grindstones on the northeast edge of Hosh el-Guruf

Figure 10. Assorted stone hammers and grinding stones from Hosh el-Guruf

5.27.1–3) in talking about gold in the rivers of Gaul says: "For in their courses the rivers have sharp bends, and since they dash against the mountains which fringe their banks and erode away great hills, they are full of gold dust. Those who occupy themselves with this business collect it and grind or break up the lumps containing the dust, and washing away the natural earthy elements, they hand it over for smelting in furnaces." Strabo (*Geography* 11.2.19) in talking about some tribes of Colchis on the Black Sea, says: "It is said that … mountain torrents swollen by melting snow carry gold down, and the locals catch it with perforated troughs and fleecy hides, and that this is the origin of the myth of the golden fleece …."

We have taken samples of sediment from the site and will also analyze them for gold content. But even if the ancient search for gold involved crushing quartz, it is likely that some of the gold would have fallen to the ground and become part of the sediment in the site itself.

This may explain why numerous local people told us that they had found gold at the site within living memory. This may also explain why we found so much disturbance to architecture in the site and why Neolithic sherds were freshly exposed on the surface of the site (unworn by wind as they would have been if they had been exposed for thousands of years) — there has been a recent gold rush at the site. Certainly local people know how to pan for gold (fig. 12). Presumably this kind of disruption has gone on at the site since its main period of use.

Figure 11. Quartz vein in bedrock at Hosh el-Guruf

Only one grindstone appears to have been found in situ, although mine sites that have previously been discovered in the Eastern Desert of Lower Nubia are also generally not clearly stratified. The predominance of Kerma period sherds at the site strongly suggests, however, that this was the main date of the extraction. The grindstones themselves are similar to grindstones found at Egyptian sites that have been dated to the New Kingdom. The site was also reused on a smaller scale in the Napatan period.

Figure 12. Hassan Ahmed Ali panning for gold in Al-Widay village

These finds are significant at two levels. First, they suggest an involvement of the ruling elite at Kerma in stimulating economic production in the Fourth Cataract. The large concentration of mills and other equipment may further imply centralized arrangements for supply, control, and security of a commodity of strategic value. Very few gold objects have been found in the Fourth Cataract itself, so it seems likely that the gold was destined for export rather than local use.

Second, they suggest that gold was a more important source of wealth (and power) in the Kingdom of Kush than previously recognized. Nubia had long been known as a source of gold, with most of the known sources being in the Eastern Desert accessible from Lower Nubia (or Wawat, as it was known in antiquity). Gold from Upper Nubia is mentioned in inscriptions of Middle Kingdom Egypt, but no source has previously been identified. When our work was presented at the Annual Fourth Cataract Conference in Lille this year, it catalyzed a discussion around gold extraction that revealed that most missions in the Fourth Cataract had recovered some installations related to gold extraction, many of them apparently dating to the Kerma period. Gold extraction continued in later periods, however, and is strongly in evidence during the Christian period. As noted above, panning of placer deposits continues today, but prospecting for veins of ore also continues as noted by one of the teams in the Fourth Cataract this past year.

Excavation Results: Al-Widay

The Oriental Institute also undertook the excavation of two cemetery areas near the village of Al-Widay (figs. 13–14). Al-Widay I had previously been identified by the Gdansk team as a cemetery, and clustered tumuli were clearly visible on the surface of the site. Al-Widay II, on the other hand, was completely denuded at the surface and was identified and excavated on the strength of information provided by a local informant who told us that a bronze mirror had been discovered there by villagers in years past. The graves at Al-Widay II contained little in the way of material culture and for the present we are unable to securely date them.

Al-Widay I is located on a natural rise approximately 500 m north of the nearest Nile channel. Of an estimated ninety graves, we excavated thirty-one. Superstructures, when preserved, were in the form of rough stone circles approximately 1.0 to 1.5 meters in diameter, the larger stones sometimes piled as high as three layers (fig. 15). Both infilled circles and tumuli with empty centers were observed. Burial shafts tended to be between about 20 and 80 cm deep, typically closer to 50 cm, excavated through a layer of crumbly stone and compressed red clay. On

Figure 13. Al-Widay I (looking north)

the strength of associated tomb goods, and comparison to other cemeteries in the Fourth Cataract region, we have dated the cemetery to the Middle and Classic Kerma periods. During the Middle Kerma period, the burial pit tended to be round and outlined with widely spaced stones (fig. 16). During the classic Kerma period, the burial pit tended to be rectangular and stone lined and occasionally also filled with stones (fig. 17).

The majority of the tombs were looted in antiquity (fig. 18), a common occurrence in the Fourth Cataract. Frequently the cranium was disturbed, which has led other excavators in the region to conclude that the majority of portable burial goods were in the form of jewelry or other adornment concentrated around the head and neck, but the lower torso and arms were also disturbed in a number of burials. We frequently encountered cranial fragments and other human skeletal fragments and small beads

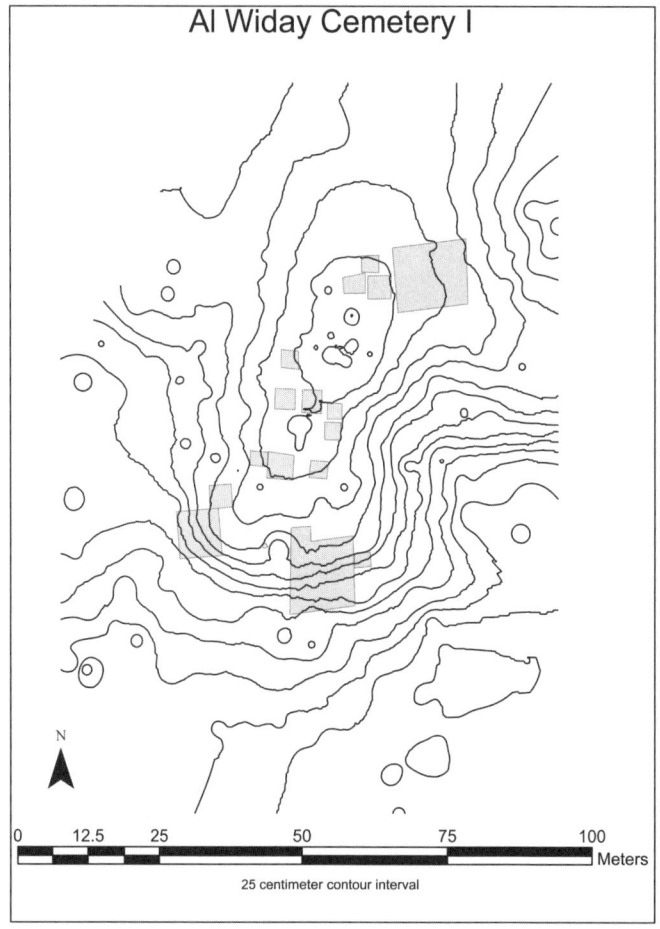

Figure 14. Topographic survey and excavation squares at Al-Widay I

Figure 15. Tomb superstructure (Al Widay I, Area I)

Figure 16. Middle Kerma burial (Al-Widay I, Area G)

Figure 17. Classic Kerma burial (Al-Widay I, Area H, tomb h)

in the secondary fill of robbed graves as well as sherds, including a few pieces that may be interpreted as digging sherds likely used by the looters themselves (fig. 19).

Preservation of skeletal remains in the graves was variable. In addition to damage caused by ancient robbers, water from the infrequent rains in the area was able to pool in the grave shafts, frequently leaving us with extremely friable skeletal remains. A preliminary analysis of the human remains by our team's osteologist, Megan Ingvoldstad, has indicated an age range from infants to middle-aged individuals. This is consistent with the demographic patterns indicated in other preliminary analyses of human skeletal remains from the Fourth Cataract. In a few cases, tentatively identified as young males, the individual was accompanied by a quadruped, probably a ram, laid on its side in front of and parallel to the body. This has been noted in other Kerma period graves in the Fourth Cataract. Interestingly, cattle are not represented as offerings in burials — a practice well attested at the site of Kerma and other sites closely associated with the Kerma state — rather, rams seem to have been favored in the Fourth Cataract. A range of burial positions were noted, though in the majority of cases the body was in a flexed position on its right side with the crown of the head pointing north. In a few cases, multiple individuals were interred in the same tomb (fig. 20). A preliminary analysis of the stratigraphy and variable preservation of such co-occurring burials suggests that the individuals were unlikely to have been buried at the same time.

Nearly all the graves included a standard set of ceramics (fig. 21) including a jar, bowl, cup, and rough cup that often contained ash, perhaps from burning incense as part of the funerary

Figure 18. Burial in which head was removed by ancient looters (Al-Widay I, Area E)

Figure 19. Worn sherd used for looting tomb in antiquity (Al-Widay I, Area H, tomb g)

ritual. A few graves contained as many as eight ceramic vessels, but none could be characterized as wealthy graves by comparison with those of Kerma itself. In addition to ceramics, a variety of beads were present, most frequently made of faience, though ostrich shell, carnelian, and a single example of a gold bead are also represented (fig. 22). Beads included simple, small disk beads made of faience or ostrich shell, larger spherical, typically carnelian, and rectangular-tube beads, often with geometric designs in sunk relief made of faience. Beads in situ were typically located around the neck, wrists, or hips. In some cases the bodies seem to have been placed on or under leather mats. Ochre was also sprinkled on the body just prior to interment in many cases, leaving a stain on bones and leather mats (fig. 23). In one tomb, an ancient razor blade was found wrapped in textile and placed near the foot of a wooden bed or bier (fig. 24).

Of the thirty-one graves excavated, about eight dated to the classic Kerma period, and these show a greater degree of connection with Kerma itself than is notable in the earlier burials. A number of these burials contained remains of wooden beds or biers (fig. 25), as often practiced at Kerma. These burials also contained the distinctive classic Kerma fine ware beakers — black-topped redware with an ash band — which was likely a high-status item made in the capital itself.

Figure 20. Double burial with ram in right foreground; note that the head of the lower burial was robbed in antiquity (Al-Widay I, Area M)

This ware was also used in a variety of other forms, including a spouted "teapot" (fig. 26). The value of these vessels is indicated by the extensive ancient repairs made to some of them (fig. 27). These burials also contained scarabs, two made of faience and undoubtedly imported from Kerma and one local imitation carved in stone (figs. 28–30).

The evidence for contact between the Fourth Cataract and Kerma thus appears to be concentrated in the classic Kerma period. Evidence from Al-Widay suggests that, in exchange,

Figure 21. Set of ceramic vessels from a single burial (Al-Widay I, Area H, tomb j)

for coordinating the extraction of gold, local elites were sent high-status gifts that included elite ceramics and occasional scarabs. That is, the Kerma state appears at present not to have been integrated by extensive economic connections between the capital and its peripheries, but more by gift exchange and tributes.

Future Work

We plan to return to the Fourth Cataract for a final season of excavation in the winter of 2007/2008 to learn more about the Kerma period occupation in this region. We will hope to be able to work on Shirri Island, and if that is not possible, the Gdansk team has kindly extended an invitation to work once again in their concession if it proves impossible to work in our own.

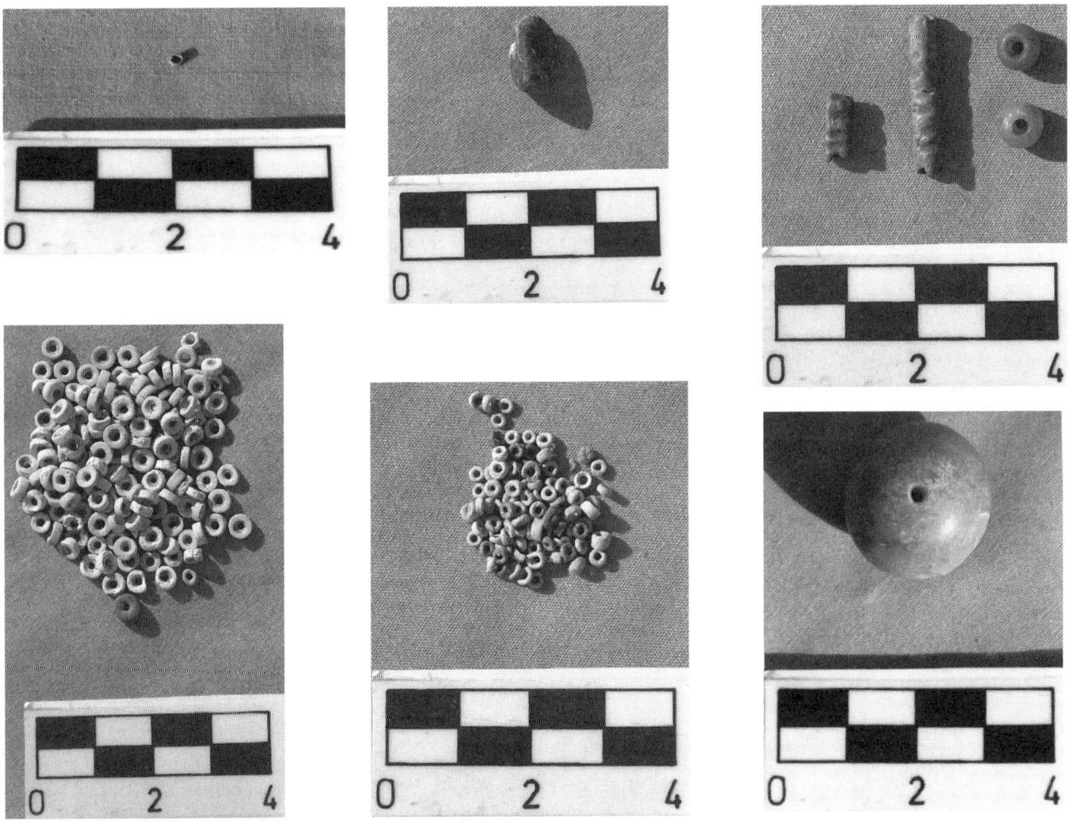

Figure 22. Carnelian, faience, ostrich shell, stone, and gold beads from various burials (Al-Widay I)

Figure 23. Ochre-stained leather mat underneath lower legs of burial (Al-Widay I Area H, tomb i)

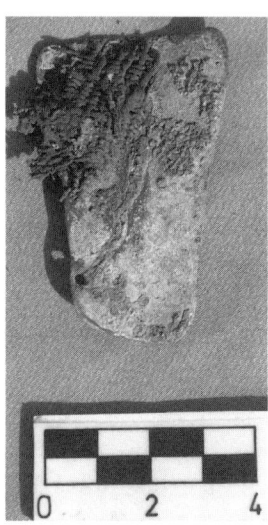

Figure 24. Razor blade from classic Kerma burial (Al-Widay I, Area L, tomb a)

Thanks

It is a pleasure to thank all those who made this season a success. Gil Stein, Oriental Institute Director, made the project possible with his support. An emergency grant from the National Geographic Society enabled us to make plans to go into the field, and extremely generous financial support from the Packard Humanities Institute allowed us to concentrate all our efforts on the excavations.

The team included Oriental Institute Research Associates Carol Meyer and Lisa Heidorn; Oriental Institute Museum Curatorial Assistant Tom James; University of Chicago students Debora Heard, Justine James, and Randy Shonkwiler; New York University student Megan Ingvoldstad; and University of Toledo Professor of Geology James Harrell. Our inspector, Mahmud Suleiman Bashir, was a truly outstanding archaeologist and colleague in addition to being extremely helpful with all the logistical issues that arose during our work. We thank them all for their good humor and hard work in sometimes trying circumstances.

It is a pleasure to thank Director General Hassan Hussein Idris and Director of Excavations Salah

Figure 25. Remains of a bed in a classic Kerma burial (Al-Widay I, Area L, tomb d)

NUBIAN EXPEDITION

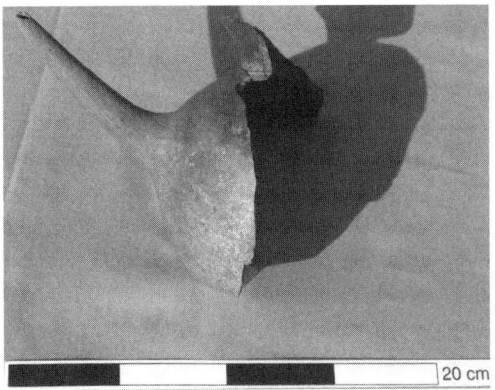

Figure 26. Classic Kerma "teapot" (Al-Widay I, Area L, tomb b)

Figure 27. Ancient repairs made to a classic Kerma beaker (Al-Widay I, Area L, tomb b)

Figure 28. Faience scarab with lotus design from a classic Kerma burial (Al-Widay I, Area D)

Figure 29. Faience scarab with design showing a Kushite man, a seated or rampant lion, and a protective Egyptian uraeus serpent from a classic Kerma burial (Al-Widay I, Area H, tomb g)

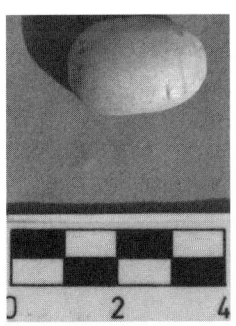
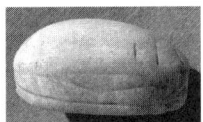

Figure 30. Stone (amazonite) imitation of a worn scarab from a classic Kerma burial (Al-Widay I, Area L, tomb c); note that there is no design carved on the flat surface of the scarab

NUBIAN EXPEDITION

Staff of the Nubian Expedition

Mohammed Ahmed of the National Corporation of Antiquities and Museums in Sudan for their hospitality and assistance.

The Acropole Hotel in Khartoum is a simple, comfortable but unassuming stop for archaeologists, journalists, and NGOs working in the country, but it is much more than that. George, Makis, and Thanasis Pagoulatos, the owners of the hotel, solved a myriad of problems efficiently and with unfailing good cheer. They helped with numerous administrative tasks, permits, and even equipment for the expedition, all of which were important to its success.

Scott Branting and Josh Trampier in the CAMEL lab helped us obtain satellite images and also gave us training on the Oriental Institute's Leica total station. Eric Rupley, graduate student at the University of Michigan, further processed the satellite images, greatly enhancing their usefulness in the field.

Here in Chicago, it is a pleasure to thank Mary Ellen Sheridan, of the University of Chicago's Research Administration, who guided us through both grant applications and the OFAC application process. It was not as simple as it sounds, and Mary Ellen was a great help.

Finally, Bill Harms of the University's News Office worked his magic and got our story out to the New York Times, Los Angeles Times, and eighteen other media outlets in eight countries (at last count). Many thanks!

PERSEPOLIS FORTIFICATION ARCHIVE PROJECT

Matthew W. Stolper

The Oriental Institute's Persian Expedition discovered the Persepolis Fortification tablets in 1933; the Iranian government loaned the tablets to the Oriental Institute for study in 1936; they became available for study in 1937; they have been under study, sometimes by teams and sometimes by individual scholars, for seventy years now. Despite this long history, however, the tablets and the work on them have rarely appeared in the *Annual Reports* of the Oriental Institute. The Fiftieth Anniversary Report for 1968/69 mentioned Richard T. Hallock's long-awaited publication of the Elamite texts from 2,000 Persepolis tablets (Hallock 1969), and in last year's report, former Oriental Institute Research Archivist and ongoing Institute Research Associate Charles E. Jones even mentioned the tablets in connection with a Project.

This is the first report of that Project, so it seems a good idea to introduce the history, contents, and significance of the Fortification tablets, and to mention the shadow of crisis under which the Persepolis Fortification Archive Project has come together, before reporting on the last year's progress. In fact, there has been much progress, so readers who already know about the past and present of the tablets from the Oriental Institute's *News & Notes*, Winter 2007, may want to skip these preliminaries.

Background of the Project

When the Oriental Institute's excavations at Persepolis began in 1931, James Henry Breasted thought of the palaces and sculptures of Darius, Xerxes, and their successors as "the full noonday of Persian civilized development, forming a noble heritage which the modern world is now only beginning to rediscover." But he also believed that "our responsibility at Persepolis could not possibly be confined to an investigation of the great group of palaces, but must include also the related evidences which surround the place and which fuse together into a great body of cultural remains" (Breasted 1933: 316f.). A few months after he wrote these words, in the autumn of 1933, the Persepolis team found the Fortification tablets. They were to answer, in ways that surpassed Breasted's expectations, his hope to have a broad, deep, and concrete historical context for the palaces.

Workers at Persepolis began to build the palaces under Darius I soon after about 520 B.C., and their successors continued to build, adorn, and renovate them until the last moments of the Persian empire, when Alexander the Great conquered Persepolis, occupied it, basked in its luxury, then looted it, and burned it in 330 B.C.. The standing ruins were still dramatic sights when the first western travelers began

PF 0698 obv.

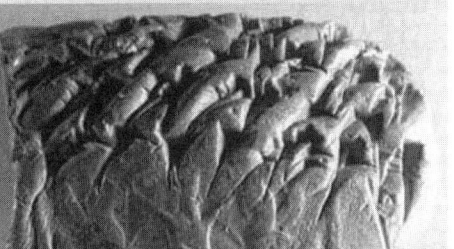

PF 0698 rev.

Persepolis Fortification tablet with Elamite text in cuneiform script (in the small, tongue-shaped format characteristic of primary records)

to look with serious attention at remains of the ancient world in the 1600s and 1700s. The decipherment of the cuneiform scripts began in the early 1800s with multilingual inscriptions that early explorers recorded at Persepolis, and that decipherment was the key that unlocked 2,000 earlier years of the ancient writing, almost doubling the sweep of the historical record. The Persian empire, whose kings left these inscriptions, had stretched from India and Central Asia to Greece and Egypt, dwarfing the ferocious Assyrian and Babylonian empires. In fact, it had incorporated all the imperial peoples of the ancient Near East, and with them, their literate cultures.

From the point of view of 1931, therefore, Persepolis was the starting gate from which the ancient history of the Near East had been explored, and it was one of the culminations that synthesized that history. It was the place where one could hope to see the Persian empire from the inside. The royal inscriptions told how great, good, and powerful Darius, Xerxes, and Artaxerxes thought they were, or wished others to think they were, but the inscriptions did not tell how they got, held, and ran their empire or how they lived in their own Persian homeland. So when the Oriental Institute found tablets with written records in the homeland, great attention was paid and great hopes were raised.

The discovery was a stroke of good luck. In 1933, the excavators were building a ramp for truck access to the terrace. They cleared away remains of a bastion in the mudbrick fortification wall on the edge of the terrace, probably at an ancient point of access to the service buildings around the palaces. They found two little rooms full of clay tablets. Hence the name, Fortification tablets, not because they say anything about fortifications, but because they were found in

PERSEPOLIS FORTIFICATION ARCHIVE PROJECT

PF 1957 obv.   1 cm

PF 1957 rev.   1 cm

Persepolis Fortification tablet with Elamite text in cuneiform script (in the large, rectangular format characteristic of secondary records)

the wall. Within six months, the excavator, Ernst Herzfeld, could give a good description of the find as a whole (Anonymous 1934: 231–32). There are three main components: first, tablets with texts in cuneiform script, in Elamite language, along with seal impressions — thousands of these, probably tens of thousands, some intact, more of them shattered; second, tablets with texts in Aramaic script, in Aramaic language, most of them also with seal impressions — fewer than a thousand of these; third, tablets without any texts, but with seal impressions — perhaps five or six thousand of these. And there are also some unique pieces: one tablet with a text in Babylonian script and language, one in Greek script and language, one in Phrygian script and language, a few with impressions not of seals, but of Persian or Athenian coins. Herzfeld guessed that there were as many as 30,000 tablets and fragments.

This first appraisal was a blow to the great hopes that the discovery had excited. It was daunting to realize that most of the texts were in Elamite. This was the indigenous language of southwestern Iran, but the least well understood of the Achaemenid languages. It was discouraging to realize that the texts were not about colorful deeds of kings and commanders and priests and eunuchs, but only about barley and flour and wine and sheep, mundane, even trivial stuff. They were not even a long record; they were all dated within less than twenty years (509–494 B.C.). They represented a single ancient information system, but a system that was dense, detailed, complex, and hard to reassemble from its bits.

So the real work of discovery began after the tablets were excavated, and it went very slowly. Only one other Achaemenid Elamite tablet of this kind had ever been found, so there was no comparison to go on, and everything had to start from the bottom. When World War II began, the team working on the tablets shrank to a few scholars, working mostly in isolation, who spent their entire lives on these puzzles. Foremost among them were Richard T. Hallock, who studied the Elamite texts, and Raymond A. Bowman, who studied the Aramaic texts. Bowman's work was not completed and published, but when Hallock published his magisterial treatment of 2,087 Elamite texts (Hallock 1969), their significance began to become clear and their information began to transform many ways of understanding the Iranian past.

The texts provided a very large new corpus for the study of the latest phase of the Elamite language, a language written in Iran for more than a thousand years before the Persians arrived there, and known to modern scholars since the first decipherment of the cuneiform scripts, but still barely comprehensible. The Elamite texts also abound in transcribed Iranian names and titles, so they also gave an immense new corpus for the study of Old Iranian languages, especially the Iranian of the Achaemenid court (otherwise represented by a few royal inscriptions) and the terminology of production and administration (otherwise represented by loanwords in other ancient languages). The texts record a complex administration, so they offer a basis for reinterpreting fragmentary administrative records from other regions of the empire. Perhaps the contents of the texts are narrow, even dull, recording storage and payouts of food and drink, yet the institution that kept the texts dealt with almost the whole gamut of imperial society, from lowly workers and craftsmen to the king's own family and in-laws. The tablets are dated and sealed, providing a vast corpus for the study of Achaemenid Persian art, its iconography, development, technique, and social context. The study of the seals on the tablets that Hallock published, undertaken in 1979 by Margaret Root (University of Michigan) and Mark Garrison (Trinity University), resulted in a definitive treatment of more than 1,400 seals represented by more than 3,000 impressions (Garrison and Root 2001, the first of three volumes).

By showing the Achaemenids no longer as gaudy, operatic despots, but as rulers of real people with real needs, no longer as illiterate barbarian rulers of more civilized subjects, but as successors to millennia of statecraft and administrative technique, no longer as borrowers of the arts of other lands, but as the patrons and creators of vital artistic programs, this large sample of Fortification texts changed the direction of every form of modern study of Achaemenid history, art, institutions, and languages. No serious treatment of the Achaemenid empire can omit the view from the imperial center that the Fortification tablets afford. In this sense, the great hopes of 1933 began to be realized after 1969.

Persepolis Fortification tablet with Aramaic text written in ink over seal impression

Sealed, uninscribed Persepolis Fortification tablet

The Tablets Today

The Oriental Institute's permit to explore Persepolis and its surroundings was the first concession granted under a newly rewritten antiquities law that ended the French archeological monopoly in Iran. The loan of the tablets in 1936 was another extraordinary expression of trust. The parties to this decision probably did not realize either how much patience the loan would entail or what historical and philological fruit the loaned material would bear.

In 2004, the Oriental Institute returned to the National Museum of Tehran three hundred of the loaned tablets that had been published by Hallock in 1969, after complete sets of digital images of them had been made and edited. This was not the first return of loaned Persepolis tablets (others had gone back in 1948 and in 1951), but it attracted wide attention.

1208-101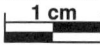

The Old Persian Persepolis Fortification tablet

PERSEPOLIS FORTIFICATION ARCHIVE PROJECT

Most of the publicity was favorable, treating this gesture as an affirmation of long-standing academic trust even in strained political circumstances. But a few months later, this attention was followed by legal proceedings that sought to have the Persepolis tablets seized and sold.

The grounds of the suit and the principles at stake were discussed by Oriental Institute Director Gil Stein in *News & Notes*, Winter 2007 (Stein 2007). Since then, the stately legal process has moved along without great changes. Motions, continuances, judgments, and appeals lie ahead, but the threat still hangs over the tablets. If the plaintiffs succeed, the tablets maybe seized, sold, and dispersed, and the integrity of the original discovery that is so crucial to interpreting it may be lost forever. If they do not prevail, Iran may demand immediate return of the material, making further study difficult, impractical, or even impossible. While the legal process moves on, the Persepolis Fortification Archive is available for recording, analysis, and reporting. Like salvage excavations in the face of a rising dam, the Persepolis Fortification Archive Project is coming together to face an emergency.

What is it that is really in peril? Of course, the tablets themselves are precious artifacts, literally priceless documents of Iranian cultural heritage. But the Oriental Institute is a research institution that deals with artifacts as vessels of knowledge. So what remains to be learned from the tablets and the archive? What knowledge is at risk? To paraphrase another assessment of another crisis, there are three kinds of things still to be learned: the known knowns, that is, more and better information of the kinds we are already using to interpret the archive; the known unknowns, that is, pending matters not yet worked out and whole classes of documents not yet thoroughly studied; and the unknown unknowns, that is, complete surprises of the kind that are often hidden in such floods of information.

There are a lot of known knowns still to be known. The texts deal with the storage and payment of food for various people on the government payroll. The records were mostly produced by five main branches of an organization: one dealing with grain, one with beer and wine, one with fruit, one with animals, and one with personnel. Records were produced at about 150 villages and about a dozen district centers, then brought into Persepolis to be compiled into six-month, twelve-month, or two-year summaries. Of course, no text actually describes all this, with an organizational chart and an information flow chart. Comprehension of the information system and the institution comes from a network of connections among texts, seal impressions, place names, personnel, commodities, work gangs, etc., forming a sort of tension structure that becomes more stable as more points are tied in. A large part of what remains to be gained is more data points and more connections in the network.

There are at least two big known unknowns. Almost everything so far known about the Persepolis Fortification Archive comes from the Elamite texts. The other large components of the archive, the Aramaic tablets and the uninscribed, sealed tablets, still await modern recording and thorough study. The Aramaic tablets, short administrative records with inked or incised texts of one to ten lines, are the largest known unpublished corpus of Imperial Aramaic. They are precisely dated and contextualized, and they are sure to challenge many of the suppositions of Aramaic paleography and epigraphy. The uninscribed tablets show impressions of thousands of different seals, making the archive one of the largest repertoires of seal imagery from anywhere in the ancient Near East. Furthermore, the seal impressions on a few Aramaic tablets and a few uninscribed tablets were made by seals that were also impressed on Elamite tablets, confirming what the findspot implies, namely, that all these classes of documents come from a common administrative setting. At the same time, most of the seal impressions on Aramaic and uninscribed tablets are new, made by unknown seals, implying that these documents originated with different individuals or offices of the overall administrative institution. The already intricate relationships among the Elamite documents are only one dimension of the Persepolis Fortification Archive; the Aramaic and uninscribed tablets present a second and a third dimension. The greatest challenge for future work on the archive will be to understand the relationships among these three information streams and their implications for the institutional context.

The unknown unknowns, of course, cannot be predicted. New words and new seal impressions are plentiful. Some texts show new details that revise old ideas. The most unexpected find so far is an ordinary-looking Persepolis tablet with a text in Old Persian language and Old Persian script (Stolper and Tavernier 2007). We are in the laughable position of explaining why it comes as a surprise that at least one Persian in Persia wrote Persian in Persian script and expected someone else to know how to file what he wrote. Yet it *is* a surprise, and an important one: hitherto, Old Persian language and writing were only found in royal inscriptions; this tablet is the first "practical" Old Persian text ever found, anywhere. It will change the way we think about language and literacy at the imperial courts.

The Persepolis Fortification Archive Project

The Persepolis Fortification Archive Project came together to deal with this wealth of information and wealth of problems in these emergency conditions, with two main aims: first, to record as much of the archive as possible, at as high quality as possible, as quickly as possible; second, to make the information available widely, quickly, and continuously as we record it. Acting on these aims means using electronic media for recording and presentation, possibilities that would not have been available to earlier workers on the Persepolis tablets.

For several years Chuck Jones and I collaborated with Gene Gragg (now emeritus Professor of Near Eastern Languages and Civilizations and emeritus Director of the Oriental Institute) and with Sandra Schloen (Oriental Institute Internet Database Specialist) on a trial project to record and present Elamite Fortification tablets that had been edited by Hallock but were not yet published. We adapted some of the programs and standards that were being developed for the electronic version of the Chicago Hittite Dictionary. The Persepolis Fortification Archive became one of the pilot projects of the Online Cultural Heritage Research Environment (OCHRE), the suite of online tools developed by David and Sandra Schloen for recording, analyzing, and presenting all kinds of textual, linguistic, and archaeological information. Because OCHRE is designed to have this range, it is particularly suitable for the Persepolis Fortification Archive, where records of different kinds that were stored together in antiquity — Elamite, Aramaic, and glyptic — are now the provinces of separate academic fields (Assyriology, Northwest Semitic, Art History), but where understanding any of them depends on integrating all of them. Our pilot project with OCHRE has become a kernel of the Persepolis Fortification Archive Project.

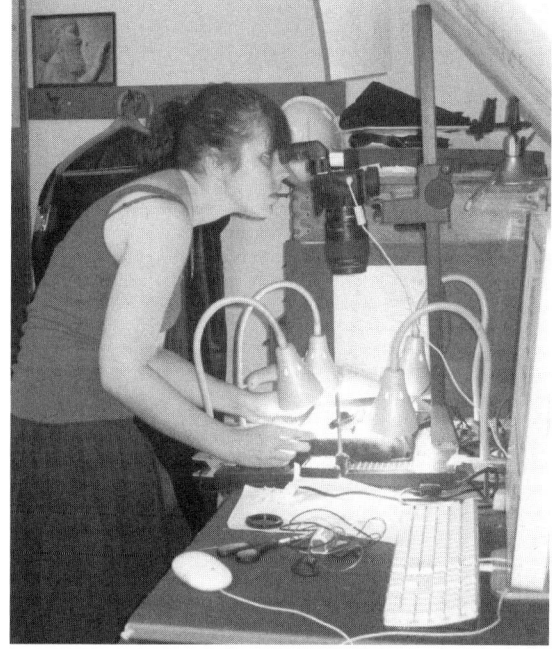

Figure 6. Jennifer Gregory photographs Elamite Fortification tablets. In the background, Darius I

PERSEPOLIS FORTIFICATION ARCHIVE PROJECT

Figure 7. Elizabeth Davidson edits photographs of Elamite Persepolis Fortification tablets

With the help of graduate student John Nielsen, I began to make and edit digital pictures of Elamite Fortification tablets in 2003. This is less simple and routine than it sounds, even for a good photographer and a good cuneiformist. Many of the tablets have more or less the size and shape of a human tongue; the script is idiosyncratic; the seal impressions are often incomplete and the images in them are not always easy to recognize. As a result, just seeing the tablet correctly takes some experience, and most tablets need many set-ups to get full coverage and good lighting of all the text and seal impressions. During the last year, we have expanded and accelerated this process, thanks to a crew of assiduous photographers and photo editors. The mainstays have been graduate students Elise McArthur, Foy Scalf, and Jennifer Gregory, undergraduates Ivan Cangemi and Elizabeth Davidson, and Oriental Institute Volunteers Irene Glassner, Louise Golland, and Joe Rosner. We also had help from graduate students Monica Crews, Toby Hartnell, Ben Thomas, and Adam Miglio. We have improved our digital cameras, computers, data transfer, storage, and backup, but thanks to these inventive photographers, we have also learned to put other technologies to better use: pot-holders for handling hot lights, for instance, or twist-ties for propping up oddly-shaped tablets.

These digital images are not only our permanent record of the tablets, they are also meant to be linked to the texts as they are put online, changing the ways in which the documents can be studied. This kind of detailed illustration has never been practical in conventional paper publication, and the large number of Fortification texts made even the conventional hand copies that are usual in publications of cuneiform texts impractical. As a result, until now most scholars who work with the Elamite Fortification texts have had very little idea what they look like.

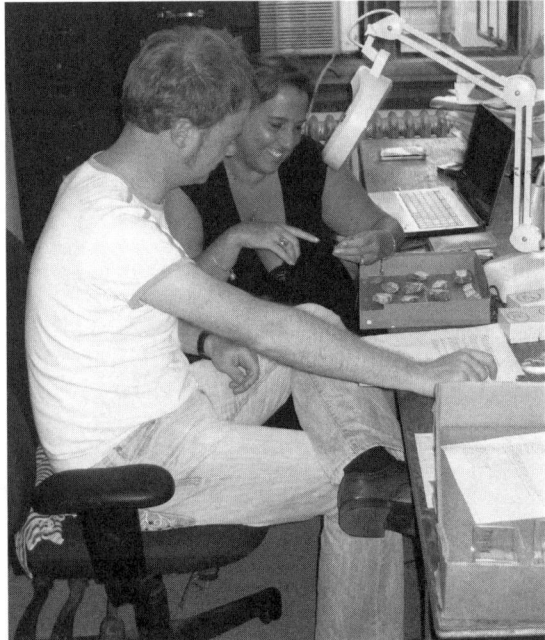

Figure 8. Persepolis Fortification Archive Project Editors Wouter Henkelman and Annalisa Azzoni find droll Aramaic epigraphs on Elamite Fortification tablets

The Elamite tablet photography began with support from a grant from the Oriental Institute Director's discretionary budget and continued with support from another grant from the Provost's Program in Academic Technology Innovation (ATI), made possible by the collaboration of Lec Maj (Research Computing, Division of Humanities). This ATI grant also allows us to employ undergraduate Jason Rosetto to scan an array of documents produced by earlier work on the Fortification Archive,

PERSEPOLIS FORTIFICATION ARCHIVE PROJECT

including photographic negatives and prints made in the early 1940s under a grant from the Works Projects Administration, as well manuscripts, indexes, notes, and sketches produced by Hallock and Bowman. The scans are held on the Humanities server and made available to Persepolis Fortification Archive Project collaborators as needed. The main purpose of the ATI grant, however, has been to allow Lec Maj to help us explore advanced technologies which may help with conserving and/or recording the tablets, including various 3-D imaging techniques, CT scanning, volumetric subsurface laser scanning, and others. So far, we have some interesting preliminary results, but we have not yet found reliable, practical miracle devices.

The biggest step of the last year has been to form an editorial board to approach all the parts of the archive in a single, concerted effort. Annalisa Azzoni (Vanderbilt University) is working on the Aramaic texts, beginning with the incomplete editions by Raymond A. Bowman of about 500 of the Aramaic Fortification tablets. Elspeth Dusinberre (University of Colorado) will treat the seal impressions on the Aramaic tablets. Wouter Henkelman (Collège de France, University of Leiden) will finish Hallock's unpublished editions of about 2,500 Elamite Fortification tablets. Mark Garrison (Trinity University) will oversee work on the daunting array of seal impressions, including those on the unpublished Hallock texts, those on new tablets as they are selected and recorded, and those on the uninscribed tablets. Gene Gragg and Chuck Jones continue their collaboration on the analysis and treatment of Elamite tablets, old and new. I survey and catalog boxes of as-yet unexamined and unrecorded tablets and fragments, helping to select items for others to work on. I also select and edit new Elamite texts.

In November 2007 most of these editors took part in a previously scheduled colloquium devoted to the Persepolis Fortification Archive in the context of first-millennium Near Eastern archives, held at the Collège de France and the University of Chicago's new Paris Center. The proceedings, including preliminary reports on several phases of the project, as well as surveys of older work on the Fortification tablets, are to be published late in 2007 (Briant, Henkelman, and Stolper n.d.). The meeting was also the occasion to recruit a few colleagues with authoritative reputations in Achaemenid studies (including Rémy Boucharlat [Lyon], Pierre Briant [Paris], Amélie Kuhrt [London], and Margaret Root [Ann Arbor]), as an advisory board to help with international liaison and longer-term policy issues.

All the editors made several visits to Chicago during 2006 to begin their assignments. During Annalisa Azzoni's first visit, we discussed the problem of making adequate images of the Aramaic texts, something that posed a range of problems that images of the cuneiform texts did not encounter. We invited advice from the reigning authority on making high-quality pictures of West Semitic inscriptions of all kinds, Bruce Zuckerman of the West Semitic Research Project (WSRP) at the University of Southern California. He came, saw, and, being in Chicago, made no small

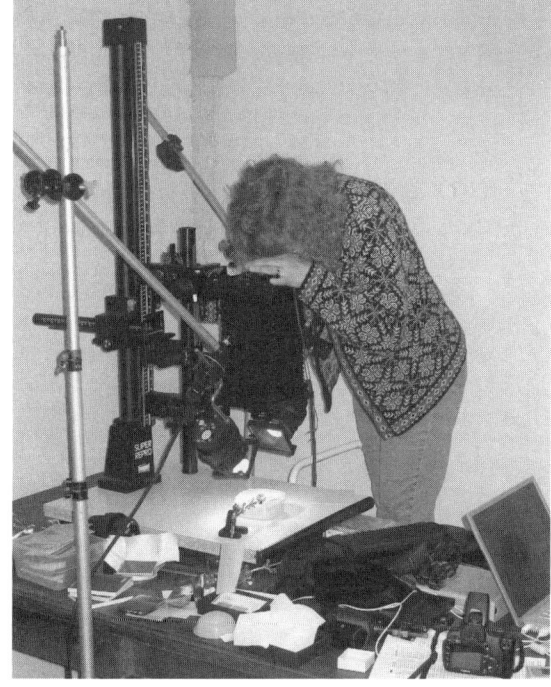

Figure 9. Marilyn Lundberg records Aramaic Persepolis Fortification tablets with large-format, very-high resolution camera and cross-polarized light

plans. By the end of the summer, thanks to Bruce's initiative, the Oriental Institute submitted a major grant proposal to the Andrew Mellon Foundation, seeking support for a two-year collaboration between the Oriental Institute and the West Semitic Research Project to make high-quality images of the Persepolis Aramaic tablets (and a selection of the uninscribed tablets) and distribute them online. The proposal was funded and the project began in January 2007; a pilot project and equipment shakedown in March went well; and the main phase is beginning as I write this, in July 2007. A Persepolis Fortification Archive Project imaging space is being set up in one of the rooms recently vacated by the Chicago Hittite Dictionary's move, and Dennis Campbell (a recent NELC Ph.D. and long-time CHD and *e*CHD worker), John Nielsen (NELC), and Clinton Moyer are being trained by members of the WSRP group (Marilyn Lundberg, John Melzian, and Ken Zuckerman) to make and process the pictures.

Figure 10. Front to back: Dennis Campbell, John Nielsen, and Ken Zuckerman setting up the Polynomial Texture Mapping dome

This project will produce two kinds of images. One set will be very high-resolution digital images, using large-format scanning backs, long exposures, and filtered or cross-polarized light as necessary. The other set will be made with a technique called Polynomial Texture Mapping (PTM), developed a few years ago by Hewlett Packard Labs. The PMT images are captured with a camera and lights mounted in a dome, and then knitted in a way that allows a viewer at a computer to manipulate the apparent light source, as if holding a tablet under a light and turning it back and forth. This is very useful, of course, for recording information in low relief that one wants to examine in shifting light, like seal impressions, incised inscriptions, or impressed cuneiform texts.

Figure 11. A box of fragments of Elamite Persepolis Fortification tablets being cataloged, not yet conserved and edited

The technology for capturing these images is the visibly glamorous part of this phase of the project. More ambitious, more challenging, and more consequential, but less immediately visible are the plans for distributing the information. It is to be done online, on a rolling, continuous basis, as quickly as the images can be edited, cataloged, and given basic editorial data. This bypasses some of the production costs and limitations of conventional hardcopy publication; it also bypasses some of the delay that arises from common conventions of academic study and publication, a delay that cannot be accepted under these emergency conditions. If this two-year project, concentrating on the comparatively small but exceptionally important group of Aramaic Fortification tablets, is successful, we hope to adapt and expand it to the entire Persepolis Fortification Archive.

The information will be presented both via OCHRE, based at the Oriental Institute, and via the WSRP's long-established Web site, InscriptiFact, (http://www.inscriptifact.com/). We also expect to collaborate with other online projects. Editions of Elamite and Aramaic texts will also be distributed via achemenet.com, and images of seal impressions and associated data also will be distributed via Achemenet and the Musée Achéménide Virtuel et Interactif (MAVI), both sites maintained by the Chair of History and Civilization of the Achaemenid empire at the Collège de France (http://www.achemenet.com/ and http://www.museum-achemenet.college-de-france.fr/). Transliterations of Elamite texts, along with scans of the tablets, will be distributed via the Cuneiform Digital Library Initiative at the University of California, Los Angeles (http://cdli.ucla.edu). There are two reasons for this apparent redundancy. First, OCHRE is the unique site and uniquely structured means for keeping all the components of the Fortification Archive linked to one another, the best electronic counterpart of the original composition of the archive as it was found; but OCHRE is in continuing development, while other relevant projects have established sites already set up to present some parts of the data immediately. Second, the several components of the Persepolis Fortification Archive material (cuneiform, Aramaic, glyptic) each have distinct, only partially overlapping audiences (Assyriologists, Semitists, Art Historians) served by these sites.

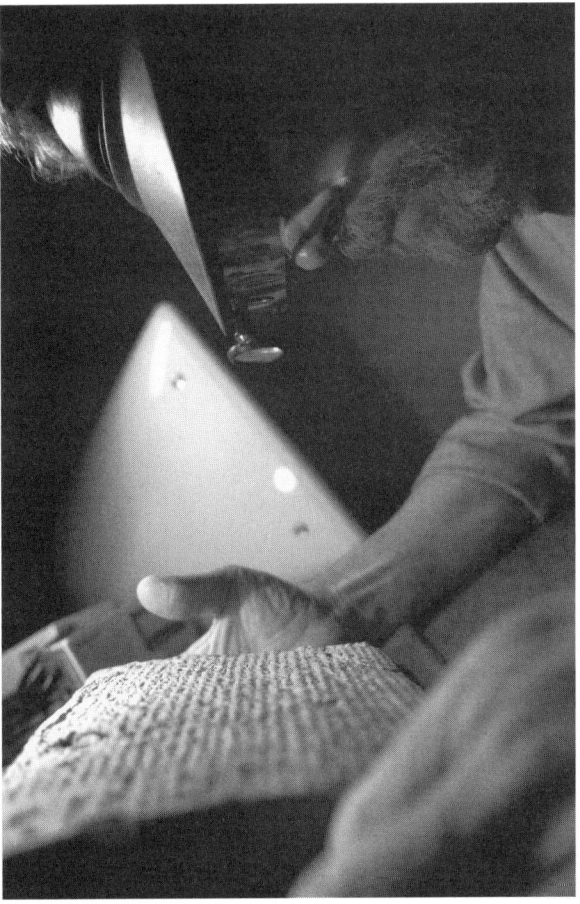

Thanks to the painstaking work of our predecessors, especially indefatigable Hallock and Bowman, we have a large number of Fortification tablets ready to record and distribute, plenty of material to prime the project pumps and get the information flow going. We also have a very large balance of tablets and fragments that have not yet been cleaned and conserved, recorded, nor, in some cases, even examined closely.

When the tablets came to Chicago in 1936, they were packed in about 2,500 cardboard boxes, each containing between one and twenty-five pieces. Hallock and Bowman removed individual tablets from these boxes as they worked on them, numbering and storing them separately. The two of them, other early team members, and the WPA project photographers examined at least 1,500 of the original boxes. By 1980 the original cardboard boxes had deteriorated seriously, so Chuck Jones led a team that transferred the pieces, box by box, to new plastic boxes of about the same size, making notes of each box as they worked.

Figure 12. Persepolis Fortification Archive Project director Matthew Stolper ponders why his predecessors left such a large and well-preserved Fortification tablet unedited. Photo courtesy of Dan Dry, University of Chicago Magazine

This outwardly simple task required four years, and the daunting appearance of the boxes explains why. Some hold well-preserved, solid tablets or large, solid fragments with apparently legible texts or beautifully clear seal impressions. Others hold pieces whose surfaces are obscured by dirt and encrustations. Others hold flakes and fragments that will never provide useful information. It takes only a few moments to realize that planning the project necessitates taking an inventory of the boxes, both to identify the items that will reward an immediate investment of time and attention and items that may reward later effort, and to estimate how many pieces of each kind there are and how many there were, the overall shape of the original Archive.

In 2006 I began a rough inventory of the boxes, recording what items had been removed and edited, what kinds of items were left (Elamite, Aramaic, uninscribed), and what condition they were in. I transcribed occasional well-preserved Elamite texts and recorded exceptional items, such as the Old Persian tablet (which looked completely unexceptional as it sat in the box next to other Fortification tablets). I entered the information in OCHRE, along with snapshots of the boxes as a guide for future planning. The first part of this inventory, covering about the quarter of the boxes, was the basis for the paper that Chuck Jones and I gave at the Paris conference, "How Many Fortification Tablets Are There?" Our estimates: 20,000–25,000 tablets and fragments, representing 15,000–18,000 original documents, about 70% Elamite, 20% uninscribed, 5% Aramaic.

Only a few thousand of these are in good enough condition to provide useful texts and seal images immediately. Thousands more need conservation, cleaning, and stabilization of the inscribed and sealed surfaces before they can be usefully recorded, requiring painstaking effort by skilled conservators working under the oversight of the Oriental Institute's chief conservator, Laura D'Alessandro. Monica Hudak has begun work on some of the tablets, giving us some idea of what we can expect, and we have received a one-year emergency grant from the National Geographic Society's Committee for Research and Exploration that allows the project to hire her full-time for a year. NGS-CRE normally makes grants only to support fieldwork, so this award is a signal recognition of the urgency and importance of our task.

We have also received a grant from the PARSA Community Foundation that will allow us to acquire a binocular microscope dedicated to the project and to hire another part-time conservator. This is also a gratifying award, since it is part of the very first funding cycle of this organization, dedicated to Iranian-American interests, including the cultural and historical heritage that the Fortification tablets embody. And thanks especially to the initiative of Laura D'Alessandro, we have also received a grant from the Women's Board of the University of Chicago that allows us to acquire a Compact Phoenix Laser Cleaning System. This is a device that will speed the delicate final part of the cleaning process. It literally blasts away the last fine layers of dirt and concretion over the cuneiform signs and seal impressions without compromising the underlying surface. We expect it to come online in 2008.

Conclusion

To describe our problem, our circumstances, and our work, I gave a talk to a combined audience of the Oriental Institute's Breasted Society and the Chicago Council on Foreign Relations in January 2007, and I gave another version of it as the first Musa Sabi Lecture on Iranian Studies at the University of California, Los Angeles, in March. Earlier, in October, *The University of Chicago Magazine* discussed the legal travails of the Fortification tablets (Puma 2006), and when we published the Old Persian tablet online (the first, I hope, in a series of such project bulletins), the University's press office sent out a news release that was picked up by the *Financial Times* and *National Geographic*'s online services, among others, and that led to an interview with the

Persian-language service of Voice of America. The best way to keep abreast of developments, to see related news items from many sources and points of view, and also to see some of the past scholarship on the tablets, is to visit the Persepolis Fortification Archive Project blog that Chuck Jones set up at http://persepolistablets.blogspot.com/, averaging about thirty visitors a day since it began in Autumn 2006).

References

Anonymous. 1934. "Recent Discoveries at Persepolis," *Journal of the Royal Asiatic Society* 1934: 226–32.

Breasted, James Henry. 1933. *The Oriental Institute*. The University of Chicago Survey 12. Chicago: University of Chicago Press.

Briant, Pierre; Wouter F. M. Henkleman; and Matthew W. Stolper, editors. Forthcoming. *Les archives des Fortifications de Persépolis dans le monde achéménide*. Persika 11. Paris: de Boccard.

Hallock, Richard T. 1969. *Persepolis Fortification Tablets*. Oriental Institute Publications 92. Chicago: University of Chicago Press.

Puma, Amy Braverman. 2006. "Worth millions ... or priceless?" *The University of Chicago Magazine*, October 2006: 16–19.

Stein, Gil J. 2007. "A Heritage Threatened: the Persepolis Tablets Lawsuit and the Oriental Institute." *Oriental Institute News & Notes* 192: 3–5.

Stolper, Matthew W. 2007. "The Persepolis Fortification Tablets." *Oriental Institute News & Notes* 192: 6–9.

Stolper, Matthew W., and Jan Tavernier. 2007. "From the Persepolis Fortification Archive Project, 1: An Old Persian Administrative Tablet from the Persepolis." ARTA 2007.001 (http://www.achemenet.com/ressources/enligne/arta/pdf/2007.001-Stolper-Tavernier.pdf).

RELIGION AND POWER: DIVINE KINGSHIP IN ANCIENT MESOPOTAMIA AND BEYOND

Nicole Brisch

The topic of the Third Annual University of Chicago Oriental Institute Seminar, held on February 23–24, 2007, was divine kingship in ancient Mesopotamia and other areas of the world, where the phenomenon of living kings that are venerated as gods, is attested. The study of kingship goes back to the roots of fields such as anthropology and religious studies (Frazer's *The Golden Bough*) or Assyriology and Near Eastern archaeology (Frankfort 1948; Labat 1939). More recently, several conferences have been held on kingship in a cross-cultural perspective (Cannadine and Price 1987; Gundlach and Weber 1992; Quigley 2005; Erkens 2002). Yet the question of the divinity of the king — the king as god — had never been examined before in a cross-cultural and multi-disciplinary perspective. Moreover, while ancient Egyptian kingship has been studied time and again (for example, O'Connor and Silverman 1995; Gundlach and Weber 1992; Gundlach and Klug 2004), Mesopotamian kingship is often neglected in cross-cultural comparisons, even though ancient Mesopotamian kings also deified themselves, at least for a brief period of time.

The last over-arching study of kingship and religion in ancient Egypt and Mesopotamia is Henri Frankfort's famous *Kingship and the Gods* (1948), a seminal study comparing the different concepts of kingship in these areas. Frankfort, who was the Oriental Institute's Field Director in Iraq, already doubted the validity of Frazer's ideas on divine kingship. However, since his study much more material has come to light, which forces us to re-evaluate some of his assessments.

While Frazer's study has received strong criticism within anthropology and religious studies, his theories on kingship in various African nations has more recently experienced a revival in anthropological and Africanist literature (especially various contributions in Quigley 2005). Frazer's model of divine kingship, however, severely limits our understanding of kingship in ancient Mesopotamia and ancient Egypt. For example, Frazer emphasized the question of regicide as part of the ideology of the divine king, who is killed when he becomes physically feeble. However, to my knowledge, regicide for ideological or religious reasons is unattested in these ancient societies. Frankfort therefore concluded that there was no divine kingship in ancient Mesopotamia.

One of the goals of this seminar was therefore to bring ancient Mesopotamia to the forefront of a discourse on kingship and to begin developing a new framework for the study of kingship in general, and divine kingship in particular, by moving beyond Frazer's models of thought that, positively or negatively, have influenced studies on kingship for the past century or so.

Seminar participants came from the fields of Assyriology (Gebhard Selz, University of Vienna; Piotr Michalowski, University of Michigan), Egyptology (Paul Frandsen, Copenhagen University), art history (Irene Winter, Harvard University; Erica Ehrenberg, New York Academy of Arts), Near Eastern Archaeology (Clemens Reichel, Oriental Institute; Reinhard Bernbeck, Binghamton University), Mayan Archaeology (David Freidel, Southern Methodist University), African Studies (Michelle Gilbert, Sarah Lawrence College), Chinese Studies (Michael Puett, Harvard University), Religious Studies (Bruce Lincoln, University of Chicago), and Roman Archaeology (Greg Woolf, St. Andrews University). Jerrold Cooper (Johns Hopkins University) and Kathy Morrison (University of Chicago) graciously served as respondents for the conference.

The seminar was divided into three sessions. The first, chaired by Emily Teeter of the Oriental Institute, focused on ancient Mesopotamia and ancient Egypt. The participants in this session all approached the topic differently. Gebhard Selz concentrated on religious aspects relating to the divine king by questioning and thereby proposing to revise our notions of the divine. Michalowski proposed a historical approach, showing that the phenomenon of kings declaring themselves divine is, at least in Mesopotamia, embedded in specific historical circumstances that made self-divinization a very instable form of government that was soon abandoned. Paul Frandsen chose a linguistic approach, in which he focused on the notion of fear of the king in ancient Egypt. His study aimed at clarifying whether the ancient Egyptians considered the pharaoh to be truly divine or human. This aura of fear can perhaps in some ways be compared to the ancient Mesopotamian concept of the divine or royal "aura," which is both fear and awe inspiring.

The second session, chaired by the Oriental Institute's Theo van den Hout, was entitled "Iconography and Anthropology of Divine Kingship." Irene Winter and Erica Ehrenberg both spoke on figurative representations of kings. Winter pointed out that divine kings appear in figural representations as deities of lower rank and suggested to not only consider representations of kings as divine, but also of gods as kings. Ehrenberg, who discussed Late Babylonian and Achaemenid kings in art, showed that the king, even though not explicitly divine, was still considered to be at the center of the cosmos. Michelle Gilbert, whose long-standing work in Ghana has given her deep insights into royal rituals of the divine Akwapim kings, illustrated fascinating beliefs and rituals associated with the cult of kings, and discussed the notion of regicide as well as the question of whether it is the king or kingship that is divine (following Evans-Pritchard's footsteps). This insight into royal rituals is especially interesting for Mesopotamianists who often do not have detailed information on such rites. David Freidel explained his theories on Maya divine kingship and especially emphasized the embeddedness of self-divinization in religion. Freidel stresses the shamanistic nature of Maya kingship, in which the king is worshipped as a god, while the gods can only be worshipped through the king. Clemens Reichel illustrated the end of the cult of divine kings as visible in the Oriental Institute's excavations in the Diyala region of Iraq. Through his painstaking efforts in reconstructing archaeological evidence and by viewing it in its historical context as visible in the textual record, Reichel was able to elucidate the only excavated example for a temple of a divine king in Mesopotamia and the changes that happened to this temple after divine kingship was abolished there. Reinhard Bernbeck as the last speaker of the first day offered some theoretical approaches to understanding royal power and possibilities for resistance against it.

The second day of the seminar was devoted to a session on "Divine Kingship and Imperialism" under the chairmanship of Adam T. Smith of the University of Chicago. The first paper by Michael Puett illustrated concepts of kingship in ancient China. Similar to Michalowski, Puett also took a historical approach and showed that different ideologies for kingship in ancient China competed against each other, thereby leading to the introduction, abolishment, and re-introduction of divine kingship. Bruce Lincoln, who spoke on the role of religion in Achaemenid imperialism, explained the Achaemenid king's central role for order in the cosmos. While, as mentioned above, Achaemenid kings did not explicitly declare themselves divine, their role at the center of the cosmos was nevertheless of utmost importance for maintaining order and stability. The last but not least lecture of the seminar by Greg Woolf was dedicated to the cult of Roman emperors. Independently of Selz, Woolf also argued for the need to rethink our (Western) notions of the human and the divine. He gave examples of emperors that were worshipped as gods despite being reluctant to such a form of adoration, and he showed that when they were worshiped, the cults were often part of local traditions in the Roman provinces that satisfied beliefs of local peoples rather than the Roman emperors. As divine emperors usually ranked among lower gods, Woolf therefore argues for contemplating different degrees of humanity and divinity with boundaries that should be fluid rather than rigid.

As one of two respondents, Jerrold Cooper summarized salient points of the papers on the ancient Near East while focusing his criticism on Ehrenberg's theory on the symbolism of the "ring and rod" in the first-millennium Achaemenid royal imagery. The second respondent, Kathleen Morrison, discussed the remaining papers. Morrison focused on the suggestion that there may be different degrees in between the categories of human and divine, and that divine kings may occupy a position somewhere in between these two opposites. She also took up Winter's point on the need to also study the way in which gods can be viewed as kings.

The seminar brought several issues to the surface that have not been discussed heretofore. In my view, one of the most interesting points of the seminar was to see the many different ways in which the topic can be approached. The main approaches, in my view, are historical, historical-religious, historical-archaeological, anthropological, art historical, and linguistic. This proves the importance of trying to integrate as many data from as many sources as possible in furthering our understanding of this phenomenon. Some of the emerging themes are:

1) The need to reconsider our notions of the human and the divine: Western notions of these categories seem to see them as a binary opposition, in which one can only occupy one *or* the other. To us, it is an anathema that a human being could be considered both, human *and* divine. But it is most likely that this was not always the case everywhere.

2) Divine kingship as a form of government is rather unstable and often not of long duration. Ancient Mesopotamia and China both exhibit similarities in that the ideology of the divine king only prevailed for a short period of time and was then replaced by an ideology that did not see kings as divine. In both areas, however, self-deification is re-introduced at certain times after it had been abolished. Rather than Frazer, who saw divine kingship as a more permanent form of government, it is now clear that it is rather fluid and ephemeral.

3) Several participants have stated that the questions that had been asked thus far may have been wrong, and that new questions have to be formulated. Gilbert, for example, proposed that the distinction between sacral and divine king should be abolished, as these are unhelpful distinctions in trying to understand kingship better. The seminar has also raised many questions for myself. For example, why did kings begin to deify themselves? What were the reasons that led to this major interference in the religious practices of that time? Why was it possible to re-introduce it after it had been abolished?

In conclusion, the two-day seminar has raised many questions, not all of which can be answered. But the emerging themes show that there still is much to be done, and it is to be hoped that this seminar will function as a stimulus for future research. The proceedings of the seminar will be published as part of the Oriental Institute Seminars (OIS) series within the next academic year (2007/2008).

I am deeply grateful to the Oriental Institute and to Gil Stein in particular for allowing me to hold this seminar. I am especially thankful to Tom Urban, Leslie Schramer, and Katie L. Johnson from the Publications Office for their amazing help with organizing the seminar, publishing the book, and being exceedingly helpful in so many other ways. Many, many thanks also to Kathryn Grossman, Carole Krucoff, and especially Joshua Best for their help.

References

Cannadine, D., and S. Price, editors. 1987. *Rituals of Royalty: Power and Ceremonial in Traditional Societies.* Cambridge: Cambridge University Press.

Erkens, F.-R., editor. 2002. *Die Sakralität der Herrschaft: Herrschaftslegitimierung im Wechsel der Zeiten und Räume.* Berlin: Akademie-Verlag.

Frankfort, H. 1948. *Kingship and the Gods: A Study of Ancient Near Eastern Religion as the Integration of Society and Man.* Chicago: University of Chicago Press.

Gundlach, R., and A. Klug, editors. 2004. *Das ägyptische Königtum im Spannungsfeld zwischen Innen- und Außenpolitik im 2. Jahrtausend v. Chr.* Wiesbaden: Harrassowitz.

Gundlach, R., and H. Weber, editors. 1992. *Legitimation und Funktion des Herrschers: Vom ägyptischen Pharao zum neuzeitlichen Diktator.* Schriften der Mainzer Philosophischen Fakultätsgesellschaft 13. Stuttgart: F. Steiner.

Labat, R. 1939. *Le caractère religieux de la royauté assyro-babylonienne.* Études d'Assyriologie 2. Paris: A. Maisonneuve.

O'Connor, D., and D. P. Silverman, editors. 1995. *Ancient Egyptian Kingship*. Leiden: Brill.

Quigley, D., editor. 2005. *The Character of Kingship*. Oxford: Berg.

SYRIAC MANUSCRIPT PROJECT
Stuart Creason

The goal of the Syriac Manuscript Project is the creation of an electronic archive of digital images of manuscripts written in the Syriac language, a variety of Aramaic that has been spoken in Middle Eastern communities for nearly 2,000 years, and the Project is focusing on two primary tasks in its efforts to reach this goal. The first task is to scan and to catalog the Professor Arthur Vööbus Collection of Syriac Manuscripts on Film, a photographic archive consisting of approximately 70,000 images found on nearly 2,600 segments of black and white 35 mm film and stored in approximately 2,000 boxes in the library of the Lutheran School of Theology at Chicago, the institution at which Arthur Vööbus served as Professor of New Testament and Early Church History prior to his death in 1988. Pictured in these images are portions of 695 different manuscripts found at twenty-three different locations in the countries of Iraq, Turkey, Syria, Lebanon, India, and Israel. The second task of the Project is to supplement the Vööbus Collection by taking digital photographs of additional manuscripts located in the Middle East. Because of the generous support of several members of the Assyrian-American community, the Syriac Manuscript Project was able to take a number of preliminary, but important, steps toward its goal during the past year.

One important step was the physical inventory of the film. At the time that the Oriental Institute acquired the rights to the Vööbus Collection in the summer of 2005, the only inventory of the film that existed was a preliminary description and count of the various segments of film based on what Professor Vööbus had written on the outside of the numerous boxes in which the film is stored. No accurate count of the total number of segments of film existed, much less an accurate count of the number of frames on each segment of film. Prior to scanning any segment of film, a precise count must be made of the number of frames on that segment, so that each frame can be given a unique identifying number and all the scanning and cataloging information about that frame can be recorded according to that number. During the past year, all the frames were counted on all the segments of film from seventeen of the twenty-three locations where Professor Vööbus photographed manuscripts. (Counts have not yet been made for the segments from Mardin, Damascus, Sharfeh, Mosul, Baghdad, and Midyat, the six locations where Vööbus took the greatest number of photographs.) One result of this count was that the estimate of the total number of images in the collection was revised downward from 80,000 to 70,000 images.

Another important step that was taken was the testing of the scanning equipment (and the software that operates the scanning equipment) using film of varying quality in order to determine the combination of settings for each type of film that would produce the best possible scan, and following that, the training of students to scan the film in the most efficient and cost-effective manner possible. This task occupied most of the year, but by April 2007, two students (Ben Thomas and Sam Boyd) had been trained, and scanning was able to proceed at a rate of approximately ten images per hour. Financial limitations dictated that scanning could only be performed between ten and fifteen hours a week; nevertheless, by June 30, 2007, Ben and Sam were able to scan 2,006 images on eighty-five segments of film depicting portions of twenty-seven manuscripts from ten different locations. The following table breaks down these numbers by location.

Location	Number of Manuscripts	Number of Film Segments	Number of Images
Bartelli	1	1	10
Pampakuda	1	3	94
Qaraqosh	1	4	104
Mar Behnam	3	7	143
Bote	2	5	153
Kerkuk	3	11	203
Tel Keph	2	8	259
Hah	1	8	278
Atshaneh	9	17	371
Mardin	4	21	391

A third step that was taken was the cataloging of the scanned images. This step is always performed after scanning, and so the number of images cataloged will always be fewer than the number of images scanned. Of the 2,006 images that had been scanned by June 30, 796 of them had also been cataloged (all the scanned images from Bartelli, Qaraqosh, Kerkuk, and Mardin, and eighty-eight of the scanned images from Atshaneh). Among the texts found on these 796 images are several poems by Narsai (a very important eastern Syriac poet), a copy of the Harklean version of the Bible with commentaries in the margins, the story of Mart ("Lady") Shmoni (a version of which is also found in the Book of Maccabees), and the story of Mar ("Lord") Gabriel (an early Syriac saint who founded the Mar Gabriel monastery, one of the places where Professor Vööbus photographed manuscripts).

In addition to these important steps, progress was also made in two other areas, though more remains to be done. These are the development of the project database, in which all the information generated by the scanning and cataloging of the images will be stored and made accessible, and the development of the project Web site, where anyone interested in the project can go to learn about its progress.

Finally, during May and June 2007, Abdul-Massih Saadi, Ph.D., Research Associate and Co-director of the Syriac Manuscript Project, traveled to Mardin, Turkey, and photographed three manuscripts, totaling 500 images, bringing the total number of images photographed over the past four years by Dr. Saadi to 4,700, representing portions of twenty-nine manuscripts.

ZINCIRLI EXPEDITION

J. David Schloen (Expedition Director) and Amir S. Fink (Associate Director)

In August and September 2006, a team from the Oriental Institute began work at Zincirli (pronounced "zin-jeer-lee"), an archaeological site in southern Turkey, on the eastern edge of the Amanus Mountains, about 100 kilometers north of Antakya (ancient Antioch). Zincirli is the site of Sam'al, a 40-hectare walled city of the Iron Age, which was ruled by an Aramaic-speaking dynasty for roughly 200 years, from the late tenth/early ninth century until the late eighth/early seventh century B.C. Zincirli was occupied much earlier, however. In the middle of the 40-hectare Iron Age mound is an 8-hectare upper mound that was settled by 2500 B.C., if not earlier, and was also occupied in subsequent periods, with occasional phases of abandonment. The upper mound was used as a royal citadel during the Iron Age, when an outer wall was constructed some distance away, forming a large lower town that encircles the upper mound. The occupation of the site spans more than two millennia, from the Early Bronze Age until the early Hellenistic period.

Zincirli was first identified as an archaeological site in 1883 and was excavated by German archaeologists in several lengthy excavation seasons from 1888 to 1902. They found impressive stone sculptures, inscriptions, palaces, and artifacts of many kinds. There were no other excavations at the site until the Oriental Institute project commenced in 2006. We are re-excavating the site in order to explore the lower town, which was not previously studied, and to clarify the stratigraphy and chronology of the upper mound and the outer fortifications. The earlier excavators uncovered and mapped a great deal of monumental architecture, but much information was lost because they did not have the benefit of modern methods of excavation and they did not understand the importance of pottery as a chronological indicator.

Our excavations are intended to date more precisely the main phases of construction at Zincirli in order to understand its political and economic role in various cultural periods. We will also excavate a large residential area in the lower town and, if possible, on the upper mound, in order to study the social and economic organization of the settlement. By applying modern archaeological methods, including the analysis of faunal and botanical remains, we hope to improve our understanding of urbanism in the region in the Bronze and Iron Ages. We will also explore the ethnic dynamics in the Zincirli region, which was exposed

A recent satellite image of Zincirli on which is superimposed Robert Koldewey's 1894 plan of the Iron Age city of Sam'al. The old city plan has been georeferenced on the basis of cornerstones still in situ in the German trenches. A modern village covers the western side of the site

The Zincirli Expedition team placing a concrete survey marker on the site during the 2006 season. Seventeen survey markers were placed on and around the site and their precise locations — accurate to one centimeter horizontally or vertically — were determined using GPS satellite readings

to a variety of cultural influences and population movements by virtue of its location in a pivotal border zone between Syria, Anatolia, and Mesopotamia. In the Iron Age, in particular, the valley around Zincirli was home to Luwian-speaking people from Anatolia, who were in many respects the heirs of Bronze Age Hittite culture, and to Aramaic-speakers who had apparently migrated into the region from the south and east. At Zincirli, we hope to examine the cultural and political interaction of these two groups from the perspective of their art, architecture, diet, and lifestyle.

In August and September 2006, we spent six weeks preparing a detailed topographical map of the site and examining the outer fortifications, which had been exposed by modern trenching in two places. By the end of the 2006 season, we had identified several promising areas for excavation and worked out the logistical details for a long-term archaeological project. In the summer of 2007, we initiated large-scale excavations in four separate areas of the site. At the time of writing, we are in the midst of a two-month season of excavation, having opened a total of 1,100 square meters with an expedition team of forty archaeologists and archaeology students.

At some point in the Iron Age, a large wall was built around the site, a few hundred meters from the central mound. This wall is unusual because it is almost perfectly circular, with a diameter of 720 meters and a circumference of 2.26 kilometers. The German excavators traced the circuit of the wall and counted 100 evenly spaced towers that project from the wall, situated approximately sixteen meters apart. Three large gates pierce the wall on the south, west, and northeast sides of the city. The southern gate in particular was extensively excavated in the 1890s. A series of sculpted basalt orthostats lined the gate passages. These orthostats are now in museums in Istanbul and Berlin.

During our 2006 season, we established seventeen precisely georeferenced inter-visible survey markers on and around the site (using differential GPS equipment) and we conducted a thorough topographical survey of the mound. In the process of doing this, we located the previously excavated corner stones of several structures around the site that are still visible in the old German trenches. This allowed us to georeference the published plans of the site within our own coordinate system. We were happy to learn that the old plans are quite accurate, with careful stone-by-

A 45-meter-wide portion of the outer city wall of Iron Age Sam'al was exposed on the northeastern side of the city during the 2006 season. The basalt stonework of the wall is 3 meters wide and 3.2 meters high. Two of the wall's 100 towers are visible in this exposure. One of the towers has partly collapsed subsequent to its initial exposure by German archaeologists in the 1890s

stone drawings that match what remains in situ. This is important because many stones were robbed from the old trenches to build the modern village on the site, which was constructed only in the twentieth century. The well-known archaeologist and architect Robert Koldewey worked at the site and drew the Zincirli plans in the 1890s, early in his career, before he moved on to his famous excavations at Babylon.

In addition to topographical mapping, in 2006 we excavated the outer city wall in two areas: near the northeast gate and on the southeast side, where a modern canal had cut across the wall. In the northeast area, we exposed 45 m of the outer face of the wall in order to examine the preserved basalt stonework, which is 3.2 m high and 3 m wide. Two of the 100 projecting towers, nos. 60 and 61 on the German excavators' plan, are visible in our exposure.

A modern canal has cut through the Iron Age city wall on the southeastern side of the site. Although it is unfortunate that the site has been damaged by this canal, it affords an opportunity to see a cross section of the fortifications, revealing both the outer wall and a matching inner wall that forms a concentric ring 7 m inside the outer wall

We determined that the stone portion of the outer wall is preserved to its original height in this area. Remnants of mudbrick material on top of the stones indicate the presence of a mudbrick superstructure — probably several meters high — which has long since eroded away. The top of the stonework is intentionally concave, forcing the bricks above it to tilt inward from each side toward the center of the wall, thereby supporting each other and increasing the stability of the wall.

We cut sections in the soil perpendicular to the wall face in order to reveal the original Iron Age field surface into which the wall was set. These sections showed that the bottom two courses (ca. 85 cm) of the wall were originally submerged below the surface; thus more than 2 m of the stonework originally stood above the ground, surmounted by a massive mudbrick wall of unknown height. Layers of downward-sloping mudbrick detritus are visible in our sections, showing the gradual dissolution of the mudbrick superstructure, which melted and slumped over the stonework after the abandonment and neglect of the Iron Age fortifications.

On the southeast side of the city, a modern canal has cut through one of the stone towers (no. 45 on the German plan), exposing a cross-section of the city's fortifications. We trimmed back the canal edges in order to examine this cross-section, revealing a unique double-wall design that had already been described by the earlier excavators. In addition to the outer wall, there is an inner wall, also 3 m wide, which is separated by a 7 m gap from the outer wall. Our excavation revealed a cobbled surface between the walls, along which the city's soldiers could have marched around the city from tower to tower and from gate to gate, on the same level as the streets inside the city.

The inner wall is founded at a higher level than the outer wall and its foundation consists of somewhat smaller stones, but it is otherwise very similar in its dimensions. The inner wall has 100 projecting towers that are lined up with the towers of the outer wall, providing a second line of defense for archers and spearmen defending the city. It is likely that the inner wall rose higher than the outer wall so that defenders could shoot down upon attackers who succeeded in capturing the outer wall. This was suggested long ago by Robert Koldewey. Our work at the site so far confirms his description of the city's Iron Age fortifications. What remains to be determined is the date of their construction — it is not at all clear in which century they were built — and whether there are phases or rebuildings of the fortifications. For this reason, we opened an excavation area in 2007 in the northeast gate, which the German plans indicate was only partially excavated. We hope to find intact floors inside and outside the gate chambers that will allow us to date their initial construction and to examine the stratigraphy of the city gate and the adjacent inner and outer walls. This would also allow us to determine more precisely when the fortifications and gates went out of use, which apparently occurred sometime during the middle or late seventh century B.C., toward the end of the Assyrian empire.

During the Iron Age, the upper mound of Zincirli was separately fortified with its own wall and with larger outer and inner gates. The extensive German excavations on the upper mound exposed these fortifications and revealed much of the royal citadel on the upper mound, although many architectural and stratigraphic details were not recorded or published by the early excavators. They unearthed sculpted stone column bases and basalt orthostats with reliefs carved in the Neo-Hittite style. These are now displayed in museums in Istanbul and Berlin.

The German excavators also found stone-carved inscriptions written in alphabetic Aramaic and Phoenician and in Akkadian cuneiform, dating from the period of the Neo-Assyrian empire. Small finds were published in a separate volume, including objects of gold, silver, ivory, and other materials. The principles of pottery chronology and stratigraphic debris-layer excavation were not known by the early excavators, with the result that building levels and stratigraphic contexts that should have been kept separate were sometimes badly mixed. However, the material collected in the early excavations gives us some idea of the periods of occupation of the site. Recent examination by Prof. Gunnar Lehmann of the Zincirli pottery stored in Berlin shows that it ranges in date from the Early Bronze Age to the early Hellenistic period, with a large proportion of late third-millennium material. This indicates that the site was occupied in various periods over a span of more than 2,000 years, from the third millennium B.C. to the first millennium B.C., even though the Iron Age and especially the Assyrian period are the best known architectural phases.

In our 2007 excavations, we opened a trench 10 m wide × 40 m long on an unexcavated portion of the citadel west of the citadel gate. This trench climbs up the southern side of the upper mound, from the lower town at the base of the mound to the top of the upper mound. The purpose of this trench is, first of all, to study the final phase of Iron Age fortifications, which consisted of a stone-faced sloping rampart leading up to a large wall on the crest of the mound. In future seasons, we will excavate more deeply in this trench to determine the occupational sequence of the site and to construct a detailed pottery chronology for the site. Eventually, we will make a stratigraphic connection from this trench to the old German trenches, in order to clarify the architectural phases of the upper mound as much as possible.

Meanwhile, we will open excavation areas in the lower city, which has not been studied before. The area between the southern gate of the outer city wall and the citadel gate on the south side of the upper mound is a promising place to start, and in the summer of 2007 we opened a 400-square-meter excavation area just north of the southern gate. It is clear at this point that a major road — an Iron Age chariot road — ran through this area, from the outer wall to the citadel, bounded by seventh-century structures on either side. In this area we hope to determine the lifespan of the road, which may have been resurfaced over its period of use, and to determine the nature of the architecture in this outermost zone of the lower town.

In the coming years, we will choose one or two additional areas in the lower town in which we will excavate broad horizontal exposures in order to study the social and economic organization of the city and changes in its organization over time, through analysis of domestic architecture and faunal, botanical, and artifactual distribution patterns. To this end, we are conducting an extensive geophysical survey in 2007 that is already revealing the outlines of buried houses and streets in the lower town. Many houses and even rooms within houses are clearly visible because their basalt foundations produce a strong magnetic signal that is picked up by the magnetic gradiometer. The geophysical survey we are conducting in 2007 will allow us to select promising areas of excavation to be opened in 2008 and subsequent years. A more detailed report on this and other aspects of the 2007 excavation season will appear in next year's *Annual Report*.

We are grateful to the Ministry of Culture and Tourism of the Republic of Turkey for making it possible for us to dig at Zincirli, and to the Ministry's representative, Ms. Aysel Çötelioğlu, who lived and worked with us during our 2006 season. We also owe whole-hearted thanks to İsmet Ersoy, the mayor of Fevzipaşa, and other government officials in the region who visited the site and helped us in various ways: Süleyman Kamçı, Governor of Gaziantep province; Bekir Yılmaz, Governor of the İslahiye district; and Mehmet Aykanat, Director of Culture and Tourism in Gaziantep province. Dr. Mehmet Önal, Acting Director of the Gaziantep Museum, and members of the museum staff, especially Ahmet Beyazlar, also gave us much encouragement and assistance for which we are very grateful.

Our expedition team consisted of the following archaeology students, whom we thank for their hard work and good spirit: Christoph Bachhuber, Olof Cannon, Annie Caruso, Leann Pace, Michele Rau, Virginia Rimmer, Melissa Rosenzweig, Eudora Struble, and Oya Topçuoğlu. Our camp manager, Mr. Zeki Cemali, and his assistant, Muhammat Kala, took care of many logistical details with great efficiency and good cheer. We would also like to express our thanks to Gil Stein, the Director of the Oriental Institute, for the invaluable support and advice he has given to us in the course of launching this new project.

All these people contributed to a very successful first season at Zincirli, which laid the groundwork for our large-scale excavations in 2007. We look forward to many more seasons of excavation at this important site.

————————

INDIVIDUAL RESEARCH

Richard H. Beal

Richard H. Beal spent much of the past year reference checking, copy editing, and entering corrections for the third fascicle of the Š volume of the Chicago Hittite Dictionary. He also worked on a number of first drafts of dictionary articles. These included three commonly occurring and complicated words with partially overlapping forms: *da-* "to take," *dai-* "to put, place," and *tiya-* "to step, take a position."

His article "Making, Preserving, and Breaking the Peace with the Hittite State" came out in the volume *War and Peace in the Ancient World,* edited by Kurt Raaflaub. In the summer he attended the 52nd Rencontre Assyriologique Internationale in Münster, whose topic, "Krieg und Frieden im Alten Vorderasien," was in memory of the peace of Westphalia, signed in Münster in 1648, which ended the Thirty Years War. At the meeting he gave a lecture "Hittite Reluctance to Go to War," which laid out the many examples of the Hittites trying to solve an international problem through diplomacy and only resorting to war when that failed.

After the meetings, he and his wife, alumna JoAnn Scurlock, went to London for several weeks to read mostly unpublished Akkadian cuneiform tablets related to her project to study ancient Mesopotamian medical treatments.

Robert D. Biggs

Robert D. Biggs devoted part of the summer of 2006 to continue reference checking for the final volume of the *Assyrian Dictionary*. He also continued work, with co-editors Jennie Myers and Martha Roth, on the papers from the 2005 Rencontre Assyriologique in Chicago. He continued the editorship of *Journal of Near Eastern Studies* until April 2007 when Wadad Kadi took over full responsibility. Having been appointed in 1971, he thus ended his editorship of more than thirty-six years. He expects shortly to resume his work on the Early Dynastic and Akkadian Period cuneiform inscriptions from the Inanna Temple at Nippur, updating his research principally in the Iraq Museum carried out over a number of years, starting in 1972. His publications include "The Human Body and Sexuality in the Babylonian Medical Texts," in *Médecine et médecins au Proche-Orient ancien*, edited by L. Battini-Villard and P. Villard (Oxford, 2006), and an article on sexual potency enhancement in the *Reallexikon der Assyriologie*.

Scott Branting

Scott Branting continued to direct the Center for Ancient Middle Eastern Landscapes (CAMEL) and to co-direct the Kerkenes Dağ archaeological project in central Turkey. He also continues to participate in the MASS project. Information on the progress of all three of these projects can be found in their separate reports. In addition, he received a Joint Theory Institute grant along with Mark Altaweel of Argonne National Laboratory to start and co-direct the SHULGI project. This

INDIVIDUAL RESEARCH

project is developing open-source agent-based computer simulation software to provide researchers with a tool by which they can model ancient and modern pedestrian based transportation systems. It is named after a king in the Third Dynasty of Ur who was known for his road building efforts and the speed with which he was purported to ambulate. The first test case for the SHULGI software, however, will be the extension and testing of the computer simulations of ancient pedestrians along the city streets at Kerkenes Dağ some 1,500 years after the reign of Shulgi.

During the year, Branting presented papers on the work at Kerkenes Dağ at the American Schools of Oriental Research Annual Meeting in Washington, D.C., and in a public lecture at Trinity International University in Deerfield, Illinois. He also presented a lecture on "The Geography and Economics of Urban Transportation" in the *Economics of Urban Policies* class taught in the Department of Economics at the University of Chicago. This was in addition to the *Ancient Landscapes I* and *II* classes he taught and a lecture he presented on "Survey and Geospatial Technologies" for the *Method and Theory in Near Eastern Archaeology* class. Within the Institute he continued to serve as chair of the Integrated Database Committee.

Branting also had a number of publications completed during the year. *Kerkenes News 9*, co-authored with Geoffrey and Françoise Summers, was published by METU Press. An article on "Technology and the Oriental Institute" appeared as well in volume 193 of the *Oriental Institute News & Notes*. In addition, two articles were accepted for publication but have yet to appear: "Using an Urban Street Network to Analyze Ancient Activities" will appear in the forthcoming volume *Computer Applications and Quantitative Methods in Archaeology 2006*, to be published by Archeaopress. While "Geospatial Data and Theory in Archaeology: A View from CAMEL," co-authored with Joshua Trampier, will appear in the edited volume *Space — The Final Frontier? An Intercontinental Approach*, to be published by Cambridge University Press.

John A. Brinkman

In the autumn, **John A. Brinkman** participated in a symposium at Cornell University honoring Peter Kuniholm on his retirement as founding director of the Malcolm and Carolyn Wiener Dendrochronology Laboratory; he delivered a lecture assessing the current status and problems of research in Mesopotamian chronology of the historical period (2350–140 B.C.). With financial support from the Mellon Foundation, he was able to continue museum research on Middle Babylonian documents in the Louvre (November–December), New York (April), and the University Museum, Philadelphia (May). He contributed three entries on Babylonian historical subjects to the *Reallexikon der Assyriologie* and wrote three notes for the French periodical *NABU* on the results of his museum research. He is currently preparing essays on Babylonian history in the second and first millennia B.C. for the catalog of a Louvre-sponsored exhibition on Babylon to be held in Paris and Berlin in 2008.

Fred M. Donner

Fred M. Donner was engaged in his usual teaching duties in 2006/2007, including a larger-than-ever survey of early Islamic history in the fall, "Introduction to the Middle East" in the spring, and at various times a seminar on the "High Caliphate," a course reading passages from the medieval Arabic historian al-Baladhuri's massive *Ansab al-ashraf*, a research seminar in early Islamic history, and several tutorials on Islamic law. He also served on sixteen dissertation committees and on three MA thesis committees.

Donner was asked to evaluate colleagues for appointment, promotion, and/or tenure at the University of Pennsylvania, Ohio State University, and University of California at Irvine and was invited to serve as external examiner for dissertation defenses at Princeton and the Sorbonne. He was also asked by the École Pratique des Hautes Études, Paris, to evaluate the application of a French colleague to become "Director of Research." He served as grant reviewer for the National Humanities Center (Research Triangle Park, North Carolina) and the American Center for Oriental Research (Amman, Jordan).

Donner delivered lectures on Islam's origins for audiences of the general public at the University's Humanities Open House (October), the German Cultural Club (Chicago, February), the Missouri Valley History Conference (Omaha, Nebraska, March), and Washington University in St. Louis (March). In February, he gave more specialized presentations on his research on Islam's origins to seminars at the Sorbonne and at the École Pratique des Hautes Études, Paris.

As usual, he continued to review manuscripts for various professional journals, including *Journal of Near Eastern Studies, International Journal of Middle Eastern Studies*, and for *Law and History Review*. He also continued to serve as editor of *Al-'Usur al-Wusta: The Bulletin of Middle East Medievalists*, which appears semi-annually.

During the year, Donner submitted to the editors the draft translation of his section of the *History of al-Ya'qubi*, a collective project to translate the works of this important ninth-century historian and geographer. He also submitted his introduction, bibliography, and other materials required for a volume of reprinted articles by various authors which he selected on the topic *The Expansion of the Early Islamic State* — to appear as volume five in the series entitled The Formation of the Classical Islamic World, published by Ashgate. He also submitted two articles, one entitled "'Umar ibn al-Khattab, 'Amr ibn al-'As, and the Muslim Invasion of Egypt," for the festschrift of a distinguished colleague, and "Umayyad Efforts at Legitimation: the Umayyads' Silent Heritage," to appear in *Umayyad Legacies/Heritages Omeyyades*, edited by A. Borrut and P. M. Cobb (forthcoming with E. J. Brill, Leiden).

At long last, he has completed the draft of his monograph, *Muhammad and the Believers: At the Origins of Islam,* and is now contacting publishers to place the work, intended for the general reader and introductory college classroom.

Two articles appeared in print during the year: "Historical Context," in *Cambridge Companion to the Qur'an*, edited by J. D. McAuliffe, pp. 23–39; and "Fight for God — But Do So With Kindness," in *War and Peace in the Ancient World*, edited by K. A. Raaflaub, pp. 297–311 (Blackwell).

Donner is continuing with his research on early Islamic history, particularly the way the early community of Believers gradually changed its self-definition and grew into what we now recognize as the Muslim community, during the first century or so following the death of the prophet Muhammad in 632 C.E. He has been awarded a Guggenheim Fellowship for 2007/2008 to pursue research on this theme on the basis of early Arabic papyri and looks forward to spending much of his time next year at the great papyrus repositories in Europe (particularly those of Paris, Vienna, and Heidelberg).

———————

Peter F. Dorman

This year **Peter F. Dorman**, together with colleague Betsy Bryan of Johns Hopkins, co-hosted the Theban Workshop in Chicago on October 14, 2006, on the general theme "Perspectives on Ptolemaic Thebes." Seven speakers chose topics that addressed the history, economics, social structure, priesthood, religion, and art history of ancient Thebes during the suzerainty of the Ptolemaic dynasty. In connection with this annual symposium, Dorman and Bryan also edited the first volume of the series "Occasional Proceedings of the Theban Workshop," consisting of the papers presented in 2003 at the British Museum in London, *Sacred Space and Sacred Function in Ancient Thebes* (SAOC 61), which the Oriental Institute published in Spring 2007.

Dorman wrote a chapter on "Epigraphy and Recording," destined for a volume entitled *Egyptology: An Introduction*, to be published by Cambridge University Press. He also prepared a book review for the *Journal of Ancient Near Eastern Religions* on *Das thebanische Grab Nr. TT 136 und der Beginn der Amarnazeit* (by co-authors A. Grimm and H. Schlögl) and another review for the *Journal of Near Eastern Studies* on the long-awaited publication of the temple of the deified form of Nebmaatre, built by Amenhotep III in Nubia, *Soleb III*, *Soleb IV*, and *Soleb V* (by M. Schiff Giorgini, edited by N. Beaux).

At the annual meeting of the American Research Center in Egypt, held in Toledo in April 2007, Dorman gave a presentation entitled "The Funerary Papyri of Hatnofer: Last of a Cursive Breed?" In addition to describing the ongoing conservation of the Hatnofer papyri in the Cairo Museum, the paper examined the physical context of the earliest attestations of Books of the Dead as found on coffins, funerary masks, and linen shrouds and suggested that the direct precursors of the "classical" funerary papyri of the Eighteenth Dynasty (in the form of cursive hieroglyphs accompanied by vignettes) were the shrouds of the early New Kingdom, on which the transition from plain hieratic had been achieved. Textual idiosyncrasies in the Hatnofer papyri likewise seem to indicate that the practice of including inscribed shrouds in burials fell into decline with the first appearance of papyrus-roll books of the dead.

The concurrent Tutankhamun and Hatshepsut exhibits in the United States gave Dorman the opportunity to lecture to various audiences in Dallas, Chicago, and Fort Worth. As part of the training program for Oriental Institute docents, he also lectured on the history of Egypt down to the beginning of the New Kingdom.

Geoff Emberling

Geoff Emberling's research this year focused on Sudan, with a field season from January to March in the Fourth Cataract region of the Nile. The team excavated a cemetery and a gold extraction site of the later Kerma period (ca. 2000–1500 B.C.) that raise questions about the internal organization of the Kerma state and the importance of the Fourth Cataract as a source of gold in many periods (see separate Nubian Expedition report). He gave a lecture on the project to the Department of Classical, Near Eastern, and Religious Studies of the University of British Columbia in Vancouver entitled "Political Economy in the Kingdom of Kush: Archaeological Salvage in the Fourth Cataract, Northern Sudan." He hopes to return to Sudan in the winter of 2008 for a final season of salvage work in the Fourth Cataract.

He continued his work toward final publication of his Tell Brak excavations (1998–2004) by working on a nearly weekly basis with his co-director Helen McDonald on the stratigraphy of Area TC, the mid-third-millennium public building that appears to be a Temple Oval. He gave a talk on the building entitled "The Brak Oval: A Sumerian Temple in Semite Lands?" in the Interdisciplinary Archaeology Workshop at the University of Chicago.

He also continued his occasional lectures on history and culture in Iraq to military units preparing to deploy to Iraq with lectures in Fort Bragg, North Carolina. Based on this work he gave a paper, "Archaeologists and the Military in Iraq: Collaboration, Compromise, or Contribution?" in a session entitled "Imperial Inspections: Archaeologists, War, and Violence" at the Society for American Archaeology conference in Austin. The relationship between archaeologists and the military in the Middle East has been problematic in many ways, not least of which is the catastrophic fact that the U.S. military did not protect the National Museum in Baghdad despite repeated warnings by McGuire Gibson and other archaeologists before the invasion. Emberling's experience with the military suggests that we need more contact, at higher levels, to prevent such destruction of cultural property in the future.

Emberling co-taught an undergraduate core class, "The Assyrian Empire" with Seth Richardson and with the help of teaching assistants (and graduate students) Virginia Rimmer and Bike Yazicioğlu. The course got good reviews, but they do not know if this was because of the exciting intellectual collaboration between archaeologist and historian, or because of the fun he and Seth had discussing and teaching the subject.

Finally, Emberling was invited to lecture in the Ancient Near Eastern Department at the Metropolitan Museum of Art on "Models for Museums: The Collection of the Oriental Institute Museum," which was an opportunity to present the Oriental Institute as a knowledge-based museum (rather than an object-based one), and to suggest that this is a model that has many advantages for the future. He is not sure how well this message was received in the Metropolitan Museum.

Walter Farber

After once more representing Chicago on the board of the International Association of Assyriologists at the 52nd Rencontre International Assyriologique in Münster (Germany), where he also chaired a session on magico-medical cuneiform texts, **Walter Farber** enjoyed traveling with Gertrud through parts of Scandinavia where they visited scores of Romanesque churches with very unusual sculptures and decorations often strongly reminding them of motifs in ancient Near Eastern art.

Having returned to Chicago in time for the academic year, the fall, winter, and spring quarters again went by very quickly with teaching, committee work, and other chores, including the occasional, and much more relaxing, time for research. A much welcomed, though non-Assyriological break came in March, when Walter was awarded the Curt-Paul-Medaille, which is given every three years for outstanding research and publications in post-World War II German postal history. He used the spring break to travel to Germany and accept this honor, before getting back to Chicago to spend much of the spring quarter seeing the festschrift for Bob Biggs through the final stages of publication.

François Gaudard

After a very interesting and productive season with the Epigraphic Survey in Luxor, under the leadership of W. Raymond Johnson, **François Gaudard** returned to the Oriental Institute to work as a Research Associate with Professor Janet Johnson on the Chicago Demotic Dictionary. It means a lot to him to have the opportunity to take part again in this project.

From 2005 through 2007, Gaudard collaborated with Rodolphe Kasser, Marvin Meyer, and Gregor Wurst on the publication of two books, namely, *The Gospel of Judas from Codex Tchacos* (National Geographic: Washington, D.C., 2006), and the critical edition of the entire codex Tchacos: *The Gospel of Judas together with the Letter of Peter to Philip, James, and a Book of Allogenes from Codex Tchacos* (National Geographic: Washington, D.C., 2007). Gaudard, along with Marvin Meyer, prepared the translation from Coptic into English of the four tractates of Codex Tchacos. He also served as a member of the National Geographic Society's *Codex Advisory Board*.

During the summer of 2006, for the seventh time, Gaudard taught the University of Chicago's intensive summer course "Ancient Egyptian Language, Culture, and History." This course, taught for credit, integrated classroom instruction with an introduction to Egyptological resources, museum experience, and the preparation of a research paper. The students had the opportunity to explore the archaeology, history, geography, religion and literature of the ancient Egyptians and began the study of Middle Egyptian. Gaudard took advantage of the resources of the Oriental Institute and is grateful to Professor Janet Johnson, Emily Teeter, Laura D'Alessandro, Geoff Emberling, Ray Johnson, Ray Tindel, John Sanders, and Tom Urban, who all contributed to the success of the course.

For the week-long seminar "The World in the Time of Tutankhamun" presented by the Oriental Institute, Gaudard delivered a lecture entitled "The Monuments of Tutankhamun," which focused on what we would know about this pharaoh if his tomb had not been discovered, including a presentation of the work of the Epigraphic Survey in Luxor (26 July).

As part of the Oriental Institute's docent training, Gaudard also spoke on the New Kingdom and the mortuary temple of Ramesses III at Medinet Habu (7 October). He also attended the 58th Annual Meeting of the American Research Center in Egypt, which took place in Toledo, Ohio, from April 20 to 22, 2007.

McGuire Gibson

McGuire Gibson had a productive year. Besides the publications related to Nippur, he sent to press an article entitled "The Dead Hand of Deimel," addressing crucial issues on the beginning of civilization, as well as a biographic essay for the *Reallexikon für Assyriologie,* on Erich F. Schmidt, the brilliant excavator of Persepolis, and two review articles. One of the review articles addresses the subject of archaeology as used in nation-building in Iraq (Magnus Bernhardsson) and the other is on a book that resulted from a conference on "Archaeology, Cultural Heritage, and the Antiquities Trade." He has also submitted two articles co-authored with Dr. Donny George on preparations made in the Iraq Museum prior to the war of 2003 and on steps that museums should make to protect themselves in the future. He also participated in international conferences in London ("Archaeology in Conflict"), in front of the Pergamum Altar in the Museum in Berlin ("Archaeology and Politics"), Salem, Oregon (Willamette College), and lectures on Mesopotamia for the Council on Foreign Affairs in Santa Fe, at Lynchburg College, and in Baltimore for the University of Chicago, Alumni Center. He took part in a small symposium on the Sumerian city of Umma, organized by Bob Adams, Peter Steinkeller, and Elizabeth Stone at the Oriental Institute. He is writing a chapter for that volume. He also spent two weeks in Amman, Jordan, working with Iraqi colleagues to reconstruct publications that they had authored but had lost in the looting of the Iraq National Museum. This work, done with Dr. Mark Altaweel, is funded by a grant from the National Endowment for the Humanities. He is also involved in an administrative and participant role in an Iraqi Oral History Project that is being conducted in Amman, London, and other cities by The American Academic Research Institute in Iraq (TAARII). The Oral History Project has recently been given an NEH grant. With the departure of Tony Wilkinson to Durham in Britain, he has taken on a larger role in the project to Model Ancient Settlement Systems (MASS), which is in its last year of a five-year grant from the National Science Foundation. He still serves as the President of TAARII and remains on the board of the Council of American Overseas Research Centers and the American Institute for Yemeni Studies.

Petra M. Goedegebuure

At the end of October 2006, **Petra M. Goedegebuure** joined the Oriental Institute and the Department of Near Eastern Languages and Civilizations from Leiden University, as Assistant Professor of Hittitology. Besides her appointment in these institutions, Goedegebuure participates half-time in the Chicago Hittite Dictionary Project as academic contributor (see Project Reports). Her research interests lie in the linguistic analysis of Hittite and related Anatolian languages, such as Hieroglyphic and Cuneiform Luwian, covering three different fields of linguistics: discourse cohesion, deixis, and information structure.

One of Goedegebuure's interests is language change in contact situations. By applying empirically tested socio-linguistic models of language change through contact to ancient Anatolia, Goedegebuure has shown that the long-held view that Hittite was heavily influenced by Hattian has to be abandoned: there is no proof for substantial Hattian substratal influence on Hittite. On the contrary, a strong case can be built for Luwian substratal influence on Hattian around the beginning of the second millennium B.C. The socio-political correlate is surprising. Instead of Indo-European nomadic warrior tribes conquering the peaceful indigenous population, we must now assume that a proto-Luwian language community quietly merged with the Hattian-speaking population in a rather subordinate socio-political position. These ideas were tested in the Historical Linguistics Discussion Group led by Sarah Thomason (University of Michigan, Ann Arbor, March 23, 2007) and submitted for publication ("Central Anatolian Languages and Language Communities in the Colony Period: A Luwian-Hattian Symbiosis and the Independent Hittites," in *Acts of the Third Leiden Symposium "Anatolia and the Jazira during the Old Assyrian Period, December 15, 2005,"* edited by J. G. Dercksen). The study of cultures and languages in contact also resulted in an appendix accompanying a publication of Oğuz Soysal (Senior Research Associate of the Chicago Hittite Dictionary Project), submitted to the *Journal of Ancient Near Eastern Religions* ("Hattian Origins of Hittite Religious Concepts: The Syntax of 'to drink (to) a deity' and other phrases").

Another strand of research explores deixis and information structure in the Anatolian languages. Goedegebuure discovered the ablative forms of the Hieroglyphic Luwian demonstrative pronouns ("The Hieroglyphic Luwian Demonstrative Ablative-instrumentals *zin* and *apin*," in *Acts of the VIth International Congress of Hittitology, September 6, 2005, Roma* [in press], edited by Alfonso Archi and Rita Francia) and uncovered the placement rules for question words in Hittite. It turned out that the placement of Hittite question words is governed by the presence or absence of counter-expectation and — if present — type of counter-expectation entertained by the speaker. This principle has not been recognized in general linguistics and will be made available to a wider audience through publication in *Linguistics* (reviewed and accepted; "Focus Structure and Q-word Questions in Hittite," in *The Interpersonal Level in Functional Discourse Grammar*, Thematic issue of *Linguistics*, edited by Evelien Keizer and Mirjam van Staden). The demonstrative system of Hittite and the use of independent third-person pronouns as focus elements will be published as a monograph, hopefully by the end of 2007 or the beginning of 2008 (*Reference, Deixis and Focus in Hittite: The Demonstratives ka- "this", apa- "that" and asi "yon,"* Studien zu den Boghazköy-Texten 49 [Wiesbaden: Harrassowitz]).

Information structure mainly deals with pragmatic and syntactic phenomena at the clausal level but is also influenced by the hierarchical organization of discourse. How information structure and discourse structure interact is the main theme of Goedegebuure's long-term research project "Exploring the Outer Limits: From Sentence to Discourse in Hittite," focusing on discourse topicality and discourse cohesion. She presented the first results of this project at one of the Wednesday luncheon meetings of the Franke Institute for the Humanities ("On Hittite and Linguistics," January 17, 2007). She also published an article in which she disproved a theory about the way discourse topicality is marked in Hittite ("The Original Function of the Hittite Sentence Particle -*kan*: Topic Reinforcer or Marker of Spatial Relations?" Review article of *Dynamics of Transformation in Hittite: The Hittite Particles -kan, -asta and -san*, by Jacqueline Boley [Innsbruck 2000], in *Bibliotheca Orientalis* 64/1–2 [2007]: 31–63).

Finally, there is no such thing as linguistics of corpus languages without sound philology. A collection of new readings in Old Hittite compositions was published in Silvin Košak's festschrift ("'Let only Neša Become Populous!,' and More. Philological Notes on Old Hittite," in *Tabularia Hethaeorum: Hethitologische Beiträge, Silvin Košak zum 65. Geburtstag*, edited by Detlev Groddek and Marina Zorman, pp. 305–12 [Wiesbaden: Harrassowitz, 2007]).

Gene Gragg

Within the general context of the Cushitic-Afroasiatic Index project, **Gene Gragg** has focused on the challenge of setting up a morphological database: how a database of paradigms can be set up and how the structures it contains can be queried, contrasted, and configured, in what in some ways might be called a "spreadsheet application for paradigms." As the current phase of the project he is proposing a comparative-historical reference archive of *all* available morphological information on the Cushitic-Omotic languages in their Afroasiatic context (selected Semitic and Berber to begin with, eventually others). The interest and importance of the planned archive lie in the fact that it will be:

- A compilation of linguistic information otherwise widely scattered or unavailable. An archive of this kind would provide a unique pool of typological-areal-genetic linguistic information. It would also be an indispensable tool for comparative Cushitic and Afroasiatic morphology, and hence for exploration of the linguistic pre-history of the ancient Near East.

- A tool for the organization, manipulation, and contrastive and analytical display of paradigmatic data, both within and among these languages, and thus an instructive model for ways of dealing with large amounts of comparative morphological data.

- With the addition of a way of accessing and comparing underlying paradigm structuring generalizations, a tool of interest to general linguistics for the exploration of the synchronic and diachronic aspects of paradigm-based approaches to morphological structure.

In this context, a relevant article from a recent conference has appeared in published form: "The 'Weak' Verb: Akkadian and Beja" *The Akkadian Language in Its Semitic Context: Studies in the Akkadian of the Third and Second Millennium B.C.*, edited by G. Deutscher and N. J. C. Kouwenberg, pp. 19–29 (Leiden: Nederlands Instituut voor het Nabije Oosten, 2006).

Still in linguistics, but on a different tack, he gave a final summarizing talk, "Synthèse: The Dynamics of Case — Recapitulation and Future Directions," at an international colloquium on Variations, concurrence et évolution des cas dans divers domaines linguistiques, held in Paris, April 2–4, 2007, at the Institut Catholique and the University of Chicago, Paris Center.

Finally, continuing also with the problem of the design, publication, systematical exploration, and maintenance of a lexically and grammatically annotated corpus, he attended a colloquium "Les archives de Persépolis" held jointly at the Collège de France and the Chicago Paris Center on November 3–4, 2006, where he gave a joint presentation with Matt Stolper and Mark Garrison of the OCHRE interface for the digital publication of the archive (concentrating on questions of glossary maintenance and of querying the corpus for grammatical and lexical information).

Rebecca Hasselbach

This academic year saw the publication of several articles by **Rebecca Hasselbach**: "Interpreting Early Akkadian Orthography — A Note on Pronominal Suffixes in Sargonic Akkadian" in the *Zeitschrift für Assyriologie*; "The Ventive / Energic in Semitic — A Morphological Study" in the *Zeitschrift der Deutschen Morgenländischen Gesellschaft*; and "The Affiliation of Sargonic Akkadian to Babylonian and Assyrian — New Insights Concerning the Subgrouping of Akkadian" in the *Journal of Semitic Studies*. She also wrote several book reviews on books dealing with Akkadian grammar and Comparative Semitics in general. In addition to these publications, Hasselbach started to work on a new research project — a detailed study of Semitic case and grammatical relations — that will be the subject of her next book. This project will make use of typological studies — studies that establish cross-linguistic tendencies on the basis of large samples of the world's languages — regarding case marking, grammatical relations, head and dependent marking, and word order, and compare these to Semitic languages in order to determine whether Semitic languages conform to typological tendencies, and whether it is possible to use typological studies to reconstruct the earliest stages of the Semitic nominal system and case inflection, which until today remain a matter of dispute.

First results of Hasselbach's ongoing investigation of the Semitic case system have been presented in March at the *Colloque Cas* in Paris, where she gave a talk about the development of case marking in Phoenician, concluding that the process underlying the loss of case inflection in this language can be explained by functional and typological tendencies. This study will be published in the conference proceedings. A similar discussion of the Akkadian case system will be presented at the Rencontre Assyriologique Internationale in July, which shows that Akkadian underwent the same basic processes in the loss of case inflection as Phoenician. The results of these two preliminary investigations strengthen the assumption that language typologies can complement internal Semitic evidence.

INDIVIDUAL RESEARCH

In April, Hasselbach took over as Book Review editor for the Ancient Near East for the *Journal of Near Eastern Studies* from Robert Biggs, who retired as editor of the journal.

In addition to these projects, Hasselbach was involved in a grant proposal submitted to and approved by the Joint Theory Institute entitled "Simulating Language Evolution in a Dynamic Social and Environmental Metamodel." This project, which is a joint project between the Department of Linguistics and the Oriental Institute, attempts to integrate language data in a previously created computer simulation of ancient Mesopotamia that works with economic and environmental factors, in order to trace language change. Hasselbach will be responsible for providing the language data for the project.

Thomas A. Holland

Thomas A. Holland is happy to report that the final volumes of the Tell es-Sweyhat excavations in Syria were computer formatted by the Publications Office at the end of 2006 and were published by the Oriental Institute in January 2007 (*Tell Es-Sweyhat, Syria, Vol. 2: Archaeology of the Bronze Age, Hellenistic, and Roman Remains at an Ancient Town on the Euphrates River* [two volumes, text and plates], Oriental Institute Publications 125 [Chicago: Oriental Institute, 2006]).

As reported in last year's *The Oriental Institute 2005–2006 Annual Report*, pp. 99–101, Holland began to edit a new volume to mark the one hundredth anniversary of Oriental Institute publications, which is entitled *Publications of the Oriental Institute 1906–2006: Exploring and Celebrating the 100th Anniversary of Investigations into the History and Civilizations of the Near East* (with an Introduction by Gil J. Stein, Director of the Oriental Institute), and will be published in the series Oriental Institute Communications, volume 30. This volume is intended to complement and serve as a guide to all Oriental Institute publications up to 2006 that will eventually be available online. Holland completed this volume towards the end of 2006 and it is now in press with the Publications Office.

At his pre-retirement celebration in December, Holland presented two in-house talks, illustrated with slides, concerning his travels in Africa and his archaeological field work in the Near East. Beginning in 1965, he worked with Peter J. Parr at Petra, Kathleen M. Kenyon at Jerusalem, and Crystal-M. Bennett at Tawilan, all in Jordan. During 1971, he worked on the first field season at Umm Dabaghiyah, Iraq, with Diana Helbaek. In 1972 he was a field supervisor on the first field season at Tell Abu Hureyra, a Neolithic site excavated by Andrew M. T. Moore beside the Euphrates River in northern Syria. From 1973 until 1975 he directed the first seasons of excavations at Tell es-Sweyhat, which was one of the sites on the east bank of the Euphrates Tabqa Dam rescue excavations that was sponsored by the Ashmolean Museum, the University of Oxford. During the years 1976, 1978, and 1980 he acted as Assistant Director of Excavations at Tell Brak, Syria, under the directorship of David Oates. Excavations were renewed at Tell es-Sweyhat under the sponsorship of the Oriental Institute and the University Museum of the University of Pennsylvania, which consisted of three field seasons conducted during 1989, 1991, and 1992.

Holland was honored at the conclusion of his talks by a splendid Oriental Institute party amidst the grand setting of the Director's Office at which time he was presented with a very beautiful mahogany and onyx plague decorated in gold lettering with the following inscription: *The Oriental Institute, University of Chicago, Presented to Tom Holland, In Recognition of 22 Outstanding Years of Service, 1984–2006.*

INDIVIDUAL RESEARCH

Holland wishes to thank all of the Oriental Institute and NELC faculty, staff, graduate students, and members who made his twenty-two years working in the Publications Office such a memorable experience.

Janet H. Johnson

During the 2006/2007 academic year, **Janet H. Johnson** divided her efforts between the Demotic Dictionary Project (see separate report) and a series of lectures which she was invited to give for various venues. Here at the Oriental Institute, she gave a lecture entitled "Women in the Time of Tutankhamun" for the Museum Education Summer Seminar on "The World in the Time of Tutankhamun," an Oriental Institute Museum "docent training" lecture on "Post-New Kingdom Egypt," and the March Oriental Institute Members' Lecture entitled "Cleopatra as CEO: Bureaucracy and Scandal in the Hostile Takeover of a First-Century (BCE) Multinational." She also gave a presentation on the Chicago Demotic Dictionary for a panel entitled "Online Dictionaries for Historic and Lesser Known Languages: An Update" at the 16th Annual Meeting of the Dictionary Society of North America, held here at the Oriental Institute in June.

Further a field, she presented a lecture on "(Women and) Sexuality in Ancient Egypt" in the Ancient Studies Colloquium "Women's Pleasure in Ancient Literature and Art" held at Johns Hopkins University in April in honor of Assyriologist Jerry Cooper on the occasion of his retirement. And in February she was in Würzburg, Germany, to present a lecture on "Gender and Marriage in Ancient Egypt" for the conference "Ehe als Ernstfall der Geschlechterdifferenz, Herausforderungen für Frau und Mann in kulturellen Symbolsystemen" sponsored by "Wahrnehmung des Geschlechterdifferenz in religiösen Symbolsystemen" of the Katholisch-Theologische Fakultät, Julius-Maximilians-Universität in Würzburg. She also attended the annual meeting of the American Research Center in Egypt, held this year in Toledo, where she represented the Oriental Institute at the meeting of the Board of Governors and accepted appointment as co-chairman of an ad hoc committee that will evaluate governance structures for the organization.

W. Raymond Johnson

This year, **W. Raymond Johnson** completed his twenty-eighth year working for the Epigraphic Survey in Luxor, and his tenth season as Field Director. On May 20th, Ray inaugurated the Barbara W. Herman Memorial Lecture series at the Boston Museum of Fine Arts with a lecture entitled "Recent Discoveries in Luxor Lead to a Reassessment of Tutankhamun's Reign." He inaugurated the Oriental Institute's dinner-lecture series, "The Oriental Institute Presents…" on July 19th with a lecture highlighting material from Luxor Temple and its blockyards, shedding new light on Tutankhamun's building activities in Luxor and fragmentary wall reliefs — including battle scenes — which may offer clues about the young king's untimely death. He has contributed an article, co-written with J. Brett McClain, "A Fragmentary Scene of Ptolemy XII Worshipping the Goddess Mut and her Divine Entourage," to be published in the forthcoming volume, *Servant of Mut: Studies in Honor of Richard A. Fazzini*, Sue D'Aurea, editor.

This spring and summer, Ray helped coordinate a multinational salvage mapping and restoration expedition to the site of Amenhotep III's palace complex of Malkata and environs on the west bank of Luxor seriously threatened by agricultural expansion, population pressures, and

Charles Ellwood Jones

Charles Ellwood Jones continued his association with the Oriental Institute's Persepolis Fortification Archive Project. For that project he completed and published a paper with Wouter Henkelman and Matthew W. Stolper, "Achaemenid Elamite Administrative Tablets, 2: The Qasr-i Abu Nasr Tablet," *ARTA: Achaemenid Researches on Texts and Archaeology* (2006) (http://www.achemenet.com/ressources/enligne/arta/pdf/2006.003-Stolper-Jones-Henkelman.pdf). In October 2006, he launched a Web site devoted to the project "The Persepolis Fortification Archives Project" (http://persepolistablets.blogspot.com), which seeks to present reliable information on the project to the wide public reading and searching the Web. To date he has made fifty-three entries in the project, republishing some existing print-based materials, linking to publications available online, and collecting news on the project. As of mid-July, 8,703 unique visitors have made 13,901 visits to the site. In November Jones attended, along with other members of the Chicago Persepolis group, a conference on "Archives des Persépolis" at the Collège de France in Paris. He traveled again to Paris in June to consult with the Achemenet on revisions to their Web site.

Jones continued work on Abzu (http://www.etana.org/abzu), cataloging more than a thousand items into the database this year. In addition the core texts corpus continues to grow, as did the Archaeological Digital Library under development at ETANA with a grant from the National Science Foundation. For all these projects see http://www.etana.org.

Jones continued in his role as moderator of the Iraq Crisis List (http://listhost.uchicago.edu/mailman.listinfo.iraqcrisis), and as co-moderator of ANE-2 (http://groups.yahoo.com/group/ANE-2).

Walter Kaegi

Completion of a draft of a book manuscript on Muslims and Byzantines in North Africa occupied most of the research time of **Walter Kaegi**. But republication of some of his older books in new formats took place during 2006/2007. Cambridge University Press has published in 2007 a paperback edition of his 2003 Cambridge University Press hardback book *Heraclius Emperor of Byzantium*. The American Council of Learned Societies has created History E-Book editions of three older books: *Byzantium and the Decline of Rome* (1968, 1970), *Byzantine Military Unrest* (1981), and *Some Thoughts on Byzantine Military Strategy* (1983). These are now available online.

Three new articles appeared: "The Aures and the Byzantine Defeat at Sbeitla in 647." It was published in a collective volume by Société d'Études et de Recherches sur l'Aurès Antique and the University of Khenchela, Algeria, in the journal *AOURAS* 3 (2006): 185–206; "The Muslim Conquests of Edessa and Amida (Diarbekir)," in *Tigranakert/Diarbekir and Edessa/Urfa*, in the series Historic Armenian Cities and Provinces 6, edited by Richard G. Hovannisian, pp. 111–36 (Costa Mesa: Mazda Publishers, 2006); "The Early Muslim Raids into Anatolia and the Byzantine Reactions under Emperor Constans II," in *The Encounter of Eastern Christianity with Early Islam*, edited by Emmanouel Grypeou, Mark N. Swanson, and David Thomas, pp. 73–93 (Leiden: Brill, 2006).

Kaegi corrected proofs for two forthcoming publications: Chapter 9 for *Cambridge History of the Byzantine Empire*, edited by Jonathan Shepard, which is entitled "Confronting Islam: Changing Intensities of Military and Political Relationships Between Byzantium and Islam, 641–1000 CE"; and "Byzantine Sardinia Threatened: Its Changing Situation in the Seventh Century," Oristano, Sardinia, Italy, Convegno sui Bizantini in Sardegna: Forme e caratteri della presenza bizantina nel Mediterraneo occidentale: la Sardegna (secoli VI–XI), which will appear in a volume edited by Paola Corrias (to be published in Italy).

He completed three book reviews: *Cambridge Companion to the Age of Justinian*, by M. Maas, for the *Journal of Near Eastern Studies* (accepted); *General Issues in the Study of Medieval Logistics*, by John Haldon, for the *Sixteenth Century Journal* (accepted); and *Noble Ideals and Bloody Realities*, edited by N. Christie and M. Yazigi, for the *Mamluk Studies Review* (accepted).

He gave several interviews to journalists: two lengthy interviews (to two different interviewers) concerned with early memories of recently deceased author (and childhood friend) Hunter S. Thompson. He also gave an interview to three Albanian journalists in Saranda, Albania (26 June 2007), concerning his impressions of Albania on his first visit to that country.

He was elected Vice-President of the University of Chicago Phi Beta Kappa Chapter and will serve in several capacities during the years 2007–2009.

He delivered lectures at two professional meetings: "Decisive Combats in Byzantine Africa," Communication in Session A.I.1, Rival Empires, 21st International Congress of Byzantine Studies, London, England, 23 August 2006; and "The African Drill in the Strategikon of Maurice," Byzantine Studies Conference, University of Missouri at St. Louis, 10 November 2006.

Walter Kaegi served as Co-Director of the University of Chicago Workshop on Late Antiquity and Byzantium. He served on a number of University of Chicago committees, including a personnel committee in the Oriental Institute as well as one to select a visiting appointee in Armenian Studies in the Department of Near Eastern Languages and Civilizations. He was a member of the Hellenistic History Search Committee, in the Department of Classics, and Member, Personnel Committee, Oriental Institute; also member, Search Committee Near Eastern Languages and Civilizations, for Armenian Studies Visiting Faculty appointee, member of a personnel committee for the appointment of a Research Scholar in the Department of History, and a member of the Committee to select nominees for Chair of the Department of History. He served as external referee for several personnel cases in the U.S. and abroad.

Walter Kaegi led a small tour group to Algeria (8–25 March 2007), which enabled him to visit familiar and new and hitherto unfamiliar (to him) archaeological sites. He visited Albanian museums and archaeological sites for the first time in June 2007.

Helen McDonald

Helen McDonald made a study trip to Tell Brak (Syria) to work on third-millennium pottery for three weeks in April/May. Some 450 pots and sherds were registered and drawn for the publication of the TC area, on which Geoff Emberling and Helen McDonald are currently working. TC was excavated between 1998 and 2004 and contains part of a substantial late Early Dynastic III building with a curving outer wall that bears a resemblance to parts of the Temple Oval complex at Khafajeh. The area also has overlying levels of Akkadian and post-Akkadian date.

Dennis Pardee

Since last reporting in these pages — yes, it has been a while — **Dennis Pardee**'s edition of the Ugaritic ritual texts has appeared in two fascicles with a total of 1,307 pages (*Les textes rituels* [Ras Shamra-Ougarit 12; Paris: Éditions Recherche sur les Civilisations, 2000]) as has a much briefer overview intended for non-specialists (*Ritual and Cult at Ugarit* [Writings from the Ancient World Series 10; Atlanta: Society of Biblical Literature, 2002]).

The excavation at Ras-Shamra (ancient Ugarit) of a building that has come to be known as the House of Urtenou was completed in 2002 and it has proven to be the richest source of inscribed tablets from that site after the Royal Palace, excavated in the middle of the last century. Some six hundred tablets and fragments were discovered in this house, of which about a fifth were in Ugaritic, the local language, the rest for the most part in Akkadian. The tablets from 1986 to 1992 were published in 2001 (*Études ougaritiques. I. Travaux 1985–1995* [Ras Shamra-Ougarit 14; Paris: Éditions Recherche sur les Civilisations): Pardee with his French colleague Pierre Bordreuil signed the edition of twenty-one texts while another, a mythological fragment, appeared under the names of A. Caquot and A.-S. Dalix. Another eighty-seven texts were unearthed in the excavations of 1994–2002; the manuscript of their edition, again signed by Bordreuil and Pardee, with the collaboration of Robert Hawley for the epistolary texts, has been submitted for publication.

Bordreuil and Pardee have also been responsible for a *Manuel d'ougaritique* (Paris: Geuthner) that appeared in 2004; an English edition is virtually complete. Both the French and the English editions are intended as a general introduction to the language, literature, and epigraphy of the Ugaritic alphabetic texts. They include a selection of fifty-five texts, covering all the major literary genres attested at Ugarit, from mythological texts to scribal exercises, and each text appears in several forms: transliteration, translation, vocalized version, hand copy, and high-resolution photograph (in the French edition, the copies were provided in both printed and electronic form, the photographs in electronic form alone). The grammar is succinct and the commentary on the texts is limited to a few brief notes, hence only those with a background in Semitics can be expected to learn Ugaritic from it without the aid of a tutor.

Pardee has also been drafted into the project of editing the Ugaritic texts discovered at the neighboring site of Ras Ibn Hani between 1977 and 2002; preliminary editions by P. Bordreuil and A. Caquot have appeared of some of these, but a comprehensive edition including copies and photographs is needed. Over one hundred and fifty Ugaritic tablets and fragments were discovered at this site, mostly of an administrative nature, including several letters, though with some interesting religious texts as well. Presently, all the texts have been copied and photographed and the time-consuming job of preparing the copies for publication is advancing well. The commentary is about one-third complete; the hope is to have the project wrapped up within two years at the most.

Producing the *Manuel* required Pardee to do new copies of several of the mythological texts excavated for the most part during the first years of the excavation of Ras Shamra (1929–1939) and he decided to follow up on this partial coverage by doing complete copies of all three of the major mythological "cycles" that go by the names of their principal protagonists, Baal (six tablets), Kirta (three tablets), and Aqhat (also three tablets). His work on tablets from earlier excavations in the museums of the Louvre, Damascus, and Aleppo has thus focused primarily on these texts (the project is nearing completion) and on the previously inaugurated project of re-editing the Ugaritic administrative texts. A series of preliminary articles in each of these areas has appeared and more are in press or in preparation.

One of the most interesting results of the re-copying of the mythological texts has been the joining of two fragments of the Baal cycle. The problem has been that all the tablets of the cycle are more or less fragmentary and their arrangement according to the original narratological sequence has thus been a matter of much discussion over the past eighty years. Pardee has established that a small fragment (RS 3.364) of which the place in the Baal stories was uncertain once belonged to the tablet that the majority of scholars have identified as the third of the principal tablets of the six-tablet cycle. What might appear superficially to be a minor join has in fact far-reaching implications because it confirms the placement of the tablet in question before the tablet conventionally identified as the fourth and thus resolves a long-standing controversy on this point. Though the new join does not fill the gap between the third and fourth tablets (the small fragment fits at the beginning of the last column of the text on the larger fragment), the presence in the new composite text of a few rare terms that re-appear near the beginning of the text on the fourth tablet leave no real doubt as to the proper sequencing of these tablets. The full details of this join will appear in an article that has been submitted to a festschrift in honor of one of our former Oriental Institute colleagues.

The study of the Ugaritic texts from Ras Ibn Hani has led to another striking discovery. One of the most interesting texts from that site is a new song to the goddess Astarte (ʿAṯtartu in Ugaritic). A preliminary presentation of the text, RIH 98/02, will appear in the acts of a conference celebrating the 75th anniversary of the discovery of Ugarit (*Ugarit at Seventy-Five*, to be published by Eisenbrauns). Shortly after completing the copy and preliminary analysis of this tablet, Pardee, while working in the museum in Damascus, happened across a tablet excavated in 1955 at Ras Shamra (RS 19.039) and was struck by the physical similarity between the two tablets, both exhibiting an extreme "cushion" form, very thick in the middle and rounded at the edges and the corners. It was too late in that year's program to take up the detailed study of RS 19.039, but he returned to it in 2006 and is currently in the process of writing up his report comparing the two tablets. A series of epigraphic and paleographic features leave little doubt that the two tablets, both of which deal with the goddess Astarte, were the work of one and the same scribe — the first clear example of texts from the hand of a single scribe occurring at both sites. This case is decided by an important number of rarely attested characteristics shared by the two tablets; it may be hoped that future paleographic research will make it possible for such identifications to be established on the basis of a greater number of less striking points of similarity.

Clemens D. Reichel

Following the 2006 excavation season at Hamoukar in September and October, and its press release in January 2007, **Clemens D. Reichel** was busy with lectures on the new discoveries at Hamoukar. They included presentations at the University of Pittsburgh in December 2006, a symposium "Archaeology of Conflict" held at George Mason University (March 2007), at Brown University (March 2007), a membership lecture at the Oriental Institute, the Illinois Arab-American Medical Association (April 2007), the Mid-America Club, and the South Suburban Archaeological Society (June 2007). In March, he participated in the symposium held on the occasion of Ray Tindel's retirement, presenting a lecture ("Digging Old Data") on the work of the Diyala Project. In May he gave a lecture on the history of the Diyala expedition called "Lobster for Dinner, Ransom Money Assured" to the Breasted Society. He also presented two lectures on the topic of divine kingship in Mesopotamia: "King and Cult: Temples to Deified Kings in Mesopotamia" at the annual meeting of the Midwest Chapter of the American Oriental Society in Beaurbonnais, and "The King is Dead — Long Live the King: The Last Days of the Shusin Cult at Eshnunna and Its Aftermath" at

INDIVIDUAL RESEARCH

the Oriental Institute's post-doc conference, "Religion and Power: Divine Kingship in the Ancient World and Beyond." Both conferences were held in February, 2007. During 2006/2007, Reichel continued his cooperation with ARCANE (www.uni-tuebingen.de/arcane/) as Regional Coordinator for Central Mesopotamia.

Reichel is overjoyed by having received a $337,000 grant from the National Endowment for the Humanities to complete the work on the "Diyala Virtual Archive." This grant will start in July 2007.

Seth Richardson

Seth Richardson spent the academic year as a Faculty Research Fellow at the University's Franke Institute for the Humanities. The time was largely devoted to research and writing for his monograph *Studies in Late Old Babylonian History: A Historical Analysis of 17th-century Babylonia and the Collapse of the First Dynasty State*. The book looks to not only historical and anthropological models of collapse, but also takes some very modern models deriving from political science, geography, and comparative literature to gain some new perspective on an old problem.

In the fall, he was also busy with co-teaching duties as the Departments of Near Eastern Civilizations and Classics launched a new undergraduate core sequence entitled "Ancient Empires," for which he and Museum Director Geoff Emberling co-taught a quarter on the Neo-Assyrian empire to forty enthusiastic students. The continued meetings of the Ancient Societies Workshop, for which he is a co-sponsor, also kept him busy. The Workshop hosted fourteen speakers during the year, speaking on subjects as diverse as the Arab conquest of Damascus, the composition and historical reliability of the Hebrew Bible book of Chronicles, and servile populations in Kassite Babylonia — but all attending to the Workshop's annual theme of historical methodology.

Richardson briefly set some time aside for other projects, including a very enjoyable trip to the annual meeting of the Association of Ancient Historians, which met at Princeton University in May, where he delivered a paper on economic regulation in the Old Babylonian period. The conference provided a welcome opportunity to extend the contacts between ancient Near Eastern and classical Greco-Roman historical discussions. Also in May, Richardson acted as co-organizer of a one-day conference on comparative methodological paradigms between the disciplines, entitled Text Envy and Artifact Allure. The conference brought together Africanists, Andeanists, Americanists, and more to share ideas about how sources and research paradigms tend to form very different research questions in different areas of the Academy. He was particularly happy to welcome as part of the event Jerry Cooper from Johns Hopkins and Jan Assmann, already on loan to Chicago as a visiting scholar from the University of Heidelberg.

Robert K. Ritner

Robert Ritner's most visible role during the past year was as the featured speaker of the donors' reception for the inauguration of Robert Zimmer, incoming President of the University of Chicago, held at The Field Museum on October 26. His lecture, entitled "Tutankhamun for the Twenty-first Century: Modern Misreadings of an Ancient Culture," defended the significance of ancient Egyptian culture against errors in the popular press and was published online on the Oriental Institute Web site: http://oi.uchicago.edu/OI/IS/RITNER/Zimmer_Lecture_2006.html, and in the *University of Chicago Record*, December 7, 2006, pp. 8–10. By request, it appeared also on the North Texas American Research Center in Egypt Web site: www.arce-ntexas.org.

This was but one of many lectures given this past year. On October 14, for the Seventh Chicago-Johns Hopkins Theban Workshop, "Perspectives on Ptolemaic Thebes," Ritner spoke on "Ptolemy IX (Soter II) at Thebes," surveying the often faulty modern copies of this king's historical records at the once great city, which was devastated by civil war during this reign. The text of the lecture will be published in a forthcoming conference volume by the Oriental Institute. At the Egyptian embassy in Washington, D.C., on April 27, he lectured on "Magic and Medicine in Theory and Practice in Ancient Egypt" for the Washington chapter of the American Research Center in Egypt. The next day, he provided a five lecture, all-day seminar for the chapter on "Creation Stories," "How a Temple Works," "The Great Deities of Mythology," "The Impact of Egyptian Religion," and "The Function of Egyptian Art." On May 14, he discussed "An Introduction to Ancient Egyptian Religion and Magic" for the Oriental Institute Volunteers.

Ritner lectured daily for the Oriental Institute from March 11 through 27, when he led "The Wonders of Ancient Egypt" tour, which featured both famous highlights and lesser-known, but highly significant, Egyptian monuments from Cairo to Abu Simbel. He then returned to Luxor for a week to assist Chicago House with the interpretation of Ptolemaic hieroglyphs carved in the remodeled Eighteenth Dynasty temple at Medinet Habu.

In addition to the publications noted above, his study "'And Each Staff Transformed into a Snake': The Serpent Wand in Ancient Egypt," was published in *Through a Glass Darkly: Magic, Dreams and Prophecy in Ancient Egypt*, edited by K. Szpakowska (Wales: University of Swansea). Brief articles on "Seti I" and "Ramses II" appeared in *World Book Encyclopedia*, and he completed a manuscript on "Graffiti and Ostraca in the Tomb of Nespakashuty" for New York's Metropolitan Museum of Art.

During the course of the year, he served as a photographic contributor for the University of Pennsylvania Museum's publication *Akhenaton and Tutankhamun*, a translator for the Frank H. McClung Museum (Knoxville, Tennessee), a publication referee for University College London, and the American member of the Academic Review Committee for the 10th International Congress of Egyptologists, to be held in Rhodes. Beyond teaching and university committee duties, Ritner served his final year as Graduate Counselor for the ancient fields in the Department of Near Eastern Languages and Civilizations.

Oğuz Soysal

In 2006/2007 **Oğuz Soysal** continued his job on the Chicago Hittite Dictionary Project. He has spent most of his time writing articles on words beginning with *te / ti* and preparing the Turkish translations of CHD L and P for *e*CHD. Aside from this, his research activities have continued to focus on Hittite history and the Hattian language. The following articles were published: "Ein Textanschluß an KBo 3.24 (CTH 39.1)," *Nouvelles Assyriologiques Brèves et Utilitaires* 2006/1 (pp. 15–16); "Review of *Hittite Etymological Dictionary*, Vol. 6 (M), by J. Puhvel, *Bibliotheca Orientalis* 63 (2006): 560–72; "Puḫanu," *Reallexikon der Assyriologie* Bd. 11, Lfg. 1/2 (2006): 110; "Hattice metinlerde dört önemli kent ve bunların rahipleri," *Tabularia Hethaeorum: Hethitologische Beiträge Silvin Košak zum 65. Geburtstag*, edited by D. Groddek and M. Zorman, pp. 653–58 (Dresdner Beiträge zur Hethitologie, Band 25; Wiesbaden: Harrassowitz, 2007); "'Tanrı

INDIVIDUAL RESEARCH

Dr. Rukiye Akdoğan and Oğuz Soysal at work on ABoT 2

içmek' Hitit kült teriminin Hatti Dili ışığında yeni bir yorumlama denemesi," *Vita, Belkıs Dinçol ve Ali Dinçol'a Armağan / Festschrift in Honor of Belkıs Dinçol and Ali Dinçol* (2007): 731–37; "Beiträge zur althethitischen Geschichte (IV): Zur Lesung des Namens "Utnapišta" im Boğazköy-Fragment KBo 54.2," *Nouvelles Assyriologiques Brèves et Utilitaires* 2007/1 (p. 7); "KBo 49.167: Ein weiteres Fragment aus dem Textensemble CTH 728 als Duplikat zu KUB 28.1 III 5′–21′" *Nouvelles Assyriologiques Brèves et Utilitaires* 2007/1 (pp. 16–17); "The Hattian-Hittite Foundation Rituals from Ortaköy (I): Fragments to CTH 725 'Rituel bilingue de consécration d'un temple'" (with Aygül Süel), *Anatolica* 33 (2007): 1–22.

Furthermore, four articles and one on necrology have been written with publication forthcoming.

Between December 2006 and January 2007 he visited Ankara where he worked with his colleague Dr. Rukiye Akdoğan, who is a curator of the Museum of Ancient Anatolian Civilizations in Ankara and the responsible person for the Boğazköy section of the museum, on some unpublished Boğazköy-Tablets which were purchased and deposited in the museum. This group of fragments bears the siglum "AnAr." In 1948, the Turkish Assyriologist Kemal Balkan from Dil ve Tarih Coğrafya Fakültesi edited sixty-five of these "AnAr" fragments in his publication Ankara Arkeoloji Müzesinde Bulunan Boğazköy Tabletleri (ABoT). For his work he had mainly selected the better-preserved pieces. Other "AnAr" fragments, however, remained untouched since the series ABoT has not continued after Balkan's only publication. The number of still unpublished "AnAr" texts is near seven hundred, and at least the half of them are of worth to edit. Dr. Akdoğan, who is recently preparing the copies of those fragments for the second volume of ABoT, has asked Soysal's contribution to comment and categorize the texts. Since she is one of the most competent copyists of the Hittite tablets, Soysal gladly accepted her invitation. This would be a further Turkish-American cooperation in the field of the Hittitology. As part of their project, Dr. Akdoğan and Soysal conducted in January 2007 the final work on the fragments (final collations and taking digital pictures of the selected tablets). Soysal's trip to Turkey and work in Ankara were made possible by the generous financial support from the Oriental Institute.

Gil J. Stein

In 2006/2007 **Gil J. Stein** presented three papers. He was invited to present the paper "Political Economy and Social Change in Models of Ancient Culture Contact" as the keynote address at the conference "Interaction and Transformations: Studying Long Distance Exchange and Interaction During the Bronze Age," held on December 2, 2006, at the Carsten Niebuhr Institute of the University of Copenhagen. This conference, organized by Mogens Larsen, focused on the Old Assyrian colony period in Anatolia during the early second millennium B.C. (the Middle Bronze Age), and aimed at integrating archaeological and textual data to develop a more holistic understanding of this important period. In February 2007, he presented a paper titled "Guess Who's Coming to Dinner? Social Identity, Mixed Marriages, and Foodways in an Ancient Mesopotamian Colony" at the Joukowsky Institute of Archaeology, Brown University. In May 2007, he presented the paper "The Global and the Local: Comparing the Dynamics of Interaction in Ubaid and Uruk Mesopotamia" to the Interdisciplinary Borderlands Study Group at the University of California, Santa Barbara.

He submitted two papers for publication as well: "A Theoretical Model for Political Economy and Social Identity in the Old Assyrian Trading Colonies of Anatolia" to the Turkish Academy of Sciences Journal of Archaeology *TÜBA-AR*; and "Local Identities and Interaction Spheres: Modeling Regional Variation in the 'Ubaid Horizon,'" to be published in *The Ubaid and Beyond: Exploring the Transmission of Culture in the Developed Prehistoric Societies of the Middle East*, edited by R. A. Carter and G. Philip, Proceedings of the International Conference on the Ubaid, Durham, 20–22 April 2006 (Leiden: E. J. Brill).

Finally, Stein has been continuing with the ongoing analysis of the stratigraphy and artifacts from his 1992–1997 excavations at the fourth-millennium B.C. town of Hacınebi in the Euphrates valley of southeast Turkey. Hacınebi was a local Anatolian town where merchants from the Uruk culture of southern Mesopotamia established a trading colony in about 3700 B.C.. This commercial expansion of Uruk Mesopotamia at Hacınebi and other sites in Turkey, Syria, and Iran formed the world's earliest known colonial network. His excavations at Hacınebi revealed the remains of both the trading colony and its Anatolian host community, thereby allowing one to investigate relations between the two groups, and the actual workings of this colonial system.

Oriental Institute Volunteer Irene Glasner made major progress by scanning the inked drawings of the Late Chalcolithic small finds from Hacınebi. Thanks in a large part to Irene, about 700 drawings have been scanned and are very close to completion. Working with research assistant Dr. Belinda Monahan, Stein has been refining the ceramic typology from Hacınebi so that the ceramic data can be integrated with the analysis of site stratigraphy. Belinda has been tracking down published comparanda of the main Uruk Mesopotamian and Local Anatolian ceramic forms. With roughly 500 different recorded forms of rims, handles, bases of jars and bowls, and assorted miscellaneous ceramic objects, this has been a large-scale and complex task. Roughly 250,000 Late Chalcolithic sherds have been recorded from the site. Stein expects to complete the ceramic typology and conduct a full diachronic analysis of this material over the course of the coming year. He plans to start writing the ceramic analysis and stratigraphy volumes of the Hacınebi final report in 2007/2008.

Matthew W. Stolper

Matthew W. Stolper spent most of his research effort during the past year on the Persepolis Fortification Archive Project, described elsewhere in this Annual Report. Related publications are two notes in a series treating scattered Achaemenid Elamite administrative in the online journal *ARTA* (see http://www.achemenet.com). The first, "Fortification Texts Sold at the Auction of the Erlenmeyer Collection," ARTA 2006.002, coauthored with Oriental Institute Research Associate Charles E. Jones, rounds up Fortification tablets that escaped the Persepolis excavators in the 1930s and are now scattered among private collections, prefiguring the gruesome threat that now hangs over the entire archive. The second, "The Qasr-i Abu Nasr Tablet," ARTA 2006.003, coauthored with Jones and Persepolis Fortification Project collaborator Wouter Henkelman, presents a similar text recovered by excavators at a nearby site, but perhaps originally taken from Persepolis.

INDIVIDUAL RESEARCH

Related lectures and presentations were a talk on the Persepolis Fortification Archive issues at the University of California; a first approach the question "How Many Fortification Tablets Are There?," presented to a symposium on the Organization of Knowledge in Antiquity: Archives and Record Management, at University of Western Washington; a discussion of the "'Diplomatics' of the Persepolis Tablets," dealing with some issues raised by tablet shape, at a colloquium on the Persepolis Fortification Archive held in Paris; a first presentation of the newly discovered Old Persian text from the Persepolis Fortification, at the American Oriental Society's annual meeting in San Antonio. He had the honor of giving the first invited Musa Sabi Lecture in Iranian Studies at the University of California, Los Angeles (though the honor really belongs to the Fortification tablets) and of showing the tablets to members of the Visiting Committee of the Division of Humanities as they gathered in the Mesopotamian Hall of the Oriental Institute Museum to meet the new dean, the Oriental Institute's Martha Roth.

Among Stolper's non-Persepolitan work is an article on "Post-Achaemenid Iranica in Babylonian Texts," a treatment of Iranian vocabulary in Babylonian documents written between the reigns of Alexander and the Parthian kings, published in the proceedings of a colloquium on the transition between the Achaemenid empire and the Hellenistic kingdoms and their successors (Persika 9; Paris: de Boccard). An article in the forthcoming festschrift for Bob Biggs, "Kasr Texts: Excavated but Not in Berlin," is another grim example of lost archival context, recording texts and fragments from the late Achaemenid Kasr archive that were once part of an excavated corpus but have been scattered by antiquities sales among many collections. An article in the forthcoming festschrift for Hermann Hunger, "From the Tattannu Archive Fragment," co-authored with Michael Jursa of the University of Vienna, deals with extraordinary texts from a nearly contemporary Babylonian legal archive whose original excavated condition can never be known.

Emily Teeter

Emily Teeter's recent research continues to be devoted to the publication of artifacts from the University of Chicago's excavations at Medinet Habu. A volume on baked clay figures and votive beds was accepted this year for publication by the Oriental Institute. Another major project is the finalization of a book on ancient Egyptian religious ritual for Cambridge University Press. Publications that appeared this year include the second revised edition of *Egypt and the Egyptians* (co-authored with Douglas Brewer), an article "Corpus of Egyptian Antiquities in Serbia: Additions and Corrections" (with Branislav Andelkovic) in the *Journal of the Serbian Archaeological Society*, and a review of the exhibit "Hatshepsut: From Queen to Pharaoh" in the *American Journal of Archaeology*. Several book reviews were published in the *Journal of Near Eastern Studies*.

Emily taught courses for the Education Department including "Tutankhamun: His Tomb and Its Treasures," and an online course "Ancient Egyptian Architecture." She gave several lectures for regional chapters of the University of Chicago Alumni Society.

Emily continues to be involved with the American Research Center in Egypt (ARCE). She serves on the Executive Committee of ARCE and she was elected vice president of the organization at the annual meeting in April. Locally, she stepped down from being president of the Chicago Chapter to serve as vice-president and program chair.

She served as a lecturer for a several tours in the Middle East.

Theo van den Hout

The past year started very well with the privilege of leading an Oriental Institute tour to Turkey where "in the footsteps of the Indo-Europeans" **Theo van den Hout** led the tour through all major sites of the Hittite empire (with a wonderful tour of Hattuša by its director, Dr. Andreas Schachner!), Phrygia, Lydia, Caria, and Lycia. With the firm hand of our excellent tour guide Tansu, it was an unforgettable trip.

Besides the work on the Chicago Hittite Dictionary (see Project Reports), classes, and committee work, there was still some time left for his own research on record management in the Hittite world. For a conference in Florence, Italy, he submitted a paper on the history of Hittite record keeping and the related question of early Hittite literacy. A request to write the entry *Schreiber* (scribe) for the *Reallexikon der Assyriologie* allowed him to research that topic and he also handed in the text for an article on general record organization for the proceedings of a conference he attended last year in Würzburg, Germany, as well an article on sealing practices for the *Journal of the American Oriental Society*. He also provided some other small entries for the *Reallexikon* as well as two book reviews.

The following articles came out in the past year: "On the Nature of the Tablet Collections of Ḫattuša," *Studi micenei ed egeo-anatolici* 47 (2005 [2006]) 277–89; "Muršili II's 'First' Plague Prayer" and "Muršili II's 'Second' Plague Prayer" (translations and explanatory notes), in *The Ancient Near East: Historical Sources in Translation*, edited by Mark W. Chavalas, pp. 259–66 (Blackwell Publishing, 2006); "The Prayers in the Haus am Hang," in *Tabularia Hethaeorum. Hethitologische Beiträge Silvin Košak zum 65. Geburtstag*, edited by D. Groddek and M. Zorman, pp. 401–09 (Dresdner Beiträge zur Hethitologie 25; Wiesbaden: Harrassowitz, 2007).

Two reviews appeared in the *Zeitschrift für Assyriologie* 96 (2006): 280–85, as well as the entry "Hittites" in the children's *World Book Encyclopedia* (pp. 269–70; Chicago, 2007).

At the 16th Conference of the Dictionary Society of North America, held at the Oriental Institute in June, he gave a presentation together with Sandy Schloen about the electronic Chicago Hittite Dictionary.

Donald Whitcomb

In early July, a repeat of the Umayyad Legacies conference of last year with reprise of ideas on Fustat provided **Donald Whitcomb** an opportunity to visit Beirut with Rana Mikati, to meet the Director of Antiquities with her, and to visit Baalbek. He had previously visited the Biqaʻ valley to see the remarkable early Islamic foundation of Anjar, the subject of many a classroom presentation and striking parallel (model?) for the remains at Aqaba. A few days after returning to Chicago, fighting destroyed much of Beirut and even damaged Baalbek; happily Rana's family was safe and she returned to Chicago.

In November Don had an opportunity to return to Damascus for a conference on Late Antiquity and early Islam sponsored by the Deutsches Archäologisches Institut, where a total of some forty papers were presented. This was an overview of the results from the Aqaba excavations with a first presentation of the Mosque and Dar al-Imara. Sadly other activities have still prevented the publication of these discoveries. There was a day-trip to the still mysterious early Islamic town at Jebel Says (also known as Usais), which reveals a pattern of settlement surprisingly different and possibly Arabian in inspiration. Finally there was a return to the "desert castle" of Hallabat, not

INDIVIDUAL RESEARCH

Don and Joy McCorriston enjoy the diwan of King Abdulaziz palace in Dawasir, Saudi Arabia

far from Amman. This site has been the subject of the painstaking and precise investigation and reconstruction of Ignacio Arce, director of the Spanish archaeological mission. He has successfully identified a Ghassanid occupation (fifth–sixth centuries), a palace and monastery building upon the Roman fort, later translated into an early Islamic *qasr*.

Upon his return Don was invited to participate in a conference at Brown University on the archaeology of Jerusalem. This paper, "Jerusalem and the Beginnings of the Islamic City," was the first public discussion of some rather unusual ideas on the initial transformation of that holy city, especially before a group of Israeli archaeologists who have excavated and studied Jerusalem for most of their careers. Their polite response and encouragement suggests that there will be more investigation of this neglected part of its history, somewhat ironic after the Israeli discovery and restoration of Islamic monuments south of the Haram al-Sharif. Participation of several Palestinian archaeologists also gives hope for a future through common understanding of archaeological research.

In the spring, Don began yet another possible project. Under the leadership of David Graf, a small group were invited to the Kingdom of Saudi Arabia under the sponsorship of the Department of Antiquities and the American Embassy. At King Saud University in Riyadh, Don gave a paper on the "Archaeology of Islamic Urbanism," which seemed rather like "bringing coals to Newcastle," considering the expertise on this subject there. This visit included a wonderful trip to Qaryat al-Fau, pre-Islamic city in the center of the Kingdom. What they witnessed was an impressive revelation after twenty-five seasons of excavations and a vital contribution to pre-Islamic antecedents of Islamic cities of Arabia and the Middle East.

Along the way, Don's students have progressed with increasingly specialized seminars on Islamic archaeology and relevant artifacts. Katherine Strange Burke took her doctorate with honors, having written her dissertation on the Sheikh's house at Quseir al-Qadim. One fruition of these studies was that, in the fall, Tanya Treptow and Don began a collaboration on the concepts and practicalities of a temporary exhibit on the medieval Persian city of Rayy, modern Tehran. Some six months later this effort to explain Islamic archaeology resulted in the opening of Daily Life Ornamented: The Medieval Persian city of Rayy. Tanya and Don gave brief talks at the opening, his on Erich Schmidt, hers on archaeology and potsherds.

Most recently, the 10th International Conference on the History and Archaeology of Jordan was held in Washington, D.C., where Don returned yet again to summarize the results in a paper, "Ayla at the Millennium," referring to the year 1000 C.E.

INDIVIDUAL RESEARCH

Magnus Widell

Magnus Widell continued to make progress on his edition of the unpublished Ur III tablets kept at the University of Notre Dame (*The Cuneiform Texts from the Ur III Period in the University of Notre Dame Theodore M. Hesburgh Library*). He also completed and submitted one scholarly article and two book reviews this year. The article, "Schiff, sumerisch," is currently being reviewed for publication in *Reallexikon der Assyriologie*.

The past year has seen the appearance of three articles, two of them, "Urbanization within a Dynamic Environment: Modeling Bronze Age Communities in Upper Mesopotamia" and "Modeling Settlement Systems in a Dynamic Environment: Case Studies from Mesopotamia" were co-authored with members of the Modeling Ancient Settlement Systems' project. The third article, "Historical Evidence for Climate Instability and Environmental Catastrophes in Northern Syria and the Jazira: The Chronicle of Michael the Syrian," appeared earlier this year in *Environment and History* 13/1, pages 47–70.

Widell gave two talks this year. In March, he presented a paper on the Sumerian expression igi-kar$_2$ at the 217th Annual Meeting of the American Oriental Society, which was held in San Antonio. In May, he was invited by the Department of Oriental Studies at Peking University to present a talk on cuneiform texts and administrative procedures in the late third millennium.

Earlier this summer, Widell accepted a position in the School of Archaeology, Classics and Egyptology at the University of Liverpool. After four and a half years at the Oriental Institute, it was a difficult decision to leave Chicago. He will start teaching at Liverpool in September 2007.

Karen L. Wilson

Karen L. Wilson is putting the finishing touches on her manuscript of the final publication of the University of Chicago's 1903–05 excavations at Bismaya (ancient Adab) thanks to the generous grant she received from the Shelby White-Leon Levy Program for Archaeological Publications. She plans to submit the completed manuscript by the end of the summer. Karen was delighted to participate in the March 26 symposium "Excavating in Museum Basements: A Conference in Honor of Raymond D. Tindel" at which she presented a paper titled "Recovering the Lost City of Adab: Edgar J. Banks and the University of Chicago Expedition to Bismaya 1903–05." Her work on Bismaya would not have been possible without Ray Tindel's generosity: he provided her with both a space to work and unrestricted access to the collections in storage, as well as moral support as the project progressed.

In May Karen submitted a completed manuscript for the Mesopotamian Gallery Guide to Museum Director Geoff Emberling. In addition, she continued to serve as Kish Project Coordinator at The Field Museum. There she worked with other museum staff to design and implement an interactive Kish Web site. The site, which is in both English and Arabic, documents archival and artifactual material that resulted from the joint excavations of The Field Museum and Oxford University at Kish from 1923 to 1933. And thanks to a recent grant from the Department of Defense, Karen is continuing as a staff member at The Field Museum for the next several years to coordinate the production of a final site report for Kish.

INDIVIDUAL RESEARCH

Christopher Woods

This year, **Christopher Woods** finished a book on grammatical voice in Sumerian, *The Grammar of Perspective: The Sumerian Conjugation Prefixes as a System of Grammatical Voice*. Brill is publishing the book as part of their Cuneiform Monograph series and it should be out by the time of the AOS meeting in Chicago next March. Some aspects of this work ("The Conjugation Prefixes, the Dative Case, and the Empathy Hierarchy in Sumerian") were presented at the 2007 AOS meeting in San Antonio in March, as well as at a conference on grammatical case, *Variations, concurrence et évolution des cas dans divers domaines linguistiques*, held in Paris this past April. Dr. Woods is the fortunate recipient of a Franke Institute Residential Fellowship for the 2007/2008 academic year. The fellowship provides a teaching and administrative reduction so that he may concentrate on his second book project, a study of Sumerian writing from typological and cognitive perspectives. This year, Woods became the editor-in-chief of the *Journal of Ancient Near Eastern Religions*. The journal will now be published bi-annually. The first volume under his direction, 2007/1, appeared as this annual report went to print.

K. Aslıhan Yener

During the year, **K. Aslıhan Yener** directed the eleventh season of the broadly based Amuq Valley Regional Projects (AVRP) in Antakya, Turkey. This included a surface survey of the mineral rich resources of the Amanus Mountains. Important for their source of gold and copper in prehistoric periods, several potentially ancient chromite mines were documented that may have supplied a necessary pigment ingredient for ancient glass and faience. The work on last year's AVRP survey (2005) season was published in (2006), "Regional Survey in the Amuq Valley, Hatay: The 2005 Season," in *24. Araştırma Sonuçları Toplantısı*, edited by Fokke Gerritsen, pp. 201–08 (Ankara: General Directorate for Cultural Heritage and Museums, 2006). Yener continued directing the third season of excavations at Tell Atchana (ancient Alalakh). Analyses and results from Alalakh are published in Açcana Höyüğü 2005 Yılı Çalışmaları, 28. *Kazı Sonuçları Toplantısı*, pp. 223–30. (Ankara: General Directorate of Antiquities and Museums, 2006).

Honors, grants, and awards during 2006/2007 included the Institute of Aegean Prehistory, "Alalakh Excavations, Turkey," and the Fund for the Amuq Valley Excavations.

She published several articles and chapters in books in "A Zoomorphic Vessel from Alalakh: Diplomatic Emblems in Three Dimensional Form?," in *Festschrift for Professor Refik Duru*, edited by Gülsün Umurtak (Turkish Historical Society, 2007). And "Transformative Impulses in Late Bronze Age Technology: A Case Study from the Amuq Valley, Southern Turkey," in *Settlement and Society: Essays Dedicated to Robert McCormick Adams,* edited by E. Stone, pp. 360–85 (Los Angeles: Cotsen Institute of Archaeology; Chicago: The Oriental Institute, 2007).

Yener was on sabbatical leave in the winter quarter last year at the University of Pennsylvania. While there, she gave a number of scholarly papers on the excavations at Göltepe and the Amuq Valley surveys. Two workshops on the Late Bronze and Middle Bronze Age levels of Alalakh at the University of Pennsylvania were well attended. Lectures on the new finds from Alalakh were given at the New York University Anthropology Department, Middle East Technical University, Turkey, and two papers at the Meetings of the International Symposium of Excavations, Surveys, and Archaeometry, May, Kocaeli Izmit, Turkey (2006).

RESEARCH SUPPORT
COMPUTER LABORATORY
John C. Sanders

PROJECTS

New Web-site Launch

After more than three years of discussions, planning, development, and testing, the Oriental Institute's new Web site was launched on February 7, 2007. As we had hoped, the new "look and feel" of the site, as well as its improved structure and query capabilities, has met with widespread approval and praise by faculty, staff, students, and the general public.

The new Web site is divided into three primary sections, Research, Museum, and Events. Each page on the Web site, with few exceptions, contains a set of links at the top and bottom for quick access to certain key pieces of information: Visit Us, Contact Us, Get Involved, Calendar of Events, Order Online, What's New, and a site-specific search function. Also present on practically all our Web pages is a "Featured Events" box, with a rotating list of links to current events, courses, sales, and opportunities that the public may take advantage of, without the need for the visitor to search for such information.

If you haven't yet visited our new Web site, point your favorite Web browser at: oi.uchicago.edu

Many faculty, staff, and former staff members within the Institute as well as staff within the University's Web Services division were involved in various ways throughout this multi-year project, and they deserve recognition at this time.

Oriental Institute Director, Gil Stein, and Executive Director, Steven Camp, have both been very supportive and approving of the overall goals of our new Web presence as the "front door" into the Institute's operations. The success of this endeavor would not have been possible without their encouragement, criticism, and guidance.

I cannot say enough about the vision and assistance offered by my partner in this project, former Research Archivist and Bibliographer, Charles Jones. Chuck was an equal participant from the earliest discussions we had back in 1993 regarding the development of the Oriental Institute's original Web site. He continued his critical role as partner in managing and maintaining our former Web site over the years, and was a critical force as we migrated the hosting of our Web site over to the University of Chicago's Networking Services and Information Technologies' (NSIT) Web Services group in March 2004. During our recent redesign process, as a member of the Institute's Web-site Design Committee, Chuck made many vital suggestions as well as operating as a sounding board for other's ideas until he left the university in July 2005, to run the Blegen Library

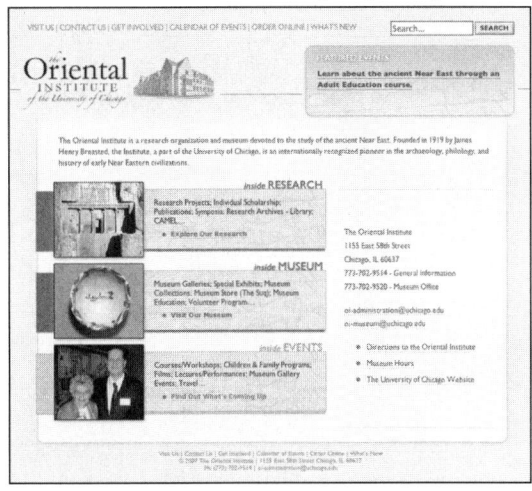

The new Oriental Institute Web site homepage

COMPUTER LABORATORY

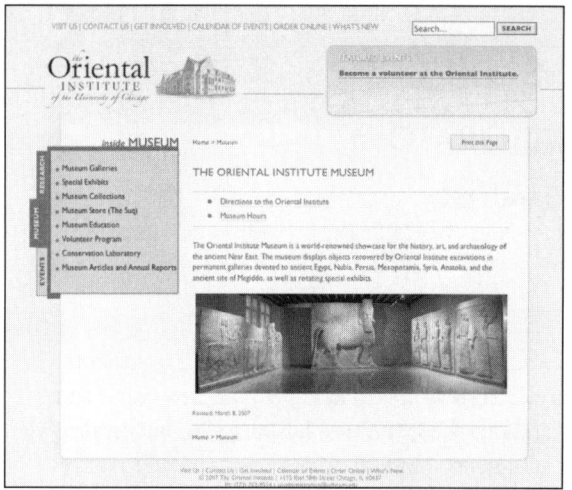

The new Oriental Institute Museum Web site homepage

of the American School of Classical Studies at Athens, Greece.

Other members of the Institute's Web site Design Committee deserve special mention because of their efforts during years of committee meetings, impromptu discussions around the water cooler, and endless e-mails involving grand scale design issues as well as miniscule arguments over font designs and color schemes. Much credit for the success of the overall design of the Web site goes to: the aforementioned Gil Stein and Steven Camp; Museum Director, Geoff Emberling; former Membership Coordinator, Maria Krasinski; Museum Education Project Coordinator, Wendy Ennes; and Development Director, Monica Witczak.

The efforts of all the above participants would be meaningless without the guidance and coordination provided by NSIT's Web Services group. The following staff members advanced the project from beginning to end, offered their advice and expertise along the way, and undertook all the behind-the-scenes code writing. The final design and deliverable product is a testament to the professional skills of the following individuals: former Web Services director, Therese Allen-Vassar; current Web Services director, John Mohr; former project coordinator, Sandor Weisz, current Web-site coordinator, Jack Auses; and programmers Megan Coleman, Sara Worrell-Berg, Stephanie Smith, Quinn Carey, Justin Sante, Lynn Barnett, Scott Bassett, and Mitchell Kim.

Lastly, I want to thank the countless Institute faculty, staff, and students who offered comments, encouragement, and criticisms of our new Web-site design during the past two years. Our design process could not incorporate all the suggestions they offered, but I hope the final product provides everyone with both a useful research tool and a pleasant web experience.

Integrated Database

Our plans to develop an integrated computer database containing all the relevant records, photographs, publications, and other documents that are the legacy of the Institute's eighty plus years of operation took several major steps forward during the past year. In the fall of 2006 the Institute's Integrated Database Committee (Gil Stein, Geoff Emberling, David Schloen, Raymond Johnson, Scott Branting, John Sanders, Thomas Urban, Steve Camp, and George Sundell) made a visit to The Field Museum, in Chicago, in order to discuss their own still ongoing computer database integration process with members of their administration and information technology staff. Although their collection management issues are more diverse than ours, the overall design and development processes they have already gone through will be very informative as we begin our efforts. Ms. Joanna McCaffrey, the Collections Database Architect who is overseeing their computer integration project, offered to assist us during our initial stage of goals assessment and program development. We greatly appreciate her willingness to help, and her insights and observations as we proceed during the coming year.

After months of discussions, and with assistance provided by Ms. McCaffrey's Field Museum experience, our Integrated Database Committee prepared a Request For Information (RFI) during the winter of 2006/2007. Once the vetting process for the document was completed, the RFP was mailed to nine software vendors in late April 2007. Responses will be received and evaluated during the summer, and a shortlist of candidates will be invited to demonstrate their proposed museum management software in the fall of 2007. We expect to choose a single software vendor for the Institute's Integrated Database by the end of the 2007 calendar year.

Oriental Institute Terabyte Storage Initiative

The Oriental Institute Archive (OIA), the Institute's terabyte (1,000,000,000,000 bytes) computer storage array maintained by NSIT, grew in two increments to its present capacity of seven terabytes in July 2007. Approximately seventy+ faculty and staff members, as well as over a dozen units and/or projects within the Institute, are currently using this long-term computer storage space for daily back up and/or archiving of their electronic data and numerous computer files. Given the ongoing plans to digitize the Museum's Photographic Archives, the continued scanning of the Research Archives' map collections by the Institute's CAMEL facility, and the ever-increasing datasets created by both the archeological and philological projects in the building, we can expect to see a continual increase in both the use and the storage capacity of the OIA throughout the coming year, and beyond.

Building-wide Document Printing and Scanning

The Institute's primary Xerox copier in room 228 and its twin in the Research Archives were replaced with newer, faster, more capable models in August and December 2006, respectively. As mentioned in last year's *Annual Report*, these new machines were installed and setup for network printing and scanning, and the predicted wave of data capture to Adobe Portable Document Format (PDF) files by the faculty and staff did occur starting immediately and shows no signs of a slowdown these many months later. Whether, however, this scanning directly to PDF files has actually reduced the amount of paper consumed in the building remains to be seen. Although having an electronic version of a paper, article, or an entire book has its definite advantages, many people still want a paper copy for ease of reading, editing, and as a backup.

During the coming year we expect to add a similar Xerox machine on the Institute's third floor as well as one in the Archaeology Lab in the basement. Once these are installed we will be able to retire the various public access laser printers located throughout the building, as these new Xerox machines are more than capable of doing double duty as both copiers, scanners, and laser printers for the faculty, staff, and students. I will report further on this issue in next year's *Annual Report*.

Macintosh Computer Upgrades

By the time you read this *Annual Report* all the Institute's faculty and staff who use Macintosh computers for their work will have been migrated to Apple's System X operating system, the vast majority of those users doing so with brand new Intel-based Apple computers purchased during summer 2006. Although a couple of the older, System 9-based Macintosh computers will remain running in the Institute's Server Room, in order to provide backwards compatibility if need be, and one or two research projects will continue to maintain System 9 Mac's because of legacy font issues relating to older document archives, all present and future Macintosh-based research will only be conducted using the much improved System X.

Because of this migration by the Institute's Macintosh users to System X, they have the added bonus of being able to take advantage of the Institute's new terabyte storage space, the OIA mentioned above, something that would not have been technologically possible had they continued

COMPUTER LABORATORY

to use their older, System 9-based computers. Needless to say, many such faculty and staff were pleased to switch knowing that the backup and archiving of their data would now be much simpler than before the upgrade.

Electronic Publications

As a part of the Institute's Electronic Publications Initiative, this is the first full year of work producing Adobe Portable Document Format (PDF) files of out-of-print volumes previously published by our Publications Office and the University of Chicago Press. In addition, this initiative dictates that current and future print publications produced by the Oriental Institute Publications Office are also made available in this same format through the Institute's Web site. I encourage everyone to read that portion of the Publications Office section of this *Annual Report* regarding the status of the Institute's Electronic Publications Initiative, then visit the Catalog of Publications page on our Web site where you will be able to download these past and current titles of our publications in electronic form:

http://oi.uchicago.edu/research/pubs/catalog/index.html

This Electronic Publications Initiative, when fully implemented through the electronic publication of all 400+ titles published by the Oriental Institute, promises to be a great benefit to scholarly research in the various fields of ancient Near Eastern studies.

For further information concerning several of the above mentioned research projects, the Institute's World-Wide Web (WWW) database, and other Electronic Resources in general refer to the What's New page on the Oriental Institute's Web site, at (NOTE: this URL is case-sensitive):

http://oi.uchicago.edu/news/

See the "Electronic Resources" section of this *Annual Report* for the complete URL to each of the Web-site resources mentioned in this article.

ELECTRONIC RESOURCES
John C. Sanders

Oriental Institute World-Wide Web Site
New and Developing Resources

(NOTE: all Web addresses below are case-sensitive)

Several Oriental Institute units and projects either updated existing pages or became a new presence on the Institute's Web site during the past year.

Museum: Special Exhibits

Wonderful Things! The Discovery of the Tomb of Tutankhamun: The Harry Burton Photographs

http://oi.uchicago.edu/museum/special/tut/

The Ancient Near East in the Time of Tutankhamun

http://oi.uchicago.edu/museum/special/tut/

Embroidering Identities: A Century of Palestinian Clothing

http://oi.uchicago.edu/museum/special/embroidering/

Through Young Eyes: Ancient Nubian Art Recreated

http://oi.uchicago.edu/museum/special/youngeyes/

Daily Life Ornamented: The Medieval Persian City of Rayy

http://oi.uchicago.edu/museum/special/rayy/

Publications Office: Electronic Publications

We are breaking with the tradition of listing in this section all titles for electronic publications made available on the Institute's Web site during the past year. Instead, the titles of those current or previous Oriental Institute publications converted to the Adobe Portable Document Format (PDF) during the past year are listed in the Publications Office section of this *Annual Report*. Links to these various electronic publications can be found on the Institute's Web site, on the appropriate series page in our Catalog of Publications:

http://oi.uchicago.edu/research/pubs/catalog/index.html

Research Archives: Research Archives Catalog Online

The Oriental Institute's online catalog of the Research Archives has received a completely new look (note the URL change below). Additionally, in order to further improve its usefulness, we have significantly increased the efforts of retrospective cataloging of material from before 1990. The total number of records stands at 233,000+.

http://oilib.uchicago.edu

Archaeology: The Zincirli Expedition

The Oriental Institute is starting a new long-term excavation project at the site of Zincirli (ancient Sam'al) in southeast Turkey.

http://oi.uchicago.edu/research/projects/zin/

Philology: Persepolis Fortification Archive

The frequently updated Persepolis Fortification Archive Project blog presents information and resources relating to the Oriental Institute's ongoing project to conserve, document, study, and publish the Elamite and Aramaic administrative documents and associated seal impressions that form the Persepolis Fortification Archive.

http://persepolistablets.blogspot.com/

Individual Scholarship: Norman Golb

An exhibition review by Prof. Norman Golb, entitled "The Dead Sea Scrolls at Seattle's Pacific Science Center."

http://oi.uchicago.edu/research/is/deadseascrolls.html

ELECTRONIC RESOURCES

An article entitled: "Museum Exhibitions Intensify Controversy Over the Dead Sea Scrolls"

http://oi.uchicago.edu/research/projects/scr/ethics_of_museology.pdf

An article entitled: "The Qumran-Essene Theory and Recent Strategies Employed in Its Defense"

http://oi.uchicago.edu/research/projects/scr/Recent_Strategies_2007.pdf

An article entitled: "Fact and Fiction in Current Exhibitions of the Dead Sea Scrolls — A Critical Notebook for Viewers"

http://oi.uchicago.edu/pdf/dss_fact_fiction_2007.pdf

Individual Scholarship: John Larson

A brief biography of Erich F. Schmidt, Field Director of the Persepolis Expedition of the Oriental Institute of the University of Chicago, from 1935 to 1939.

http://oi.uchicago.edu/pdf/erich_f_schmidt_bio.pdf

Individual Scholarship: Robert K. Ritner

Address at the first inaugural celebration for incoming University of Chicago President Robert J. Zimmer.

http://oi.uchicago.edu/research/is/ritner2006.html

Individual Scholarship: Charles E. Jones

Although Charles Jones is no longer director of the Oriental Institute's Research Archives, he still actively maintains several vital electronic resources for ancient Near Eastern studies just as he had done during his tenure in Chicago. Thank you, Chuck, for your continuing service to the field and our faculty, staff, and students.

ABZU: Guide to Resources for the Study of the Ancient Near East Available on the Internet

http://www.etana.org/abzu

ETANA: Electronic Tools and Ancient Near Eastern Archives — Core Texts

A substantial selection of digitized titles from the collections of the Research Archives has been added to the ETANA Core Texts this year.

http://www.etana.org/coretexts.shtml

IraqCrisis

A moderated list for communicating substantive information on cultural property damaged, destroyed, or lost from Libraries and Museums in Iraq during and after the war in April 2003, and on the worldwide response to the crisis. A component of the Oriental Institute's response to the cultural heritage crisis in the aftermath of the war in Iraq, this list provides a moderated forum for the distribution of information.

https://listhost.uchicago.edu/mailman/listinfo/iraqcrisis

PUBLICATIONS OFFICE

Thomas G. Urban

The full-time staff of the Publications Office decreased this year with the retirement of Thomas Holland. The full-time staff of the editorial office consists of Thomas Urban and Leslie Schramer. Happily, Leslie was promoted to Associate Editor. Student Editorial Assistants Lindsay DeCarlo and Katie L. Johnson continued to provide invaluable assistance. Sadly, Lindsay resigned at the end of the year and is pursuing other interests.

The Publications Office continues to assist the Membership Office with the publication of *News & Notes* and the *Annual Report*; and new this year was the assistance with various postcards, brochures, and posters given to the Membership and Development Offices.

Sales

The David Brown Book Company and Oxbow Books Ltd., U.K., continue to represent the Institute for its book distribution. Although a limited number of titles are available for in-house sales in the Suq shop, please note that all external orders for Institute publications should be addressed to: The David Brown Book Company, P.O. Box 511, Oakville, CT 06779; Telephone Toll Free: 1-800-791-9354; Fax: 1-860-945-9468; E-mail: david.brown.bk.co@snet.net; Web site: www.oxbowbooks.com.

Information related to the sales of Oriental Institute titles may be obtained via e-mail:

oi-publications@uchicago.edu

The Chicago Demotic Dictionary and InDesign

Readers of Oriental Institute *Annual Reports* will remember the printing test that the office tried a few years ago (*2003–2004 Annual Report*, page 160) for the Chicago Demotic Dictionary (CDD). The goal was to place CDD files created in Microsoft Word with 20,000+ embedded graphics into page layout files in the most efficient manner so that the clarity of the graphics is not compromised. When the experiment was tried using Adobe PageMaker in 2004, the graphics inverted to negatives. The Publications Office now uses Adobe InDesign as its page layout application, and it is time for another test. On pages 39–41 of this report three words in Demotic script were converted to TIFF files and placed in the text as inline graphics. Here, one word in Demotic script, in two forms, is placed directly from a Word file: ⲥⲩ ⲥⲩ.

Electronic Publications

All new titles are simultaneously issued in print and as PDF files delivered through the Oriental Institute's Web site. The Oriental Institute chose Northern MicroGraphics (NMT Corporation), located in La Crosse, Wisconsin, to scan its published and either out-of-print titles or titles whose electronic files are too old and to convert them to PDF files. The Publications Office oversaw the scanning of the following forty-six titles of the latter type, archiving high resolution TIFF and PDF files and posting them on the Web in reduced file size, searchable, and secure PDF files: Assyriological Studies (AS) 5, 17, and 22; Chicago Assyrian Dictionary (CAD) L; Materials for the Assyrian Dictionary (MAD) 1, 4, and 5; Oriental Institute Communications (OIC) 13, 14, 16, 17, 19, 20, 22, and 23; Oriental Institute Publications (OIP) 11, 15, 16, 21, 42, 43, 44, 53, 58, 60, 63, 72, 78, 79, 88, 92, 97, 98, 99, 102, 104, 111, 114, and 115; Studies in Ancient Oriental Civilization (SAOC) 20, 31, 44, and 51; Uch Tepe 1 and 2; and R. McC. Adams' *The Uruk Countryside*. In next year's *Annual Report* the office hopes to announce that more than 100 titles are available as downloadable PDF files and that all 300+ titles published by the Oriental Institute since its founding are listed online. The office is still trying to work out how best to make the out-of-print titles available as books-on-demand.

Volumes Published

1. *The Assyrian Dictionary of the Oriental Institute of the University of Chicago*, Volume 18 (T). Martha T. Roth, editor-in-charge. 2006.

2. *The Assyrian Dictionary of the Oriental Institute of the University of Chicago*, Volume 19 (Ṭ). Martha T. Roth, editor-in-charge. 2006.

3. *Daily Life Ornamented: The Medieval Persian City of Rayy*. Tanya Treptow, with Donald Whitcomb. OIMP 26. 2007.

4. *Embroidering Identities: A Century of Palestinian Clothing*. Iman Saca. OIMP 25. 2006.

5. *Excavations at Tell es-Sweyhat, Syria*, Volume 2. *Archaeology of the Bronze Age, Hellenistic, and Roman Remains from an Ancient Town on the Euphrates River*. (2 vols.). Thomas A. Holland. OIP 125. 2006.

6. *Nippur* V. *The Early Dynastic to Akkadian Transition: The Area WF Sounding*. Augusta McMahon. OIP 129. 2006.

7. *The Origins of State Organizations in Prehistoric Fars, Southern Iran: Excavations at Tall-e Bakun*. Abbas Alizadeh. OIP 128. 2006.

8. *Performing Death: Social Analyses of Funerary Traditions in the Ancient Near East and Mediterranean*. Nicola Laneri, editor. OIS 3. 2007.

9. *Sacred Space and Sacred Function in Ancient Thebes*. Peter F. Dorman and Betsy M. Bryan, editors. SAOC 61. 2007.

10. *Settlement and Society: Essays Dedicated to Robert McCormick Adams*. Elizabeth C. Stone, editor. Joint Publication with the Cotsen Institute of Archaeology, University of California, Los Angeles. 2007.

Volumes in Preparation

1. *Chogha Mish*, Volume 2. *Final Report on the Last Six Seasons of Excavations, 1972–1978: A Prehistoric Regional Center in Lowland Susiana, Southwestern Iran*. Abbas Alizadeh. OIP 130.

2. *European Cartographers and the Ottoman World, 1500–1750: Maps from the Collection of O. J. Sopranos*. Ian Manners and M. Pınar Emiralioğlu. OIMP 27.

3. *The Monumental Complex of King Ahmose at Abydos*, Volume 1. *The Pyramid Temple of Ahmose and Its Environs: Architecture and Decoration*. Stephen P. Harvey.

4. *Studies in Semitic and Afroasiatic Linguistics in Honor of Gene B. Gragg*. Cynthia L. Miller, editor. SAOC 60.

5. *Proceedings of the Fifty-first Rencontre Assyriologique Internationale Held at the Oriental Institute of the University of Chicago, July 18–22, 2005*. Robert D. Biggs, Jennie Myers, and Martha T. Roth, editors. AS 28.

6. *Studies Presented to Robert D. Biggs, June 4, 2004*. From the Workshop of the Chicago Assyrian Dictionary, Volume 2. Walter Farber, Martha T. Roth, and Matthew W. Stolper, editors. AS 27.

RESEARCH ARCHIVES
Magnus Widell

Introduction

Over the last two years, the Research Archives have undergone some very significant changes and updates. I have truly enjoyed being a part of these exciting developments, but I have recently decided to undertake new opportunities as a new faculty member at the School of Archaeology, Classics and Egyptology at the University of Liverpool. The decision to move to England was a difficult one. It has been a truly wonderful experience to be part of a vibrant institution such as the Oriental Institute of the University of Chicago. I am positive that my successor as the Head of the Research Archives will continue to develop and improve this valuable resource in the fields of ancient Near Eastern studies.

Acquisitions and Online Catalog

The library's holdings have increased significantly in 2006/2007. In addition to the continued effort to acquire important older publications that are missing in our holdings, we have received several thousand volumes, primarily from the generous donations of Erika Reiner and Gregory Areshian. Despite the extra work on these collections, we have continued to develop the electronic catalog of the Research Archives into a powerful, comprehensive, and modern research tool. The ultimate goal is to make this catalog an indispensable research tool for all scholars of the ancient Near East. The electronic catalog, which is available online at http://oilib.uchicago.edu/, includes all books and articles/reviews in journals acquired since 1990. We have continued last year's intensive effort to finish the retrospective cataloging of pre-1990 monographs and journals. At the time of writing (August 29, 2007), the catalog contains over 245,000 records. More than 41,000 entries (primarily journal articles) are linked directly to PDFs available online through JSTOR, EBSCO, ETANA, BRILL, PEETERS, etc. In the coming year, we will add another 30,000 links to online PDFs. We are very close to our goal of creating an online database of the holdings of our library that is completely integrated with both the free and the subscription-based Internet resources in our fields of study.

We have completely cataloged all SERIES and all FOLIOS in the Elizabeth Morse Genius Reading Room. There is nothing more to catalog in this room. There is still work to be done in the New Stacks. This room has a total of eighty-eight bookcases. As of today, we have finished fifty-six of these bookcases. This means that we have done roughly 64% of the monographs in the library, slightly more than estimated in last year's report. The progress with journal articles has been modest in 2006/2007. While all major journals have been covered, there are still many articles and reviews in peripheral journals that need to be cataloged in the coming year.

We expect to be completely done with all journal articles/reviews and have all the monographs done by the end of next year. The catalog will finally (after twenty-one years!) be complete and include all the holdings of the library.

Staff and Acknowledgments

Our team this past year included Foy Scalf, Annie Caruso, Kamran Cross, and Seunghee Yie. The large number of primarily Armenian and Russian publications in the donated books by Gregory Areshian were processed by Armine Harutyunyan. I am most grateful to my assistants for all their help in the past year, and for their hard work cataloging new acquisitions as well as retrospective cataloging of monographs, series, and journal articles.

THE TABLET COLLECTION

Walter Farber

During the past year, the Tablet Room, under the daily care of Jonathan Tenney, continued to accommodate visitors for short, or sometimes extended, visits to work on cuneiform texts in our collection, as well as on materials from the Persepolis archives housed in the Oriental Institute. As in the past, the Tablet Room also opened its space to several of our own graduate students who, for their dissertations or for other projects, have used original texts from our collection. We are glad to be able to offer this convenient and, according to most users, very adequate facility to all colleagues wishing to do research on our tablets, sealings, and other small objects from our collections.

Overleaf. Head of a Nubian. Sandstone, pigment. Luxor, Egypt. Mortuary Temple of Ramesses III. Reign of Ramesses III (ca. 1184–1153 B.C.). OIM 14648. The Egyptians portrayed foreigners in stereotyped and often unflattering ways. This head of a Nubian emphasizes elements that would be perceived as distinctly un-Egyptian: tightly curled hair, a large earring, and scars across the brow that identified the individual's tribe or village.

MUSEUM

Geoff Emberling

The museum was an extremely lively place in 2006/2007, the first full year since our permanent galleries have been open. Our special exhibit program presented no less than four different exhibits. The Education Department developed outstanding activities and programs for many different audiences. We have never been so busy assisting research projects, cataloging and digitizing the collection, and improving storage conditions. And the museum galleries have hosted a wide variety of dinners and events. The vitality of the museum is not simply the result of having beautiful gallery spaces or a magnificent collection, however — it is due to the remarkable dedication and knowledge of the museum staff.

The Marshall and Doris Holleb Family Special Exhibits Gallery hosted a wide range of exhibits that illustrate some of the potential of our special exhibit program to broaden the appeal of the museum. We displayed beautiful photographs documenting the discovery of Tutankhamun's tomb; early twentieth century hand-embroidered dresses from Palestine; Middle School students' art and writing inspired by ancient Nubia; and ceramics from medieval Persia that are some of our most beautiful sherds. We are developing a very high standard for excellence in display due to the outstanding eye and skillful hands of Erik Lindahl and his Prep Shop staff and our graphic designer, Dianne Hanau-Strain of Hanau-Strain Associates.

Dress from Bir Sabe (Beersheva) in the exhibit Embroidering Identities: A Century of Palestinian Clothing

These exhibits provided opportunities for Oriental Institute faculty, research associates, and staff to present their work, both in the exhibits themselves and in the catalogs we have produced for the exhibits, and we hope to continue these collaborations in the future. The exhibits have presented opportunities for a wide range of education programs and activities, which have enriched the exhibits beyond the displays themselves. And it must be said that these exhibits kept the museum staff extremely busy.

Registration and Archives have been extremely busy this year, particularly with three active projects to publish Amuq sites excavated in the 1930s, but also with a wide range of other important research noted below. Between our special exhibits program and our international reputation, we have also had a high volume of incoming and outgoing loans that have taken a remarkable amount of time. It is a credit to the importance of these positions for the research role of the museum that Oriental Institute Director Gil Stein approved two new positions in these areas this year: an Archives Assistant, Margaret Schröeder, and an Assistant Registrar, a position we hope to fill in the coming year.

It is difficult to summarize the contributions of the Education Department and Volunteer Program in just a few lines because they are both so active, and highlighting one program or another would simply leave others out. I can only recommend their descriptions below.

One exciting collaboration across the museum that began last year was with the MAPSS program at the University. This is a one-year MA program in which Ray Fogelson and Morris Fred offer a two-quarter course on the Anthropology of Museums. The Oriental Institute has been the subject of their ethnographic project as well as a final exam paper, and we have been fortunate this past year to have the help of no less than seven students from this program as interns and work-study students in Special Exhibits, Publicity (and Membership), Education, and Archives. These students contributed greatly to many aspects of work in the museum over the past year, and we are hopeful that this collaboration with the MAPSS program will continue in years to come.

The attendance numbers were not as good as they have been in previous years. Attendance was down slightly — the increased attendance from the presence of the Tut exhibit at The Field Museum did not last much beyond its opening months in May and June. Contributions in our "cash box" in the lobby were down 6%.

On the positive side, activities of the museum were supported by a wide range of grants in this past year. Education projects were funded by the Polk Bros. Foundation, Fry Foundation, Joyce Foundation, and by a major two-year grant from the National Endowment for the Humanities that we received due to the vision and grant-writing skills of Wendy Ennes. Conservation had a record-breaking year, receiving grants from the Institute for Museum and Library Services, the National Endowment of the Humanities, and the University of Chicago Women's Board. Details of these grant-funded projects can be found below.

We have had quite a few changes in staff over the past year.

Ray Tindel retired as Registrar after twenty-one years, having left Registration in excellent shape to continue cataloging the collection in the database he had set up. Ray's contributions to the museum have been so important and so wide-ranging that it is no exaggeration to say, as Ray did at the retirement symposium organized by Gil Stein, that it had become "his" museum. We will all miss Ray's daily presence as a colleague and friend and are glad that he is able to continue volunteering for the next year or two.

Ray Tindel speaking at his retirement symposium

Helen McDonald has eased some of our concerns over Ray's departure as she has mastered the work of Registration since her arrival two years ago. She moved into Ray's position as Registrar on July 1.

The position of Reinstallation Coordinator for the permanent galleries ended with the opening of the Nubia Gallery in February 2005, and although we were able to find funds to keep Markus Dohner for months after that, this was not a permanent position. I am happy to report that Markus is now working at the Art Institute.

Erik Lindahl has now moved into the senior position in the Prep Shop and Design. We are fortunate to have his many contributions to exhibits and to the museum and the Oriental Institute more broadly.

Margaret Schröeder has moved from her position at the lobby desk to Archives Assistant, where she is thriving.

And we are pleased to welcome Adam Lubin as the Head of Security and Visitor Services.

It is a pleasure to thank, first of all, everyone on the museum staff for our successes this past year. Gil Stein has been consistently energetic, helpful, and supportive of museum programs. Tom Urban and Leslie Schramer in Publications have been nothing short of remarkable in their ability to produce well-designed and carefully edited catalogs for special exhibits on tight deadlines. Bill Harms in the University News Office has helped greatly with publicity for a wide range of museum (and Institute) activities. Candace Walters in the University Office of Risk Management has been extremely helpful with all our loans, some of which have been complicated indeed. Morrie Fred, Lecturer on museum studies in the MAPSS program and former Director of the Spertus Museum, has been actively interested in our museum at many levels and has been a source of advice and inspiration. And last, but not least, I would like to thank Dianne Hanau-Strain for her continuing work as exhibit designer and graphic designer for the museum.

The Year to Come

We are looking forward to next year in the museum. We plan to have two exciting special exhibits. The first, opening in November, will display European maps of the Ottoman world; the second, opening in April, will present the ongoing looting of archaeological sites in Iraq. We are working on a single-volume guide to the galleries as well as six volumes that will present highlights of the museum collection — at present we have manuscripts for Mesopotamia and Megiddo, with active work on Nubia and Persia. We are hoping to inaugurate audioguide tours. We are working to put our galleries online so that the objects and information in them is widely available. We are developing a rotating set of posters for the "Star Chamber" — the small hallway between Egypt, Persia, and Nubia — that will present current Oriental Institute research. We are also developing a simulated dig based on the model of the Spertus Museum's Artifact Center (which itself was designed in consultation with Oriental Institute archaeologist Doug Esse). These projects all serve to present the collection and research of the Oriental Institute to the public to encourage ongoing interest and support for our work.

It will also be a busy year behind the scenes, with active work cataloging and digitizing the collections, installing new state-of-the-art storage cabinets and rehousing objects, and facilitating a wide range of research projects. Particularly exciting will be the intensive conservation training programs of conservators from the Middle East.

SPECIAL EXHIBITS

Emily Teeter

The first show of the period covered by this report was Wonderful Things: The Discovery of the Tomb of Tutankhamun: The Harry Burton Photographs (see further details in the *2005–2006 Annual Report*, p. 132). This exhibit, which was warmly received, closed October 9.

Our next exhibit, Embroidering Identities: A Century of Palestinian Clothing ran from November 11, 2006, to March 25, 2007, and was curated by Dr. Iman Saca, Research Associate of the Oriental Institute and Assistant Professor of Anthropology at St. Xavier University.

SPECIAL EXHIBITS

This exhibit illustrated some of the challenges that special exhibits pose to museum staff. A fundamental part of the look of the show was how the garments were to be exhibited. We toyed with all sorts of possibilities, from department store mannequins to simple rods. Finally Museum Preparator Erik Lindahl, working with the Conservation Department, devised an ingenious and flexible series of armatures that Laura and her staff padded and dressed. This was also our first foray into international loans. It was a true trial by fire that, in the end, was successful. As originally conceived, the exhibit was to be made up of garments from our collection augmented by a significant number of others from the Palestine Heritage Center in Bethlehem. As the political situation in the West Bank deteriorated, we found ourselves in a maze of complications, particularly moving and insuring the loan materials from Bethlehem to Jerusalem and then to Chicago, fearing that it might get stuck in customs leaving the West Bank. Registrar Helen McDonald was on a very sharp learning curve investigating insurance and shipping, aided by the ever-helpful Candace Walters in the University's Office of Risk Management. At the darkest, it looked as if we would receive no additional materials, but through team effort and coordination, shortly before the opening, a shipment of key garments arrived.

The exhibit had a very different look for us. Not only were we showing garments that were only a century old, but the delicacy of the fabrics necessitated low light levels. Erik Lindahl achieved a safe level of attractive lighting after experimenting with various types of bulbs and shielding. The exhibit also necessitated additional security because the garments were on pedestals with no solid barriers to protect them from curious visitors.

The visitor comment book recorded a wide variety of reactions, ranging from the prosaic: "Beauty for my eyes; cultural information for my mind; appreciation for my heart"; to comments from those with a special interest: "As a Palestinian-American 1st generation, it's strengthening to see and learn about the various regional differences in clothing"; and "As a Palestinian, I was exposed to different aspects of my culture unknown to me. Thank you for your exhibit." Other comments made us very proud: "Excellent exhibit! The explanations were concise and informative. Very interesting to see the parts of other cultures (like coins from Russia and France) which were part of clothing," while a few contained complaints that the exhibit had a political or cultural agenda (which we assiduously tried to avoid). Other comments had us scratching our heads ("reminds me of people in my neighborhood (63rd and Kedzie)") or shaking our heads ("boring!"). We are grateful (and sometimes amused) by the comments, and we are eager to receive positive, as well as critical, feedback from our visitors.

It was very touching to meet the sons of the late Mrs. Clara Klingeman who donated most of the garments to the Oriental Institute (see *News & Notes,* no. 191, pp. 6–7). They visited several times and related amusing anecdotes about their childhood memories of the clothing.

After Embroidering Identities closed, the gallery was prepared for an Education Department exhibit entitled Through Young Eyes: Nubian Art Recreated that ran from April 11 to May 6, 2007. Information about that exhibit can be found in the report of the Education Department.

On May 15, our next exhibit Daily Life Ornamented: The Medieval Persian City of Rayy opened in conjunction with a reception for the annual meeting of the American Association of Museums. It continues to October 14, 2007. This show is a good illustration of collaboration between the museum, faculty and graduate students. Don Whitcomb, Research Associate (Associate Professor) of Islamic Archaeology, mentioned to Geoff that one of his graduate students, Tanya Treptow, had done a thoughtful paper on how Islamic art is represented in museum galleries. From that paper came the idea for an exhibit that examines how archaeologists deal with fragments of a culture (in this case, beautifully decorated sherds), and how they can use those shattered records to reconstruct a culture. Objects in the exhibit are from the collection

SPECIAL EXHIBITS

View of the Special Exhibit Daily Life Ornamented: The Medieval Persian City of Rayy

of the Oriental Institute. The beautiful exhibit had a number of good outcomes; it provided a graduate student with valuable curatorial experience and an important and attractive publication, and a great number of previously unaccessioned and unpublished sherds were registered and photographed in preparation for the exhibit.

As the temporary exhibits evolve, the catalog component has become an essential part of each show. Iman Saca, in collaboration with Maha Saca, authored the Embroidering Identities volume, and Tanya Treptow, with contributions by Don Whitcomb, Oliver Watson, and John Larson, was responsible for the Rayy catalog. There is no possibility that the museum could produce these catalogs without the skill, good humor, and patience of Tom Urban and Leslie Schramer in our Publications Office. They have thrown themselves into the challenge of producing publications with a completely different look, feel, and market than the highly academic books that they usually produce, and they have made a seamless transition. Each catalog is more handsome than the last. Dianne Hanau-Strain designed the elegant covers of the last two catalogs. The volumes have experienced strong sales. Denise Browning of the Suq has promoted them by featuring each on the back page of *News & Notes* and through prominent placement in the shop. News releases about the exhibits mention the availability of the catalog. Our international book distributor, David Brown Book Co., has likewise promoted them. We are still feeling our way through the complexities of price points and print runs, but we are gratified to know that the catalogs have a market.

Upcoming Exhibits

- European Cartographers and the Ottoman World, 1500–1750: Maps from the Collection of O. J. Sopranos. November 2, 2007–March 2, 2008 (members' opening, Tuesday, October 30). This exhibit of maps, sea charts, and atlases explores how the intellectual and geographical discoveries of the fifteenth century modified the medieval view of the cosmos, and how cartographers sought to produce world maps that reconciled classical ideas

SPECIAL EXHIBITS

and theories with the information collected and brought back by travelers and voyagers. Presented in conjunction with the citywide Festival of Maps.

- Catastrophe! The Looting of Iraq's Past. April 10–December 31, 2008. This exhibit reviews the appalling damage to archaeological sites and the cultural heritage of Iraq by illicit digging that still continues five years after the looting of the Iraq Museum in Baghdad.

We are working with faculty, staff and graduate students as well as with our colleagues in other institutions to develop exhibits and to find funding sources for them. A priority in our planning is to offer a variety of themes that represent various geographic areas. A special exhibits committee has been formed to evaluate exhibits proposals. The reality of the time and budget required to produce two special exhibits with catalogs has sunk in, especially as we work on multiple exhibits simultaneously.

PUBLICITY

Emily Teeter

This year posed particular challenges for publicity because of the near absence of a budget for paid promotion. In previous years, we had some funds associated with the corporate sponsorship of permanent galleries. Despite that shortfall, we received considerable press coverage in the form of feature stories on the work of faculty and staff and special exhibits. As always, our efforts have been supported and our successes ensured by the continuing assistance of William Harms of the News Office.

We continue to work closely with city cultural organizations developing programming which ensures that we are listed in their publications. As in the past, much of that success is due to the ingenuity of the Education Department and Carole Krucoff, who are able to devise programs that seem to fit any theme. For example, we had a listing in the city's "Winter Delights" promotion (a brochure with a print run of 400,000 copies that was included as a supplement to *Chicago Magazine*), and we offered "Games Pharaoh Played" for the "Art of Play" promotion (200,000 copies). Our program was so appealing that it was given a full page in the program. Likewise, we were featured in the Department of Cultural Affairs "Chicago Immersion Weekends" program under "Intimate Look at Chicago's Museums." We continue to be included in the Chicago Neighborhood Tours whose brochure has a print run of 55,000. Not only does the city produce enormous numbers of their promotional pieces, but the brochures are very widely distributed, giving us far broader reach than we could ever achieve on our own.

We received good coverage in major media. The *New York Times* reported on Professor Norman Golb and his research on the Dead Sea Scrolls, and there were major stories on the excavations of Clemens Reichel at Hamoukar and Geoff Emberling and Bruce Williams in Sudan. These stories were picked up by the wire services and widely reprinted (as far away as Kazakstan!). A *New York Times* article on "Must See Neighborhoods" specifically suggested a visit to the Oriental Institute. Local press was also attentive. The *Chicago Sun-Times* ran an article on Scott Branting and the CAMEL Lab in their "E-Biz" column. The *University of*

PUBLICITY

Chicago Magazine had a very amusing feature on an origami lamassu by noted artist Robert Lang. The piece was photographed in front of its much larger prototype, and the resulting image later turned up on the magazine's fund raising letter, giving us additional exposure. The story of the Persepolis tablets (see *News & Notes,* no. 192, pp. 3–9) was covered by media from *Archaeology* to the *New York Times.*

In the effort to learn more about how the Oriental Institute and its museum can be promoted, we served as subjects for a marketing class at Roosevelt University, a collaboration proposed by Gil Stein. Two student teams presented detailed reports on how to increase our visibility on a limited budget. Some ideas were very good and worthy of implementation. I also met with a class on social entrepreneurs from Manchester College that was studying the Institute and its publicity efforts.

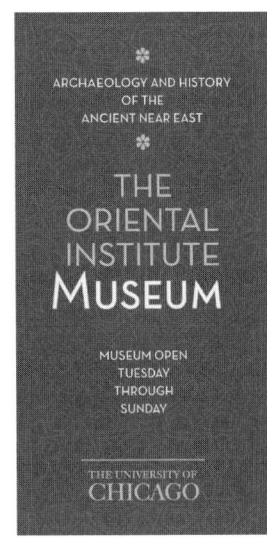

Eye-catching banner promoting the exhibit Daily Life Ornamented: The Medieval Persian City of Rayy at the 58th Street entrance. Design by Hanau-Strain Associates, Inc.

As we hoped, the special exhibits have generated publicity. *Saudi Aramco World* ran a very impressive feature on the forthcoming map exhibit. *Time Out Chicago* has been very supportive, running features on the Palestine show and the Rayy exhibit. In the effort to reach new audiences, we did a direct mail campaign to Muslim groups (mosques, community centers) to make them aware of the Embroidering Identities exhibit.

I was thankful for the help of intern Eric Rogers who spent fall and part of winter quarter helping me and others at the Institute. He was able to use his impressive technology skills to design a new image-imbedded e-mail notification system for lectures and events. Another of his lasting contributions was unsnarling and streamlining the various media mailing lists, making it easier and more effective to communicate with the press via e-mail. He also developed and administered a survey of museum visitors to try to establish, in the absence of paid promotion, how people know about us, and what they know. One of the surprises was that a full 28% of the visitors learned of us "through word of mouth," and another 22% from teachers.

In the past, we have communicated the opening of temporary exhibits to the media at a press preview. We dispensed with this for the Palestine and Rayy exhibits, substituting more targeted contact with specific press. Indeed, at least for these two exhibits, the revised strategy seems to have been effective, for we managed to receive a number of feature stories. Although our budget has not allowed us to produce another round of street pole banners, each temporary exhibit is prominently advertised by banners at the 58th Street entrance.

We are experimenting with new technology for publicity. Working with William Harms and Tim Gutowski in the University of Chicago News and Information Office, we produced a "vodcast" (brief digital video) featuring Geoff Emberling and Rayy exhibit curators Tanya Treptow and Don Whitcomb. It was mounted on the news office's Web site. We all learned a lot through this experience, and with Bill and Tim's help, we hope to produce another for the upcoming map exhibit.

REGISTRATION

Helen McDonald

The most significant event of the year for Registration was the retirement of Ray Tindel after twenty-one years as Museum Registrar (and prior to that Museum Preparator). A conference organized by the Oriental Institute to mark Ray's years of service included papers by several researchers who had used the Institute's museum collections extensively in their research on old excavations. These included Mark Garrison (Persepolis seal designs), Clemens Reichel (Diyala), Bruce Williams (Nubian Salvage excavations), and Karen Wilson (Bismaya). The lectures were followed by a reception in the Persian Gallery, and many of the museum's volunteers past and present were able to be there.

The registration department has moved over 52,000 objects this year (an increase of around 40% on the previous year). Just over 600 of these objects were used in teaching and over 5,500 were the subject of research of all kinds. Over 27,000 were newly registered objects (a 33% increase on the previous year) and over 300 related to the special exhibits. The museum database now has over 188,000 object numbers.

We received the final batch of storage cabinets from our last IMLS grant at the end of February and these were used to re-house Nubian pottery from Adindan and Ballana (850 items). We also took delivery of two textile cabinets, into which the conservators are presently re-housing a large portion of our Nubian textiles. Two banks of new Delta shelving have now been filled with heavy objects. In May of this year, we heard that Laura D'Alessandro's latest application to the IMLS has also been successful and so during the next two years we will be receiving a further forty-three storage cabinets, a run of pallet racks for more of our heavy objects, and a final textile cabinet. The first delivery will take place at the end of the summer.

One of Registration's main foci of activity this year has been hosting and assisting three outside researchers who are working on final publications of the later levels at three of the Amuq sites. Lynn Swartz Dodd (Tell Judaidah), Marina Pucci (Chatal Höyük), and Heather Snow (Tayinat) have all been working on both archival records, pottery, and objects from their various sites. The material of the fourth and third millennia from these and other Amuq sites has already been published in *Excavations in the Plain of Antioch* by Robert and Linda Braidwood (OIP 61), but much remains to be done with the Middle and Late Bronze age, the Iron Age, and later material. The Amuq researchers have studied over 2,600 objects this year and are still hard at work on both our collections and Amuq material held in the Antakya Museum. All three of our Amuq researchers are compiling computer databases of their material, so it was decided to register all of the sherds now in order that the OIM registration number could be used as the unique identifier in the databases. This registration of all the Amuq sherds has occupied both of our museum assistants and almost all our hard-working volunteers this year and accounts for the majority of new registrations.

The collections continue to be used for teaching and research. Users include the following:

Donald Whitcomb used Islamic sherds from the Amuq for a class held in the spring quarter.

Robert Ritner used parts of one of the copies of the Book of the Dead (the Hynes papyrus) for a class in the autumn, and several inscribed scarabs for another class in the spring quarter.

Persis Berlekamp taught a class on the Islamic art of the book in the spring quarter for which she used some of our Arabic and Persian manuscripts.

Janet Johnson used some of the large Demotic marriage contracts for a class in the spring quarter.

Hratch Papazian used two hieratic ostraca for a class in the autumn quarter.

Students taking part in Aslıhan Yener's museum installation course in the autumn quarter used a selection of Amuq objects to research and plan a small exhibit.

Foy Scalf and Jackie Jay continued to read Demotic ostraca.

François Gaudard has also been reading Demotic ostraca.

Dominique Bonatz (who has recently begun to excavate at Tell Fakhariyah, Syria) visited to examine both objects and archival records from the Oriental Institute's excavations at that site.

Rebecca Ward visited to examine both objects and excavation records from temple 2048 at Megiddo (strata 8 and 7).

Hanan Charaf Mullins visited to record the bichrome pottery from Megiddo for a project re-examining all the bichrome pottery from the eastern Mediterranean.

Alex Nagel came to work on Persepolis excavation records and objects, with particular reference to the use of color on the reliefs.

Hamid Reza Valipour visited to study and photograph the collection of newly registered Chalcolithic sherds from Cheshmeh Ali (Iran). This is for a computer database that will be used to publish the Cheshmeh Ali ceramics including not only those in the Oriental Institute Museum, but also those in Tehran and the University Museum in Philadelphia.

Karen Wilson continues to work on material from Bismaya and the preparation of a guide to the Edgar and Deborah Jannotta Mesopotamia Gallery. She has also used Nippur pottery for a class in a course on Nippur by McGuire Gibson.

With the success of his recent National Endowment for the Humanities grant application, Clemens Reichel has continued to work on Diyala material. At the time of writing, Angela Altenhofen is drawing seal impressions for this project.

We have been involved in making preparations for incoming loans for our next special exhibit, entitled European Cartographers and the Ottoman World, 1500–1750: Maps from the Collection of O. J. Sopranos, as well as work on outgoing loans that will take place in the next twelve months. We have had requests to borrow objects from the Louvre (Paris), the Staatliche Museen zu Berlin, the Metropolitan Museum of Art (New York), and the Institute of Humanities of the University of Michigan. We may also be lending objects to the Smart Museum on campus.

We have answered queries on subjects as diverse as the molded figurines from Medinet Habu, Hellenistic coinage, oil lamps, Meroitic pottery, and whether our collection contains any baboon mummies (it does not).

These accomplishments have been made possible by the capable and efficient efforts of museum assistants Dennis Campbell and Courtney Jacobson, with the help of a wonderful group of volunteers, including Joan Barghusen, Gretel Braidwood, Elizabeth Davidson, Joe Diamond, Janet Helman, Barbara Levin, Daila Shefner, Toni Smith, and Jim Sopranos. The volunteers have altogether contributed well over a thousand hours of their time to Museum Registration. Following his retirement, Ray Tindel joined our group of volunteers. At the time of writing, Dennis Campbell had just heard that he has a post-graduate position working with the Persepolis tablets project (in addition to his work on the Hittite Dictionary). While this is great news for him, we will miss him greatly down here in Registration. Dennis has been museum assistant since 2002 and has helped during the recent gallery re-installations and with the unpacking of the collection as we have acquired new cabinets. Both Ray Tindel and Helen McDonald have valued his care with object handling, attention to detail, and his cheerful demeanor. We wish him all the best.

————————

ARCHIVES

John A. Larson

In early December 2006, John Larson passed his twenty-sixth anniversary as Museum Archivist.

Photographic Services

Until December 2006, John Larson was assisted by graduate-student assistant Tobin Hartnell. Among many other projects, Toby scanned the field negatives of the Aerial Survey of Iran and a selection of images for the Rayy exhibit. On October 1, 2006, Margaret Schröeder was appointed Assistant Archivist, with the responsibility for preparing the necessary paperwork and handling all the other details that are involved in processing the requests that we receive for photographic image materials and reproduction permissions. Margaret has also scanned several large record groups of black-and-white negatives in the Archives and entered the metadata for the images into our photo image database. Between July 1, 2006, and June 30, 2007, we processed 234 requests for photographic images, reproduction permission, and information. Income from sales of Oriental Institute photographic images and permission fees for the fiscal year 2006/2007 totaled $13,513. The income from photo sales and reproduction fees enables us to purchase archival supplies and equipment for the Archives and for Photography.

Archives

Visiting scholars during fiscal year 2006/2007 included Jeffrey Abt, Dominik Bonatz, Eric Cline, Lynn Schwarz Dodd, Michael Jones, Suzanne Loibl, Timothy Matney, Alexander Nagel, Wayne Pitard, Marina Pucci, Heather Snow, Hamid Reza Valipour, Rasool Vatandoust, and Ruth Ward. From within our own Oriental Institute community, Vanessa Davies, Peter Dorman, Robert Ritner, Emily Teeter, Tanya Treptow, Theo van den Hout, Donald Whitcomb, and Karen L. Wilson have conducted research using Archives materials. We would also like to thank Thomas James for his many contributions to the operation of the Archives.

Donald Nash, artist of the Sakkarah Expedition, in the courtyard of Memphis House, season of 1932/1933. Photograph by Leslie F. Thompson

Recent Acquisitions

In September 2006, Mr. Peter Sharp contacted the Oriental Institute with the offer of a collection of photographic materials and other records of Leslie Frederick Thompson, who had served as the only official photographer of the Oriental Institute's Sakkarah Expedition from October 1, 1931, through June 30, 1936. Leslie ("Tom") Thompson had given his collection to Mr. Sharp's mother, who left the material to her son when she passed away. The Thompson Collection arrived in Chicago in October, and it gives us great pleasure to acknowledge here Mr.

Sharp's generous gift of photographic negatives, prints, motion picture film, and related materials of Leslie F. Thompson. This archive is a wonderful addition to our existing record of the work of the Sakkarah Expedition and its principal project, the two-volume publication of the Mastaba of Mereruka. Mr. Thompson was a meticulous record-keeper, and his negatives are numbered and identified. We have been adding names and dates to a number of previously unidentified or poorly identified pictures in our collection. It is particularly nice to have so many "new" candid photographs of personnel and their work (and play) activities in Egypt. We have had virtually no visual documentation of the Sakkarah House itself, and now, thanks to Mr. Sharp, we have a number of good photographs of interiors and exteriors of the expedition headquarters. There are also pictures taken on holiday, including some of Chicago House and the Epigraphic Survey Staff, the Cairo Zoo, and the old Shepheard's Hotel in Cairo. In November 2006 Mr. Sharp very kindly sent us an addition to the Thompson Collection, a note card containing photographs of Prentice Duell (Field Director of the Sakkarah Expedition), "Tom" Thompson and his wife Hilda, and Marina Kossoff, another member of the expedition.

The transition on the third floor of the Oriental Institute building, putting the Chicago Hittite Dictionary Project in the space that formerly housed the Chicago Assyrian Dictionary files, has resulted in the transfer of some additional papers of A. Leo Oppenheim and I. J. Gelb to the Archives. We would also like to thank Prof. Emer. Robert Biggs for a number of contributions of Oriental Institute-related ephemera to the Archives during the past year.

Volunteers and Student Assistants

The following people have contributed their time during fiscal year 2006/2007 and have made it possible for us to begin, continue, and complete a number of projects in the Oriental Institute Archives that would not have been possible without their generosity and dedication: Hazel Cramer, Peggy Grant, Patricia Hume, Sandra Jacobsohn, Roberta Kovitz, Bryan Moles, Lillian Schwartz, Robert Wagner, and Carole Yoshida. We are very grateful for the services of these volunteers, and it is a pleasure to acknowledge them here for their efforts on behalf of the Archives.

Throughout the summer of 2006, four student interns — Julia van den Hout, Jessica Henderson, Kaitlin Ford, and Rachel Kreiter — worked on new shelf lists for the Archives Storage Room and other tasks, under the supervision of John Larson. During the academic year, John was assisted by Bryan Moles and by two graduate students from the MAPSS program, Steve Catania and Sheena Finnigan.

CONSERVATION

Laura D'Alessandro

It is very true that life in the conservation laboratory is seldom boring. Conservation was faced with a variety of challenges this past year that kept the conservation staff on its toes. Each of the special exhibits that Conservation was involved in this year presented interesting challenges. Alison Whyte, the Assistant Conservator, spearheaded the conservation efforts of both the Embroidered Identities and Rayy exhibits. The Embroidered Identities special exhibit involved

CONSERVATION

the dressing of two-dimensional wooden armatures with clothing intended for three dimensional bodies. Alison and Monica Hudak, our Contract Conservator, performed miracles on the imaginative human-size stick figures produced by Erik Lindahl and Brian Zimerle. The Rayy exhibit provided its own challenges. In addition to carrying out cleaning and mending treatments on over sixty ceramics, objects conservators performed the very basic paper conservation technique of applying hinges of Japanese tissue to the wonderful Rayy watercolors.

Alison returned in late July from her work in Sardis, Turkey, conserving wall paintings from the ancient city of Sardis. She presented an illustrated lecture of her excavation experience to the museum staff upon her return. The following spring, Alison attended the annual meeting of the American Institute of Conservation in Richmond, Virginia. The focus of this year's meeting was fakes, forgeries, and fabrications in the art world.

In addition to working under Alison's supervision on the conservation needs of the special exhibits, Monica spent a portion of her time working on the Persepolis Fortification Tablet project. Monica's contribution is important to the overall success of the tablet imaging project and her work on the tablets is an ongoing concern. In further aid of the Persepolis tablet project, the Conservation Laboratory received a very generous grant from the Women's Board of the University of Chicago to purchase a Class IV laser cleaning device. The laser equipment will allow a high level of accuracy and control in cleaning the very fragile clay tablets. The laser equipment will have a life after the Persepolis tablet project is completed as it will serve as a specialized cleaning tool for the museum and research collections.

No sooner had the 2005 IMLS rehousing grant activities been completed than the Oriental Institute Museum received a 2007 Conservation Project Support grant from the Institute of Museum and Library Services (IMLS). This two-year grant will allow the museum staff to continue to rehouse portions of the collections that are still in cardboard boxes from the "great migration," more commonly known as the construction project. The collections that will be rehoused during this project include Nubian organic materials of leather, wood, and textile; ceramic vessels from Serra (Nubia); human remains from the sites of Megiddo, Alishar, and Nippur; and large stone sculptural fragments from Khorsabad. A total of forty-three new, museum-quality cabinets and industrial pallet racks will be purchased with these funds, including a customized textile cabinet for several of the oversized Nubian textiles.

Under the direction of Gil Stein, the Institute received another training grant from the National Endowment for the Humanities (NEH) for a second conservation training program for conservators from war-ravaged countries of the Middle East. The Institute conservators are busy preparing the laboratory and formulating the curriculum for this six-month course that will encompass both scientific theory and practical work. As part of the preparations for the arrival of the participants, Gil contacted Dr. Ra'id Abdullah in the Department of Pediatric Medicine at the University of Chicago. Dr. Abdullah had expressed interest in trying to help with the programs in some way, soon after the Institute received the first training grant. After meeting with Gil and Laura, Dr. Abdullah sent out an e-mail to the entire hospital asking for donations of binocular microscopes for the participants. The response has been overwhelming as doctors all over the hospital opened their hearts and their storage closets, looking for "retired" microscopes. We are very appreciative of Dr. Abdullah's assistance in reaching out to the medical community and to all of the doctors who contributed to the program. With the help of funding from an anonymous donor, we are currently in the process of outfitting several of the donated microscopes to adapt them to the particular needs of archaeological conservation. As the seemingly endless visa process proceeds, the entire Institute is looking forward to the arrival of the first participants.

PREP SHOP

Erik Lindahl

As I look around the prep shop I see the remnants of the year past. Taped to the wall above my desk are the Palestinian Heritage Foundation postcards that we used as reference when putting together the Embroidering Identities show; next to them is the invitation to Ray Tindel's Retirement conference. Under one of our worktables is the first model that Brian Zimerle and I made as part of a feasibility study on the possibility of moving the Spertus Institute's "Artifact Center" to the Oriental Institute. This year has been a busy one. The large permanent gallery reinstallation projects have been replaced with many less monumental and more diverse tasks. This new workload has caused us to have to solve more problems faster while collaborating with more people.

The Marshall and Doris Holleb Family Special Exhibits Gallery has been a busy place with materials coming and going from lands near and far. It was the home to photos of the opening of King Tut's tomb taken by Henry Burton and loaned to us by the Metropolitan Museum of Art, Palestinian traditional dress loaned to us by the Palestinian Heritage Foundation, art inspired by pieces in the Robert F. Picken Family Nubia Gallery created by students from Fiske Elementary at Little Black Pearl, and some of the remnants of the Persian city Rayy accompanied by two miniatures loaned to us from the Art Institute of Chicago. Pulling together these exhibits required quite a lot of cooperation and creativity.

Erik Lindahl and Brian Zimerle preparing for Embroidering Identities

The beauty of the photos in the Tut show made it very rewarding. This show is also noteworthy because of its use of modern technology. All that was exchanged between the Oriental Institute and the Metropolitan Museum of Art was a DVD containing high-resolution scans of Burton's original prints that were digitally printed, mounted, and framed. Embroidering Identities, an exhibit of fairly modern (for the Oriental Institute, at least) Palestinian dress, was new ground for the Oriental Institute. Brian Zimerle, Markus Dohner, the conservation lab, the curators Iman and Maha Saca, and I all collaborated in the many stages of the design and fabrication of the armatures used to display the dresses. This cooperation allowed us to devise a way to display the material as true to form as possible.

Through Young Eyes, sponsored by the Joyce Foundation, was a joint project of Fiske Elementary, the Oriental Institute Museum, and Little Black Pearl art studio. Students from Fiske produced work inspired by artifacts found in the Picken Family Nubia Gallery that was then displayed at both the Oriental Institute Museum and Little Black Pearl. The prep shop produced and installed the exhibits at both venues and it was a pleasure to work with the Little Black Pearl staff. The Rayy show was our biggest challenge of the year. Due to issues with loan material, the show went through a lot of changes. Tanya Treptow and Donald Whitcomb, working with Dianne Hanau-Strain, did a wonderful job with the design and curation of the exhibit. Andrew Furse,

PREP SHOP

Elizabeth Beggs, and I had an exciting time changing over from the Through Young Eyes exhibit to Rayy. We had a window that was much smaller than we would have liked to make the change. The absence of Geoff Emberling and Tom James due to the excavation in the Sudan also added to the excitement of install week.

The prep shop does not just build exhibits, it also assists with collections management, builds fixtures for the museum, and is the keeper of the keys to the Oriental Institute's off-site storage space. Furthermore, this year Andrew Furse and I tried our hands at animal rescue. Some of these non-exhibit accomplishments include assisting Helen McDonald with the rearrangement of heavy object storage to make way for a visiting scholar who will be studying our Assyrian relief fragments. The prep shop worked with Museum Education once again to build another computer kiosk, this time for the Picken Family Nubia Gallery. We also took advantage of assisting in the relocation of items for the Chicago Assyrian Dictionary to off-site storage to do a little organizing. With the assistance of Hogan Movers, off-site storage was totally reorganized. This has helped not only free up space in the basement, but has also made it easier to select and move cases in and out for temporary exhibits.

The rescue of a duck family was by far, however, our most memorable moment of the year. The night of the opening of the Rayy exhibit, Andrew Furse and I were enlisted to go to Botany Pond and rescue some ducklings that had been relocated there without the mother and found themselves in the territory of several other extremely aggressive duck families. Wielding a net, we rolled up our pant legs and waded in. Safe and sound, our ten ducklings, reunited with their mother, are now happily days away from flying.

SUQ

Denise Browning

This was another busy and exciting year for the Suq. We started the year off in October with the annual dinner. Kitty and Rita Picken came up with the wonderful idea of decorating the tables with Suq merchandise! So we ordered lots of new merchandise that complemented the dinner table decorations and promoted our sales as well.

The Tut exhibit at The Field Museum drew many new customers to the Suq so our Egyptian merchandise flew off the shelves. They all raved about our museum and the Suq, many wishing they had just come to the Oriental Institute instead.

We barely had time to catch our breath to prepare for the Embroidering Identities exhibit. We ordered lots of handmade Palestinian embroidery and jewelry from a woman's cooperative in Bethlehem. The colorful, mostly geometric embroideries have always been a favorite of mine. We complemented it with Dead Sea salts, olive soap, and the colorful ceramics of the region.

The Smart Museum invited us to help stock and redesign their shop for their Cosmophilia exhibit. It was an exciting experience, plus we also gained sales from the sale of our merchandise at the Smart.

In our normal tasks we updated the Web page and instituted an e-mail listhost mailing list through the university and also an e-mail sign up in the Suq, which gave us over 500 addresses.

We also photographed several objects for our online Web page, which John Sanders added to our Web site, further increasing our sales.

But unfortunately for us we also saw the retirement of one of our most loyal volunteers, Muriel Brauer. Muriel has been with the Suq for over thirty years! She was always so cheerful and courteous to our customers, as well as informative. According to Muriel, she was also one of our best shoppers! I'm glad to report she is still full of energy!

Special thanks to our other great volunteers, Peggy Grant, Marda Gross, and Norma van der Meulen! Norma continues as our much valued in-house jewelry designer. Florence Ovadia tirelessly brings order and design to the store every Monday after a week's worth of customer abuse.

Jennifer Westerfeld, Ph.D. candidate in Egyptology, was our book buyer, photographer, and mail order specialist. Also of great help were Amanda Finney, Nicole Lasky, Alycia Hesse, and Klara Scharnagl.

MUSEUM EDUCATION

Carole Krucoff

Collaboration was the watchword for Museum Education this past year. Partnership programs broadened our services and horizons as we joined with long-time associates and new friends to provide a wide variety of educational activities for adults, youth, and families. Special exhibits were the springboard for many of our collaborative events, including an array of programs with The Field Museum in conjunction with special exhibits on Tutankhamun at their museum and our own. We also reached out to the community to partner with a range of city-wide initiatives, including Silk Road Chicago, Arab Heritage Month, Winter Delights, and Mayor Daley's Kids and Kites. Other joint ventures ranged from media campaigns to a grant-funded exhibit of artwork by local youth.

Support from the Joyce Foundation, the Polk Bros. Foundation, and the Chicago Public Schools helped us provide in-depth museum learning experiences for children and their families. A grant from the Lloyd A. Fry Foundation helped us develop a unique teacher-training and school programming initiative on ancient Nubia. This report also describes how support from the Institute of Museum and Library Services, a federal agency, and a major new grant from the National Endowment for the Humanities, are enabling us to continue our ground-breaking work in online education, which will serve teachers and students from across the nation and around the world.

Special Exhibit Programming

Tutankhamun Collaborations

The special exhibit Wonderful Things: The Discovery of the Tomb of Tutankhamun: The Photos of Harry Burton, opened at the Oriental Institute in May, complementing Tutankhamun and the Golden Age of the Pharaohs, a major traveling exhibition that was on view at The Field Museum.

MUSEUM EDUCATION

Hosting these exhibitions gave the Oriental Institute and Field Museum the opportunity to jointly plan, present, and publicize a wide variety of programs.

- "Tut and His Treasures," an adult education course taught by Emily Teeter, met at the Oriental Institute to focus on the special nature of our photographic collection and Egyptian Gallery. It also met at The Field Museum to concentrate on the grandeur of the special Tutankhamun exhibition.

Fascinating examples of Egyptian-style decor inspired many photographs during the Egyptomania, Chicago Style bus tour this past summer. Photo by Carole Krucoff

- "Egyptian Exploration," a professional development seminar for teachers of grades K–12, met for sessions at The Field Museum, the Oriental Institute, and also at the Chicago Botanic Garden, where teachers discovered plants from the land of the pharaohs.

- "Egyptomania, Chicago-Style," a city-wide bus tour led by Egyptologist Michael Berger, visited the Oriental Institute as one of its sites and encouraged visits to The Field Museum.

- "Meet King Tut," a hands-on program for children and their families, began at The Field Museum and then traveled to the Oriental Institute, where youngsters and their parents created versions of King Tut's golden headdress.

- "The World in the Time of Tutankhamun," a week-long summer seminar, was the centerpiece of our Tutankhamun programming. Publicized widely for us by The Field Museum, this program was held in collaboration with the University of Chicago's Graham School of General Studies. Along with local participants, the seminar attracted registrants from states near and far as well as from Canada and Europe. The program featured lectures on the life and the times of Tutankhamun by Oriental Institute faculty including Peter Dorman, Associate Professor of Egyptology and Chairman of the Department of Near Eastern Languages and Civilizations; Janet H. Johnson, Morton D. Hull Distinguished Service Professor of Egyptology and Editor of the Chicago Demotic Dictionary Project; Seth Richardson, Assistant Professor of Ancient Near Eastern History; and Theo van den Hout, Professor of Hittite and Anatolian Languages and Executive Editor of the Chicago Hittite Dictionary Project. Museum and Institute staff presenters included: Geoff Emberling, Oriental Institute Museum Director; François Gaudard, Research Associate; John Larson, Museum Archivist; and Emily Teeter, Curator of the Egyptian and Special Exhibits Galleries. Advanced graduate student presenters included Dennis Campbell, Vanessa Davies, Debora Heard, and Eudora Struble. Participants also enjoyed a behind-the-scenes visit led by Curatorial Assistant Tom James, a Middle Eastern dinner at Maza Restaurant, a visit to the Tutankhamun and the Golden Age of the Pharaohs exhibition led by Oriental Institute Egyptologists, and a closing banquet at the University of Chicago's Quadrangle Club. Interns Katharyn

A beaming boy proudly displays the royal headdress he made during the "Meet King Tut" workshop co-sponsored by The Field Museum. Photo by Carole Krucoff

Hanson and Rozenn Bailleul-LeSeur made sure every aspect of this multi-faceted program ran smoothly.

Joint programming with the national Elderhostel organization was another major partnership featuring Tutankhamun as one of their "Day of Discovery" programs. These events encourage senior citizens to become acquainted with the cultural resources local universities provide for the public. We were delighted to be selected by Elderhostel for a joint program with them. Our event featured a slide lecture by Geoff Emberling on the ancient Near East during the reign of Tutankhamun, and a slide lecture by Emily Teeter on the spectacular photographs in the Wonderful Things exhibit. A docent-led tour of the museum's galleries was another program highlight. Luncheon at the Quadrangle Club was also included in this program that drew more than 100 participants from the entire metropolitan area, many of whom had never visited the Oriental Institute.

Egyptologist Emily Teeter, right, listens to a question inspired by her lecture during Tutankhamun: His Tomb and Treasures, a special museum event for Elderhostel members in the Chicago area. Photo by Carole Krucoff

Wonderful Things also inspired a collaboration with the City of Chicago. During the summer, city-wide publicity funded as part of the Silk Road Chicago initiative drew visitors from throughout the area for a gallery talk on the Burton photographs by Emily Teeter and a museum tour by Geoff Emberling featuring artifacts from the time of Tutankhamun.

Embroidering Identities and Daily Life Ornamented Programming

Collaborations inspired by the special exhibit Embroidering Identities: A Century of Palestinian Clothing included partnerships on campus and with the city of Chicago. In conjunction with Arab Heritage Month in November the University of Chicago's Middle East Music Ensemble came to the Oriental Institute to present a special concert of historic and contemporary Palestinian music. Visitors

Members of the Middle Eastern Music Ensemble get ready for the concert of Palestinian music held in Breasted Hall. Photo by Carole Krucoff

also enjoyed film screenings of "Palestinian National Costume," which featured nineteenth- and early twentieth-century garments, headdresses, and jewelry presented to the beat of Arabic music. Gallery talks by Iman Saca, exhibit curator and Assistant Professor of Anthropology at St. Xavier College, were special highlights. The exhibit also inspired Museum Education intern Jared Jeffers to create a self-guided treasure hunt that invited children and their families to seek out and discover meanings of the many symbols embroidered in the colorful garments. The hunt was so popular that copies disappeared almost as soon as they were stacked in the gallery.

The springtime opening of the special exhibit Daily Life Ornamented: The Medieval Persian City of Rayy led to collaborations with the Smart Museum, which was hosting an exhibit of

MUSEUM EDUCATION

Maha Saca, left, listens to a gallery talk presented by Guest Curator Iman Saca, her daughter. Mrs. Saca, Director of the Palestinian Heritage Center in Jerusalem, collaborated with her daughter on the development of the special exhibit Embroidering Identities: A Century of Palestinian Clothing. Photo by Carole Krucoff

Islamic art. A cross-campus tour of both exhibits focused on ways archaeology provides context for Islamic art as well as the enduring legacies of Islamic artistic traditions. Tanya Treptow, Daily Life Ornamented co-curator, led the Oriental Institute portion of this joint program that quickly filled to capacity. "Islamic Art and Archeology," an adult education course taught by A. Asa Eger was also sponsored by and featured study sessions at both museums.

Daily Life Ornamented was the springboard for a new Oriental Institute partnership with the Chicago Architecture Foundation (CAF). Frances Laidlaw, CAF Docent, worked with Donald Whitcomb, Associate Professor of Islamic and Medieval Archaeology; Tanya Treptow; and Carole Krucoff, Head of Public and Museum Education, to develop a bus tour highlighting Islamic-style architecture throughout the city. The tour, which also featured docent-led gallery talks in the Daily Life Ornamented exhibit, sold out during its first presentation in the spring. The second trip, held in summer, also filled to capacity.

Our Sunday film showings included special screenings for Daily Life Ornamented. Tanya Treptow introduced and led a discussion of "Persian Miniature: The Gardens of Paradise," a documentary film on medieval Persian art and culture. "Children of Heaven," an Iranian feature film nominated for an Academy Award as Best Foreign Language Film in 1998, was shown at the Oriental Institute courtesy of the University of Chicago's Film Center.

Adult Education

Along with programs related to special exhibits, we provided many other adult education opportunities this past year. These included multi-session courses on campus and at the Gleacher Center; correspondence courses for distance learning, single session adult education programs; and free drop-by events throughout the year.

Courses

Correspondence courses this past year included "Hieroglyphs by Mail" taught by Andrew Baumann and Jacqueline Jay, and "Intermediate Hieroglyphs" by Andrew Baumann. Both these courses now provide a special certificate of completion for all students who finish assigned class work. While all our courses are non-credit adult education opportunities, students have been requesting such certificates for many years and appreciate them as mementos of their learning experiences. Certificates were also provided for students who completed "Ancient Egyptian Architecture," an audio course developed by Emily Teeter. This course, which drew students from locales across the United States as well as Canada, South Africa, and even Egypt, included a Web component with slide presentations featuring full-color views of ancient sites, artifacts from the Oriental Institutes collections, and photographs from Teeter's own collection.

Nearly all our on-campus and Gleacher Center courses are presented in collaboration with the University of Chicago's Graham School of General Studies, which joins us on course development, advertising, and registration. The Graham School also works with the Illinois

State Board of Education to offer continuing education credits to all K–12 teachers who take our courses.

This year our joint Graham School courses included:

- "Merchants of the Desert: The Lost Kingdom of the Nabateans," taught by Joey Corbett
- "Khorsabad: Capital of the Assyrian Empire," taught by Geoff Emberling
- "Excavating Armageddon: The Ancient Israelite City of Megiddo," "Lo, the Vile Asiatic: Ancient Egypt's Love/Hate Relationship with Canaan and Ancient Israel," and "With Bible and Trowel: An Exploration of the Historicity of Ancient Israel," all taught by Gabrielle V. Novacek
- "The Dead Sea Scrolls: The Texts and Their Meaning," taught by Israel Sandman
- "Cultures of the Silk Road," taught by Ilya Yakubovich

Special Programs and Drop-by Events

In addition to formal courses, Museum Education provided a broad spectrum of special adult education programs and free events designed to explore themes related to ancient or contemporary Middle Eastern culture. Our series of Middle Eastern cuisine and cookery experiences continued this year with two new dining experiences. At "A Taste of Ethiopia," held at Ethiopian Diamond Restaurant, owner Almaz Yiguzaw invited everyone to savor the unique cuisine and dining experiences of her homeland. At "A Taste of the Levant," held at Maza Restaurant, owner and master chef Joseph Kuri highlighted the elegant cuisine of his Lebanese homeland and taught everyone the secrets of one of his favorite recipes. This series has become one of our most sought-after programs and has introduced many Chicagoans to the Oriental Institute.

"Ancient Arts/Contemporary Artists," held in March, was the start of new collaborative series with The Field Museum featuring the work of local artists inspired by the techniques and processes of ancient times. This first program, which focused on ancient writing processes and materials, began with a guided tour of the Oriental Institute's galleries led by docent Kathleen Mineck, a Ph.D. candidate in the department of Near Eastern Languages and Civilizations, who introduced the scripts, languages, and writing tools highlighted in our exhibits. During the program's second half, held at the Hyde Park Art Center, paper artist Mary Tepper demonstrated the making of papyrus and invited everyone to create their own ancient-style paper. The day ended with a wine-and-cheese reception where the whole group urged us to make this a permanent series.

Widespread media attention brought many new visitors to the Oriental Institute for three special lectures this year. These free lectures took advantage of seasonal celebrations and the publicity available to us through city-wide initiatives. Timed to coincide with Valentine's Day, February's highlight was "Love and Sex in Ancient Egypt." Presented by Emily Teeter, this lecture captured headlines in several city newspapers and — no surprise! — drew a large crowd. Jacqueline Jay also inscribed special

Pounding plant fibers to make papyrus was a special feature during Ancient Arts/Contemporary Artists, an event co-sponsored by The Field Museum and Hyde Park Art Center. Photo by Carole Krucoff

MUSEUM EDUCATION

Docent Mary Shea, right, introduces new University of Chicago students to the Oriental Institute during Orientation Week in September. Photo by Carole Krucoff

Valentine sentiments in ancient Egyptian hieroglyphs for visitors.

Two additional lectures were co-sponsored by Museum Education and the Oriental Institute Membership Office. In conjunction with Womens' History Month in March, Janet H. Johnson presented a new take on a famous queen with a lecture entitled "Cleopatra as CEO: Bureaucracy and Scandal in the Hostile Takeover of a First Millennium (B.C.) Multinational." In April, the city's Silk Road Chicago initiative featured guest lecturer Pavel Lurye, a Russian scholar associated with the Institut für Iranistik in Vienna, who presented "The Road Map of the Silk Road: How Did Caravans Reach China in the Early Middle Ages?"

Other free drop-by events focused on outreach to the University community. During Student Orientation Week in September we welcomed newcomers with docent-led gallery tours. Guided tours for the University's Humanities Day and Parents Weekend programs are a long-standing tradition. The University community, along with local residents and visitors from throughout the area, also continue to enjoy our free Sunday film showings, which feature documentary and feature films on the ancient and contemporary Middle East.

Youth and Family Services

Museum Education presented an array of long-time favorites as well as special new programs for children and families this past year. Three outreach programs used off-site formats to reach new audiences. In the fall we joined the 57th Street Children's Book Fair in celebrating their twentieth anniversary as well as the Oriental Institute's twenty years of participation. Special thanks to Nicole Brisch, Oriental Institute Post-Doctoral Fellow, for her help in showing children what it's like to "dig into history." This simulation of an archaeological dig was one of the fair's most popular events.

For the ninth straight summer, we traveled to the Lill Street Art Center on the city's north side, where teaching artists Mary Tepper and Ashley Golden took part in two week-long sessions of "Be An Ancient Egyptian Artist," a summer day-camp program for children ages 8–12. The program, which filled to capacity for both sessions, included a visit to the Oriental Institute, where Jessica Caracci, Education Programs Assistant, developed the art-making sessions and arranged guided tours for the campers.

Jessica Caracci also joined with educators from other Hyde Park cultural organizations to plan and then present

Education interns (left to right) Rupa Pillai, Elizabeth Beggs, and Clare Brody prepare for the hundreds of kite-making families who visited the Oriental Institute booth during Mayor Daley's Kids and Kites Festival, which was held on the grounds of the Museum of Science and Industry this past spring. Photo by Jessica Caracci

MUSEUM EDUCATION

activities for our neighborhood's first booth at Mayor Daley's Kids and Kites Festival, which is held on the lawn of the Museum of Science and Industry each spring. Hundreds of children and their families stopped at the Oriental Institute table where museum staff and interns helped them create kites and kite-tails decorated with ancient Egyptian designs.

Back at the museum, Jessica developed and presented a special tour and hands-on activities for University Alumni and their families during this year's celebration of June Reunion. She was also involved in our three largest on-site events for families, which took place as part of seasonal initiatives promoted by the city's Department of Cultural Affairs. Mummies took center stage in October during our annual "Mummies Night" pre-Halloween celebration in conjunction with Chicago Book Month. City-wide publicity brought us more than 350 children and their families who joined us for a "tomb-full" of programming. Breasted Hall was filled to overflowing as the acclaimed Kidworks Theater Company brought ancient Egyptian stories and tales to life with a rousing presentation of "The Pharaoh, the Sphinx, and the Curse of the Mummy."

Dressing like ancient Egyptian royalty was a new experience for this shy young visitor during the annual pre-Halloween celebration for families. Photo by Wendy Ennes

Docents and interns offered a round of activities that ranged from origami bat-making to a "Guess the Gummy Mummies" contest to dressing up like ancient Egyptians with costumes from "King Tut's Closet." Holiday Adventures, a new initiative for the holiday season, gave us city-wide promotion for a weekend program in December that featured hands-on activities, family treasure hunts, and wonderful shopping opportunities during the Suq's holiday sale.

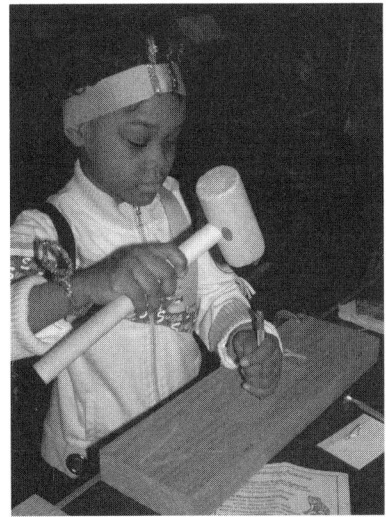

A young visitor tries her hand at working leather like the ancient Nubians during the Awesome Ancient African Arts festival for families. Photo by Wendy Ennes

In February we celebrated African American Heritage Month with "Awesome Ancient African Arts: A Festival for Families." Promoted by the City of Chicago's Winter Delights initiative, this program attracted close to 500 children and their families for an afternoon filled with hands-on activities, treasure hunts, films, crafts projects, and more. Docents wearing "Ask Me" badges staffed the Egyptian and Nubian Galleries to answer countless questions from visitors. Leather worker Carol Jackson and ceramic artists Theaster Gates and Meghan Peterson involved families in recreating arts processes from ancient times. Awad Abdelgadir, Nubian artist and educator, returned to repeat the stellar performance he presented for us last year during the opening of the Picken Family Nubia Gallery. Breasted Hall was filled to capacity for "Life on the Nile," his fascinating multi-media journey to today's Nubia.

MUSEUM EDUCATION

Nubian educator Awad Abdelgadir tells visitors about his homeland during the Awesome African Arts event. Photo by Wendy Ennes

Education intern Jared Jeffers helps Claremont Academy students analyze animal bones to learn about the past during Museum Connections, a school outreach program funded by Chicago Public Schools. Photo by Jessica Caracci

Many of the parents and children who joined us for "Awesome Ancient African Arts" could do so due to support from Museum Connections: Beyond the Classroom Walls, a special museum/schools outreach program for families that is funded by the Department of Mathematics and Science of the Chicago Public Schools. The Oriental Institute Museum was invited to take part in Museum Connections in partnership with Bret Harte School, Claremont Academy, and Henry Elementary School, three Chicago public schools where the parent populations do not often consider museums as learning venues for their families. We used at-school sessions to involve students and their families in arts processes and techniques from ancient times, and also to introduce ways archaeologists learn about the past through analysis of animal bones and the scientific study of mummies. We then invited the families to come to the museum for "Awesome Ancient African Arts" using bus transportation provided by Museum Connections. We were gratified when close to 100 children and their families from these schools joined us that day. Special thanks go to the following people who made this program happen: Jessica Caracci, Jared Jeffers, Rupa Pillai, and Mary O'Shea from Museum Education, and Catherine Dueñas, Volunteer Coordinator from the Volunteer Program; teaching artists Mary Tepper and Pam Robinson; and Belinda Monahan, Oriental Institute Research Associate in Zooarchaeology.

The African Heritage Project

This past year, a major grant from the Joyce Foundation allowed the Oriental Institute to develop and implement the African Heritage Project, an intensive new program that built new bridges of collaboration to serve the youth of our community. The project enabled Chicago public school teachers and administrators, Oriental Institute Museum staff, and artists from the Little Black Pearl Art and Design Center to serve a sector of the population of Woodlawn by providing school outreach services that enriched the learning experiences of sixty 7th and 8th grade students and their families.

Using the Oriental Institute's Picken Family Nubia Gallery as the springboard, educators from Fiske School, the Oriental Institute, and Little Black Pearl introduced the students to the rich history and heritage of ancient Nubia with specially developed curriculum materials for the classroom and a series of gallery tours and discussion sessions at the museum. During their museum visits, students selected and then photographed their favorite artifact from the Nubia exhibit. This work readied them to interpret their chosen artifacts in drawings, sculpture, poetry,

MUSEUM EDUCATION

and prose during writing workshops at their school and hands-on arts sessions with teaching artists at Little Black Pearl.

Development of students' literacy, research, social studies, art, and critical thinking skills was a fundamental goal of the African Heritage Project. The project's culmination was Through Young Eyes: Nubian Art Recreated, a two-part exhibit of student artwork at two venues — the Holleb Family Special Exhibit Gallery at the Oriental Institute and the central galleries at Little Black Pearl.

The time and talents of many people were crucial to the success of the African Heritage Project. Wendy Ennes, Oriental Institute Teacher Services and e-Learning Coordinator, served as overall Project Manager, providing leadership and support for all project activities. Her contributions ranged

Wendy Ennes, Teacher Services and e-Learning Coordinator (center, with camera) helps Fiske public school students photograph their favorite ancient Nubian artifact as part of The African Heritage Project supported by Joyce Foundation. Photo by Jessica Caracci

from scheduling and organizing every event to guiding students during the museum photography sessions to planning the exhibits at both its venues. Other Oriental Institute contributors included Emily Teeter, who took students on guided tours of the Nubia exhibit, and Erik Lindahl, Museum Preparator, who brilliantly installed the student artwork with the aide of Elizabeth Beggs, Andrew Furse, and Curatorial Assistant Tom James.

Stephanie Pearson, social studies teacher at Fiske School, was Wendy Ennes' full partner in the African Heritage Project. She developed and taught the Nubia curriculum, helped to plan and prepare students for the museum visits, and ensured student participation at all project events. The support of Cynthia Miller, Fiske Principal, was also vital to the project's success, as were the contributions of Valesta Cobb, Wilbert Miller, and Donna Turner.

Teaching artists Gwen Pruitt and Carla Carr led the art-making sessions at Little Black Pearl. Their guidance enabled the students, most of whom had no art making experience, to create artwork that was intriguing and moving. Monica Haslip, Executive Director, as well as Leon Haslip, Heidi Hickman, and Chinyeia Moody, also provided assistance and encouragement.

Fiske school student creates a drawing of his favorite ancient Nubian artifact in preparation for the student exhibit that was part of The African Heritage Project. Photo by Erik Treese

A student from Fiske school proudly displays her drawing and sculpture in the exhibit "Through Young Eyes: Ancient Nubia Recreated" in conjunction with The African Heritage Project. Photo by Erik Treese

MUSEUM EDUCATION

This special program, which united members of the Woodlawn, Hyde Park, and North Kenwood/Oakland communities, helped us create a collaborative model for educational partnerships that we can all build upon for the future

From Anatolia to Africa: Museum Learning for Families

Over the past several years the Oriental Institute has received major support from the Polk Bros. Foundation to develop a comprehensive program of self-guided museum learning experiences for children and parents who seldom visit our museum. These include many of the African-American families living in neighborhoods surrounding the University of Chicago as well as the city's growing population of Hispanic families.

Polk Bros. Foundation support from 2000 to 2003 enabled us to create a rich array of self-guided activities for the Egyptian and Mesopotamian Galleries. This success inspired the foundation to award the Oriental Institute a new two-year grant to develop similar services for the Empires in the Fertile Crescent: Ancient Assyria, Anatolia, and Israel exhibit and the Picken Family Nubia Gallery. With the completion of From Anatolia to Africa this past year, the Oriental Institute Museum has become an important family learning venue in the City of Chicago.

A mother and daughter from Nightingale School test the bilingual prototype Family Activity Cards in the Nubia Gallery. This project is part of Families in the Museum, an initiative supported by the Polk Bros. Foundation. Photo by Wendy Ennes

Like its predecessors, the primary objectives for From Anatolia to Africa were to:

- Create bilingual self-guided print materials and touch-screen computer activities that provide underserved families with engaging and educationally sound learning experiences in our museum.

- Develop and pilot these learning experiences through an ongoing dialogue and collaborative relationship with parents, students, and educators from schools representing the city's African American and Hispanic communities.

- Establish a comprehensive program of self-guided family activities that are sustainable with manageable overhead.

- Build increased awareness among families and teachers about the educational opportunities provided by the Oriental Institute's self-guided program.

Over the past two years all these goals were met through the involvement of a broad spectrum of collaborators who were crucial to the project's success. An advisory panel of parents and children from local schools were our major partners for developing the self-guided activities now in place in the Empires exhibit and Nubia Gallery. Five families from the North Kenwood/Oakland Charter School (NK/O), where the student population is almost entirely African-American, joined us, with Marvin Hoffman, NK/O founding director, as educational advisor. Eight families from Nightingale School, where the student population is largely Hispanic, also worked with

MUSEUM EDUCATION

us, with Principal Maureen Savas and Vice-Principal Carmen Lehotan as educational advisors. During the projects' first year, these families toured the Empires in the Fertile Crescent exhibit, identified objects they found intriguing, and suggested the kinds of activities they would find meaningful and enjoyable. They then returned to test and evaluate prototype activities that staff had developed. This past year these activities were repeated for the Nubia Gallery.

The outcomes of this process are rich and rewarding. Museum visitors can now explore and make discoveries about artifacts in the Empires exhibit and Nubia Gallery using full-color Family Activity Cards in English and Spanish. We have also produced a broad spectrum of exciting and instructive "hands-on" computer activities which introduce families to experiences that range from taking part in an archaeological excavation to "meeting" an educator from Sudan who explains what life is like in Nubia today.

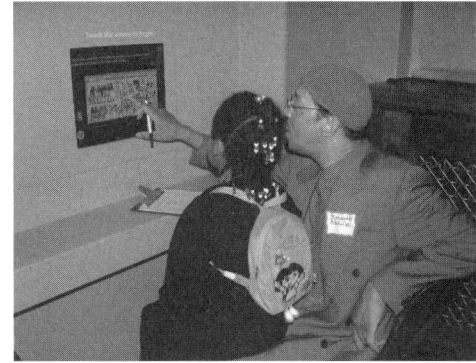

A grandfather and granddaughter from North Kenwood/Oakland Charter School test prototype computer activities for the Nubia Gallery as part of the Families in the Museum project. Photo by Wendy Ennes

Faculty from both partner schools became project collaborators this year, helping us determine the most effective ways the self-guided activities now in place throughout the museum could also be used as teaching and learning tools for the city's schools. The entire faculty of Nightingale School — seventy teachers from grades K–8 — and nearly twenty teachers from NK/O came to the museum in spring, and all were amazed at the depth and richness of these activities. Their suggestions ranged from ways the Family Activity Cards could be used to prepare students for a museum tour to methods for using the computer activities for student research projects. They also urged us to host similar museum visits to introduce faculty from other schools to our resources, advice we are taking to heart, especially since we learned that nearly all the teachers had never visited the Oriental Institute!

The successes of From Anatolia to Africa would have been impossible to achieve without the expertise and creativity of the project's staff and consultants. Geoff Emberling was our academic advisor. For the Nubia activities he was joined by Emily Teeter and Peter Dorman. Their involvement ensured that all materials would reflect the authenticity and most recent research of the Oriental Institute. Jessica Caracci shaped the content and copy for the Family Activity cards. To publicize the completed project she also researched and directed a major marketing campaign that included press release information and family-friendly advertisements for key media, as well as the distribution of posters declaring that "Every Day is Family Day at the Oriental Institute" to all Chicago Public Library branches. Wendy Ennes played a central role as the project's art director. Nitzan Mekel-Bobrov, who has just received a Ph.D. in Genetics from the Committee on Genetics at the University of Chicago, was content researcher, computer

Principal of Nightingale School Maureen Savas, right, joins her faculty to listen as docent Joe Diamond, center left, leads a tour of the museum galleries. The tour was sponsored by the Polk Bros. Foundation. Photo by Wendy Ennes

2006–2007 ANNUAL REPORT 175

MUSEUM EDUCATION

programmer, and multi-media architect. Ennes and Mekel-Bobrov obtained the latest equipment to outfit all Oriental Institute computer kiosks, ensuring their ability to serve the public for several years to come. Erik Lindahl installed the handsome gallery displays that house the project's self-guided activities.

Maria Chagnon, University of Chicago graduate in Romance Languages, translated all the Family Activity cards into Spanish. Her fluency in Spanish was complemented by the Spanish language skills of Volunteer Coordinator Catherine Dueñas, who served as advisor, museum guide for the Spanish-speaking families, and editor for the bilingual Family Activity Cards.

Teresa Vazquez, the project's evaluation consultant, was crucial to its success. She helped us set goals and objectives, prepared evaluation instruments in both English and Spanish for all family meetings, led discussion sessions in both languages so the families could communicate with each other, and wrote comprehensive reports to guide us in all aspects of our work. She also helped develop the survey instruments used during faculty visits this spring and helped shape these teacher programs in ways that have given us important information on how to integrate our family activities into school curricula.

The long-standing interest and generosity of the Polk Bros. Foundation has allowed us to provide a rich, comprehensive, and lasting program of self-guided learning experiences for all who come to the Oriental Institute Museum. Due to the Foundation's vision and support, every day will be "Family Day" at the Oriental Institute for many years to come.

Teacher Services

Empowering teachers to enrich student learning though meaningful classroom and museum study of ancient civilizations is a major mandate for Museum Education. A vital way for us to reach this goal is to provide K–12 teachers and other educators with professional development and student learning opportunities based on the renowned collections, scholarly expertise, award-winning curriculum materials, and unique online resources of the Oriental Institute. This past year we completed two ground-breaking programs for teachers and began a major new initiative that will set our course for teacher training in the upcoming years.

Ancient Nubia, Teaching Training, and Student Achievement

Generous grants from the Lloyd A. Fry Foundation have been supporting teacher training at the Oriental Institute for many years. This year we completed a new initiative entitled Ancient Nubia: Teacher Training and Student Achievement, a project that moved beyond professional development to track student learning based upon the academic enrichment their teachers had received during training at the Oriental Institute.

This new project focused on the Institute's exhibit of art and artifacts from ancient Nubia, whose rich artistic and cultural history are almost entirely missing

Debora Heard, center, Curatorial Assistant for the Nubia Gallery, presents a slide lecture for teachers attending an Oriental Institute professional development seminar on ancient Nubia. The lecture was part of Teacher Training and Student Achievement, a project sponsored by the Lloyd A. Fry Foundation. Photo by Wendy Ennes

MUSEUM EDUCATION

from school curricula. The exhibit, combined with our broad array of curriculum materials and online resources, made the Oriental Institute ideally suited to provide meaningful professional development on Nubia for teachers of ancient civilizations, world history, global studies, African, and African-American studies.

Over the years, support from the Fry Foundation enabled us to create an online Teacher Resource Center that provided teachers nationwide with artifact images, online lessons, and interactive components for ancient Egypt and Mesopotamia. The first component of our new project, which is explained in the Oriental Institute's *Annual Report* for 2005–2006, focused on creating equally rich online resources for ancient Nubia. Developed by Wendy Ennes with the support of a panel of teacher advisors, these Web-based resources were launched in time to serve as a springboard for the project's second component, an intensive two-week summer seminar designed to attract and serve teachers from inner city schools surrounding the University of Chicago. Seminar publicity took place in collaboration with Duel Richardson, Director of Neighborhood Relations/Education in the University's Department of Community Affairs; Richardson's associate, Yelene Modley; and Lisa Perez, Area Library Coordinator for the Chicago Public Schools. Thanks to their efforts seventeen elementary and high school educators from sixteen different schools — most on the city's south side — registered for the seminar.

Students decorate pottery with ancient Nubian designs during a museum lesson their teacher created during an Oriental Institute professional development seminar. The seminar and student visit were supported by the Lloyd A. Fry Foundation

Coordinated by Wendy Ennes, the seminar focused on enhancing teacher understanding of the Oriental Institute's academic and collections resources on ancient Nubia. Seminar lecturers included Geoff Emberling, who introduced the land and peoples of ancient Nubia; Debora Heard, who lectured on religion and burial practices in ancient Nubia; John Larson, who provided a history of the Oriental Institute's archaeological explorations in Sudan; and Emily Teeter, who lectured on ancient Nubian society and also on the relationship between ancient Nubia and ancient Egypt. Wendy Ennes also involved the teachers in creating museum and classroom learning experiences on ancient Nubia that would fulfill state mandates for social studies content, literacy, critical thinking skills, and the integration of web resources into the curriculum.

The project's third component was a partnership with the teachers in assessing and documenting student achievement as their classes took part in the museum and school-based learning experiences the teachers had created during the seminar. We documented student outcomes in a variety of ways. Education staff visited classrooms to see performances and exhibits of student work. We also observed classes as they took part in museum activities designed by their teachers. These ranged from a tour where students took digital photos of Nubian artifacts to create a slide show set to the beat of hip-hop music to a visit where students made drawings of designs on Nubian pottery and then used their research to decorate the pots they had created in the classroom. The students' excitement and involvement in such projects provided us with many informal examples of positive outcomes, but we also partnered with nine of the teachers for more formal assessment. Using a survey instrument created by Wendy Ennes, these teachers reported on learning outcomes for 500 students. All the teachers indicated that classroom work and museum visits had brought about improvements in the students' retention of content; development of

MUSEUM EDUCATION

observation, critical thinking, and writing skills; and increased understanding of ancient Nubian history, culture, geography, and its role in world history. The teachers determined improvement using a wide variety of testing instruments, including quizzes, writing assignments, art projects, library and internet research projects, portfolio production, and map and timeline making.

Analysis such as this is crucial for a project that has student achievement as its ultimate goal. Ancient Nubia: Teacher Training and Student Achievement provides vital information on the relationship between professional development and student outcomes and has given us a model to build upon for all our future teacher training programs. It has also provided important documentation for us to share with the education community in Chicago and beyond.

Ancient Mesopotamia: This History, Our History

Another ground-breaking project to provide resources for teachers and their students came to an end this year with the completion of Ancient Mesopotamia: This History, Our History. Supported by a prestigious National Leadership Grant from the Institute of Museum and Library Services, a federal agency, Ancient Mesopotamia is a unique Web-based project that includes three major components: a searchable database called "The Learning Collection," which features key artifacts from the museum's Mesopotamia collection; a curriculum-based simulated archaeological excavation called "Dig into History"; and an online course on ancient Mesopotamia that will provide professional development and graduate credit for teachers nationwide.

Wendy Ennes, Project Coordinator, was the driving force of this major initiative. She was joined by two University of Chicago collaborators — Chicago WebDocent and e-CUIP Digital Library, both a part of CUIP, the University of Chicago Internet Project.

"The Learning Collection," launched online in February 2006, was the first project component to be completed. Designed for teachers and students of grades 6–12, it provides a state-of-the-art format for browsing, researching, and interacting with artifacts in a myriad of ways, ranging from zooming in to examine all aspects of an ancient sculpture to "rolling out" a cylinder seal to discover the intricacies and beauty of ancient Mesopotamian art. The production of such a resource was a labor-intensive process that demanded the time, talents, and expertise of a whole host of dedicated people. All the participants, and the entire process, are described in full detail in the Museum Education section of the Oriental Institute's *Annual Report* for 2005–2006.

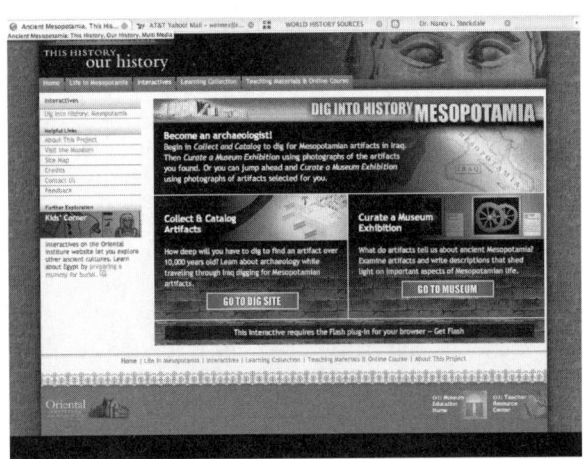

Home page for Dig into History, a simulated archaeological excavation that is part of Ancient Mesopotamia: This History, Our History, a major online project supported by the Institute of Museum and Library Sciences

Wendy Ennes shaped the format and structure of the online professional development course, using the expertise she gained from two years of study in the University of Illinois Master Online Teaching Certification Program. Ancient Mesopotamia's second major component, this online course was researched and written by Leslie Schramer, former graduate student in the Department of Near Eastern Languages and Civilizations, and edited by volunteer David Berry. Their work was guided and reviewed by numerous Oriental Institute faculty members, whose contributions are documented in the 2005–2006 Oriental Institute *Annual Report*.

MUSEUM EDUCATION

This fall the online course will be offered for graduate credit to non-degree seeking educators nationwide in collaboration with the University of Chicago Graham School of General Studies.

This past year, the Ancient Mesopotamia team was involved in the extensive production required to complete and launch "Dig into History," the project's third major component. An archaeological simulation game that K–12 students and their teachers can access nationwide, "Dig into History" teaches the principles of archaeology and Mesopotamian history an engaging way. Game play begins with students choosing a "quest statement" that relates to a major idea or concept about ancient Mesopotamia. After selecting a quest, students begin unearthing artifacts, guided by Fahima Muhammed, an Iraqi archaeologist avatar. Students meet challenges, decide work schedules, and observe and catalog their finds. They end the game by creating an online photographic exhibit of their discoveries that they "install" a virtual museum gallery.

The archaeological quests for "Dig into History" were developed by the project's panel of teacher advisors so that they would relate to key concepts in the nationally mandated social studies curriculum. Advisors who worked with us this year included: Paula Andries, Educational Coordinator for Hephzibah Children's Association; Mary Cobb, Ray School Technology Coordinator; JoAnne Groshek, Bell School 6th Grade Teacher; Mia Henry, Director of Youth-Led Social Change, Chicago Freedom School; Lisa Perez, Area Library Coordinator, Department of Libraries and Information Services, Chicago Public Schools; and Mike Shea, Social Studies Teacher, Kenwood Academy High School.

Christie Thomas, Steven Lane, and Glen Biggus, all of e-CUIP, along with Flash Developer Sean York as consultant, were the extraordinarily talented team who joined Wendy Ennes in creating "Dig into History." Geoff Emberling was also a key contributor, drawing upon his expertise as an archaeologist and museum professional to help us create authentic scenarios for the site. We invite you to visit the entire Ancient Mesopotamia: This History, Our History project at http://mesopotamia.lib.uchicago.edu, where you can experience this unique computer-learning opportunity that will be available to enrich teacher and student knowledge about ancient Mesopotamia for many years to come.

A Look to the Future

Late this spring, the National Endowment for the Humanities recognized Museum Education's vision and commitment to online education by awarding the Oriental Institute a major new grant for Teaching the Middle East: A Resource for High School Educators. The goal of this two-year project is to provide the nations' high school teachers with online resources that draw upon the best in humanities scholarship to help build student understanding of the ancient and contemporary Middle East. At present such materials are in short supply.

Wendy Ennes will be at the helm of this major online project, joined again by the staff of the e-CUIP Digital Library and also a new campus partner — the University of Chicago's center for Middle Eastern studies. The project's online materials will be developed by faculty members of the Department of Near Eastern Languages and Civilizations, with the involvement of a panel of teacher advisors from a cross-section of public and private schools throughout the City of Chicago. Our aim over the next two years will be to produce resources that enable high school educators to focus on key issues and events, shape meaningful lesson plans, and help their students examine stereotypes about the Middle East that abound in today's society.

MUSEUM EDUCATION

Behind the Scenes

Taking stock of all that has been accomplished this past year, I'd like to say how much Museum Education appreciates the encouragement, support, and involvement of Oriental Institute faculty, staff, and students, many of whom are mentioned in this report. A special thank you goes to Geoff Emberling, who provides assistance and support at every turn and has even presented some of our most engaging educational programming. Grateful thanks also go to the Museum Education and Family Program volunteers. None of our gallery-based public programs could have taken place without the time and talents of these men, women, and young people. A record of all their names appears in the Volunteer section of this Oriental Institute *Annual Report*.

More than 15,000 participants joined us for educational programming this year, a decrease from the record number of last year but more in line with general programming attendance during years without major gallery openings. This spring we sent a survey to the 5,000 members and friends who receive our quarterly program and events brochure. Still being returned, this survey is providing valuable information on ways we can meet visitor needs and interests now that our museum is fully open.

The creativity, spirit, and dedication of the department's staff are what make everything happen in Museum Education. Wendy Ennes, Teacher Services and e-Learning Coordinator, is the key figure in all of our major grant-funded initiatives for teachers and students. Her vision, commitment, and drive, along with her grant-writing skills, dedication to excellence in educational programming, and her expertise in online teaching and learning, make her an invaluable asset to the entire Oriental Institute. Along with all her accomplishments described in this report, Wendy makes every effort to share the successes of Oriental Institute Museum Education with local, regional, and national education and museum communities. This year alone she made presentations about our Web-based resources for the Illinois Technology Conference for Educators in St. Charles, Illinois; the Illinois Council for the Social Studies Conference in Lisle, Illinois; the Knowledge is Power Program (KIPP) National School Summit in New Orleans, Louisiana; the National Council for the Social Studies (NCSS) Conference in Washington, D.C.; the Museums and the Web Conference for educators worldwide, which was held in San Francisco in April 2007; and the American Association of Museums National Meeting in Chicago in May 2007. She also made several appearances on the Web, including presentations for TAPPED IN, an online resource funded by the National Science Foundation and Sun Microsystems, and she joined Christie Thomas of e-CUIP to present a online teacher training program in "Second Life," a virtual world filled with a myriad of experiences that reach more than eight million "residents" from around the globe.

The contributions of Jessica Caracci, Education and Public Programs Assistant, are visible throughout this report. Jessica has been central to the development and implementation of all our programs for youth and families this past year, and her expertise as writer, editor, graphic designer, and program presenter have been crucial to

Carole Yoshida helps visitors make ancient Egyptian-style rubbings during the Holiday Adventures program. Carole was one of the many volunteers who contributed time and talents to all our public programs this past year. Photo by Carole Krucoff

MUSEUM EDUCATION

the success of all our grant-funded initiatives for families, teachers, and students. This year she also assumed a supervisory role for the department's new internship program, a collaboration between the museum and the University of Chicago's Master of Arts Program in the Social Sciences. Work-study student Jared Jeffers, and volunteer interns Elizabeth Beggs and Rupa Pillai, aided us in countless ways that ranged from office and programmatic support to materials development and exhibit evaluation. Clare Brody also joined us as an intern from the University of Chicago Laboratory School. Jessica's guidance assured all these interns a meaningful and rewarding experience that combined assistance to our department with an introduction to the role museum education can play at a major university museum.

Education Programs Assistant Jessica Caracci, left, joins intern Elizabeth Beggs at "King Tut's Closet" during Mummies Night. Supervising Education interns is but one of the many and varied responsibilites that make Jessica "command central" in the Museum Education Office. Photo by Wendy Ennes

Jessica's public relations, design, and organizational skills also make her "command central" in the Museum Education Office. She supervises the registration, confirmation, and financial record-keeping for all adult education, family, and guided tour programs. She also serves as our media specialist; writing and distributing our quarterly press packets and targeted press releases, as well as designing and supervising production for most of our educational and marketing materials. As with all her other responsibilities, Jessica handles these tasks with poise, grace, and a genuine concern for the needs and interests of others. Museum Education is truly fortunate to have such a creative, insightful, and multi-talented museum professional with us.

In the following section you will learn about the achievements of the Oriental Institute Volunteer Program, supervised by Volunteer Coordinators Catherine Dueñas and Terry Friedman, who are our colleagues in the Education Office. These extraordinarily gifted and dedicated women are continually inspired by the creativity and commitment of their remarkable corps of volunteers. Read on to see how the institute and the community have benefited from the work of our volunteers, and all that Cathy and Terry have helped them accomplish.

VOLUNTEER PROGRAM

Catherine Dueñas and Terry Friedman

Since the Oriental Institute Volunteer Program's inception in 1966, its mission has always been to make ancient Near Eastern research, scholarship, and archaeological discoveries more accessible and engaging to the general public. Over the past four decades, museum docents have served as educators and good will ambassadors to visitors of all ages. This unique relationship is strengthened and enriched by the docent's individual initiatives and motivations to understand and to expand their knowledge of the ancient Near East. Throughout the years, not only has a devoted cadre of museum docents served the Institute, but also in more recent years, the program has expanded to meet the changing needs of the Oriental Institute's faculty and staff. Volunteer participation is institute wide, allowing individuals to express their interest in supporting the Oriental Institute's ongoing operation.

This year marked the first opportunity to implement a comprehensive Volunteer Training Class for the docents and volunteers since the museum closed for renovation and climate control in 1996. After a dynamic recruitment campaign during the summer, the new volunteers, along with current and returning volunteers, participated in an extensive lecture series covering a wide range of topics. However, volunteer training does not end with the last training class; the Volunteer Program is an ongoing educational experience designed to engage and to inspire its participants as well as to foster support for individual research and interpretation. Beyond Volunteer Day lectures, one-on-one interactions with professors and access to the Docent Library, multiple opportunities exist to encourage intellectual curiosity among members. By dedicating themselves to the Oriental Institute's mission, volunteers are able to connect to cultural histories and to discuss the modern relevance of scholars' work, while successfully bringing ancient Near Eastern civilization to life for visitors of all ages.

Recruitment

The past year has been a very busy and productive period in the Volunteer Office. With all the museum galleries now reopened and the development of a structured training program, we turned our attention to implementing an active recruitment campaign.

Under the guidance of Debby Halpern, who researched and organized a marketing campaign which successfully met our recruitment goals, and Jessica Caracci, who creatively designed and placed informative advertisements promoting the Oriental Institute's Volunteer Program, we were able to attract many eager recruits.

We were very pleased to welcome thirty-one new members into the volunteer corps this past year: Erin Baker, Susan Barzargan, Elizabeth Beggs, Irene Berkey, Roman Bilik, Marc Block, Louise Boyd, Maureen Brierton, Roberta Buchanan, Kristin Buskirk, Morgan Campbell, Bob Cantu, John DeWerd, Jennifer Douglass, Alexander Elwyn, Barbara Freidell, Jill Gosser, Erin Guinn-Villareal, Morton Jaffee, Larry Lissak, Brittany Luberda, Sherry McGuire, Jorge Montes, Alexander Muir, Rupa Pillai, Claire Pritchard, Gerladine Rowden, Ljubica Sarenac, Mae Simon, Ronald Wideman, and Kenneth Yu.

Volunteer Training Fall 2006

Fall 2006 saw the production of the first comprehensive volunteer training series since 1994. The classes were designed to cover a broad range of historical, cultural, and archaeological background about the ancient Near East as well as provide interesting contrasts and comparisons between the cultures. The course provided newly recruited, current, and returning docents and volunteers with an extraordinary learning experience.

The twelve-session training series was a monumental organizational endeavor that included twenty separate lectures and gallery workshops led by Oriental Institute faculty, staff, and volunteers. Each session was professionally video taped through the services of the Chicago Media Initiatives Group at the University of Chicago. The DVDs produced will be an extremely valuable educational resource for all future volunteers and will add a dimension of professionalism to current training materials.

Upon completion of the training classes, all new museum docents along with those who have joined the program since 1994, were strongly encouraged to produce a "Highlights of the Collection" gallery tour outline. This assignment was designed to help clarify and consolidate a docent's knowledge of the museum's collection into a workable format, while developing his or her own individual tour. It has also proved to be an excellent tool to evaluate a docent's preparation to serve as a tour guide. Many of the "Highlights" tours have been compiled into a binder, making them readily available to help other new volunteers develop their tours.

We would like to thank all of the presenters who gave outstanding lectures or demonstrated interactive touring techniques during each of the sessions. Kudos to: Joe Diamond, Peter Dorman, Geoff Emberling, Margaret Foorman, François Gaudard, McGuire Gibson, Tobin Hartnell, Debora Heard, Janet Johnson, W. Ray Johnson, Kathleen Mineck, Seth Richardson, Stephen Ritzel, Martha Roth, David Schloen, Mary Shea, Emily Teeter, Theo van den Hout, Bruce Williams, Karen Wilson, and Christopher Woods.

We would like to give special thanks to the numerous volunteers, who were so helpful with checking in participants and setting up refreshments for each event. In particular, we would like to recognize Dennis Kelley and Mary O'Shea, who took charge of these tasks and thus made our job much easier.

Tour Program

For over forty years, docent-led tours of the museum galleries have continued to engage and to delight visitors of all ages, because the Oriental Institute Museum Docents have been eager to share their knowledge and pride for the museum's collection with all our guests. With the completion of the reinstallation and renovation project, the docents now have the opportunity to guide groups through the museum's galleries without detours or construction zone interruptions. They are delighted to be able to finally present the artifacts in a cohesive and comprehensive manner.

Despite the passage of time, the role of a museum docent has not been significantly altered. Perhaps the original function of a museum docent can best be described in this brief excerpt from an article written by former museum docent and volunteer Ida De Pencier. She was in the first docent training class in 1966 and guided youngsters through the galleries for almost thirty years. Her insightful observations hold true to this day.

> The Oriental Institute in establishing the Docent program is providing an outstanding service to a wide community. The Museum is a gem, but Docents are needed to interpret the displays, especially to younger visitors. To be sure, the artifacts are well chosen and charmingly displayed, but it is the human voice, explaining and describing, which gives emphasis to what the eyes see. Ida De Pencier, "Reflections of a Volunteer," *News & Notes*, 1974.

VOLUNTEER PROGRAM

This past year, many museum docents enjoyed informal study sessions that focused on the development of special interest tour topics. Docents independently researched an area of special interest and shared this knowledge with others in the group. These study sessions helped to enhance their own understanding of specific areas within the collection as well as to encourage unique approaches to engage audiences with interactive touring techniques.

Docents were also introduced to the new Assistive Listening Devices (ALD) this year. The ALD is a wonderful way to enhance a visitor's museum experience. The new equipment will be available to any museum visitor who requests it at the reception desk. We are pleased to proactively reach out to the hearing impaired.

We are very proud to announce that 10,706 visitors enjoyed a docent-led tour this past year.

Docent Captain System

As the primary link between museum docents and the administrative staff, the Docent Captain System continues to play a pivotal role in the ongoing excellence and efficiency of the Volunteer Program. The captains' supervision of the docents and tour staffing are vital components of the program. Captains are mentors for docents-in-training, helping to foster both a positive attitude and rewarding interaction among their group members. Our thanks and appreciation to Docent Captains: Myllicent Buchanan, Gabriele DaSilva, Joe Diamond, Teresa Hintzke, Dennis Kelley, Roy Miller, Donald Payne, Patrick Regnery, Stephen Ritzel, Lucie Sandel, Deloris Sanders, Pierangelo Taschini, Pramrudee Townsend, and Carole Yoshida for all their efforts on behalf of the Volunteer Program.

Docent Advisory Committee

The Docent Advisory Committee was formed two years ago to give the Volunteers a greater voice in the decision-making process of the Volunteer Program and Education Office. The Committee serves as an open forum for the docents and the volunteers to discuss concerns and to work on productive solutions for problems. We thank the committee for its comprehensive report, which focused on a variety of issues expressed by the docents and volunteers. This group's initiatives have been a catalyst for improvement. Under the leadership of its executive members, Joe Diamond, Dennis Kelley, and Mary Shea, many of the concerns expressed in the initial July 2005 report have been successfully resolved over the past year.

We were very pleased to have Geoff Emberling, Oriental Institute Museum Director, become actively involved with the committee and its recommendations. His pragmatic and insightful observations helped direct the committee toward creative and innovative solutions to improve the Volunteer Program's structure.

Volunteer Survey

A Volunteer Survey was developed in order to solicit relevant information from the Volunteer Corps. Oriental Institute Volunteers were asked to participate in this questionnaire to help identify their needs and expectations. In these changing times with shifting priorities, the information gleamed from this survey will be useful and provide valuable advice, when reviewing the program's future objectives.

VOLUNTEER PROGRAM

Docent Library

Margaret Foorman, Head Docent Librarian, has continued to expand and improve the outstanding collection of books, ephemera, and reference materials for volunteers. Her monthly updates in the *Volunteer Voice* highlight new additions to the library and offer suggested readings to enhance members' knowledge and understanding of the ancient Near East. Through numerous and generous donations from faculty, staff, and volunteers, along with many new purchases, the Docent Library's collection continues to thrive both as an educational resource and a valuable research archive. Our thanks also to Sandra Jacobsohn for assisting Margaret with the library's ongoing maintenance.

Our guest speaker for January Volunteer Day was Ray Tindel, who reminisced about his tenure as the Oriental Institute Registrar and the many different staff members and volunteers with whom he has worked over the years. It was a rare opportunity to hear how registration methods have changed as well as to see many of the smaller pieces of registered objects stored in the basement. Ray explains some of these rare sherds as Helen McDonald, Margaret Foorman, and Mary Shea listen. Photo by Wendy Ennes

April Volunteer Day featured Clemens Reichel who gave a full-day seminar on Mesopotamia. The morning lecture featured a revisit to the Mesopotamian Gallery, while the afternoon program was an interactive workshop on building a tour narrative. The two sessions were designed to give the volunteers a fresh perspective on how to effectively work with the museum collection. Photo by Terry Friedman

Gil Stein, Oriental Institute Director, was our guest speaker for June Volunteer Day. Gil spoke about the Ubaid period in Mesopotamian history. At the conclusion of the program docents and volunteers joined Gil in the Mesopotamian Gallery for a closer look at the Ubaid objects. Photo by Terry Friedman

2006–2007 ANNUAL REPORT

VOLUNTEER PROGRAM

Our thanks to Mary Shea for contributing her book review of *How Writing Came About* by Denise Schmandt-Besserat to the June Volunteer Voice. We hope to continue to offer a book review as a quarterly feature in our monthly newsletter.

We were pleased to add the entire DVD series from the Fall 2006 Training Class to the library's reference materials. The addition of these lectures in digital format gives both new and current volunteers an opportunity to experience the sessions from a fresh, first-hand perspective. We look forward to incorporating these DVDs into future volunteer training classes.

Adam Lubin, Security and Visitors Services Supervisor, explains evacuation procedures to museum docents during our spring fire safety drill. Photo by Terry Friedman

Volunteer Days

Volunteer Day programming continues to provide an outstanding educational opportunity for all Oriental Institute docents and volunteers. These monthly educational seminars blend current research and discoveries with broader historical and cultural overviews to expand everyone's knowledge of the ancient Near East. These informative lectures and gallery workshops have been at the heart of the program's longevity and success. They have helped to sustain a high level of interest and participation among the volunteers and have fostered an atmosphere conducive to learning and exploring new interpretations. Our thanks and appreciation to presenters, Steve Beaudoin, John Brinkman, John Larson, Adam Lubin, Clemens Reichel, Robert Ritner, Gil Stein, Ray Tindel, and Tanya Treptow, for their outstanding programs.

Evacuation Drill

During June's Volunteer Day, the Oriental Institute had an evacuation drill under the guidance of Adam Lubin, Head of Security and Visitor Services. Docents and volunteers were instructed to position themselves throughout the galleries before the practice. The entire drill lasted only a few minutes, but all the participants including the Oriental Institute's faculty and staff members appreciated the opportunity to take part in this important exercise. The Institute and the Office of Security and Visitor Services plans to conduct this drill on an annual basis as a precautionary measure for everyone's safety.

Several of this year's recognition award recipients pause for a moment before the annual holiday luncheon at the Quadrangle Club. Top row left to right: Margaret Foorman, Jim Sopranos, Carlotta Maher, Peggy Grant; bottom row left to right: Joan Curry, Stephen Ritzel, and Andrew Buncis. Photo by Wendy Ennes

Summer Field Trip

On July 10th, volunteers gathered at The Field Museum to view Tutankhamun and the Golden Age of the Pharaohs. This spectacular exhibit showcased some of the priceless treasures from the tombs of Tutankhamun and his royal ancestors. We were very pleased to have Emily Teeter join us on this special field trip. Her wealth of knowledge and insightful comments brought these magnificent artifacts to life.

December Volunteer Day and Volunteer Recognition Ceremony

As an annual tradition, faculty, staff, and volunteers gather to enjoy a festive holiday celebration for December Volunteer Day. This popular program includes a guest speaker, the introduction of new volunteers, and the volunteer recognition ceremony. The program culminates with a lovely holiday luncheon at the Quadrangle Club. This year's special event took place on Monday, December 4.

Our guest speaker for this year's program was John Larson, who gave a brilliant slide presentation entitled "The Breasted Family and King Tut's Tomb: Words and Pictures from the Oriental Institute Archives." John's fascinating discussion, along with the beautifully chosen archival photographs, truly brought to life James Henry Breasted, his family, and the extraordinary time in which they lived.

Volunteer Services Coordinators Cathy Dueñas (left) and Terry Friedman (right), along with three of their predecessors, Janet Helman, Peggy Grant, and Carlotta Maher, helped celebrate the fortieth anniversary of the Volunteer Program. Photo by Wendy Ennes

This year the Volunteer Recognition Ceremony was divided into two sections: one for the entire Volunteer Program and one for those individuals with several years of service.

The year 2006 marked an important turning point for the Volunteer Program as it celebrated its fortieth anniversary. Although its founder, Carolyn Livingood, passed away in 1994, we are very fortunate to still have three former volunteer coordinators: Carlotta Maher, Peggy Grant, and Janet Helman, as advisors and mentors. Their hard work, determination, and collective vision has served as a driving force in the continued development of the Oriental Institute's Volunteer Program as it stands today. In their speeches at the ceremony, each one of these amazing ladies shared their memories and reminisced about the past four decades.

Eleven individuals were recognized for their distinguished support and loyal commitment to the Oriental Institute and the museum. Their combined years of service represent a total of 220 years! Congratulations to this year's Recognition Award Recipients:

5 Years

| Andrew Buncis | Joan Curry | Lo Luong Lo |
| Charlotte Noble | Toni Smith | |

20 Years

Margaret Foorman

25 Years

Stephen Ritzel

35 Years

Peggy Grant

40 Years

| Cissy Haas | Carlotta Maher | O. J. Sopranos |

VOLUNTEER PROGRAM

As a yearly tradition, faculty, staff, and volunteers gather to enjoy a festive holiday luncheon at the Quadrangle Club. This year's special event took place on Monday, December 4. Photo by Wendy Ennes

Cissy Haas, Jim Sopranos, and Carlotta Maher, members of the first Docent Training Class, in 1967, were recognized for forty years of service. Photo by Wendy Ennes

Congratulations again to all the Recognition Award recipients and to all the volunteers, who have given an extraordinary year of service to the Oriental Institute.

This December Volunteer Day Program would not have been possible without the support and cooperation of many people. We want to express our appreciation to:

Gil Stein and the Office of the Director of the Oriental Institute for underwriting the annual holiday luncheon for the Docents, Faculty, Staff, and Volunteers.

Monica Witczak, Development Director, for awarding complimentary memberships to the Volunteer Recognition Award recipients.

Wendy Ennes for photographing this very special occasion.

Denise Browning for her assistance with the recognition awards and gift selection.

Stephen Ritzel for helping with the parking validation for the Volunteers.

Olivia Boyd for her technical assistance with the audio-visual aspect of the program.

Gabriele DaSilva and Semra Prescott, who were so helpful with the setup and the cleanup of the morning coffee reception.

Chris Nogulich and the Quadrangle Club staff for preparing and serving another wonderful holiday luncheon.

Jessica Caracci for designing the beautiful certificates for the recognition award recipients.

Outreach on the Move

The Outreach Program has continued to delight and engage audiences of all ages. Outreach has grown in popularity over the past eleven years as it continues to generate a loyal following in schools as well as attract new audiences, who enjoy this alternative "in-house field trip" experience. From Chicago's north side to its southwest and western suburbs, Oriental Institute Volunteers have been on the move taking the "show on the road." We were pleased to make our annual visit to James Hart Millennium School in Homewood and to Springbrook Elementary School in Naperville, Illinois. Audiences on the north side were also thrilled to meet our Outreach team at the Lake Shore Retirement Health Center and at the Sultzer Public Library. For over a decade, students, educators, parents, and adults have continued to give the program rave reviews. This year 390 participants enjoyed the advantage of an outreach visit.

VOLUNTEER PROGRAM

Interns and Staff Support

We were very fortunate this past academic year to have Elizabeth Beggs and Rupa Pillai as interns in the Volunteer and Education Offices. From administrative tasks to assisting on special projects, all who worked with them appreciated their energetic spirit and excellent work. Throughout this past year their numerous contributions have helped to enhance and to support many vital areas of the Volunteer Program's ongoing operation.

We are delighted to welcome Elizabeth Kisor and Alyssa Price as our summer interns. We look forward to working with them on many exciting and challenging projects throughout the next few months.

"On the road again" with outreach. Outreach docents pause for a break in the teachers' lounge at James Hart Millennium School during our annual visit. Photo by Terry Friedman

We would also like to thank our colleagues in Museum Education for their unwavering support and prudent advice throughout this past year: Jessica Caracci, Education Programs Assistant; Carole Krucoff, Head of Education and Public Programs; and Wendy Ennes, Teachers' Services and Family Project Coordinator. In an environment filled with activity and interruptions, their calm demeanor and sense of humor foster a congenial and productive atmosphere.

A special note of thanks to Jessica Caracci whose incredible organization and communication skills are at the very core of the program's success. Her patience and attention to detail are greatly appreciated by everyone.

In Memoriam

The Volunteer Program lost three loyal friends and supporters of the Oriental Institute: Lillian Cropsey, Dr. Larry Scheff, and Peggy Wick. These individuals exemplified the essence of an ideal volunteer. Each devoted decades of time to share their unique talents and skills to help further the goals and mission of the Oriental Institute. We will greatly miss these three remarkable people and we are thankful that they spent a substantial portion of their volunteer time with us.

Reflections

Building on over forty years of expansion and growth, the Volunteer Program has attempted to meet the many challenges and opportunities in a changing world through a plurality of initiatives. Throughout its forty-year history, the program has been able to expand to offer other options for volunteer service and support within the museum and the Oriental Institute itself. Since 1966 the Volunteer Corps has grown to over 150 people, who form a community of uniquely talented individuals; all of whom are devoted to serving the Institute and to enriching its mission. We thank them for their numerous past and present contributions and look forward to their future support. This year the Oriental Institute Docents and Volunteers have demonstrated their commitment by contributing over 12,000 hours of service.

Our thanks and appreciation to our summer intern Alyssa Price for her assistance and patience with the production of this year's *Annual Report*.

VOLUNTEER PROGRAM

Honorary Volunteers-at-Large

Carol Randel   Elizabeth Sonnenschein

Volunteers: Class of 2006/2007

Erin Baker	Susan Barzargan	Elizabeth Beggs
Irene Berkey	Roman Bilik	Marc Block
Louise Boyd	Maureen Brierton	Roberta Buchanan
Kristin Buskirk	Morgan Campbell	Bob Cantu
John DeWerd	Jennifer Douglass	Alexander Elwyn
Barbara Freidell	Jill Gosser	Erin Guinn-Villareal
Morton Jaffee	Larry Lissak	Brittany Luberda
Sherry McGuire	Jorge Montes	Alexander Muir
Rupa Pillai	Claire Pritchard	Gerladine Rowden
Ljubica Sarenac	Mae Simon	Ronald Wideman
Kenneth Yu		

Advisers to the Volunteer Program

Peggy Grant   Janet Helman   Carlotta Maher

Volunteer Program Consultant

Shel Newman

Volunteers Emeritus

Debbie Aliber	Charlotte Collier	Lilian Cropsey†
Erl Dordal	Patty Dunkel	Mary D'Ouville
Bettie Dwinell	Carol Green	Mary Grimshaw
Cissy Haas	Alice James	MaryJo Khuri
Nina Longley	Jo Lucas	Masako Matsumoto
Dorothy Mozinski	Janet Russell	Larry Scheff†
Peggy Wick†		

Docent Library - Head Librarian

Margaret Foorman

Library Committee

Sandra Jacobsohn   Deloris Sanders   Mary Shea

Docent Advisory Committee Executive Board

Joe Diamond   Dennis Kelly   Mary Shea

Museum Docents

John Aldrin	Sylwia Aldrin	Douglas Baldwin
Nancy Baum	Susan Bazargan	Irene Berkey
Christel Betz	Rebecca Binkley	Dorothy Blindt
Maureen Brierton	Myllicent Buchanan	Roberta Buchanan
Andrew Buncis	Kristin Buskirk	Gabriella Cohen
David Covill	Joan Curry	Gabriele Da Silva
John DeWerd	Joe Diamond	Jennifer Douglass
Sam Dreessen	Djanie Edwards	Mary Finn
Margaret Foorman	Barbara Freidell	Joan Friedmann
Dario Giacomoni	C. Azure Gillman	Ruth Goldman
Louise Golland	Anita Greenberg	Debby Halpern
Ira Hardman	Janet Helman	Lee Herbst
Teresa Hintzke	Morton Jaffee	Dennis Kelley
Henriette Klawans	Lo Luong Lo	Margaret Manteufel
Pat McLaughlin	Sherry McGuire	Robert McGuiness
Roy Miller	Kathy Mineck	Alexander Muir
Alice Mulberry	Austin O'Malley	Mary O'Shea
Nancy Patterson	Denise Paul	Donald Payne
Kitty Picken	Rita Picken	Diane Posner

VOLUNTEER PROGRAM

Semra Prescott	Claire Pritchard	Melissa Ratkovich
David Ray	Patrick Regnery	Stephen Ritzel
Gerladine Rowden	Lucie Sandel	Deloris Sanders
Sarah Sapperstein	Larry Scheff†	Joy Schochet
Anne Schumacher	Mary Shea	Daila Shefner
Mae Simon	Toni Smith	Bernadette Strnad
Pierangelo Taschini	Mari Terman	Karen Terras
Pramerudee Townsend	Arveal Turner	Ronald Wideman
Inge Winer	Carole Yoshida	Kemmeth Yu

Volunteer Interns

Elizabeth Beggs   Elizabeth Kizior (summer)   Rupa Pillai
Alyssa Price (summer)

Work Study Intern
Jared Jeffers

Museum Archives

Hazel Cramer	Peggy Grant	Adam Hemmings
Patricia Hume	Sandra Jacobsohn	Roberta Kovitz
Bryan Moles	Lillian Schwartz	Robert Wagner
Carole Yoshida		

Museum Registration

Joan Barghusen	Gretel Braidwood	Elizabeth Davidson
Joe Diamond	Janet Helman	Barbara Levin
Daila Shefner	Toni Smith	Jim Sopranos
Ray Tindel		

Suq

Muriel Brauer   Peggy Grant   Marda Gross
Norma van der Meulen

Suq Jewelry Designer
Norma van der Meulen

Persepolis Tablets
Irene Glasner   Louise Golland

Computer Lab
Alexander Elwyn

CAMEL Lab
Alexander Elwyn   Ron Wideman

Demotic Dictionary
Verena Lepper   Janelle Pisarik

Diyala Project
Betsy Kremers   George Sundell   Karen Terras

Epigraphic Survey and Chicago House
Mary Grimshaw   Carlotta Maher   Crennan Ray
David Ray

Hacinebi Excavations
Irene Glassner

2006–2007 Annual Report

VOLUNTEER PROGRAM

Hamoukar Project
Karen Terras

Iraq Museum Database
Muhammad Abdallah

Tell Brak
Serra Jackman Sonia Gollance

ROMANCING THE PAST: 2006
Gala Committee

Gretel Braidwood	Andrea Dudek	Margaret Foorman
Debby Halpern	Janet Helman	Carlotta Maher
Kitty Picken	Rita Picken	Mary Shea
Mari Terman		

Behind the Scenes
Jo Lucas Mary O'Shea Agnes Zellner

Set-up
Djannie Edwards

Registration and Greeting
Catherine Dueñas Sarah Sapperstein Mae Thornburgh
Tobin Hartnell

Museum Education and Family Programs Volunteers

Rozenn Bailleul-LeSeur	Erin Baker	Elizabeth Beggs
Christel Betz	Rebecca Binkley	Myllicent Buchanan
Andrew Buncis	Bob Cantu	Joan Curry
Gabriele Da Silva	Joe Diamond	Stephen Esposito
Margaret Foorman	Dario Giacomoni	Louise Golland
Erin Guinn-Villareal	Debby Halpern	Katharyn Hanson
Ira Hardman	Teresa Hintzke	Tom Hunter
Dennis Kelley	Robert McGuiness	Sherry McGuire
Roy Miller	Kathy Mineck	Mary O'Shea
Nancy Patterson	Donald Payne	Rupa Pillai
Rita Picken	Semra Prescott	Diane Posner
Patrick Regnery	Stephen Ritzel	Lucie Sandel
Deloris Sanders	Joy Schochet	Anne Schumacher
Mary Shea	Toni Smith	Bernadette Strnad
Pierangelo Taschini	Mari Terman	Inge Winer
Carole Yoshida		

Junior Volunteers
Clare Brody Kristina Cooper Cameron Kelley
Carl Mineck

Outreach Docents and Volunteers

Rebecca Binkley	Myllicent Buchanan	Andrew Buncis
Janet Calkins	John DeWerd	Joe Diamond
Bettie Dwinell	Bill and Terry Gillespie	Ira Hardman
Robert McGuiness	Caryl Mikrut	Roy Miller
Kathy Mineck	Mary O'Shea	Stephen Ritzel
Larry Scheff†	Joy Schochet	Anne Schumacher
Carole Yoshida	Agnes Zellner	

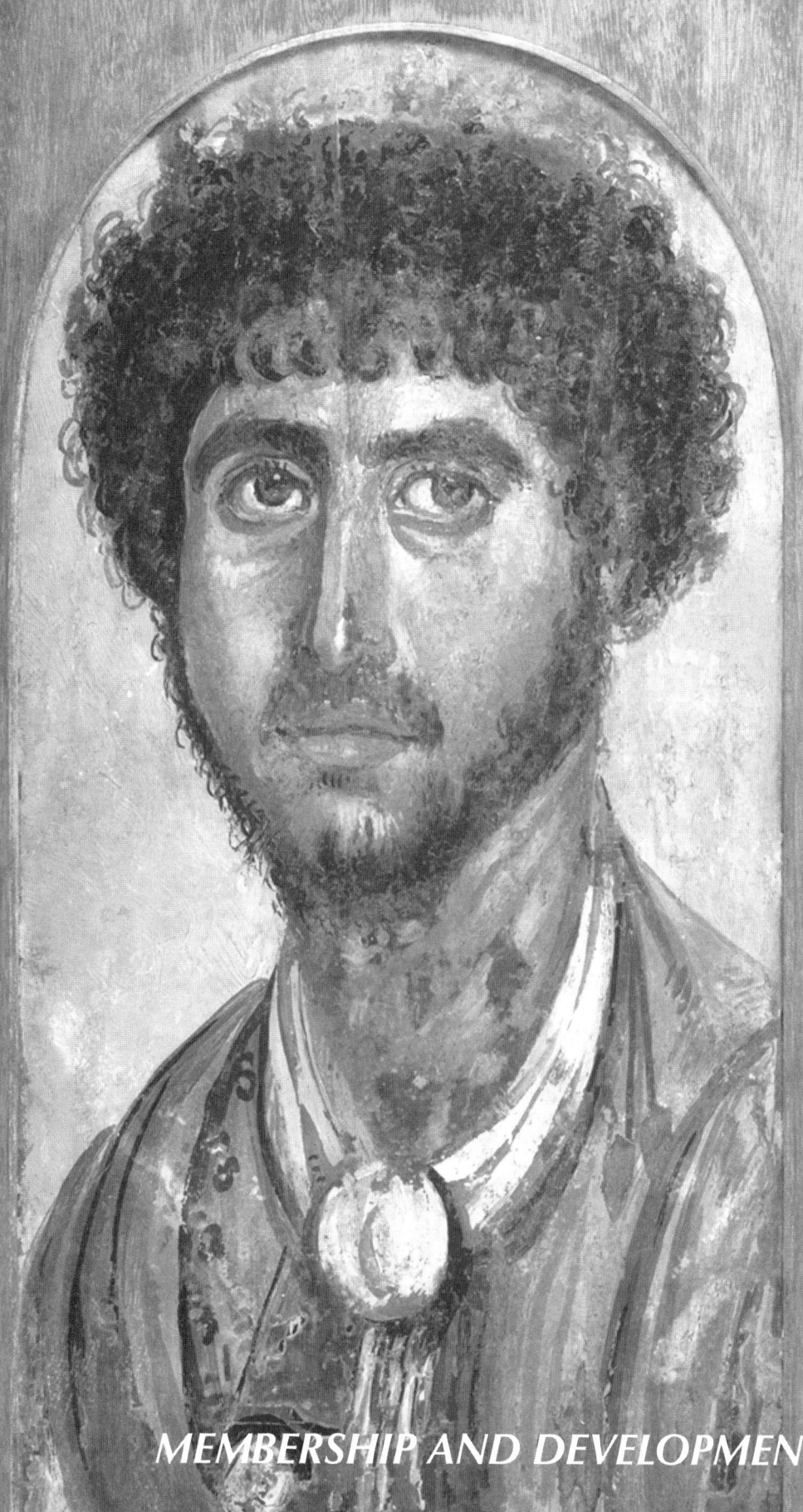

MEMBERSHIP AND DEVELOPMENT

Overleaf. Mummy Portrait of a Young Man. Wood, wax, pigment. Roman period, First century A.D. Hawara, Egypt. OIM 2053. The Egyptian tradition of mummification survived well into the Roman period. During that time, new styles emerged to accommodate foreign influence. Some people chose to have a Greco-Roman style realistic portrait of themselves attached to the mummy rather than to employ a traditional Egyptian idealized head cover.

MEMBERSHIP AND DEVELOPMENT

MEMBERSHIP

Sarah Sapperstein

Statistics

At the close of the fiscal year, the Oriental Institute had 2,072 active members. Between July 1, 2006, and June 30, 2007, 178 new members joined the Institute.

Publications

With the assistance and guidance of the Publications Office, the Membership Office continued to publish *News & Notes* on a quarterly basis. The Fall 2006 issue focused on the special exhibit Embroidering Identities: A Century of Palestinian Clothing with a lead article by curator Iman Saca. In Winter 2007, our members were introduced to the Persepolis Fortification Tablets and the international legal case surrounding their future and past, with articles by Matthew Stolper and Gil Stein. The Spring 2007 issue featured the technological advancement pioneered by the Oriental Institute in an article by Scott Branting of the CAMEL project, as well as an illuminating, full color article on the special exhibit Daily Life Ornamented: The Medieval Persian City of Rayy, by Don Whitcomb and student curator Tanya Treptow. In Summer 2007, we celebrated the contributions of Raymond Tindel. Ray himself, as well as Mark Garrison of Trinity University, contributed pieces which were presented at a spring symposium in honor of Ray's retirement. The Summer 2007 issue also featured updates from the Oriental Institute excavation in Nubia, the forthcoming Megiddo Gallery guide, and Museum Education's youth and family programming.

Events

The 2006/2007 year was full of events for members and supporters of the Oriental Institute. The academic year began with a very successful Stars and Tombs event in collaboration with the Adler Planetarium and The Field Museum. Members were treated to a planetarium presentation, a presentation by University of Chicago Near Eastern Languages and Civilizations graduate students, and admission to the exhibit Tutankhamun and the Golden Age of the Pharaohs at The Field Museum.

Janet Richards joined us to present the first Members' Lecture of the 2006/2007 year, which was entitled "The Lost Tombs and the Archaeology of Individuals in Late Old Kingdom Egypt." Many members took part in the gallery talks led by Emily Teeter and Geoff Emberling focusing on the discovery of and the culture surrounding King Tutankamun.

Members also enjoyed a preview of the autumn 2006 special exhibit, Embroidering Identities: A Century of Palestinian Clothing, as well as a Members' Lecture given by Maha Saca, Director of the Palestinian Heritage Center. Members took part in a concert given by the University of Chicago's Middle East Music Ensemble, a performance presented in conjunction with the Palestinian Clothing exhibit.

On October 5, over 150 members, donors, supporters, volunteers, and scholars came together to celebrate seventy-five years of scholarship in the Oriental Institute building with the Oriental Institute Gala, Romancing the Past. With a silent and live auction of over thirty items from around

MEMBERSHIP

the world, the Gala event raised over $100,000 for the Oriental Institute. Guests enjoyed a gallery dinner, music by the Middle Eastern Music Ensemble, and a living-history portrayal of James Henry Breasted himself by Chicago-based actor R. J. Lindsey.

The Gala event would not have been possible without the tireless efforts of Monica Witczak and Maria Krasinski, along with the Oriental Institute Visiting Committee's Events Committee. We express our infinite gratitude to Debby Halpern, Gretel Braidwood, Andrea Dudek, Margaret Foorman, Janet Helman, Kitty Picken, Rita Picken, Mary Shea, and Mari Terman. Thank you to both Emily Teeter and Denise Browning for their participation and leadership on the Gala Committee. Special thanks are also due to the many volunteers who helped the evening run smoothly.

In January 2007, our members were treated to a lecture on Afghanistan's Hidden Past by Frederik Hiebert of the National Geographic Society. On January 31, Breasted Society members enjoyed an exclusive presentation on the Persepolis Fortification Tablets — their cultural and archaeological context and modern legal ramifications. Breasted Society members got a chance to see some of the tablets in an intimate setting with the guidance of Dr. Matthew Stolper, after which members enjoyed an evening gallery reception.

In spring, the Members' Lecture schedule was very busy with five lectures in six weeks. In March, members learned about Canaanites and Minoans in the Middle Bronze Age palace of Tel Kabri, Israel, from Eric Cline of George Washington University, as well as recent research in the Hittite capital of Hattuša, presented by Andreas Schachner of the German Archaeological Institute. Over 100 people attended the lecture Cleopatra as CEO: Bureaucracy and Scandal in the Hostile Takeover of a First Millennium B.C. Multinational" presented by Janet Johnson, Oriental Institute Egyptologist.

In April, Clemens Reichel presented the lecture "City, Craft Specialization, and Conflict at Hamoukar"; Pavel Lurye from the Austrian Academy of Sciences in Vienna discussed "Silk Road Geography"; and Josef Wegner of the University of Pennsylvania presented a lecture to an audience of over 120 on the excavations "Beneath the Mountain of Anubis in Abydos, Egypt."

Our Associate Members enjoyed an exclusive lecture and reception with Kathryn Gleason of Cornell University. Dr. Gleason presented her research on the palaces, gardens, and archaeology of banqueting in her lecture "Dining Al Fresco with Herod the Great." Members enjoyed the Beatrix Farrand Memorial Courtyard garden at the Oriental Institute during our gallery reception. Less than twenty-four hours later, the tomb of Herod was discovered in Israel, giving this lecture a most timely application.

This year we not only celebrated the great developments made in the field, in the lab, and in the research facilities of the Oriental Institute, we also had an occasion to celebrate two very important individuals and their personal and professional contributions to our one-of-a-kind institution.

In February 2007, Robert McCormick Adams was honored with a presentation of a festschrift, or felicitation volume, in his honor. Bob Adams is not only a past Director of the Oriental Institute and Provost of the University of Chicago, but is also viewed as one of the greatest American archaeologists, redefining our understanding about the development of urbanization in early Mesopotamia. Members, donors, friends, and family attended the gallery reception honoring Bob Adams.

On March 26, 2007, the staff, faculty, and researchers of the Oriental Institute came together to celebrate Raymond Tindel, long-time Museum Registrar, on the occasion of his retirement. A symposium was held in his honor and five scholars from the Oriental Institute and across the United States presented papers on the value of a "well-excavated museum collection." Ray's statements on the value of the Oriental Institute and it's museum collection, as well as Mark

Garrison's presentation from the symposium in Ray's honor, are featured in the Summer 2007 edition of *News & Notes*.

Travel

The year 2006/2007 was a popular year for travel, with three international Oriental Institute departures.

In September of 2006, Theo van den Hout led a group through the Lands of the Hittites, Lycians, and Carians. The group travel through Turkey was a successful exploration of Anatolia and proved to be one of our most popular and best-loved trips of the year.

In early 2007, Robert Ritner escorted a group of one dozen members through the Wonders of Ancient Egypt, visiting the famous sites of the Nile Valley and the Oriental Institute's historical research and archaeological excavations.

In June 2007, the Oriental Institute had scheduled a departure to Israel, escorted by graduating Ph.D. student and guest curator of the Oriental Institute Megiddo Gallery, Gabrielle Novacek. The program unfortunately had to be canceled.

We will be conducting trips to Israel and the surrounding areas in the future, most likely in 2008 or 2009. We are looking forward to creating itineraries that are more thematically focused so that travelers are able to fully engage in not only a country and its culture, but also a topic or focus of study they may reference throughout their journey.

Administration and Behind the Scenes

The Membership Office saw a lot of change in 2006/2007. I had the pleasure of transitioning from volunteer docent at the Oriental Institute to the Membership Coordinator at the end of January 2007. I am incredibly grateful to Maria Krasinski, the former Membership Coordinator, for her kindness, mentorship, and continuing help in learning the position and this wonderful place. Maria is responsible for so many of the year's advancements in membership, including the leaps and bounds made in the graphic imagery and design of membership materials, including the members' newsletter, *News & Notes*. I am sure you all join me in wishing Maria well as she embarks on a graduate degree in International Relations here at the University of Chicago.

The Membership Office also is pleased to announce the graduation of Ms. Tera Ellefson from the College at the University of Chicago. Tera graduates with honors in the Department of English Language and Literature and is on her way to great things in Boston, Massachusetts. She has been a vital part of this office for more than this fiscal year alone, and I am personally immensely appreciative of her patience and help in the office and at our many events.

I am also grateful for the help of Tanvi Solanki and Joseph Apodaca, who worked extensively in the Membership and Development offices respectively, before my arrival in the office. Both have stepped up and gone above and beyond the call of duty on multiple occasions, and have been indispensable to me in learning the membership system, as well as coordinating the development of this office and its services.

Publicity and Advertising

The Membership Office has continued to utilize postal correspondence to communicate its advertising — this has not been without frustration, however. We have filed multiple complaints with the local and regional Postmasters, with issues such as pre-addressed Oriental Institute envelopes returned as "address unknown," members' mail returned to us as "undeliverable" once we have

MEMBERSHIP

confirmed the address, and a postcard mailing that was sent first class but took over three weeks to deliver to local addresses, and to some, not at all. One must, however, find the humor, and frequently, sad irony, in each situation, as we face the federal system in what appears to be somewhat of a hopeless battle. Such a case is exemplified by the good humor of Don Whitcomb, curator of the Medieval Persian City of Rayy exhibit, when he failed to receive his postcard invitation to the May 14 Members' Preview of his own exhibit project. We are grateful that he attended anyway, and I am thrilled to report that this Members' Preview invitation postcard, mailed in the end of April, reached Professor Whitcomb's Chicago mailbox in the beginning of August.

In an attempt to circumvent postal communication as much as possible, over the past nine months, the Membership Office has developed, with the help and guidance of Eric Rogers and Emily Teeter, an html, image embedded e-mail template that greatly enhances the quality and image of the Oriental Institute event programming to members as well as the general public. Graphic e-mail, maintaining continuity with the imagery of the Web site, http://oi.uchicago.edu, has been used to publicize lectures, travel opportunities, and community building events at the Oriental Institute. Through use of the University of Chicago list-serves, we are able to advertise our events to not only Oriental Institute members, but also to the Humanities Department and other major staff and faculty interest groups across the University of Chicago, as well as external organizations with whom we have worked in cooperation.

The Membership Office has also established itself on the new Oriental Institute Web site, oi.uchicago.edu, where members and supporters can find out about events, membership opportunities, and travel programs. All members' events, including lectures, symposia, formal museum gallery events, and travel programs now have contact information and a presence on both the Oriental Institute calendar as well as the members' pages online. We are seeing a secondary benefit of a Web presence through the multitudes of people who are contacting us based off their Web searches for travel, lecture, or research topics. In the next fiscal year, we plan to further develop a membership sign-up site that automatically processes joining and renewing members into our system here at the Oriental Institute.

The Membership Office has also utilized media advertising to help cultivate new members and donors, increase public awareness of the Oriental Institute's museum and research programs, and the events through which the public can become involved in the ancient Near East. The Graham School for General Studies at the University of Chicago has kindly engaged in reciprocal advertising of our travel programs; Oriental Institute members and donors are notified about other travel opportunities through the Graham School that might be of interest to them, and reciprocally, the Graham School advertises the Oriental Institute's travel programs to over 50,000 names across the nation.

We have worked in conjunction with the Smart Museum to develop a reciprocal membership program which has come into effect through enrollment in the NARM program: Oriental Institute Associate Members (supporters who contribute $100 or more) receive reciprocal membership benefits at over 100 museums across the North American continent during their visits to those institutions. Meanwhile, members from other museums who enroll in the NARM program at their "home institutions" learn about the Oriental Institute and can receive our members' benefits during their visits here. Because the Smart and Oriental Institute museums are both enrolled in this program, we have effectively created a system of reciprocal membership between these two prominent cultural institutions of the University of Chicago. For more information about the NARM program, contact the Membership Office or visit http://www.greenvillemuseum.org/narm_mem.html.

Lastly, we have developed somewhat of a consistent media presence, both in the Chicago vicinity as well as in national publications. This is very much the fruit of the tireless efforts of Emily Teeter, whose publicity report is featured earlier in this volume, as well as our many wonderful researchers who continue to work on groundbreaking projects that speak to people from across our country and around the globe. The Membership Office has purchased advertisements for our new travel programs: Unseen Egypt, departing March 2008, and On the Path of the Umayyads: Syria and Spain, departing April 2008. By fall of 2007, we will have been featured in two issues of *Archaeology* magazine, with a targeted, global readership of over 600,000, both on paper and internet subscriptions. We will advertise one more time in winter of 2007, and then evaluate the results of this advertising campaign.

Furthermore, we purchased a set of six advertisements to be placed in the *Chicago Jewish News*, a popular weekly publication for the greater Chicagoland Jewish community, with a readership of over 40,000 households. We placed ads for the Dead Sea Scrolls domestic travel program, taking place in October 2007, and the editors of the publication featured us as a cover story in their mid-summer issue — a two-page spread on the work of Professor Norman Golb.

Many thanks are owed to Tom Urban and Leslie Schramer in the Oriental Institute Publications Office for their enduring patience, diligence, and kindness in helping me coordinate design and publication projects for members and supporters over the past nine months. With the recent increase in postage, we are exploring ways to consolidate information into more graphically appealing, high quality event notices that we hope members and donors will not only use to learn about our events, but also enjoy.

I owe a debt of gratitude to the entire Oriental Institute research and administrative staff for their warm welcome over these past six months. Special thanks go to Emily Teeter, Robert Ritner, Theo van den Hout, Norman Golb, and Clemens Reichel for their kindness and leadership for our travel program and other programming. A thank you to Geoff Emberling, Don Whitcomb, Erik Lindahl, and Adam Lubin for their patience and help with organizing museum events in our galleries for members and supporters this spring. A special thank you also to Carole Krucoff, Jessica Caracci, Wendy Ennes, and both Cathy Dueñas and Terry Friedman for their kindness and support of membership and our programming.

Finally, a very big thank you to Gil Stein, Steve Camp, Monica Witczak, and Carla Hosein for their warm welcome into the Oriental Institute administration and for their patience, support, and enthusiasm for the Membership Program and its future. Over the next year, members can look forward to increased members' benefits, a more concise schedule of members' programming, and the expansion of the benefits of membership to all donors and supporters of the Oriental Institute. Additionally, we will be working on new graphic advertising and announcements for our events, increased public and media outreach, and more opportunities for families to enjoy both programming and membership at the Oriental Institute. I look forward to a great year ahead.

DEVELOPMENT
Monica Witczak

Overview

For fiscal year 2006, the Oriental Institute raised $2,094,090 in non-federal private gifts and grants. Among the notable contributions received were a gift from Dr. and Mrs. Arthur Herbst in support of the annual Post-Doc Symposium, a grant from the Andrew W. Mellon Foundation for the Persepolis Fortification Archive, a grant from the Packard Humanities Institute to fund a salvage excavation in Sudan, and a gift from the Neubauer Family Foundation to support the Institute's newest excavation at the site of Zincirli in Turkey. Additionally, the following foundations and corporations provided support for our programs: The Amsted Corporation, The Joyce Foundation, LaSalle Bank, The Luther I. Replogle Foundation, National Geographic, the William Blair & Company LLC Foundation, and the Women's Board of the University of Chicago. We thank all our generous supporters who made this financial success possible.

The Research Endowment Campaign

One of the great strengths of the Oriental Institute is its ability to undertake large scale, long-term research projects focused on the major questions and issues in the study of ancient Near Eastern civilizations. These projects require significant financial resources and the need will only increase over time.

The Research Endowment Campaign, launched in the fall of 2006, is a five-year campaign to increase funding for the core research areas of the Oriental Institute providing a stable and predictable level of support for this work. To reach this goal, the Campaign will raise $3 million between 2006 and 2011 to boost our research endowments from their current level of $2.2 million to $5.2 million.

The Research Endowment Campaign targets five crucial areas that require long-term financial resources:

- **Ancient Languages**

This endowment will support the writing of dictionaries such as the Chicago Assyrian Dictionary, the Chicago Demotic Dictionary, and the Chicago Hittite Dictionary. It will also support text-based research in Egyptology, Assyriology, Iranian languages, ancient Hebrew, and Northwest Semitic studies by funding:
  1. Research travel costs
  2. Programming support
  3. Editing support

- **Archaeological Fieldwork**

This endowment will support current excavations in Egypt, Syria, and Turkey and provide resources for future fieldwork throughout the Middle East by funding:
  1. Field project start-up costs
  2. Building infrastructure and security to protect the excavation sites
  3. Student travel costs
  4. Laboratory work such as radiocarbon dating

DEVELOPMENT

- **Research Archives**

This endowment will support the Oriental Institute's research archives. Containing more than 45,000 volumes, it is the foremost library on the ancient Near East in the Western hemisphere. This endowment will fund:
1. The purchase of new collections;
2. The transition to digital holdings (in parallel to print holdings);
3. The construction of new stacks and other infrastructure to house collections and address growing space restrictions due to the natural growth of collections;
4. The completion of the online catalog to cover all acquisitions made prior to 1990.

- **Technology**

This endowment will support the technological needs of all areas of the Institute by funding:
1. Computers
2. Programming support
3. Satellite imagery
4. Remote sensing equipment

- **Museum Holdings and Special Collections**

The Oriental Institute's museum holds a position of extraordinary importance for researchers. Many of these collections form the primary or only stratigraphic record for key regions of the Fertile Crescent. The goal is to make these collections more accessible for study and publication by Institute scholars as well as scholars from other institutions. Museum exhibits are also a key part of the Oriental Institute's mission to communicate the results of its research to the public. We plan a regularized program of mounting two rotating special exhibits each year, to be displayed in the Marshall and Doris Holleb Family Special Exhibits Gallery. This endowment will fund:
1. Grants to researchers
2. Curatorial fees
3. Exhibit installation
4. Loan fees
5. Special exhibit development

Visiting Committee

The fall meeting of the Visiting Committee was held on December 13 in the Director's Office at the Oriental Institute. David Schloen, recently returned from the field, gave a presentation on his preliminary excavation at Zincirli, the Institute's newest archaeological dig in southeastern Turkey. Cocktails and dinner at the Quadrangle Club followed the meeting.

The spring Visiting Committee meeting was held on May 17 at the Fortnightly Club. Provost Tom Rosenbaum attended the meeting and addressed the committee members. The faculty presentation was given by Museum Director Geoff Emberling, who briefed the Committee on his recent salvage expedition of a Nubian site in Sudan, located near the fourth cataract of the Nile. An elegant dinner was served in the Club's ballroom following the meeting.

DEVELOPMENT

It is with sadness that I report the passing of three members of the Visiting Committee during the course of this academic year: Joan Armstrong, Marion Cowan, and William J. O. Roberts. Together, they contributed a total of twenty-eight years of service on the Visiting Committee. They will be greatly missed.

Romancing the Past, The Oriental Institute's 2006 Gala

Romancing the Past, the Oriental Institute's gala, was held on October 5, 2006, and raised over $100,000 to benefit the Research Endowment Campaign. For the first time in more than twenty years, the gala was held in the museum itself, affording guests the unique opportunity to dine among the reliefs which once lined the courtyard of Sargon II's palace, at the feet of a monumental statue of King Tutankhamun, or under the watchful gaze of the Persepolis bull. Guests of honor at Romancing the Past included all those for whom the newly installed galleries and renovated courtyard garden are named: Robert and Deborah Aliber, Mary Grimshaw, Cissy Haas, the Herbolsheimer Family, Marshall and Doris Holleb, Edgar and Deborah Jannotta, Rita and Kitty Picken, Lois Schwartz, the Norman Solhkhah Family, Nicole Williams and Larry Becker, and the Sharukin Yelda Family. Silent and live auction items included a life-size reproduction of the Rosetta Stone, a customized children's birthday party in the museum, a week-long stay at Chicago House in Luxor, Egypt, and a private dinner in the museum with Elizabeth Peters, author of the Amelia Peabody mystery series. Guests were also treated to a living history portrayal of the Institute's founder, James Henry Breasted, who spoke convincingly and with fondness of his memories of the Institute's early days. Professor Breasted also proved himself to be an able and entertaining auctioneer.

This wonderful event would not have been possible without the tireless dedication and creativity of the Special Events Committee:

Debby Halpern, Chair
Gretel Braidwood
Denise Browning
Andrea Dudek
Margaret Foorman
Janet Helman
Kitty Picken
Rita Picken
Mary Shea
Emily Teeter
Mari Terman

May your names live forever!

Waterfowl Management

Many of you may have noticed that the Institute entertained a number of long-term visitors this spring. They never set foot in the museum, did no research in the archives, and presented no lectures in Breasted Hall. These guests were drawn to the Oriental Institute for its luxe accommodations, including three swimming pools, daily housekeeping service, and predator-free environment — all of which are quite important if one is a duck in search of a secure place to nest and raise a family.

In mid-May, the alert went out — a mother duck and ten ducklings had taken up residence in the courtyard, newly replanted and restored to according to landscaper architect Beatrix Farrand's original design. The building's animal lovers (and a few amused accomplices) swung into ac-

DEVELOPMENT

tion — the above-mentioned wading pools were installed, complete with ramps for ease of access, and a daily feeding and cleaning schedule was put into place. A donation jar was set up to help support the care and feeding of the ducks. While many unknown donors contributed to this effort, the ducks and their caretakers especially wish to thank François Gaudard and Ruth O'Brien for their contributions.

Most of the ducklings have now left the courtyard in search of open water — as of this writing, three holdouts remain. We wish them a fond farewell and hope that when the nesting season comes around next year, they might consider the Peabody Hotel in Memphis, where a marble fountain and red carpet await them.

Many thanks to the Spring 2007 duckling nannies: Joey Apodaca, Rozenn Bailleul-LeSuer, Laura D'Alessandro, Monica Hudak, Tom James, Helen McDonald, Margaret Schröeder, Allison Whyte, and Monica Witczak. Special thanks to Andrew Furse and to Erik Lindahl, duck wrangler and net-maker extraordinaire.

HONOR ROLL OF DONORS AND MEMBERS

Director's Circle ($50,000 and Above)

Trust Estate of Alwin Clemens Carus, Dickinson, North Dakota
Dr. Marjorie M. Fisher, Bloomfield Hills, Michigan
Misty and Lewis Gruber, Chicago, Illinois
Dr. Arthur Herbst and Mrs. Lee Herbst, Chicago, Illinois
The Joyce Foundation, Chicago, Illinois
The Andrew W. Mellon Foundation, New York, New York
Mr. Joseph Neubauer and Ms. Jeanette Lerman-Neubauer, Philadelphia, Pennsylvania
Friends of the Oriental Institute
Packard Humanities Institute, Los Altos, California

Director's Circle ($25,000–$49,999)

Mr. Thomas C. Heagy and Mrs. Linda Hutton Heagy, Chicago, Illinois
LaSalle Bank, Chicago, Illinois
Mr. Robert Parrillo and Mrs. Elizabeth Parrillo, Chicago, Illinois
Mr. and Mrs. John W. Rowe, Chicago, Illinois
Trust Estate of Erica Reiner, Chicago, Illinois
Mr. and Mrs. O. J. Sopranos, Winnetka, Illinois
Mrs. Roderick Webster, Winnetka, Illinois
Ms. Nicole Suzann Williams and Mr. Lawrence J. Becker, Ph.D., Glencoe, Illinois

Director's Circle ($10,000–$24,999)

Mr. Alan R. Brodie, Chicago, Illinois
Eric and Andrea Colombel, New York, New York
Ms. Andrea Dudek, Orland Park, Illinois
Global Heritage Fund, Palo Alto, California
Mr. Richard and Mrs. Mary L. Gray, Chicago, Illinois
Mr. Howard E. Hallengren, New York, New York
Harvard University, Cambridge, Massachusetts
Mr. Neil King and Mrs. Diana Hunt King, Chicago, Illinois
Mrs. Elisabeth F. Lanzl, Chicago, Illinois
Leon Levy Foundation, New York, New York
Mr. David W. and Mrs. Jill Carlotta Maher, Chicago, Illinois
Mrs. Barbara G. Mertz, Frederick, Maryland
Mr. Roger R. Nelson and Mrs. Marjorie Nelson, Chicago, Illinois
The Rathmann Family Foundation, Arnold, Maryland
Mrs. William J. O. Roberts, Lake Forest, Illinois
Mr. Mark Rudkin, France
Mrs. Maurice Schwartz, Los Angeles, California
St. Lucas Charitable Foundation, Burr Ridge, Illinois
Dr. Francis H. Straus II and Mrs. Lorna Straus, Chicago, Illinois
Estate of Chester D. Tripp, Chicago, Illinois
Mrs. Barbara Breasted Whitesides, Newton, Massachusetts
The Women's Board of the University of Chicago

HONOR ROLL OF DONORS AND MEMBERS

Director's Circle ($5,000–$9,999)

The Assyrian National Council of Illinois, Inc., Chicago, Illinois
Dr. Vallo Benjamin, New York, New York
William Blair & Company LLC Foundation, Chicago, Illinois
Alwin Clemens Carus Mineral Trust, Dickinson, North Dakota
R. Crusoe & Son, Chicago, Illinois
Mr. and George L. Estes III, West Hartford, Connecticut
Far Horizons Archaeological & Cultural Trips, Inc., San Anselmo, California
Mrs. Margaret E. Foorman and Mr. James Foorman, Winnetka, Illinois
Dr. François Gaudard, Chicago, Illinois
Mr. Isak V. and Mrs. Nancy Hopkins Gerson, Chicago, Illinois
Mr. Howard G. Haas and Mrs. Carolyn Werbner Haas, Glencoe, Illinois
Mrs. Janet W. and Mr. Robert A. Helman, Chicago, Illinois
Mr. Edgar Jannotta and Mrs. Deborah Jannotta, Winnetka, Illinois
National Philanthropic Trust DAF, Jenkintown, Pennsylvania
Mrs. Beth Noujaim, Boca Grande, Florida
Mrs. Robert F. Picken, Chicago, Illinois
Luther I. Replogle Foundation, Washington, D.C.
Mr. Norman J. and Mrs. Alice E. Rubash, Evanston, Illinois
Mr. and Mrs. Robert G. Schloerb, Chicago, Illinois
Toni S. Smith, Chicago, Illinois
Dr. Norman Solhkhah, Lincolnwood, Illinois
The Jane and Stuart Watson Foundation, Inc., Boca Grande, Florida
World Monuments Fund, New York, New York

Director's Circle ($2,500–$4,999)

Professor and Mrs. Robert Z. Aliber, Hanover, New Hampshire
Mrs. James W. Alsdorf, Chicago, Illinois
Mr. Raymond Tindel and Ms. Gretel Braidwood, Chicago, Illinois
Dr. Mary Chuman and Dr. Charles Chuman, Chesterton, Indiana
Ms. Katharine P. Darrow, Brooklyn, New York
Dr. Sarmed G. Elias, Chicago, Illinois
Ms. Joan Fortune, St. Louis, Missouri
Mr. Byron Gregory, Wilmette, Illinois
Mr. Dietrich Gross and Mrs. Erika Gross, Wilmette, Illinois
Mr. Donald H. J. Hermann, Chicago, Illinois
Mr. and Mrs. Marshall M. Holleb, Chicago, Illinois
Mr. Jonathan Janott, Chicago, Illinois
Joukowsky Family Foundation, New York, New York
Mrs. Marjorie H. Buchanan Kiewit, Chestnut Hill, Massachusetts
Mr. Jack A. Koefoot, Evanston, Illinois
Mr. Richard Kron and Mrs. Deborah Bekken, Chicago, Illinois
Trust Estate of Susanne E. Larsh, Chicago, Illinois
Mr. Robert Levy and Mrs. Diane Levy, Chicago, Illinois
Mrs. Janina Marks, Chicago, Illinois
Museum Tours, Inc., Littleton, Colorado
Mr. Andrew Nourse, Woodside, California
Nuveen Benevolent Trust, Berkeley, California
Mr. William D. Petty, Littleton, Colorado
Mrs. Crennan M. and Mr. David K. Ray, Santa Fe, New Mexico
Dr. Miriam Reitz Baer, Chicago, Illinois
Mr. H. Warren and Mrs. Janet Siegel, San Juan Capistrano, California

HONOR ROLL OF DONORS AND MEMBERS

Director's Circle ($2,500–$4,999) (cont.)

Ms. Anna M. White, Terre Haute, Indiana
Ms. Flora Yelda, Chicago, Illinois
Mrs. Jeanette Yelda, Chicago, Illinois
Dr. and Mrs. Sharukin Yelda, Chicago, Illinois

Patrons ($1,000–$2,499)

Thomas G. Akers, Ph.D., and Dr. Ann B. Akers, New Orleans, Louisiana
Mr. Stanley N. Allan and Mrs. Mary S. Allan, Chicago, Illinois
Archaelogical Tours, New York, New York
Assyrian Academic Society, Skokie, Illinois
Mr. E. M. Bakwin, La Porte, Indiana
Mr. John J. Barbie, Chicago, Illinois
Ms. Margaret C. Brandt and Mr. Albert Wallace Lyons, Eminence, Kentucky
Mr. Jonathan Barry Brookner and Ms. Rita M. Joyce, Fairfield, Connecticut
Mr. Dennis A. Calvanese, Oak Brook, Illinois
Mr. Thomas J. and Mrs. Ann J. Charters, New York, New York
The Chicago Community Foundation, Chicago, Illinois
Mr. Charles Custer and Mrs. Irene Custer, Chicago, Illinois
Mr. Joseph M. and Mrs. Helen R. Diamond, Hazel Crest, Illinois
Dr. Erl Dordal, Atlanta, Georgia
Ms. Aimee Leigh Drolet, Los Angeles, California
Estate of John J. Armstrong, Jr., Chicago, Illinois
ExxonMobil Foundation, Princeton, New Jersey
Ms. Linda Gail Feinstone, New York, New York
Mr. Robert and Mrs. Joan Feitler, Chicago, Illinois
Ms. Emily Huggins Fine, San Francisco, California
Mrs. John W. Fritz II, Kenilworth, Illinois
Mrs. Dorothy V. and Dr. Tawfik F. Girgis, Burr Ridge, Illinois
Mrs. Margaret Grant and Mr. Robert Grant, Chicago, Illinois
Mrs. Joseph N. Grimshaw, Wilmette, Illinois
Mr. I. A. Grodzins and Mrs. Diana Grodzins, Chicago, Illinois
Dr. Benjamin Gruber and Dr. Petra Maria Blix, Chicago, Illinois
Ms. Louise Grunwald, New York, New York
Mrs. Deborah G. and Mr. Philip Halpern, Chicago, Illinois
Mr. William Harms and Mrs. Myra Harms, Grayslake, Illinois
Mr. David P. Harris and Mrs. Judith A. Harris, Lake Forest, Illinois
Dr. Rex Charles Haydon and Ms. Maria Cecilia Lozada, Chicago, Illinois
Mr. Roger H. and Mrs. Jane B. Hildebrand, Chicago, Illinois
Mr. Roger David Isaacs and Mrs. Joyce R. Isaacs, Glencoe, Illinois
Mr. William R. and Mrs. Janet Jentes, Chicago, Illinois
Dr. Donald Whitcomb and Dr. Janet H. Johnson, Chicago, Illinois
Mr. Jack Josephson and Ms. Magda Saleh, New York, New York
Mr. Michael L. Keiser and Mrs. Rosalind C. Keiser, Chicago, Illinois
Mr. Marvin Leibowitz and Ms. Isabel Leibowitz, Aventura, Florida
Mr. Julius Lewis, Chicago, Illinois
Mr. James Lichtenstein, Chicago, Illinois
Dr. John M. and Mrs. Amy Livingood, Bethesda, Maryland
Mr. and Mrs. Barry L. MacLean, Mettawa, Illinois
Mayer, Brown, Rowe & Maw LLP, Chicago, Illinois
Mr. and Mrs. John McCarter, Northfield, Illinois
Merrill Lynch and Co. Foundation, Inc., Princeton, New Jersey

HONOR ROLL OF DONORS AND MEMBERS

Patrons ($1,000–$2,499) (cont.)

Mr. Martin and Mrs. Jany Mirza, Wheeling, Illinois
Ms. Vivian B. Morales, St. Paul, Minnesota
Mr. Phil C. and Mrs. Linda Thoren Neal, Chicago, Illinois
New York Times Company Foundation, Princeton, New Jersey
Mr. Donald Oster, United Kingdom
Miss Kathleen Picken, Chicago, Illinois
Miss M. Kate Pitcairn, Kempton, Pennsylvania
Mr. Harvey B. Plotnick, Chicago, Illinois
Mr. Don Michael Randel and Mrs. Carol E. Randel, New York, New York
Dr. Randi Rubovits-Seitz, Washington, D.C.
Harold and Deloris Sanders, Chicago, Illinois
Mrs. Lawrence J. Scheff, Chicago, Illinois
Schnitzer Family Foundation, Chicago, Illinois
Mr. Thomas and Mrs. Barbara Schnitzer, Chicago, Illinois
The Schwab Fund for Charitable Giving, San Francisco, California
Mr. Charles N. Secchia, Grand Rapids, Michigan
Mr. Peter Secchia, Grand Rapids, Michigan
Mr. and Mrs. Charles M. Shea, Wilmette, Illinois
The Honorable George P. Shultz, Stanford, California
Mr. Matthew Sideman, Chicago, Illinois
Ms. Lowri Sprung, San Pedro, California
Mr. Joseph Daniel Cain and Ms. Emily Teeter, Chicago, Illinois
Dr. and Mrs. David Terman, Wilmette, Illinois
Mr. Ed Thayer and Mrs. Sandi Thayer, Illinois
Mrs. Barbara A. and Mr. Randolph Frank Thomas, Chicago, Illinois
Mrs. Rose and Mr. Robert Wagner, Chicago, Illinois
Mr. Kenneth C. Williams and Ms. Theresa S. Williams, Houston, Texas
Mr. Robert I. Wilson, Peoria, Illinois
Lucia Woods Lindley and Daniel A. Lindley, Jr., Evanston, Illinois
Mr. Robert R. Yohanan and Ms. Joan Yohanan, Kenilworth, Illinois

Sponsoring Associate Supporters ($500–$999)

Joseph C. and Kathleen A. Anderson, M.D., Torrance, California
Mrs. Julie Antelman, Chicago, Illinois
Mrs. Joan Barghusen and Dr. Herbert Barghusen, Portage, Indiana
Mr. John Batchelor and Ms. Suzanne Bell, Fernandina Beach, Florida
Mr. James N. Bay and Mrs. James N. Bay, Chicago, Illinois
Mr. Mark Bergner and Mrs. Nancy Bergner, Chicago, Illinois
Ms. Julia A. Beringer, Lawn Springs, Illinois
Mr. Charles E. Bidwell and Mrs. Helen Lewis Bidwell, Chicago, Illinois
Dr. Sidney J. and Ms. LaMoyne C. Blair, Oak Park, Illinois
Ms. Marion Cowan, Illinois
Mr. David L. Crabb and Mrs. Dorothy Mixter Crabb, Chicago, Illinois
Anthony T. and Lawrie C. Dean, Illinois
Mrs. Bettie Dwinell, Chicago, Illinois
Ms. Ann Esse, Sioux Falls, South Dakota
Mrs. Ann B. Fallon, Tucson, Arizona
Mr. Wolfgang Frye, Phoenix, Arizona
Mr. James J. and Mrs. Louise Glasser, Lake Forest, Illinois
Mr. M. Hill Hammock and Mrs. Cheryl W. Hammock, Chicago, Illinois

HONOR ROLL OF DONORS AND MEMBERS

Sponsoring Associate Supporters ($500–$999) (cont.)

Mr. Robert Haselkorn and Mrs. Margot Haselkorn, Chicago, Illinois
Mr. John P. and Ms. Jan Isaacs Henry, Colorado Springs, Colorado
Mr. Scott E. Hertenstein, Cary, North Carolina
Mr. Peter G. and Ms. Gwen Jones, Chicago, Illinois
Mr. John H. Kelly, Conyers, Georgia
Mr. Dee Morgan Kilpatrick, Chicago, Illinois
Mr. H. David Kirby and Mrs. Faye Taylor Kirby, West Linn, Oregon
Mr. Joseph T. Lach, Evanston, Illinois
Mr. Martin S. Lazor, Butler, Pennsylvania
Mr. Michael D. and Mrs. Kristina Lockhart, Lancaster, Pennsylvania
Mr. Frank D. and Mrs. Linda M. Mayer Jr., Glencoe, Illinois
McGraw-Hill Companies, Inc., Princeton, New Jersey
Mrs. Jean S. Meltzer, Chicago, Illinois
Ms. Holly J. Mulvey, Evanston, Illinois
Ms. Mary Jane Myers, Los Angeles, California
Mr. Michael Nabholz and Ms. Pamela Martin, San Diego, California
Mr. Charles R. Nelson, Seattle, Washington
Northrup Grumman Foundation, Los Angeles, California
Mr. John K. Notz, Jr. and Mrs. Janis W. Notz, Chicago, Illinois
Mr. James Ringenoldus and Ms. Maxine Cohen, Arlington Heights, Illinois
Mr. Daniel B. Ritter, Seattle, Washington
Mr. F. Garland Russell, Jr. and Mrs. Peggy Lee Cowie Russell, Columbia, Missouri
Mr. M. Moin Sadeq, Chicago, Illinois
Mr. John Eric Schaal, Burr Ridge, Illinois
Mr. Howard J. Schulz II, Davison, Michigan
Mr. Todd D. H. Schwebel and Mr. Thomas C. Driscoll III, Chicago, Illinois
Dr. Coleman R. Seskind, Chicago, Illinois
Seven Wonders Travel, La Salle, Illinois
Mrs. Miriam and Mr. Henry Shapiro, Culver City, California
Mr. Clyde Curry Smith, Ph.D. and Mrs. Ellen Marie Smith, River Falls, Wisconsin
Ms. Dorothy J. Speidel, Wilmette, Illinois
Mr. Gil Stein and Ms. Elise Levin, Evanston, Illinois
Mr. George R. Sundell, Wheaton, Illinois
Ms. Ann S. and Mr. Anthony Syrett, APO, Military - A.E.
Mr. Thomas G. and Mrs. Mary C. Urban, Chicago, Illinois
Vanguard Charitable Endowment Program, Southeastern, Pennsylvania
Ms. Connie Vari, Williamsville, New York
Mr. Marcus Wedner and Mrs. Anne Louise Wedner, Winnetka, Illinois
Mr. Douglas R. and Mrs. Jill A. White, Taneytown, Maryland
Mr. Charles Mack Wills Jr., East Palatka, Florida
Dr. Wendall W. Wilson, Victoria, Texas
Ms. Sinclair Winton, Winnetka, Illinois
Woodland Travel, Woodland, California
Ms. Carole Y. Yoshida, Orland Park, Illinois

Contributing Associate Supporters ($250–$499)

The Honorable James Akins and Mrs. Marjorie Akins
Mrs. Lee W. Alberts, Chicago, Illinois
Dr. J. Marshall and Mrs. Alison Igo Ash, Winnetka, Illinois
Mr. Gordon Atkins, Eau Claire, Michigan
Mr. Roger Atkinson and Ms. Janet Arey, Riverside, California

HONOR ROLL OF DONORS AND MEMBERS

Contributing Associate Supporters ($250–$499) (cont.)

Mr. and Mrs. Ronald R. Baade, Winnetka, Illinois
Miss Janice V. Bacchi, Encinitas, California
Mrs. Guity Nashat Becker, Chicago, Illinois
Benjamin Foundation, Inc., Chicago, Illinois
Mr. Geogre W. Benson and Ms. Ellen C. Benson, Chicago, Illinois
Ms. Lynn M. Bishop, Tustin, California
Mr. Robert Bordeman and Mrs. Cathy Bordeman, Hinsdale, Illinois
Mr. James T. Bradbury III and Mrs. Mary Louise B, Knoxville, Tennessee
Ms. Janice Brannon, La Salle, Illinois
Mr. Charles N. Callahan and Mrs. Naila Britain, Chicago, Illinois
Mr. John A. Bross, Chicago, Illinois
Mr. Cameron and Mrs. Jean McGrew Brown, Lake Forest, Illinois
Mr. Bruce P. Burbage, Nokomis, Florida
Mr. Jay Carson, El Cajon, California
Mr. Bruce Chelberg and Mrs. Joyce Chelberg, Arlington Heights, Illinois
Mr. Richard L. Cook and Ms. Sally W. Cook, Sherman Oaks, California
Dr. Thomas Field Cope, Denver, Colorado
Mr. Robert D. Corey, Brockton, Massachusetts
Barbara E. Corkey, Boston, Massachusetts
Mr. Charles Custer and Mrs. Irene Custer, Chicago, Illinois
Ms. Barbara Wilson D'Andrea, Wainscott, New York
Mr. Nirmal Dhesi and Mrs. Gwendolyn Dhesi, Santa Rosa, California
Ms. Lisa and Mr. Lynn R. Dyrdahl, Kent, Washington
Ms. Delores Eckrich and Mr. Richard Eckrich, Denver, Colorado
Ms. Karen Evans, Batavia, Illinois
Fair Isaac Corporation, San Rafael, California
Ms. Jean Fincher, Chicago, Illinois
Mrs. Eleanor B. Frew, Flossmoor, Illinois
Dr. Gary S. Garofalo, Palos Hills, Illinois
Mr. Dario Giacomoni and Mrs. Mary Giacomoni, Chicago, Illinois
Ms. Ruth Goldman, Wilmette, Illinois
Mr. Eugene Goldwasser and Ms. Deone Griffith Jac, Chicago, Illinois
Ms. Louise Ahrndt Golland, Chicago, Illinois
Ms. Marcia E. Goodman and Mr. Hiroyoshi Noto, Chicago, Illinois
Mr. Howard A. and Mrs. Barbara L. Gradet, Reisterstown, Maryland
Ms. Leigh Grant and Mr. Tony Doumlele, Norwalk, Connecticut
Mr. David Gratner and Mrs. Marsha Gratner, Sulpher Springs, Indiana
Mr. Donald M. Green and Dr. Joni Grant Green, Coral Gables, Florida
Mr. Francis P. Green, Bloomington, Illinois
Ms. Jane Davis Haight, Napa, California
Mr. and Mrs. Richard Harwood, Colorado Springs, Colorado
C. Luckey Heath, Ogden, Utah
Ms. Laura N. Heller, Englewood, Colorado
Mrs. Joan L. Hoatson, Burr Ridge, Illinois
Mrs. Gail T. and Mr. Thomas H. Hodges, Evanston, Illinois
Ms. Debbie Holm, Chicago, Illinois
Rev. Elizabeth Hopp-Peters and Mr. Kurt Peters, Evanston, Illinois
Mr. Paul Houdek and Ms. Linda Houdek, Berwyn, Illinois
Mr. George T. Jacobi and Mrs. Angela C. Jacobi, Milwaukee, Wisconsin
Mrs. Sandra Jacobsohn, Chicago, Illinois
Dr. Joseph Jarabak and Dr. Rebecca Jarabak, Hinsdale, Illinois
Mr. Thomas Jedele and Dr. Nancy J. Skon Jedele, Laurel, Maryland
Mr. Richard Jones, Wilmette, Illinois

HONOR ROLL OF DONORS AND MEMBERS

Contributing Associate Supporters ($250–$499) (cont.)

Mrs. Joyce J. and Mr. John A. Kelly, Winnetka, Illinois
Peter S. and Beth Berson Kolevzon, Bronx, New York
Mr. Martin Kozak and Mrs. Susan Kozak, Wilmette, Illinois
Ms. Abigail Krystall, Kenya
Mr. Peter Lacovara, Atlanta, Georgia
Mr. John P. and Mrs. Sarah V. Lafare, Newport Beach, California
Mr. William J. and Mrs. Blair S. Lawlor III, Kenilworth, Illinois
Mr. Richard Lee, Holland, Pennsylvania
Mr. Douglas and Mrs. Marilyn Liddicoat, Watsonville, California
Mr. Paul Linsay and Ms. Roni Lipton, Newton, Massachusetts
Ms. Johanna W. and Mr. Jo Desha Lucas, Chicago, Illinois
Mr. Arthur and Mrs. Jane S. Mason, Washington, D.C.
McCollum & Bunch, Fresno, California
Mr. Timothy D. McCollum, Fresno, California
Mr. Gene Miller, Madison, Wisconsin
The Honorable Martha A. Mills, Chicago, Illinois
Mr. Jeffrey E. Miripol and Mrs. Patricia A. Miripol, Hockessin, Delaware
Mr. Richard Morrow, Glenview, Illinois
Elizabeth Mueller, Chicago, Illinois
Mr. Douglas G. and Mrs. Isobel M. Murray, Santa Barbara, California
Mr. Walter A. and Dawn Clark Netsch, Jr., Chicago, Illinois
Mr. John P. Nielsen, Lombard, Illinois
Nuveen Investments, Inc., Chicago, Illinois
Mr. David Paldan and Mrs. Karen Paldan, Scottsdale, Arizona
Mr. Larry Paragano, Basking Ridge, New Jersey
Valentin Parks, Jr., Austin, Texas
Mrs. Denise G. Paul, Chicago, Illinois
Mr. Gaetano Fernando Perego, Chicago, Illinois
Mrs. Elizabeth M. Postell, Chicago, Illinois
R. B. Industries, Inc., Niles, Illinois
Mr. Gary W. Rexford and Mrs. Lillian K. Rexford, Topeka, Kansas
Dr. Barry H. Rich and Dr. Nancy E. Rich, Richland Center, Wisconsin
Francesa Rochberg, Morena Valley, California
Dr. Bonnie Sampsell, Chapel Hill, North Carolina
Christine Scardina-Gazzo, Pittsburgh, Pennsylvania
Mr. Timothy J. Schilling, Hammond, Indiana
Mr. Vincent F. Seyfried, Franklin Square, New York
Mrs. Deborah Shefner, Chicago, Illinois
Ms. Mary Ellen Sheridan, Chicago, Illinois
Mr. George N. Sherman, San Diego, California
Dr. Henry D. Slosser, Pasadena, California
Mr. Allen R. Smart, Chicago, Illinois
Mr. Harold and Mrs. Linda Stringer, Garland, Texas
Ted Studios, Inc., Chicago, Illinois
Mr. Frederick Teeter and Mrs. Shirley Teeter, Ransomville, New York
Mr. James Tomes and Mrs. Josie Tomes, Chicago, Illinois
Dr. Nohad Toulan and Mrs. Dirce Toulan, Portland, Oregon
Mr. and Mrs. Theo van den Hout, Chicago, Illinois
Mrs. Norma Van der Meulen, Chicago, Illinois
Mr. Karl H. Velde, Jr., Lake Forest, Illinois
Mr. Jonathan R. Warner, Pelham, New York
Mr. Thomas J. White and Ms. Leslie Scalapino, Oakland, California
Professor Irene Winter, Cambridge, Massachusetts

HONOR ROLL OF DONORS AND MEMBERS

Contributing Associate Supporters ($250–$499) (cont.)
Ms. Patricia Woodburn, Chicago, Illinois
Ms. Debra F. Yates and Ms. Carolyn Yates, Chicago, Illinois

Associate Supporters ($100–$249)
3M Company, St. Paul, Minnesota
Mr. D. M. Abadi and Ms. Mary C. Abadi, Iowa City, Iowa
Mr. Daniel L. Ables and Mrs. Susan M. Ables, Scottsdale, Arizona
Dr. Charles Martin Adelman, Cedar Falls, Iowa
Mr. Nick Ahrens and Mr. C. J. Ahrens, Chicago, Illinois
Ms. Judith Akers, Wilmette, Illinois
Mrs. Karen B. Alexander, Geneva, Illinois
Mr. James P. and Mrs. Susan J. Allen, Providence, Rhode Island
Mrs. Geraldine Smithwick Alvarez, Burr Ridge, Illinois
American Archaeology Group LLC, Lampasas, Texas
American Electric Power Company, Inc., Canton, Ohio
Mr. Edward Anders and Mrs. Joan Anders, Burlingame, California
Mrs. Carolyn S. Anderson, Lincoln, Nebraska
Mr. Richard J. Anderson, Chicago, Illinois
Dr. Thomas Andrews, Hinsdale, Illinois
Mr. Evan Appelman and Mrs. Mary Appelman, Kensington, California
Mr. James Armstrong and Ms. Beverly Armstrong, Cambridge, Massachusetts
Mr. Richard E. and Mrs. Melinda C. Averbeck, Deerfield, Illinois
Ayco Charitable Foundation, Clifton Park, New York
Mrs. Doris J. Ayers, Chicago, Illinois
Dr. and Mrs. Robert M. Ball, Amarillo, Texas
Marjorie C. Barnett, M.D., Chicago, Illinois
Mr. Paul Barron and Ms. Mary Anton, Chicago, Illinois
Mr. Kevin Rock and Ms. Cynthia Bates, Evanston, Illinois
Mr. Frederick Bates and Dr. Ellen Benjamin, Illinois
Ms. Margaret Bates, Sarasota, Florida
Mr. James Baughman and Mrs. Deborah Morris Baughman, Chicago, Illinois
Mrs. Robert Baumgarten, Winnetka, Illinois
Dr. David Bawden and Ms. Jan E. Bawden, Northfield, Illinois
Mr. John M. Beal, Chicago, Illinois
Dr. Kathleen Beavis Mr. Bruce Beavis, Chicago, Illinois
Ms. Jane E. Belcher, Chicago, Illinois
Bell Jones & Quinlisk, Chicago, Illinois
Mrs. John F. Benjamin, Chicago, Illinois
Mr. John F. Benjamin and Mrs. Esther R. Benjamin, Chicago, Illinois
Ms. Catherine Bennett, Des Moines, Iowa
Clive Davies and Phoebe Bennett, Arlington, Virginia
Mr. and Mrs. Thomas Bennett, New York, New York
Mr. Keki R. Bhote and Mrs. Mehroo K. Bhote, Glencoe, Illinois
Mr. Howard Birnberg and Mrs. Diane Birnberg, Chicago, Illinois
Mr. F. Gordon Bitter, Chicago, Illinois
Mr. Edward McCormick Blair, Lake Bluff, Illinois
Mr. Edward C. Blau, Alexandria, Virginia
Dr. Harriet Blitzer, Buffalo, New York
Mrs. George V. Bobrinskoy, Jr., Chicago, Illinois
Paul J. Bollheimer, Chicago, Illinois
Mr. Norman M. Bradburn and Ms. Wendy McAneny Bradburn, Arlington, Virginia

HONOR ROLL OF DONORS AND MEMBERS

Associate Supporters ($100–$249) (cont.)

Mr. Michael and Mrs. Julie Bradle, Lampasas, Texas
Addison and Catherine Braendel, Chicago, Illinois
Mr. O. John Brahos, Wilmette, Illinois
Mr. James A. Brandt and Mrs. Nancy H. Brandt, Chicago, Illinois
Mrs. Jerald C. Brauer, Chicago, Illinois
Ms. Catherine Novotny Brehm, Chicago, Illinois
Ms. Meta Brown, Chicago, Illinois
Mr. Stephen Hayze Brown, Junior, Chicago, Illinois
Mr. Willard W. Brown Jr., Bucksport, Maine
Ms. Myllicent Buchanan, Chicago, Illinois
Mr. James Nicholson and Ms. Patricia L. Callis, Pickerington, Ohio
Miss Anne Carlisle Campbell, Chicago, Illinois
Mr. and Mrs. Blouke Carus, Peru, Illinois
Mr. Thomas Cassidy, Littleton, Colorado
Claire Chamberlain, Houston, Texas
Dr. Allan G. Charles and Mrs. Phyllis V. Charles, Chicago, Illinois
Ms. Elsa Charlston, Chicago, Illinois
Miss Mary E. Chase, Olympia Fields, Illinois
Chicago Children's Museum, Chicago, Illinois
Mr. William A. Claire, Washington, D.C.
Mr. Steven Anthony Clark, Oak Lawn, Illinois
CNA Foundation, Chicago, Illinois
Mr. Brian L. Cochran, Tucson, Arizona
Mrs. Lydia G. Cochrane, Chicago, Illinois
Mrs. Zdzislawa Coleman, Chicago, Illinois
Ms. Cynthia Green Colin, New York, New York
Mr. Dennis Collins and Mrs. Julia Collins, Downers Grove, Illinois
Mr. James Comiskey, Chicago, Illinois
Community Unit School District No. 220, Barrington, Illinois
Ms. Johna S. Compton, Chancellor, Alabama
Mr. Courtney B. Conte, Santa Monica, California
Dr. Jerrold Stephen Cooper, Berkeley, California
Mr. William Cottle and Mrs. Judith Cottle, Winnetka, Illinois
Mr. Philip Couture and Mrs. Rebecca Couture, Lakeside, California
Mr. Albert Crewe and Mrs. Doreen Crewe, Dune Acres, Indiana
Dr. Eugene D. Cruz-Uribe and Dr. Kathryn Cruz-Uribe, Marina, California
Ms. Helen M. Cunningham, Arlington Heights, Illinois
Mrs. Barbara Flynn and Mr. David P. Currie, Chicago, Illinois
Ms. Deborah Davis, Chicago, Illinois
Mr. Richard A. Davis and Mrs. Sheila H. Davis, Evanston, Illinois
Mr. Mark Dawson and Mrs. Susan Dawson, Chicago, Illinois
Mr. Walter E. De Lise, Indian Head Park, Illinois
Mr. Robert O. Delaney and Mrs. Quinn E. Delaney, Winnetka, Illinois
Mr. Glen Wilson and Ms. Patricia Dihel, Grayslake, Illinois
Ms. Mary Dimperio, Washington, D.C.
Mr. Henry S. Dixon and Ms. Linda Giesen, Dixon, Illinois
Ms. Yvonne C. Donahue, Portola Valley, California
Dr. Patty L. Dunkel, Chicago, Illinois
Mrs. Rose B. Dyrud, Chicago, Illinois
Dr. Robert H. Dyson Jr., Essex, New York
Ms. Eaves and Mr. Boebel, Chicago, Illinois
Mrs. Cynthia Echols, Chicago, Illinois
Ms. Deborah J. Eddy, Chicago, Illinois

HONOR ROLL OF DONORS AND MEMBERS

Associate Supporters ($100–$249) (cont.)

Ms. Margaret Hart Edwards and Mr. William Thomas Espey, Lafayette, California
Mr. C. David Eeles, Columbus, Ohio
Mr. Lawrence R. Eicher and Mrs. Vicky C. Eicher, Charlottesville, Virginia
Mr. Philip Elenko, New York, New York
Endodontics Limited, Chicago, Illinois
Mr. S. Cody Engle, Chicago, Illinois
The Sidney Epstein and Sondra Berman Epstein Fdn., Chicago, Illinois
Mr. and Mrs. Richard Evans, Chicago, Illinois
Mr. Robert B. Faber, Bulgaria
Hazel S. Fackler, Chicago, Illinois
Mr. Eugene F. Fama and Mrs. Sallyann Dimeco Fama, Chicago, Illinois
Dr. Martin J. Fee and Dr. Janis D. Fee, North Tustin, California
Ms. Mary G. Finn, Chicago, Illinois
Mrs. Lois Finney, Winnetka, Illinois
Gerrit D. Fitch, San Francisco, California
Dr. Michael Flom, Boynton Beach, Florida
Mr. Richard E. Ford, Wabash, Indiana
Mrs. Adrian Foster, Chicago, Illinois
Mr. John L. Foster and Ms. Gloria W. Foster, Evanston, Illinois
Leila M. Foster, J.D., Ph.D., Evanston, Illinois
Dr. Samuel Ethan Fox and Mrs. Beverly F. Fox, Chicago, Illinois
Janet Franklin, Alameda, California
Mr. Paul E. Freehling and Ms. Susan S. Freehling, Chicago, Illinois
Mr. Kere Frey, Chicago, Illinois
Mrs. Barbara Heller Friedell and Dr. Peter Friedell, Chicago, Illinois
Mr. Charles Barry Friedman and Mrs. Terry Friedman, Chicago, Illinois
Ms. Deborah Gordon Friedrich, Chicago, Illinois
Sylvia and Jim Furner, Chicago, Illinois
Mr. Gregory Gajda, Mount Prospect, Illinois
Dr. Thomas Gajewski and Dr. Maria-Luisa Alegre, Chicago, Illinois
Prof. McGuire Gibson, Chicago, Illinois
Mr. Lyle Gillman, Bloomingdale, Illinois
Rev. Raymond Goehring, Lansing, Michigan
Mr. William H. Gofen and Mrs. Ethel Gofen, Chicago, Illinois
Mr. Marvin J. Goldblatt and Dr. Phyllis K. Goldblatt, Evanston, Illinois
Mrs. Betty Goldiamond, Chicago, Illinois
Mrs. Ethel Frank Goldsmith, Chicago, Illinois
Mr. Morris Goodman, Evanston, Illinois
Ms. Ingrid E. Gould and Dr. Robert Hsiung, Chicago, Illinois
Mr. Frederick Graboske and Mrs. Patricia Graboske, Rockville, Maryland
The Professors Gene and Michele Gragg, Chicago, Illinois
Mr. Charles W. Graham, Camden, Maine
Mr. Kenneth Granath and Mrs. Doris Granath, St. John, Indiana
Mr. Phillip and Ms. Sharon Green, Portage, Michigan
Mr. Ray H. Greenblatt, Winnetka, Illinois
Dr. Joseph Greene and Mrs. Eileen Caves, Belmont, Massachusetts
Ms. Ann Marie Gromme, Edina, Minnesota
Mr. Edmund P. Grondine, Jr., Kempton, Illinois
Mrs. Paul W. Guenzel, Winnetka, Illinois
Dr. Richard J. Guillory and Dr. Stella J. Guillory, Washougal, Washington
Mrs. Hans G. Guterbock, Chicago, Illinois
Mr. Ronald B. Guttman, Washington, D.C.
Mr. Richard Haines and Mrs. Susan Haines, Atlanta, Georgia

HONOR ROLL OF DONORS AND MEMBERS

Associate Supporters ($100–$249) (cont.)

Ms. Pamela N. Halfman, Ballinger, Texas
Ms. Ellen R. Hall and Ms. Betty Ann Cronin, West Allis, Wisconsin
Mrs. Mary and Dr. George Hallenbeck, Burr Ridge, Illinois
Mrs. Lynda and Mr. Mark Hamilton, Barbados
Mr. Joel L. Handelman and Ms. Sarah R. Wolff, Chicago, Illinois
Dr. Lowell Kent Handy, Des Plaines, Illinois
Commissioner Carl R. Hansen, Mount Prospect, Illinois
Ms. Ednalyn Hansen, Chicago, Illinois
Mrs. Beth Alison and Mr. Duncan Harris, Chicago, Illinois
Mr. Richard Harter and Mrs. Mary Harter, Chicago, Illinois
Mr. James B. Hartle, Santa Barbara, California
Ms. Caroline Haskell Simpson, Geneva, Illinois
Mr. Edward Day Hatcher and Ms. Valerie Hoffman Hatcher, Morris, Illinois
Ms. Alice J. Hayes, Illinois
Ms. Brittany Haynes, Deerfield, Illinois
Mrs. Jacqueline A. Haynes, Deerfield, Illinois
Mr. Matthew Hedman, Ithaca, New York
Dr. H. Lawrence Helfer and Ms. Joanne S. Helfer, Pittsford, New York
Thomas E. Hemminger, Peotone, Illinois
Mr. John A. Herschkorn, Jr. and Mrs. Gloria Herschkorn, San Jose, California
Dr. David C. and Mrs. Betty S. Hess, Downers Grove, Illinois
Ms. Hedda Hess, Chicago, Illinois
Mr. David C. Hilliard and Mrs. Celia Hilliard, Chicago, Illinois
Prince Abbas Hilmi, Egypt
Mrs. Harold Hines, Winnetka, Illinois
Ms. Christy Hoberecht, Santa Fe, New Mexico
Mr. William A. Hoffman, Chicago, Illinois
Mr. and Mrs. Marshall Hoke, Elkins, New Hampshire
Ms. Jayne Honeck, Streamwood, Illinois
Mr. Wayne Hoppe, Chicago, Illinois
John E. Horn, Attorney at Law, Tinley Park, Illinois
Mr. John Horn and Ms. Elizabeth Kelley, Oak Forest, Illinois
Mrs. Leonard J. Horwich, Chicago, Illinois
Mr. and Mrs. Lawrence Howe, Winnetka, Illinois
Mr. Richard Huff, Oak Park, Illinois
Mr. Herbert B. Huffmon, Madison, New Jersey
Dr. Kevin Hughes, Boston, Massachusetts
Mr. Arthur T. and Ms. Susan L. Hurley, Napa, California
Dr. Henry S. Inouye and Mrs. Tomi Inouye, Chicago, Illinois
J.P. Morgan Chase Foundation, Princeton, New Jersey
Ms. Lise K. Jacobson, Evanston, Illinois
Mr. Richard D. Jaffe and Mrs. Evelyn D. Jaffe, Chicago, Illinois
Kineret Jaffe, Chicago, Illinois
Dr. William R. Jeffery, Dickerson, Maryland
Johnson Controls Foundation, Milwaukee, Wisconsin
Mr. Kenneth P. Jones, Chicago, Illinois
Ms. Pamela Jordan, Chicago, Illinois
JS Charitable Trust, Chicago, Illinois
Mr. Michael Kadinsky-Cade and Ms. Ann Kadinsky-Cade, Chicago, Illinois
Ms. Loretta Kahn, Evanston, Illinois
Mr. John Kaminski and Ms. Maria Duran, Chicago, Illinois
Dr. Michael Kaplan and Dr. Maureen Kaplan, Lexington, Massachusetts
Mr. Stephen Katz, Chicago, Illinois

HONOR ROLL OF DONORS AND MEMBERS

Associate Supporters ($100–$249) (cont.)

Ms. Toyoko Kawase, Japan
Mrs. Constance T. and Mr. Dennis J. Keller, Oak Brook, Illinois
Mr. Don Kelm, Port Angeles, Washington
Professor Anne Draffkorn Kilmer, Tucson, Arizona
Ms. Henriette Klawans, Chicago, Illinois
Mr. William J. Knight and Mrs. Julia F. Knight, South Bend, Indiana
Mr. Michael E. Koen, Chicago, Illinois
Mr. Henry H. and Mrs. Annie A. Kohl, Media, Pennsylvania
Roger and Karen Konwal, Elmhurst, Illinois
Mr. Martin Krasnitz and Ms. Betsy Levin, Chicago, Illinois
Mr. Bernard L. Krawczyk, Chicago, Illinois
Mr. Ernest A. Krumbein, Munster, Indiana
Ms. Lottie J. Krzywda, Chicago, Illinois
Mr. Nikolai M. Kushner, Chicago, Illinois
Jennifer Ladisch-Douglass and Mr. Richard Douglass, Chicago, Illinois
Mr. Carl Lambrecht and Mrs. Catherine A. Lambrecht, Highland Park, Illinois
Daniel P. and Genifer Lara, Lake Havasu City, Arizona
Mr. and Mrs. Victor Lary, Springfield, Illinois
Mr. John Lawrence, Ann Arbor, Michigan
Dr. Mark Lehner, Milton, Massachusetts
Dr. Leonard H. Lesko and Mrs. Barbara S. Lesko, Seekonk, Massachusetts
Ms. Marie Levesque, Chicago, Illinois
Mr. John G. Levi and Mrs. Jill F. Levi, Chicago, Illinois
Mr. Josef B. and Mrs. Gail E. Levi, Chicago, Illinois
Mrs. Barbara Levin and Mr. Marvin Bogdanoff, Evanston, Illinois
Mr. Donald H. Levy and Ms. Susan Miller Levy, Chicago, Illinois
Mr. Thaddeus Walczak and Mrs. Carole J. Lewis, Hailey, Idaho
Mr. Robert B. Lifton and Ms. Carol Rosofsky, Chicago, Illinois
Mr. Robert Lipman and Mrs. Lynn Lipman, Evanston, Illinois
Mr. & Mrs. David Lipsey, McLean, Virginia
Mr. Alfred R. Lipton and Ms. Kathleen Roseborough, Glencoe, Illinois
Mr. Laurence Lissak, Lombard, Illinois
Ms. Beth Ann Lodal, Oak Park, Illinois
Mr. John Patrick and Ms. Rochelle Cohen Lodder, Chicago, Illinois
Mrs. Nina A. Longley, Park Forest, Illinois
Mr. David Loy, Los Angeles, California
Mr. David Lubell, Chicago, Illinois
Mr. Philip R. Luhmann and Mrs. Dianne C. Luhmann, Chicago, Illinois
Mr. Gary Lyall, Willowbrook, Illinois
Dr. Ross D.E. MacPhee, New York, New York
Dr. Jennifer L. Magnabosco, Santa Monica, California
The Malcolm Gibbs Foundation, Inc., New York, New York
Mr. Daniel R. Malecki, Kensington, California
Ms. Leah Maneaty, Chicago, Illinois
Dr. Glennda Susan Marsh-Letts, Australia
Ms. Eva C. May, New Rochelle, New York
Mrs. Marie Therese McDermott, Chicago, Illinois
Ms. Catherine McDonald, Philadelphia, Pennsylvania
Dr. William B. McDonald and Glen A. Khant, Chicago, Illinois
Mr. Willis McDonald IV, Cody, Wyoming
Mr. George McElroy, Grosse Pointe Park, Michigan
Ms. Harriet B. McKay, Huntsville, Alabama
Mrs. Patricia McKiernan, Chicago, Illinois

Associate Supporters ($100–$249) (cont.)

Ms. Mary E. Meier, Shelby Township, Michigan
Ms. Sarah Meisels, Wheaton, Illinois
Professor R.D. Bock and Mrs. Renee Menegaz-Bock, Chicago, Illinois
Dr. Carol Meyer, Hinsdale, Illinois
Dr. and Mrs. Alvin Michaels, West Bloomfield, Michigan
Ms. Melissa Brisley Mickey, Chicago, Illinois
Mr. Phillip L. Miller and Mrs. Barbara Miller, Chicago, Illinois
Mr. Richard A. Miller, Oak Lawn, Illinois
Mr. Walter R. Miller, Glenwood, Illinois
Dr. William K. Miller, Duluth, Minnesota
Morton Millman, MD, and Ann K. Millman, MD, Chicago, Illinois
Mr. Sam Mirkin, Mishawaka, Indiana
Mr. Mark Christopher Mitera and Mr. Edwin Wald, Forest Park, Illinois
Mr. J. Y. Miyamoto, Los Angeles, California
Mr. Robert Moeller and Ms. Lois Moeller, Evanston, Illinois
Mr. Keith and Mrs. Anne S. Moffat, Chicago, Illinois
Dr. D. Read Moffett and Mrs. Jane M. Moffett, Chatham, Massachusetts
Ms. Catherine Moore, Gurnee, Illinois
Ms. Shirley A. Morningstar, Los Angeles, California
Mr. William L. Morrison and Mrs. Kate B. Morrison, Chicago, Illinois
Vivian Mosby, Woodland, Washington
Mr. Charles H. Mottier, Chicago, Illinois
Mr. Anthony Mourek and Dr. Karole Shafer Mourek, Riverside, Illinois
Mr. Henry Moy, Idabel, Oklahoma
Ms. Maureen Mullen, Greenfield, Wisconsin
Mrs. Luigi Mumford, Chicago, Illinois
Mr. David E. Muschler and Ms. Ann L. Becker, Chicago, Illinois
Mrs. Margaret Wislon Myers, Blue Hill, Maine
Ms. Demetria D. Nanos, Chicago, Illinois
Mr. Robert M. Newbury and Mrs. Diane S. Newbury, Chicago, Illinois
Mr. and Mrs. Nicholas, Chicago, Illinois
Mr. Dale George Niewoehner, Rugby, North Dakota
The Northern Trust Company Charitable Trust, Chicago, Illinois
The Northern Trust Company, Chicago, Illinois
Mr. Theodore Norton, Los Gatos, California
Notre Dame Academy, Toledo, Ohio
Dorinda J. Oliver, New York, New York
Mr. Wayne R. Olson, Prior Lake, Minnesota
Mr. J. Reed O'Malley and Ms. Ute O'Malley, Wheaton, Illinois
Mrs. William R. Oostenbrug, Hinsdale, Illinois
Mr. Gary A Oppenhuis and Ms. Mary E. Oppenhuis, Flossmoor, Illinois
Mr. Mark Osgood, Burr Ridge, Illinois
Mr. Myras Osman and Ms. Linda Osman, Flossmoor, Illinois
Mrs. China Oughton, Dwight, Illinois
Park Tudor School, Indianapolis, Indiana
Kisoon and Moonyoung Park, Chicago, Illinois
Ms. Joan Hunt Parks, Chicago, Illinois
Dr. Richard F. Pedersen and Mrs. Nelda N. Pedersen, Claremont, California
Mr. Eric Pelander and Dr. Evalyn Gates, Chicago, Illinois
Ms. Carolyn and Mr. Peter Pereira, Chicago, Illinois
Mr. Roger Perkins and Mrs. Betty Perkins, Los Alamos, New Mexico
Mr. Norman and Mrs. Lorraine Perman, Chicago, Illinois
Mr. Thomas D. and Mrs. Betty A. Philipsborn, Chicago, Illinois

HONOR ROLL OF DONORS AND MEMBERS

Associate Supporters ($100–$249) (cont.)

Mr. David Pierce, Cleveland, Ohio
Ms. Genevieve Plamondon, Telluride, Colorado
Mr. Jeffrey Pommerville and Mrs. Yvonne Pommerville, Scottsdale, Arizona
Mrs. Charlene Posner, Chicago, Illinois
Mr. Cameron Poulter, Chicago, Illinois
Mrs. Dorothy M. Price, Maumee, Ohio
Mr. Richard H. Prins and Mrs. Marion L. Prins, Chicago, Illinois
Mr. Joseph Putz and Mrs. JoAnn Putz, Palos Heights, Illinois
Ms. Elaine Quinn and Mr. Robert Andersen, Chicago, Illinois
Mr. Richard Rapp, Chicago, Illinois
Raytheon Foundation, Princeton, New Jersey
Mr. David E. Reese, Chicago, Illinois
Louise Lee Reid, Clarendon Hills, Illinois
Mr. Alan Reinstein and Mrs. Laurie Reinstein, Highland Park, Illinois
Ms. Carole Reisman, Great Neck, New York
Mr. Seth Richardson and Ms. Molly Herron, Chicago, Illinois
Mr. James J. Richerson and Ms. Judy Lee, Peoria, Illinois
Mr. George G. Rinder and Mrs. Shirley L. Rinder, Burr Ridge, Illinois
William S. and Marianna Roberts, Poway, California
Mr. Chris Roling, United Kingdom
Mr. Howard J. Romanek, Skokie, Illinois
Mrs. Ludwig Rosenberger, Chicago, Illinois
Mrs. Lucia B. Rothman-Denes, Chicago, Illinois
Mrs. Edwin A. Rothschild, Chicago, Illinois
Mrs. Treadwell Ruml, New York, New York
Ms. Sally Black Ruscitti, Phoenix, Arizona
Mr. Cihan Kemal Saclioglu and Mrs. Virginia L. Taylor-Saclioglu, Turkey
Dr. Leo Sadow and Mrs. Carol Sadow, Chicago, Illinois
Mr. Mazin Safar and Mr. Michal Safar, Chicago, Illinois
Mr. Dan Saltzman, Portland, Oregon
Mr. John Sanders and Mrs. Peggy Sanders, Chicago, Illinois
Mr. John Sarr, Portland, Oregon
Ms. Roberta Schaffner, Chicago, Illinois
Mr. Paul Benjamin Schechter, Denver, Colorado
Ms. Erika L. Schmidt, Ottawa, Illinois
Mr. Frank L. Schneider and Mrs. Karen M. Schneider, Chicago, Illinois
Mr. Paul Schoessow and Ms. Patricia Cavenee, Lakewood, Colorado
Dr. Hans Schreiber and Ms. Karin Schreiber, Chicago, Illinois
Mrs. Jane C. and Mr. Albert M. Schwuchow, Chicago, Illinois
Ms. Jane Ayer Scott, West Newton, Massachusetts
Dr. Michael Sha, Carmel, Indiana
Mr. Robert E. Shapiro and Mrs. Susan H. Shapiro, Chicago, Illinois
Mr. Khaled Shawwaf, Chicago, Illinois
Mr. Thomas Sheffield, Jr., Chicago, Illinois
Ms. Emma Shelton and Ms. Florence Kate Millar, Bethesda, Maryland
Mrs. Raymond Shlaustas, Chicago, Illinois
Ms. Deborah Shmalcs, Roselle, Illinois
Ms. Lois Siegel, Chicago, Illinois
Ms. Susan R. Silver, Playa Vista, California
Mr. Michael A. Sisinger and Ms. Judith E. Waggoner, Columbus, Ohio
Mr. Charles and Mrs. Elizabeth A. Sklarsky, Chicago, Illinois
Mrs. Adair Small, Irvine, California
Mr. Robert K. Smither, Hinsdale, Illinois

Associate Supporters ($100–$249) (cont.)

Mr. Hugo F. and Mrs. Elizabeth Sonnenschein, Chicago, Illinois
Mr. Stephen C. Sperry, Litchfield, Minnesota
Mrs. Elizabeth Spiegel, Chicago, Illinois
Mr. Jim Sredzinski, LaGrange, Illinois
Mr. Ted and Mrs. Alyssa Stamatakos, Chicago, Illinois
Mr. Ronald W. Steele and Mrs. Mary J. Steele, Fairfax, Virginia
Mr. Jerome L. Stein and Mrs. Hadassah L. Stein, Providence, Rhode Island
Mr. David A. Steinberg and Mrs. Tracy Steinberg, Fiddletown, California
Mr. Stephen M. Stigler and Mrs. Virginia Stigler, Chicago, Illinois
Mr. Frederick H. Stitt and Mrs. Suzanne B. Stitt, Wilmette, Illinois
Mrs. Patricia Study, Chicago, Illinois
Mr. Louis Sudler, Chicago, Illinois
Mr. Gerald Sufrin, Snyder, New York
Mr. Damon R. Swank, Rancho Palos Verdes, California
Mrs. Peggy Lewis Sweesy, San Diego, California
Mr. Gustavus F. and Mrs. Linda Swift IV, Chicago, Illinois
Dr. Arnold Tanis and Mrs. Maxine Tanis, Fernandina Beach, Florida
Dr. Pierangelo Taschini, Chicago, Illinois
Mrs. John Tatum, Massachusetts
Mr. James W. Tedrow and Mrs. Virginia Vlack Tedrow, Menlo Park, California
Mr. Justin Tedrowe, Downers Grove, Illinois
Mr. Barry E. Thompson and Ms. Judithe A. Thompson, Gallipolis, Ohio
Miss Kristin Thompson, Madison, Wisconsin
Mr. John Tonkinson and Mrs. Jane Tonkinson, Torrance, California
Mr. Robert L. Toth and Mrs. Rosemary A. Toth, Medina, Ohio
Mr. John E. and Mrs. Eva L. Townsend, Winnetka, Illinois
Irme Tracy, Novi, Michigan
Miss Janice Trimble, Chicago, Illinois
Mrs. Harriet M. Turk, Joliet, Illinois
Dr. Robert Y. Turner, Philadelphia, Pennsylvania
Mrs. Frances and Mr. Atwell R. Turquette, Champaign, Illinois
Mr. Russell Tuttle and Mrs. Marlene Tuttle, Chicago, Illinois
Mr. Sugihiko Uchida, Japan
Ms. Lucia Uihlein, Lake Bluff, Illinois
Ms. Vachher and Mr. Selitto, Chicago, Illinois
Dr. Walter Vandaele and Mrs. Annette Vandaele, Washington, D.C.
Vincennes University, Vincennes, Indiana
Mr. Tom Vosmer, Oman
Mrs. Marguerite A. Walk, Chicago, Illinois
Nancy E. Warner, M.D., Pasadena, California
Mr. and Mrs. Washburn, Chicago, Illinois
Professor Richard Watson and Professor Patty Jo Watson, Missoula, Montana
Mr. LeRoy Weber, Jr., Rio Vista, California
Mr. Jerry Wegner, Munster, Indiana
Dr. David B. Weisberg and Mrs. Ophra Weisberg, Cincinnati, Ohio
Mr. Edward Wente and Mrs. Leila Wente, Chicago, Illinois
Linda Wheatley-Irving, Chicago, Illinois
Dr. Willard E. White, Riverside, Illinois
Mr. Vic Whitmore, Boise, Idaho
Mr. Ralph Wiggen, Los Angeles, California
Mr. Clifton J. Wilkow, Chicago, Illinois
Mr. Wayne M. Wille and Mrs. Lois J. Wille, Chicago, Illinois
Dr. Jerome A. Winer and Mrs. Inge K. Winer, Chicago, Illinois

HONOR ROLL OF DONORS AND MEMBERS

Associate Supporters ($100–$249) (cont.)

Ms. Debra Wingfield, Tucson, Arizona
Ms. Melanie R. Wojtulewicz, Chicago, Illinois
Rabbi Arnold Jacob Wolf and Mrs. Grace W. Wolf, Chicago, Illinois
Mr. Michael Wolf, Chicago, Illinois
Mr. Arnold R. Wolff and Mrs. Ann Wolff, Winnetka, Illinois
Ms. Paula Wolff, Chicago, Illinois
Mrs. Judith M. Wright, Carson City, Nevada
Mr. Donald Yesnik, Arlington, Virginia
Mr. Thomas K. Yoder, Chicago, Illinois
Carol L. Yohanan, Evanston, Illinois
Ms. Machiko Yoshinaga, Bethesda, Maryland
Mrs. George B. Young, Chicago, Illinois
Zoula Pyle Zein-Eldin, Galveston, Texas
Mrs. Agnes Zellner, Chicago, Illinois

Friends ($1–$99)

Ms. Kate Abele, Wilmette, Illinois
Mrs. Annabel Abraham, Oak Park, Illinois
Ms. Virginia Lee Adi, Portola Valley, California
Mr. Russell Alberding and Mrs. Ellen P. Alberding, Chicago, Illinois
Dr. John R. Alden, Ann Arbor, Michigan
Mr. John Aldrin and Mrs. Sylwia Aldrin, Gurnee, Illinois
Ms. Carolyn Allison, Rockford, Illinois
Mr. Kenneth Alterman, Roslyn Heights, New York
Ms. Elizabeth Ames, Blue Jay, California
Mr. Christian A. Anderson, Loves Park, Illinois
Ms. Kathryn E. Anderson, Amherst, Ohio
Mr. Roger W. Anderson, Jr., and Mrs. Arletta Anderson, Mukilteo, Washington
Ms. Rebecca Andis, Crown Point, Indiana
Mr. George Autos, Monroe, Wisconsin
Aquinas College, Grand Rapids, Michigan
Dr. and Mrs. Barry Arnason, Chicago, Illinois
Ms. Carolyn Arnolds, Chicago, Illinois
Ms. Ardell Arthur, Chicago, Illinois
Ms. Julie Auger and Mr. Roger Sciammas, Chicago, Illinois
Dr. James Harper Andrews and Dr. Donna M. Avery, Chicago, Illinois
Ms. Sharon Avery and Mr. Philip Rychel, Tulsa, Oklahoma
Ms. Hilsa Ayonayon, Brisbane, California
Dr. Diana Backus, Tannersville, Pennsylvania
Mrs. Barbara Baechler, El Cajon, California
Dr. Leah R. Baer, Skokie, Illinois
Ms. Rozenn Bailleul-LeSuer, Chicago, Illinois
Mrs. Glenda H. and Mr. Kirby A. Baker, Pacific Palisades, California
Ms. Erin Baker, Chicago, Illinois
Ms. Isabelle Balzer, Australia
Dr. Barry Bandstra, Holland, Michigan
Bank of America Foundation, Charlotte, North Carolina
Mr. Joseph Barabe, Oak Park, Illinois
Mr. John P. Baril, Lincoln Park, Michigan
Ms. Lynn A. Baril, Culver City, California
Ms. Kate Barnash, Chicago, Illinois

HONOR ROLL OF DONORS AND MEMBERS

Friends ($1–$99) (cont.)

Carol and Dr. Erwin P. Barrington, Lincolnwood, Illinois
Ms. Joyce Bartels, Lombard, Illinois
Professor Jost Baum and Mrs. Heidi Baum, Palo Alto, California
Mr. William F. Bayer, Chesterfield, Missouri
Ms. Bazargan and Mr. Raskin, Chicago, Illinois
Mr. Michael C. Behnke and Ms. Lee Behnke, Chicago, Illinois
Mr. William L. Belew, Fair Oaks, California
Ms. Laurel V. Bell-Cahill, Sacramento, California
Mr. Stephen Bencze, Ocala, Florida
Mr. John David Bender, Pinole, California
Miss Kitty Benjamin, San Francisco, California
Col. William T. Bennett and Mrs. Deanna J. Bennett, Palm Harbor, Florida
Mr. William Joseph Berger, Philadelphia, Pennsylvania
Mr. Richard Bertoldi and Mrs. Donna Bertoldi, Chicago, Illinois
Mr. Hans Dieter Betz and Mrs. Christel Betz, Chicago, Illinois
Mr. David Bevington and Mrs. Margaret Bevington, Chicago, Illinois
Ms. Elise Jordan Beyer, Chicago, Illinois
Mr. Norman Beyer and Ms. Ann Beyer, Penney Farms, Florida
Mr. Roger J. Bialcik, Downers Grove, Illinois
Mr. Paul Bialobrzeski, Middlebury, Connecticut
Miss Rae Ellen Bichell, Brentwood, Tennessee
Ms. Terry Jo Bichell, Chicago, Illinois
Mr. Roman W. Bilik, Chicago, Illinois
Mrs. Bette Rose Blair, Chicago, Illinois
Dr. Anita Blanchard, Chicago, Illinois
Mrs. Judy Blau, Highland Park, Illinois
Mr. Richard Blindt and Mrs. Dorothy Blindt, Naperville, Illinois
Walter and Marguerite Bloch, River Forest, Illinois
Mr. Marc Block and Manuel Block, Lake Zurich, Illinois
Ms. Nancy Bloomstrand, Rockford, Illinois
Ms. Betty Blum, Chicago, Illinois
Mr. David L. Blumberg and Mrs. Linda Horween Blumberg, Highland Park, Illinois
Ms. Barbara Boczar and Mr. William Widner, Davis, California
Mr. John Bodenmann and Ms. Tracy Bodenmann, Chicago, Illinois
Ms. Katherine Mary Bolger, New York, New York
Dr. Sara J. Denning Bolle, Biddeford, Maine
Mrs. Abraham Bookstein, Chicago, Illinois
Ms. Jocelyn Boor, Shorewood, Wisconsin
Mrs. Charles D. Borst, Illinois
Mr. Seymour Bortz, Highland Park, Illinois
Mr. William Bosron, Indianapolis, Indiana
Ms. Louise Boyd, Chicago, Illinois
Mr. Douglas Braidwood and Mrs. Patricia Braidwood, Virgina Beach, Virginia
Mr. John Bramwell and Ms. Dolores Janicki, Mesa, Arizona
Mr. Paul Brankin, Rapid City, South Dakota
Mrs. Lylus Brash, Chicago, Illinois
Dr. and Mrs. Ethan M. Braunstein, Phoenix, Arizona
Ms. Olive N. Brewster, San Antonio, Texas
Ms. Maureen Brierton, Chicago, Illinois
Dawn Bronson, Palos Heights, Illinois
Mr. Jack E. Brown, Akron, Ohio
Mr. Langston Brown, Dublin, Ohio
Mr. Timothy Arthur Brown, Franconia, New Hampshire

HONOR ROLL OF DONORS AND MEMBERS

Friends ($1–$99) (cont.)

Mr. James F. Brownfield, Uniontown, Pennsylvania
Ms. Denise Browning, Chicago, Illinois
Ms. Marie Bryan, Woodland, California
Mrs. Roberta Buchanan, Evanston, Illinois
Ms. Dorathea G. Bucher, Dublin, Ohio
Mr. Glenn Bucher and Mrs. Denise Bucher, Evanston, Illinois
Ms. Moira Buhse, Downers Grove, Illinois
Mr. Aaron Alexander Burke and Mrs. Katherine Strange Burke, Los Angeles, California
Mr. Richard W. Burke, St. Louis, Missouri
Mr. Robert A. Burke, Lutherville, Maryland
Ms. Patricia Burton, Kirksville, Missouri
Ms. Kristin Buskirk, Oak Park, Illinois
Ms. Jennifer Butchart, Park Hills, Missouri
Ms. Carolyn Byron, Oxford, Ohio
Mr. Salvatore Calomino and Mr. James Zychowicz, Madison, Wisconsin
Ms. Christine Calvillo, Blue Island, Illinois
Mr. Robert Calvin and Mrs. Jane Calvin, Chicago, Illinois
Mr. Morgan Campbell, Wilmette, Illinois
Mr. and Mrs. Parks Campbell, Fort Worth, Texas
Mrs. Jeanny Canby, Haverford, Pennsylvania
Mr. Robert Cantu, Romeoville, Illinois
Mr. Arthur Caraher and Mrs. Ruth Caraher, Chicago, Illinois
Mr. William Carlberg and Ms. Shirley Carlberg, Evergreen Park, Illinois
Mr. Richard Carli, Chicago, Illinois
Mr. Stephen C. Carlson and Mrs. Patricia Brown Carlson, Chicago, Illinois
Ms. Gale Carter, East Chicago, Indiana
Mr. Tim Cashion, Canada
Ms. Mary Cerven, Downers Grove, Illinois
Mr. Richard L. Chambers, Montgomery, Alabama
Anne Champagne, Chicago, Illinois
Roberta Chanin, Chicago, Illinois
Dr. J. Harley Chapman, Jr., Palatine, Illinois
Mr. Norman Chenven, Austin, Texas
Mr. Gary Chiavetta, St Charles, Missouri
Mr. Martin T. and Ms. Evangeline S. Choate, Chandler, Arizona
Christies's Incorporated, Chicago, Illinois
Miss Lucille Christopher, Greenville, Pennsylvania
Mr. James Chrobak, Chicago, Illinois
Mr. Robert Chwedyk and Mrs. Kathy Chwedyk, Algonquin, Illinois
Ms. Sandi Ciesielski, Southgate, Michigan
Jean P. Cioffi, Pompton Plains, New Jersey
Mr. David Foster Clapp, Chattanooga, Tennessee
Ms. Heinke K. Clark, Seattle, Washington
Ms. Carol Clausen, Highland, Indiana
Mrs. Ahira Cobb, Princeton, New Jersey
Mrs. Gabriella Cohen, Highland Park, Illinois
Lila L. Cohen, Valparaiso, Indiana
Mrs. Susan S. Conklin, Grand Rapids, Michigan
Dr. Lewis W. Coppel and Mrs. Marilyn Coppel, Chillicothe, Ohio
Prof. Lorelei H. Corcoran, Memphis, Tennessee
Mr. Jason Cordero, Australia
Cornfield and Feldman, Chicago, Illinois
Ms. Maria Corpuz and Mr. John A. Hug, Chicago, Illinois

HONOR ROLL OF DONORS AND MEMBERS

Friends ($1–$99) (cont.)

Ms. Leah Cozzi, Oak Park, Illinois
Ms. Hazel Cramer, Darien, Illinois
Ms. Mary Jane Crotty, Evanston, Illinois
Cathy Cunningham, Chicago, Illinois
Ms. Katherine M. Damitz, Wheaton, Illinois
Mr. Joseph N. Darguzas and Ms. Christine A. Toohey, Homewood, Illinois
Mr. Robert Koos and Ms. Diane Dau-Koos, Kenosha, Wisconsin
Mr. Sidney Davidson and Mrs. Freda Davidson, Chicago, Illinois
Mr. Claude Davis, Hillsborough, North Carolina
Ms. Jennifer Davis, Canada
Mrs. Vivan Davis, Chicago, Illinois
Ms. Maybrit S. De Miranda, Chicago, Illinois
Mr. Matthew Charles and Ms. Katherine Lynn Dean, Oak Park, Illinois
Fanny and Catherine Delisle, Bedford, New Hampshire
Mr. Richard DeMaris, Valparaiso, Indiana
Mr. Robert Demos, Chicago, Illinois
Mr. R. L. Den Adel, Pella, Iowa
Ms. Stephanie Denkowicz, Manhasset, New York
Mr. Kevin M. Dent, Bloomington, Indiana
Mr. James Despot, Richmond, California
Mr. Richard Diaz, Chicago, Illinois
Ms. Michaelann Dievendorf, Hummelstown, Pennsylvania
Ms. Ursula Digman, Elgin, Illinois
Ms. Lynn Swartz Dodd, Los Angeles, California
Mr. J. McGregor Dodds, Grosse Pointe Farms, Michigan
Mr. Richard J. and Ms. Diane F. Donaher, Warrington, Pennsylvania
Mr. Jim Douglas, Jr., West Lafayette, Indiana
Mrs. Edmond L. d'Ouville, Willowbrook, Illinois
Mr. and Mrs. George T. Drake, Wilmette, Illinois
Ms. Margaret Drake, Austin, Texas
Mr. Andrew Drazdik, Jeannette, Pennsylvania
Mr. John Dreibelbis and Mrs. Patricia Dreibelbis, Evanston, Illinois
Mr. Kenneth Drobena, Chicago, Illinois
Drs. Adilman, Katin, Lubar, Ltd., Northbrook, Illinois
Mr. and Mrs. Pedro A. Duenas, Chicago, Illinois
Mr. William A. Dumbleton, Chicago, Illinois
Dr. George Dunea, Chicago, Illinois
Ms. Sally S. Dunham, Westport, Connecticut
Dr. Jim Dunlap and Ms. Judy Dunlap, Glenview, Illinois
Mr. Ronald K. Eagle, Northbrook, Illinois
Mr. David Eckert, Chicago, Illinois
Mrs. Nancy A. Elliott, Yuma, Arizona
Mr. Chris Ellis, Kirkland, Washington
Mr. Stephen A. Ellis, Rockford, Illinois
Mr. Alexander Elwyn and Mrs. Sheila Elwyn, Chicago, Illinois
Mrs. Doris E. Evans, Des Plaines, Illinois
Ms. Rhoda Ewert, Atlanta, Georgia
Mr. John Cochrane and Ms. Beth Fama, Chicago, Illinois
Dr. Valerie Fargo, Midland, Michigan
Mr. William Farina, Evanston, Illinois
Mr. Edward Farnham, Chicago, Illinois
Dr. Wendy Fish, Nashville, Tennessee
Mr. Dale Fisher, Cicero, Illinois

HONOR ROLL OF DONORS AND MEMBERS

Friends ($1–$99) (cont.)

Mr. John H. Fisher and Mrs. Carol A. Fisher, River Forest, Illinois
Mr. Barry Fitzpatrick, United Kingdom
Dr. Laurel Flentye, Kenilworth, Illinois
Mr. Carl G. Fonden, Milford, New Hampshire
Mr. Scott Forsythe and Mrs. Carol Forsythe, Forest Park, Illinois
Ms. Ann L. Foster, Evanston, Illinois
Ms. Janet Fourticq and Mr. Michael Fourticq, Los Angeles, California
Ms. Tara Fowler, Chicago, Illinois
Mr. Charles J. Fraas and Mrs. Judy S. Fraas, Jefferson City, Missouri
Ms. Thea Francel, Piedmont, Oklahoma
Judith A. Franke, Lewistown, Illinois
Mr. Jay and Mrs. Marlene M. Frankel, Chicago, Illinois
Mrs. Jon Freiler, Bethany, Connecticut
Mr. Thomas F. Frey and Mrs. Barbara D. Frey, Sarasota, Florida
Mrs. Joan Friedmann, Chicago, Illinois
Mr. John Frye, Elmwood Park, Illinois
Ms. Angie R. Fudge, Sturgis, Michigan
Mr. Brad Gangler and Ms. Betty Gangler, Monee, Illinois
Mr. Mark B. Garrison, San Antonio, Texas
Ms. Leanna Gaskins, San Francisco, California
Mr. Ben Gatch, Jr., and Mrs. Carole J. Gatch, Chicago Heights, Illinois
Mrs. Vanessa Gavin, Skokie, Illinois
Mr. John G. Gay, Willowbrook, Illinois
Mr. James Gelbort, Chicago, Illinois
Mr. Phillip K. George, Ravenna, Ohio
Mr. Ken Gerleve, Chicago, Illinois
Prof. Gilbert Ghez, Chicago, Illinois
Mrs. Constance M. Gibbon, River Forest, Illinois
Ms. Christina Gibbons, Brattleboro, Vermont
Ms. Judith Gillespie, Alexandria, Virginia
Mr. Robert W. Gillespie, Urbana, Illinois
Dr. and Mrs. John Gills, Elmhurst, Illinois
Ms. Andrea Gilmore, Chicago, Illinois
Ms. Irene Dorotea Glasner, Chicago, Illinois
Ms. Gloria Goetsch, Chesterfield, Missouri
Ms. Leah Goldberg, Chicago, Illinois
Dr. Steve Goldstein and Ms. Emily Novick, Chicago, Illinois
Mr. Marvin Gordon, Chicago, Illinois
Ms. Jill Gosser, Chicago, Illinois
Mr. James M. Govoni, Malden, Massachusetts
Mr. Robert W. Graham, Johnson City, Tennessee
Mr. Robert Grasso, Las Vegas, Nevada
Mr. Thomas Greiner, Canada
Miss Elizabeth Griffin, Winter Haven, Florida
Dr. B. Herold Griffith and Mrs. Jeanne B. Griffith, Evanston, Illinois
Ms. JoAnn and Dr. Mortimer D. Gross, Highland Park, Illinois
Mr. Robert Grutz and Mrs. Jane Grutz, Houston, Texas
Mr. Stanley Gucwa, Grayslake, Illinois
Mr. John Guhin, Pierre, South Dakota
Mr. David Guillory, Lake Charles, Louisiana
Ms. Margaret S. Gulley, Bay Village, Ohio
Mrs. Eleanor A. Guralnick, Chicago, Illinois
Ms. Joanna H. Gwinn, Evanston, Illinois

HONOR ROLL OF DONORS AND MEMBERS

Friends ($1–$99) (cont.)

Mrs. Joan M. and Mr. Joseph R. Gyulay, Panama City Beach, Florida
Dale Haber, Beardstown, Illinois
Ms. Barbara Hale, Park Ridge, Illinois
Ms. Maureen Hale, Chicago, Illinois
Mr. Christopher Hall, Saint Joseph, Illinois
Ms. Ruth Hallowell, Westwood, Massachusetts
Mr. Robert Hanawalt and Mrs. Arnetta N. Hanawalt, Aurora, Colorado
Arden Handler, Evanston, Illinois
Dr. C. Rollins and Mrs. Margaret H. Hanlon, Kenilworth, Illinois
Mrs. Theresa Hannah, Glenview, Illinois
Mr. Ira Hardman, Matteson, Illinois
Dr. W. Harer, Seattle, Washington
Ms. Peggy Hargrove, Chicago, Illinois
Mr. Tony Harper, Lake Zurich, Illinois
Ms. Leslie Harris, Chicago, Illinois
Mr. Philip Harrison, Virginia Beach, Virginia
Prof. Timothy P. Harrison, Canada
Mr. Tobin Hartnell, Chicago, Illinois
Mr. Henry A. and Mrs. Billie Black Hauser, Homewood, Illinois
Mrs. Dorothy D. Hawley, Winnetka, Illinois
Ms. Anne Hay, South Africa
Mr. John C. Hayman, Mokena, Illinois
Mrs. Virginia L. and Mr. Harold Martin Hays, Westfield, Indiana
Mr. James Heckman and Ms. Lynne Heckman, Chicago, Illinois
Ms. Mary Hegarty, Northumberland, Pennsylvania
Ms. Jennifer L. Hegedus, Chicago, Illinois
Mr. Adrii Helgren, Salinas, California
Mr. Douglas Hempel, Milwaukee, Wisconsin
Mrs. Arles Hendershott-Love, Rockford, Illinois
The Reverend Richard Henshaw, Rochester, New York
C. A. Hertenstein, Cary, North Carolina
Mr. Charles Herzer, New York, New York
Mr. Todd Michael Hickey and Mrs. Mary Iacono, Benicia, California
Ms. Helen Hift, Madison, Wisconsin
Mr. Laurence Dean Hill, Chicago, Illinois
Mr. Roger Hilpp, Aurora, Illinois
Mrs. Patricia Hirsh and Mr. George Hirsh, Chicago, Illinois
Ms. Rachael Hirt, Saugatuck, Michigan
Mr. Donald H. Hoffman, Chicago, Illinois
Dr. Harry A. Hoffner Jr. and Mrs. Winifred Hoffner, Darien, Illinois
Ms. Joanmarie Hofmann, Wesley Chapel, Florida
Mr. Thomas Holland, Chicago, Illinois
Dr. Susan T. Hollis, Penfield, New York
Mr. Steven Winford Holloway, Chicago, Illinois
Ms. Ruth Holmes, Bloomfield Hills, Michigan
Mr. Stephen L. Holst, Ossining, New York
Ms. Kay and Mr. David Holz, Iola, Wisconsin
Mr. Rodney J. Holzkamp, Chicago, Illinois
Dr. Sylvia Hood-Washington, Winfield, Illinois
Mrs. Audrey A. and Mr. John C. Hook, McLean, Virginia
Hope College, Holland, Michigan
Mr. Michael D. Hopkins and Mrs. Rosemary Hopkins, Chicago, Illinois
Mr. and Mrs. Joseph Howicz, Orland Park, Illinois

HONOR ROLL OF DONORS AND MEMBERS

Friends ($1–$99) (cont.)

Mr. Joe Hubbard and Mrs. Linda Hubbard, Schaumburg, Illinois
Mr. Michael Hyman and Ms. Stephanie Young, Chicago, Illinois
Mr. A. A. Imberman, Evanston, Illinois
Mr. Philip W. and Mrs. Josephine Jackson, Chicago, Illinois
Mr. Gary Jacob, River Forest, Illinois
Ms. Terri Jacobs, Chicago, Illinois
Mrs. Elise Jacobson, Chicago, Illinois
Ms. Judith Jaeger-Hoffmann, Chicago, Illinois
Mrs. Barbara Schaffer Jaffe, Chicago, Illinois
Mr. Jeffrey Jahns and Mrs. Jill Metcoff-Jahns, Chicago, Illinois
Mr. Martin David Jankowiak, Chicago, Illinois
Mrs. Morris Janowitz, Chicago, Illinois
Ms. Rebecca Janowitz, Chicago, Illinois
Ms. Caroline January, New York, New York
Mr. Lawrence E. Jarchow, Chicago, Illinois
Mr. Richard Lewis Jasnow, Baltimore, Maryland
Margit Javor, Chicago, Illinois
Ms. Fran Jennaro, Milwaukee, Wisconsin
Arthur A. and Patricia D. Johannes, Homewood, Illinois
Mr. Paul Johnson and Mrs. Cynthia Johnson, Chicago, Illinois
Dr. Albert Johnston, Acton, Massachusettes
Mr. Hugh W. Johnston, Spokane, Washington
Mr. Charles E. Jones and Dr. Alexandra A. O'Brien, Greece
Mr. Stanley Jones, Bloomington, Indiana
Ms. Yvonne Jones, Chicago, Illinois
Ms. Georgette Joseph, Chicago, Illinois
Mrs. Bette Kalichman, Chicago, Illinois
Ms. Katrina Kalomas, Darien, Illinois
Mr. Robert Kao, West Linn, Oregon
Mr. Larry Katkin, Fairbanks, Alaska
Mr. Lawrence Kauffman, Commack, New York
Mr. Preston B. Kavanagh and Mrs. Lois L. Kavanagh, Gaithersburg, Maryland
Mr. Alan J. Kawaters, Chicago Heights, Illinois
Ms. Jane Keeley, Ho Ho Kus, New Jersey
Ms. Alicia Kehr, Cresskill, New Jersey
Mr. Dennis L. Kelley, Elmhurst, Illinois
Mrs. Eva Kelly, Chicago, Illinois
Ms. Janet Zell Kessler, Chicago, Illinois
Mr. Chad Kieffer, Fayetteville, Arkansas
Ms. Cleo Kiergaard, McFarland, Wisconsin
Mr. James A. Kilgore, Sun Lakes, Arizona
Mr. Jerome C. Kindred, Arlington, Virginia
Mr. Tim King, Chicago, Illinois
Jacqueline Kinnaman, Chicago, Illinois
Mr. William R. Schick and Ms. Jacqueline P. Kirley, Chicago, Illinois
Mr. Richard Kirschner and Mr. Kurt Kirschner, Pacific Palisades, California
Mr. Kenneth Kitchen, United Kingdom
Mr. Dirk W. Kitzmiller and Mrs. Mildred L. Kitzmiller, Lake Forest, Illinois
Mr. Ron and Mrs. Carol Klaus, Muskego, Wisconsin
Mr. Glenn Klinksiek, Chicago, Illinois
Mr. Gunnar Klintberg, Old Greenwich, Connecticut
Ms. Karen Kobylarz, Chicago, Illinois
Ms. Maurine Kornfeld, Los Angeles, California

Friends ($1–$99) (cont.)

Shelley Korshak, M.D., Chicago, Illinois
Mr. Nicholas M. Kotcherha and Mrs. Maruchi Kotcherha, Buffalo Grove, Illinois
Ms. Paula Kowalczyk, Illinois
Miss Aletha A. Kowitz, Arlington Heights, Illinois
Dr. Arthur A. Krawetz, Evanston, Illinois
Carole and Larry Krucoff, Chicago, Illinois
Mr. Ernest A. Krumbein, Munster, Indiana
Ms. Lena Ksarjian, Chicago, Illinois
Mr. James Kulikauskas, Arlington Heights, Illinois
Mr. Arthur Yuan Ao Kuo, Cerritos, California
Ms. Joan Kuric, Chicago, Illinois
Ms. Jean I. Ladendorf, Springfield, Illinois
Mr. Jack B. Lambke, Poplar Grove, Illinois
Ms. Harriet E. Lang, San Francisco, California
Mrs. Martyl S. Langsdorf, Schaumburg, Illinois
Mr. Charles Larmore and Mrs. Amey Larmore, Providence, Rhode Island
Ms. Laura L. Larner-Farnum, Yorba Linda, California
Dr. David L. Laske, Niles, Illinois
Mr. Tim Later and Ms. Mary Field, Chicago, Illinois
Mrs. Gail D. LeBow, Boise, Idaho
Dr. Erle Leichty and Mrs. Annette Leichty, Media, Pennsylvania
Mr. Michael Patrick Lemke, Arlington Heights, Illinois
Ms. Kathy Lentz, Washington, Missouri
Ms. Sara Leonard, Beverly Shores, Indiana
Mrs. Gabrielle M. Liese, Prescott, Arizona
Ms. Stephanie Lindeburg, Canada
Ms. Donna Lipsky, Seattle, Washington
Mr. John W. Lissack and Mrs. Bernadine Lissack, Redondo Beach, California
Mr. John Litster, Western Springs, Illinois
Ms. Helen A. Lloyd, Libertyville, Illinois
Mr. Richard Loescher, Appleton, Wisconsin
Dr. Robert Tor Lofberg, El Paso, Texas
Mr. Thomas J. Logan, Carmel, California
Ms. Helen Lowell and Ms. Eileen Nash, United Kingdom
Ms. Gail W. Lowry, Berkeley, California
Ms. Brittany Luberda, Chicago, Illinois
Mrs. Beatrice Lumpkin, Chicago, Illinois
Mr. Michael J. Lutz, Chicago, Illinois
Ms. Corinne Lyon, Chicago, Illinois
Mr. Michael Macaluso, Chicago, Illinois
Mrs. Lillian MacBrayne, Geneva, Illinois
Mr. Andrew M. MacDonald, Santurce, Puerto Rico
Mrs. Osa MacLane, Bethesda, Maryland
Ms. F. Rachel Magdalene, Rock Island, Illinois
Mr. James Maish and Mrs. Roberta Maish, Barrington, Illinois
Dr. Eugene I. Majerowicz, California
Mr. Moses M. Malkin and Mrs. Hannah L. Malkin, Sun City Center, Florida
Mr. Paul Mallory, Chicago, Illinois
Mrs. Barbara J. Malone, Summerfield, Florida
Ms. Geraldine Manar, Chicago, Illinois
Ms. Margaret Manteufel, Highwood, Illinois
Ms. Paula G. Manzuk, Summit, Illinois
Mr. Alvin Markovitz and Mrs. Harriet June Markovitz, San Francisco, California

HONOR ROLL OF DONORS AND MEMBERS

Friends ($1–$99) (cont.)

Ms. Elizabeth Martin, Chicago, Illinois
Mrs. Judith G. and Mr. Donald Martin, Evanston, Illinois
Mr. Andrew H. Massie, Jr., San Francisco, California
Mr. Robert Masters, Newport Beach, California
Mr. Frank D. and Mrs. Linda M. Mayer, Jr., Glencoe, Illinois
Dr. Joseph A. McCaffrey, Bettendorf, Iowa
Mr. Kevin McDonald and Ms. Judy Chan, Wilmette, Illinois
Mr. Kevin McDonald, Santa Ana, California
Bernard McGinn and Patricial McGinn, Chicago, Illinois
Ms. Sherry McGuire, River Grove, Illinois
Mr. Michael J. McInerney, Chicago, Illinois
Mr. Glen McIntyre, Kingfisher, Oklahoma
Ms. Sandra McNaughton, Chicago, Illinois
Ms. Simone McNeil, Chicago, Illinois
Mr. Michael D. Meacham, Berkeley, California
Ms. Betty D. Meador, Ramona, California
Mr. Richard H. Meadow, Canton, Massachusetts
Mr. Ben Meeker and Mrs. Mila Maria Meeker, Chicago, Illinois
Ms. Rachael Mellon, Peru, Illinois
Dr. Grier H. Merwin, Brookline, Massachusetts
Mr. John Merza and Mrs. Ophelia Merza, Chicago, Illinois
Ms. Susan Messinger, Chicago, Illinois
Mr. Gerard Metzger, Chicago, Illinois
Mrs. Marilyn K. Metzger, Chicago, Illinois
Mrs. Henry Meyer, Shreveport, Louisiana
Mrs. Suzanne Millan, Gilbert, Arizona
Dr. Michael Millar and Mrs. Ruth Millar, Cedar Falls, Iowa
Mr. Andrew K. Miller, Millersville, Pennsylvania
Ms. Mary Miller, Evanston, Illinois
Ms. Sue E. Miller, Cincinnati, Ohio
Mr. Steven Mintz, Madison, Wisconsin
Mr. Gene Mitchell, Madison, Wisconsin
Professor Heshmat Moayyad and Mrs. Ruth Moayyad, Chicago, Illinois
Mr. Wayne N. Moles, Jacksonville, Florida
Mr. James M. Monson, Wheaton, Illinois
Mr. Jorge Montes Mr. Alberto Montes, Chicago, Illinois
Moody Bible Institute, Chicago, Illinois
Ms. Helen Louise Moorman, Chicago, Illinois
Ms. Suzanne Morgan, Chicago, Illinois
Ms. Morgan Moroney, Shavano Park, Texas
Dr. W. Brown Morton III, Fredricksburg, Virginia
Dr. Jonathan Moss, Chicago, Illinois
Mrs. Margaret Mottier, Chicago, Illinois
Mr. Ian S. Moyer, Southfield, Michigan
Ms. Janet Mryan, Lyons, Illinois
Mr. Van D. Mueller and Ms. Mildred I. Mueller, Andover, Minnesota
Mr. Alexander Muir, Chicago, Illinois
Mr. Jay F. Mulberry and Mrs. Alice J. Mulberry, Chicago, Illinois
Mr. Casey James Murray, Crown Point, Indiana
Mr. Michael J. Murrin, Chicago, Illinois
Mr. David Musgrave, Milford, Ohio
Mr. Dan Myers and Mrs. Joanne Myers, Coon Rapids, Minnesota
Ms. Marion Myers and Mr. Jim Myers, Chicago, Illinois

Friends ($1–$99) (cont.)

Mr. Robert Naftzger and Mrs. Mary O. Naftzger, Chicago, Illinois
Professor Sidney Nagel and Ms. Young-Kee Kim, Chicago, Illinois
Mrs. F. Esther Naser, Evanston, Illinois
Dr. Keith Shelby Naunheim and Dr. Rosanne S. Naunheim, St. Louis, Missouri
Mr. Jeffrey N. Nelson, Bismarck, North Dakota
Mr. Charles Newell and Ms. Kathleen Collins, Chicago, Illinois
Ms. Anne and Mr. John Newton, Natick, Massachusetts
Mr. Roy Ng, Skokie, Illinois
Dr. Peter Nichols, Chicago, Illinois
Leslie Nickels, Evanston, Illinois
Ms. Lucille M. Nikodym, Inver Grove Heights, Minnesota
Dr. Ruprecht and Ms. Elizabeth Nitschke, Middleton, Wisconsin
Timothy M. Nolan, Attorney at Law, Chicago, Illinois
Mr. Timothy Michael and Mrs. Mary Ann Nolan, Palos Park, Illinois
Dr. Edward Brovarski and Mrs. Del Nord, Brookline, Massachusetts
Mr. Joseph T. and Ms. Monetta K. Novak, Bloomingdale, Illinois
Mr. John Michael O'Donnell, Chicago, Illinois
Ms. Kelly Olmstead, Stoughton, Wisconsin
Mr. Lee R. Olson, Somers, New York
Ms. Erin Oluanaigh, Cheshire, Connecticut
Ms. Caryl Osborn, Las Vegas, Nevada
Dr. Allen L. and Mrs. Amy C. Oseroff, Greenville, North Carolina
Ms. Mary O'Shea, Chicago, Illinois
Ms. Kathleen O'Toole, Oak Lawn, Illinois
Ms. Maxine Otto, Chicago, Illinois
Dr. Jacques Ovadia and Mrs. Florence Ovadia, Chicago, Illinois
Mr. John Overbey, Benton, Arkansas
Mrs. Sarah R. Packard, Westmont, Illinois
Mr. David Padfield, Zion, Illinois
Mr. Gary Palm, Chicago, Illinois
Mr. Lewis K. Panion and Ms. Ruth P. Panion, Titusville, Pennsylvania
Mr. Courtenay Wright, Chicago, Illinois
Erika O. Parker, M.D., Evanston, Illinois
Ms. Sylvia Parks, Chicago, Illinois
Mrs. Rose Pashigian, Chicago, Illinois
Ms. Ila Patlogan, Flossmoor, Illinois
Mr. Hiram Patterson, Dallas, Texas
Mr. Mark R. Pattis, Highland Park, Illinois
Dr. Robert Paulissian, Tarzana, California
Mr. Richard Paulsen, Elmhurst, Illinois
Ms. Laurie E. Pearce, San Francisco, California
Mr. William H. Peck, Detroit, Michigan
Mrs. Evelyn Perodeau, Haddonfield, New Jersey
Mrs. Mildred G. Peters and Mr. Victor S. Peters, Winnetka, Illinois
Ms. Gloria Phares and Mr. Richard Dannay, New York, New York
John F. Philipps, Dyer, Indiana
Ms. Janelle Pisarik, Wentzville, Missouri
Dr. Audrius Vaclovas Plioplys, Chicago, Illinois
Ms. Elizabeth Frances Plocharczyk and Mr. Geoffrey Daniel Callander, Upper Arlington, Ohio
Mrs. Barbara B. Pope, Cincinnati, Ohio
Dr. Barbara A. Porter, Boston, Massachusetts
Mr. Michael Pratts, Chicago, Illinois
Ms. Claire Pritchard, Chicago, Illinois

HONOR ROLL OF DONORS AND MEMBERS

Friends ($1–$99) (cont.)

Mr. William Pritchard, Ridgewood, New Jersey
Mr. James Provins, Wexford, Pennsylvania
Ms. Kim Della Puca, Stafford, Virginia
Ms. Lynne Puckett, Billings, Montana
Ms. Jane Pugh, Chicago, Illinois
Dr. Smilja Rabinowitz, Chicago, Illinois
Mr. Joseph Radov, Northfield, Illinois
Mrs. Celestina Raineri, Chicago, Illinois
Mr. Francis B. Randall, New York, New York
Kristin Rankin, Chicago, Illinois
Mr. James M. Ratcliffe, Chicago, Illinois
Ms. Melissa Ratkovich, Bridgeview, Illinois
Ms. Lynne Rauscher-Davoust, Elmhurst, Illinois
Dr. Charles Dean Ray, Santa Barbara, California
Razor Soft, St. Joseph, Illinois
Ms. Margaret W. Redding, Winnetka, Illinois
Ms. Jane Reese, Bremerton, Washington
Mr. William Reinke, Granger, Indiana
Mrs. Olga M. Reiss, Falls Church, Virginia
Mrs. Charlotte B. and Mr. David Reiter, Chicago, Illinois
Mr. Joseph J. Rembusch, De Kalb, Illinois
Mr. Paul Remeczki, Carteret, New Jersey
Mrs. Merle Reskin, Northbrook, Illinois
Gerhard and N. Linn Reusswig, Jopiln, Missouri
Mr. Charles S. and Mrs. Barbara B. Rhyne, Portland, Oregon
Mr. David Rice and Ms. Carol Jackson Rice, Barrington, Illinois
Mr. Andrew Rich, Richland Center, Wisconsin
Robert and Cynthia Richardson, Old Chatham, New York
Mr. Harold A. Richman and Mrs. Marlene F. Richman, Chicago, Illinois
Mr. Thomas Riggins, New York, New York
Ms. Elizabeth Caswell, Denver, Colorado
Mr. and Mrs. Burton Rissman, Chicago, Illinois
Ms. Joan Robbins, Scottsdale, Arizona
Prof. John F. Robertson, Mount Pleasant, Michigan
Mr. and Mrs. Burton H. Robin, Chicago, Illinois
Mr. Norman Robins and Ms. Sandra Robins, Chicago, Illinois
Mr. Jon Robison and Mrs. Sandra Robison, Bayfield, Colorado
Ms. Traci Rodriguez, Costa Mesa, California
Mr. Michael A. Rom, Chicago, Illinois
Ms. Kristi Rose, East Windsor, New Jersey
Mr. Richard Rosenberg and Mrs. Donna Green Rosenberg, Winnetka, Illinois
Mr. Andrew Rosenfield and Mrs. Betsy Rosenfield, Lake Forest, Illinois
Mr. Robert Rosner and Mrs. Marsha Rosner, Chicago, Illinois
Ms. Geraldine Rowden, Crete, Illinois
Mr. Sidney Rowland, Lawrenceville, New Jersey
Mr. Bernard Wolf Rozran, Switzerland
Ms. Betsy Rubin, Chicago, Illinois
Mr. Mark Rubin, Arlington, Virginia
Ms. Janet Russell, Concord, California
Ms. Diane M. Ruszczyk, Lancaster, California
Ms. Margaret Rutledge, Costa Mesa, California
Mr. and Mrs. Patrick G. Ryan, Winnetka, Illinois
Maria L. Rydstedt, Grand Rapids, Michigan

Friends ($1–$99) (cont.)

Mrs. Marguerite L. Saecker, River Forest, Illinois
Tobi Jean Saidel, Lyons, Colorado
Ms. Christina Salowey, Buchanan, Virginia
Ms. Doris Saltzman, West Henrietta, New York
Ms. Helen Samuels and Mr. Greg Anderson, Chicago, Illinois
Dr. Gonzalo Sanchez, Fort Pierre, South Dakota
Mr. Michael Sandalow, Skokie, Illinois
Ms. Lucie Sandel, Homewood, Illinois
Mr. James L. Sanders and Ms. Emma A. Loredo, Cedar Hill, Texas
Ms. Zabrina Santiago, Wheaton, Illinois
Ms. Ljubica Sarenac, Chicago, Illinois
Dr. Shahan Sarrafian, Skokie, Illinois
Ms. Judith Sayad and Mr. Lorne Temes, Chicago, Illinois
Mr. Jack Scaparro, New York, New York
Mr. R. Thomas Schaub, Pittsburgh, Pennsylvania
Mr. Martin Scheckner, Miami, Florida
Mrs. Sheldon K. Schiff, Chicago, Illinois
Mr. Steven Schilderout, Youngstown, Ohio
Ms. Hilda Schlatter, Oak Park, Illinois
Ms. Denise Schmandt-Besserat, Austin, Texas
Mr. Paul and Mrs. Nell Schneider, Oak Park, Illinois
Ms. Margaret Schröeder, Chicago, Illinois
Mr. David Schultz, Omaha, Nebraska
Mr. Warren C. Schultz, Chicago, Illinois
Mrs. Anne Rose and Dr. Gebhard F. Schumacher, Homewood, Illinois
Ms. Paula Scully, Manahawkin, New Jersey
Seecago Tours, Inc., Crete, Illinois
Mr. Richard Sefton, Posey, California
Mrs. Charlotte Sere, Chicago, Illinois
Dr. Byron E. Shafer, Yonkers, New York
Ms. Judith Shaltry, Deerfield, Illinois
Dr. Arthur M. Shapiro and Mr. Bernard S. Shapiro, Chicago, Illinois
Isaac B. and Ruth Shapiro, Chicago, Illinois
Mr. William Shapiro, Wilmette, Illinois
Dr. Peter G. Sheldrick, Canada
Ms. Ki Shih, Chicago, Illinois
Mr. Randy Shonkwiler, Chicago, Illinois
Ms. Roberta and Mr. Howard Siegel, Chicago, Illinois
Ms. Janet Silvers and Ms. Teri Tebelman, Burke, Virginia
Peter and Charlotte Silvers, Lake Mills, Wisconsin
Prof. Bernice Kern Simon, Chicago, Illinois
Ms. Mae Simon, Chicago, Illinois
Ms. Mary Small, Kensington, California
Ms. Bright Smith and Mr. Carl Sandrock, Bolinas, California
Mr. Gary N. Smith, Sacramento, California
Mr. Joe Smolik, Switzerland
Mr. Eugene Soltes, Chicago, Illinois
Miss Nancy A. Spencer, Chicago, Illinois
Mr. David A. Spetrino, Wilmington, North Carolina
Dr. Wolfgang Spindler, Park Ridge, Illinois
Mr. Richardson L. and Mrs. Janice B. Spofford, Chicago, Illinois
Mr. Fred E. Stafford and Mrs. Barbara Maria Stafford, Chicago, Illinois
Mr. Paul Stanwick, New York, New York

HONOR ROLL OF DONORS AND MEMBERS

Friends ($1–$99) (cont.)

Ms. Jody Stawicki, Chicago, Illinois
Mr. John Gerald Steenken, Chicago, Illinois
Mr. Richard Stein, Oak Lawn, Illinois
Mr. Bob Steiner, Glenview, Illinois
Mr. Roger Stelle, Trout Valley, Illinois
Ms. Gwen Stern, Chicago, Illinois
Mr. Thomas Sternau and Mrs. Phyllis Sternau, New York, New York
The Honorable Adlai E. Stevenson III and Mrs. Nancy A. Stevenson, Chicago, Illinois
Ms. Barbara Stewart, Nashville, Tennessee
Mr. Robert N. Stewart, Columbus, Indiana
Dr. W. Forrest Stinespring and Mrs. Marjorie Moretz Stinespring, Chicago, Illinois
Dr. Houston Hobson Stokes and Mrs. Diana A. Stokes, Chicago, Illinois
Professor Geoffrey Stone, Chicago, Illinois
Mr. Herbert Storck, Canada
Mr. Edward P. Stratford, Trumbull, Connecticut
Dr. Jonathan Strauss, Chicago, Illinois
Ms. Holly Strebe, Grand Blanc, Michigan
Clay W. Stuckey, DDS, Bedford, Indiana
Dr. Rabi Sulayman and Mrs. Aida Sulayman, Chicago, Illinois
Ms. Mary D. Sullivan and Mr. Joseph T. Sullivan, Oak Park, Illinois
Mr. Michael K. Sullivan, Madison, Wisconsin
Mr. William M. Sumner and Ms. Kathleen J. Sumner, Columbus, Ohio
Dr. Ronald F. G. Sweet, Canada
Mr. Stuart Swenson, Dyer, Indiana
Mr. Warren Swindell, Baton Rouge, Louisiana
Mr. John Taaffe, Chicago, Illinois
Rev. Shunjo Takahashi, Evanston, Illinois
Grace Takata, Park Forest, Illinois
Mrs. Faye E. Takeuchi, Canada
Mrs. Lorna Tang, Chicago, Illinois
Mr. Robert M. Taras, Las Vegas, Nevada
Ms. Betsy Teeter, San Francisco, California
Mr. George M. Telthorst, Bloomington, Indiana
Dr. Eric Terman and Ms. Mari Philipsborn, Chicago, Illinois
Mr. Joost Dupon and Ms. Lieve Teugels, Chicago, Illinois
Mrs. Richard J. Thain, Chicago, Illinois
Ms. Peggy Tharp, Atlanta, Georgia
The Quiet Investor Inc, Willowbrook, Illinois
Mr. Gregory Thomas, Grandview, Texas
R. R. Thomason, Tohatchi, New Mexico
Mr. Tigerman and Ms. McCurry, Chicago, Illinois
Ms. Marianne Tomita McDonald, Oakland, California
William M and Ann L. Toneff, Brecksville, Ohio
Levon K. Topouzian, M.D., and Nancy B. Topouzian, Ph.D., Skokie, Illinois
Mrs. Pramerudee Townsend, Chicago, Illinois
Ms. Marie-Claude Tremouille, Italy
Ms. Cynthia Tripp, Las Vegas, Nevada
Ms. Tatyana Tsirlin, Woodridge, Illinois
Ms. Patricia Tuchman, Champaign, Illinois
Ms. Janet Tuffing, Evanston, Illinois
Ms. Tanya Tuffing, Austin, Texas
Mrs. Nancy E. Turchi, Indian River, Michigan
Ms. Marilyn Underwood, Chicago, Illinois

HONOR ROLL OF DONORS AND MEMBERS

Friends ($1–$99) (cont.)

Mr. Jason Ur, Cambridge, Massachusetts
Dr. John D. Utley, Dixon, Illinois
Ms. Annelize van der Ryst, South Africa
Margaret Van Wissink, Mount Prospect, Illinois
Mr. John S. Vandenberg, Jenison, Michigan
Ms. Deloris Vanderhoof, Laingsburg, Michigan
Mr. K. R. Veenhof, Netherlands
Ms. Judith Vessely, Berwyn, Illinois
Ms. Erin Villareal, Chicago, Illinois
Mr. Gregory L. Vogel, Naperville, Illinois
Mr. Don and Mary W. Wacker, Issaquah, Washington
Mrs. Lynne M. Wait and Mr. Douglas Baum, Homewood, Illinois
Mr. Doug Walter and Ms. Pam Walter, Chicago, Illinois
Ms. Sarah Walter, Homewood, Illinois
Ms. Stephanie Walters, Park Ridge, Illinois
Dr. Kelvin Ward, Chicago, Illinois
Mr. John F. Warnock, Mason City, Illinois
Mr. Mark Watkins, Mint Hill, North Carolina
Mr. John Watrous, Beloit, Wisconsin
Mr. Leroy Webb and Ms. Carolyn Webb, Spanaway, Washington
Ms. Dorothy Anne Wedner, Winnetka, Illinois
Mr. Norman Weinberg and Mrs. Eve Weinberg, Chicago, Illinois
Mr. Steven Weingartner and Mrs. Sally Weingartner, La Grange Park, Illinois
Professor June M. Weisberger and Professor Converse H. Blanchard, Madison, Wisconsin
Mr. Erwin and Mrs. Estelle Weiss, Northbrook, Illinois
Ms. Nancy Wenzler, Glendale, Wisconsin
Mr. Arthur P. Wheatley, East Chicago, Indiana
Mrs. Carmel Whitcomb, Decatur, Georgia
Mr. John F. Whitehouse, Australia
Mr. Ronald Wideman, Chicago, Illinois
Mr. William D. Wiener, Chicago, Illinois
Dr. Henry Wildberger, Mount Prospect, Illinois
Mr. Terry G. Wilfong, Ann Arbor, Michigan
Ms. Alexandra Helen Wilkinson, United Kingdom
Mr. Jon Nicholson Will, Chicago, Illinois
Ms. Emily Marie Williams, Canada
Mr. Andrew Wilson and Ms. Christine Wilson, Chicago, Illinois
Mrs. Muriel B. Wilson, Chicago, Illinois
Ms. Nancy O. Wilson, Munroe Falls, Ohio
Dr. Robert W. Wissler and Mrs. Elizabeth A. Wissler, Illinois
Ms. Corin Wood, Fraser, Colorado
Mr. Daniel Wood, Three Rivers, Michigan
Ms. Monica Wood, Chicago, Illinois
Ms. Jane F. Woodruff, Pleasant Valley, Missouri
Mr. James D. Worrell, Raleigh, North Carolina
Ms. Carol Ann Woskey, Philadelphia, Pennsylvania
Ms. Rita P. Wright, Manchester, Vermont
Ms. Louise M. Wrobel, Chicago, Illinois
Ms. Claire Yasher, Chicago, Illinois
Ms. Carolyn Yates, Chicago, Illinois
Mrs. Deborah M. Yerman, Citrus Springs, Florida
Ms. Bonnie Young, Chandler, Arizona
Ms. Susan N. Young, La Grange, Illinois

Friends ($1–$99) (cont.)

Mr. Kenneth Yu, Chicago, Illinois
Ms. Susan L. Zayac, New York, New York
Mr. Emil Edward Zbella, Chicago, Illinois
Mrs. Anna M. Zelisko, Hinsdale, Illinois
Prof. Wendy Zhang, Chicago, Illinois
Ms. Barbara Zoub, Chicago, Illinois
Mr. Gregory Zuck, Estes Park, Colorado

MEMORIAL

In Memory of Larry Scheff

Carol and Dr. Erwin P. Barrington, Lincolnwood, Illinois
Lylus Brash, Chicago, Illinois
Chris and Motria Caudill, Chicago, Illinois
Jean P. Cioffi, Pompton Plains, New Jersey
Lila L. Cohen, Valparaiso, Illinois
Cornfield and Feldman, Chicago, Illinois
Drs. Adilman, Katin, Lubar, Ltd., Northbrook, Illinois
Endodontics Limited, Chicago, Illinois
Mr. S. Cody Engle, Chicago, Illinois
Sylvia and Jim Furner, Chicago, Illinois
Ms. Leah Goldberg, Chicago, Illinois
Mrs. Betty Goldiamond, Chicago, Illinois
Mrs. Deborah G. and Mr. Philip Halpern, Chicago, Illinois
Arden Handler, Evanston, Illinois
Dr. Sylvia Hood-Washington, Winfield, Illinois
Margit Javor, Chicago, Illinois
Mrs. Bette Kalichman, Chicago, Illinois
Jacqueline Kinnaman, Chicago, Illinois
Mr. David Lubell, Chicago, Illinois
Leslie Nickels, Evanston, Illinois
Dr. Allen L. and Mrs. Amy C. Oseroff, Greenville, North Carolina
Mrs. Rita Picken, Chicago, Illinois
Kristin Rankin, Chicago, Illinois
Ms. Claudia Roberson, Chicago, Illinois
Mr. and Mrs. Burton H. Robin, Chicago, Illinois
Miriam Rogers-Singer, Clayton, Missouri
Ms. Betsy Rubin, Chicago, Illinois
Tobi Jean Saidel, Lyons, Colorado
Mrs. Dorothy Scheff, Chicago, Illinois
Mr. Steven Schilderout, Youngstown, Ohio
Mr. Paul and Mrs. Nell Schneider, Oak Park, Illinois
Ms. Lillian H. Schwartz, Chicago, Illinois
Isaac B. and Ruth Shapiro, Chicago, Illinois
Professor Bernece Simon, Chicago, Illinois
Anne Slavich, Chicago, Illinois
Grace Takata, Park Forest, Illinois
William M. and Ann L. Toneff, Brecksville, Ohio
Mr. Norbert Voit, Chicago, Illinois
Mr. Donald Yesnik, Arlington, Virginia

In Memory of Peggy Wick

Ms. Denise Browning, Chicago, Illinois
Ms. Hazel Cramer, Darien, Illinois
Mr. David L. Crabb and Mrs. Dorothy Mixter Crabb, Chicago, Illinois
Dr. Erl Dordal, Atlanta, Georgia
Ms. Ruth Hallowell, Westwood, Massachusetts
Ms. Anne and Mr. John Newton Natick, Massachusetts
Mrs. Anne Rose and Dr. Gebhard F. Schumacher, Homewood, Illinois
Mrs. Elizabeth Spiegel, Chicago, Illinois
Mr. Jon Nicholson Will, Chicago, Illinois

In Memory of William J. O. Roberts
Mr. and Mrs. George L. Estes III, West Hartford, Connecticut
Mrs. William J. O. Roberts, Lake Forest, Illinois

In Memory of Marion Cowan
Mrs. Susan S. Conklin, Grand Rapids, Michigan

HONORARY

In Honor of Tom Van Eynde
Ms. Ingrid E. Gould and Dr. Robert Hsiung, Chicago, Illinois
Mr. Laurence Dean Hill, Chicago, Illinois
Mr. Glenn Klinksiek, Chicago, Illinois
Professor Gene Mazenko, Chicago, Illinois
Mr. Donald H. Levy and Ms. Susan Miller, Chicago, Illinois
Mr. Keith and Mrs. Anne S. Moffat, Chicago, Illinois
Dr. Jonathan Moss, Chicago, Illinois
Mr. Casey James Murray, Crown Point, Indiana
John F. Philipps, Dyer, Indiana
Mr. Robert Rosner and Mrs. Marsha Rosner, Chicago, Illinois
Professor Geoffrey Stone, Chicago, Illinois

In Honor of Ray Tindel's Retirement
Mrs. Joan Barghusen and Dr. Herbert Barghusen, Portage, Indiana
Ms. Aimee Drolet, Los Angeles, California
Mrs. Cynthia Echols, Chicago, Illinois
Mrs. Joseph N. Grimshaw, Wilmette, Illinois
Mrs. Rita Picken, Chicago, Illinois
Mr. James J. Richerson and Ms. Judy Lee, Peoria, Illinois

In Honor of Anne Schumacher's Birthday
Mr. Joseph N. Darguzas and Ms. Christine A. Toohey, Homewood, Illinois
Mr. Henry A. and Mrs. Billie Black Hauser, Homewood, Illinois
Arthur A. and Patricia D. Johannes, Homewood, Illinois
Ms. Masako I. Matsumoto, Napa, California
Dr. Ruprecht and Ms. Elizabeth Nitschke, Middleton, Wisconsin
Erika O. Parker, M.D., Evanston, Illinois
Ms. Kathleen Picken, Chicago, Illinois
Mrs. Rita Picken, Chicago, Illinois
Mrs. Deborah Shefner, Chicago, Illinois
Ms. Emily Teeter, Chicago, Illinois

In Honor of O. J. Sopranos
Mr. Karl H. Velde, Jr., Lake Forest, Illinois

HONOR ROLL OF DONORS AND MEMBERS

In Honor of Elizabeth Speigel
Mrs. Deborah Shefner, Chicago, Illinois

In Honor of Roger Isaacs
Mr. John P. and Ms. Jan Isaacs Henry, Colorado Springs, Colorado

In Honor of Dr. Salim Nasser
Maria L. Rydstedt, Grand Rapids, Michigan

In Honor of Raja Khuri's 70th Birthday
Mrs. Terry Friedman, Chicago, Illinois

In Honor of Dennis Campbell's Elevation to Ph.D.
Andrea Dudek, Orland Park, Illinois

In Honor of Gabrielle Novacek's Elevation to Ph.D.
Andrea Dudek, Orland Park, Illinois

ORIENTAL INSTITUTE VISITING COMMITTEE
2006–2007

Janet W. Helman, Chair

Mrs. James W. Alsdorf	Donald H. J. Hermann
Joan Armstrong†	Marshall M. Holleb
Gretel Braidwood	Doris B. Holleb
Alan R. Brodie	Neil J. King
Jean McGrew Brown	Daniel A. Lindley, Jr.
Marian Cowan†	Lucia Woods Lindley
Matthew Dickie	Jill Carlotta Maher
Andrea Dudek	Janina Marks
Emily Huggins Fine	John W. McCarter, Jr.
Dr. Marjorie M. Fisher	Roger Nelson
Margaret E. Foorman	Muriel Kallis Newman
Joan Fortune	Rita T. Picken
Mrs. Isak V. Gerson	Crennan M. Ray
Isak V. Gerson	Patrick Regnery
Margaret H. Grant	William J. O. Roberts†
Mary L. Gray	John W. Rowe
Mary J. Grimshaw	Robert G. Schloerb
Diana L. Grodzins	Lois M. Schwartz
Lewis Gruber	Mary G. Shea
Misty Gruber	Toni Smith
Howard G. Haas	O. J. Sopranos, Vice-Chair
Deborah Halpern	Mari Terman
Thomas Heagy	Marjorie K. Webster
Arthur L. Herbst, M.D.	Anna White

FACULTY AND STAFF OF THE ORIENTAL INSTITUTE
July 1, 2006–June 30, 2007

EMERITUS FACULTY

Lanny Bell, Associate Professor Emeritus of Egyptology

Robert D. Biggs, Professor Emeritus of Assyriology & Editor of Journal of Near Eastern Studies
r-biggs@uchicago.edu, 702-9540

John A. Brinkman, Charles H. Swift Distinguished Service Professor Emeritus of Mesopotamian History
j-brinkman@uchicago.edu, 702-9545

Miguel Civil, Professor Emeritus of Sumerology
m-civil@uchicago.edu, 702-9542

Gene B. Gragg, Professor Emeritus of Near Eastern Languages
g-gragg@uchicago.edu, 702-9511

Harry A. Hoffner, Jr., John A. Wilson Professor Emeritus of Hittitology & Co-editor of Chicago Hittite Dictionary Project
h-hoffner@uchicago.edu, 702-9527

William M. Sumner, Professor Emeritus, Archaeology
sumner.1@osu.edu

Edward F. Wente, Professor Emeritus of Egyptology
e-wente@uchicago.edu, 702-9539

FACULTY

Fred M. Donner, Professor of Islamic History
f-donner@uchicago.edu, 702-9544

Peter F. Dorman, Professor of Egyptology & Chairman of the Department of Near Eastern Languages and Civilizations
p-dorman@uchicago.edu, 702-9533

Walter T. Farber, Professor of Assyriology
w-farber@uchicago.edu, 702-9546

McGuire Gibson, Professor of Mesopotamian Archaeology
m-gibson@uchicago.edu, 702-9525

Petra Goedegebuure, Assistant Professor of Hittitology
pgoedegebuure@uchicago.edu, 702-9550

Norman Golb, Ludwig Rosenberger Professor in Jewish History and Civilization
n-golb@uchicago.edu, 702-9526

Stephen P. Harvey, Assistant Professor of Egyptian Archaeology (until 12/31/06)

FACULTY AND STAFF

Rebecca Hasselbach, Assistant Professor of Comparative Semitics
hasselb@uchicago.edu, 834-3290

Janet H. Johnson, Morton D. Hull Distinguished Service Professor of Egyptology & Editor of Chicago Demotic Dictionary Project
j-johnson@uchicago.edu, 702-9530

W. Raymond Johnson, Associate Professor (Research Associate) & Field Director, Epigraphic Survey
wr-johnson@uchicago.edu, 834-4355

Walter E. Kaegi, Professor of Byzantine-Islamic Studies
kwal@midway.uchicago.edu, 702-8346, 702-8397

Dennis G. Pardee, Professor of Northwest Semitic Philology
d-pardee@uchicago.edu, 702-9541

Seth Richardson, Assistant Professor of Ancient Near Eastern History
seth1@uchicago.edu, 702-9552

Robert K. Ritner, Professor of Egyptology
r-ritner@uchicago.edu, 702-9547

Martha T. Roth, Professor of Assyriology & Editor-in-Charge of Chicago Assyrian Dictionary Project
m-roth@uchicago.edu, 702-9551

David Schloen, Associate Professor of Syro-Palestinian Archaeology
d-schloen@uchicago.edu, 702-1382

Gil J. Stein, Professor of Near Eastern Archaeology & Director of the Oriental Institute
gstein@uchicago.edu, 702-4098

Matthew W. Stolper, John A. Wilson Professor of Assyriology
m-stolper@uchicago.edu, 702-9553

Theo P. J. van den Hout, Professor of Hittite and Anatolian Languages & Executive Editor of Chicago Hittite Dictionary Project
tvdhout@uchicago.edu, 834-4688, 702-9527

Donald Whitcomb, Associate Professor (Research Associate), Islamic and Medieval Archaeology
d-whitcomb@uchicago.edu, 702-9530

Christopher Woods, Assistant Professor of Sumerology
woods@uchicago.edu, 834-8560

K. Aslıhan Yener, Associate Professor of Archaeology
a-yener@uchicago.edu, 702-0568

FACULTY AND STAFF

RESEARCH ASSOCIATES

Abbas Alizadeh, Senior Research Associate, Iranian Prehistoric Project
  a-alizadeh@uchicago.edu, 702-9531

Richard H. Beal, Senior Research Associate, Chicago Hittite Dictionary Project
  r-beal@uchicago.edu, 702-3644

Scott Branting, Director, CAMEL Laboratory
  branting@uchicago.edu, 834-1152

Nicole Brisch, Postdoctoral Fellow (from 9/18/06 to 8/31/07)
  Nbrisch@uchicago.edu, 702-3291

Stuart Creason, Research Associate, Syriac Manuscript Project
  s-creason@uchicago.edu, 834-8348

Geoff Emberling, Research Associate & Museum Director
  geoffe@uchicago.edu, 702-9863

Gertrud Farber, Research Associate, Sumerian Lexicon Project
  g-farber@uchicago.edu, 702-9548

John L. Foster, Research Associate, Egyptian Poetry
  jlfoster@uchicago.edu, (847) 475-2613

François P. Gaudard, Research Associate, Epigraphic Survey & Chicago Demotic Dictionary Project
  fgaudard@uchicago.edu, 702-9524, 702-9528

Ronald Gorny, Research Associate, Alişar Regional Project
  rlg2@uchicago.edu, 702-8624

Thomas A. Holland, Research Associate, Tell es-Sweyhat Project & Co-Managing Editor, Publications Office
  t-holland@uchicago.edu, 702-1240

Carrie Hritz, Research Associate, Ayvalipinar Archaeological Project

Charles E. Jones, Research Associate
  cejo@uchicago.edu, 702-9537

Nicola Laneri, Postdoctoral Fellow (from 09/01/05 to 08/31/06)

Mark Lehner, Research Associate, Giza Plateau Mapping Project
  MarkLehner@aol.com

Carol Meyer, Research Associate, Bir Umm Fawakhir Project
  c-meyer@uchicago.edu

Jennie Myers, Research Associate, Chicago Assyrian Dictionary Project
  jmyers1@uchicago.edu

Clemens D. Reichel, Research Associate, Diyala Project
  cdreiche@uchicago.edu, 702-1352

Abdul-Massih Saadi, Research Associate, Syriac Manuscript Project
  asaadi@nd.edu, (574) 631-8419

FACULTY AND STAFF

Iman Saca, Research Associate
isaca@uchicago.edu

Mohammed Moin Sadeq, Research Associate (until 08/14/05)

John Sanders, Senior Research Associate & Head, Computer Laboratory
jc-sanders@uchicago.edu, 702-0989

Oğuz Soysal, Senior Research Associate, Chicago Hittite Dictionary Project
o-soysal@uchicago.edu, 702-3644

Benjamin Studevant-Hickman, Research Associate, MASS Project (from 10/24/05)
Studeven@uchicago.edu, 834-2249

Emily Teeter, Research Associate & Coordinator of Special Exhibits
e-teeter@uchicago.edu, 702-1062

Raymond Tindel, Research Associate (from 06/15/07)
R-tindel@uchicago.edu

Magnus Widell, Research Associate, Head Research Archivist
widell@uchicago.edu, 702-9537

Bruce Williams, Research Associate (from 01/01/06)
Bbwillia@uchicago.edu, 702-3686

Karen L. Wilson, Research Associate
k-wilson@uchicago.edu

STAFF

Joshua Best, Assistant to the Director (from 02/01/07 to 04/02/07)

Olivia Boyd, Assistant to the Director (until 01/14/07)

Denise Browning, Manager, Suq
d-browning1@uchicago.edu, 702-9509

Marie Bryan, Librarian, Epigraphic Survey
702-9524

Steven Camp, Executive Director
shcamp@uchicago.edu, 702-1404

Jessica Caracci, Museum Programs Assistant, Museum Education
j-caracci@uchicago.edu, 702-9507

Laura D'Alessandro, Head, Conservation Laboratory, Museum
l-dalessandro@uchicago.edu, 702-9519

Vanessa Davies, Epigrapher, Epigraphic Survey
vdavies@uchicago.edu, 702-9524

Margaret DeJong, Artist, Epigraphic Survey
702-9524

Christina DiCerbo, Artist, Epigraphic Survey
702-9524

FACULTY AND STAFF

Markus Dohner, Museum Installation Coordinator, Museum (until 07/09/06)

Catherine Dueñas, Volunteer Services Coordinator, Volunteer Office
c-duenas@uchicago.edu, 702-1845

Wendy Ennes, Teacher Services and e-Learning Coordinator, Museum Education
wennes@uchicago.edu, 834-7606

Amir Sumaka'i Fink, Research Professional, The Tell Atchana (Alalakh) Project
asumakai@uchicago.edu, 702-1407

Terry Friedman, Volunteer Services Coordinator, Volunteer Office
et-friedman@uchicago.edu, 702-1845

Jean Grant, Photographer, Museum
jm-grant@uchicago.edu, 702-9517

Lotfi Hassan, Conservator, Epigraphic Survey
702-9524

Carla Hosein, Financial Manager
cchosein@uchicago.edu, 834-9886

Monica Hudak, Conservator
mhudak@uchicago.edu, 702-9519

Thomas James, Curatorial Assistant, Museum
trjames@uchicago.edu, 834-8950

Helen Jacquet, Egyptologist Consultant, Epigraphic Survey
702-9524

Jean Jacquet, Architect Consultant, Epigraphic Survey
702-9524

Hiroko Kariya, Conservator, Epigraphic Survey
702-9524

Jen Kimpton, Epigrapher, Epigraphic Survey
702-9524

Yarko Kobylecky, Photographer, Epigraphic Survey
702-9524

Maria Krasinski, Membership Coordinator, Membership Office (until 12/01/06)

Carole Krucoff, Head, Public and Museum Education, Museum Education
c-krucoff@uchicago.edu, 702-9507

John Larson, Museum Archivist, Museum
ja-larson@uchicago.edu, 702-9924

Susan Lezon, Photo Archivist and Photographer, Epigraphic Survey
702-9524

Erik Lindahl, Gallery Preparator, Museum
lindahl@uchicago.edu, 702-9516

FACULTY AND STAFF

Adam Lubin, Security and Visitor Services Supervisor (from 11/13/06)
alubin@uchicago.edu, 702-5112

Jill Carlotta Maher, Assistant to the Director of the Epigraphic Survey
702-9524

J. Brett McClain, Epigrapher, Epigraphic Survey
jbmcclai@uchicago.edu, 702-9524

Helen McDonald, Assistant Registrar, Museum
helenmcd@uchicago.edu, 702-9518

Linda McLarnan, Manuscript Editor, Chicago Assyrian Dictionary Project (until 10/29/06)

Kathleen Mineck, Research Project Professional, Chicago Hittite Dictionary Project
kmineck@uchicago.edu, 702-9527

Marlin Nassim, Accountant, Epigraphic Survey
702-9524

Susan Osgood, Artist, Epigraphic Survey
702-9524

Safinaz Ouri, Financial Manager, Epigraphic Survey
702-9524

Mariana Perlinac, Assistant to the Director (from 05/01/07)
oi-administration@uchicago.edu, 834-8098

Conor Power, Structural Engineer, Epigraphic Survey
702-9524

Dany Roy, Stonecutter, Epigraphic Survey
702-9524

Sarah Sapperstein, Membership Coordinator (from 01/31/07)
oi-membership@uchicago.edu, 834-9777

Leslie Schramer, Associate Editor, Publications Office
leslie@uchicago.edu, 702-5967

Margaret Schröeder, Security Supervisor, Museum (until 08/31/06)
Photo Research Assistant, Museum (from 09/01/06)
m-schroeder@uchicago.edu, 702-9522

Elinor Smith, Photo Archives Registrar, Epigraphic Survey
702-9524

John Stewart, Conservator, Epigraphic Survey
702-9524

Raymond Tindel, Registrar and Senior Curator, Museum (until 06/04/07)
r-tindel@uchicago.edu, 702-9518

Thomas Urban, Senior Editor and Co-Managing Editor, Publications Office
t-urban@uchicago.edu, 702-5967

FACULTY AND STAFF

Paula von Bechtolsheim, Managing Editor, Journal of Near Eastern Studies
702-9592

Alison Whyte, Assistant Conservator, Conservation Laboratory, Museum
aawhyte@uchicago.edu, 702-9519

Monica Witczak, Development Director, Development Office
mwitczak@uchicago.edu, 834-9775

INFORMATION

The Oriental Institute
1155 East 58th Street
Chicago, Illinois 60637

Museum gallery hours:
 Tuesday and Thursday to Saturday 10:00 AM–6:00 PM
 Wednesday 10:00 AM–8:30 PM
 Sunday 12:00 NOON–6:00 PM

Telephone Numbers (Area Code 773) and Electronic Addresses

Administrative Office, oi-admin@uchicago.edu, 702-9514
Archaeology Laboratory, 702-1407
Assyrian Dictionary Project, 702-9543
Computer Laboratory, 702-9538
Conservation Laboratory, 702-9519
Department of Near Eastern Languages and Civilizations, 702-9512
Demotic Dictionary Project, 702-9528
Development Office, 834-9775
Director's Office, 834-8098
Epigraphic Survey, 702-9524
Executive Director's Office, 702-1404
Facsimile, 702-9853
Hittite Dictionary Project, 702-9527
Journal of Near Eastern Studies, 702-9592
Membership Office, oi-membership@uchicago.edu, 834-9777
Museum Archives, 702-9520
Museum Education and Public Programs, oi-education@uchicago.edu, 702-9507
Museum Information, 702-9520
Museum Office, oi-museum@uchicago.edu, 702-9520
Museum Registration, 702-9518
Publications Editorial Office, oi-publications@uchicago.edu, 702-5967
Research Archives, oi-library@uchicago.edu, 702-9537
Security, 702-9522
Suq Gift and Book Shop, 702-9510
Suq Office, 702-9509
Volunteer Guides, 702-1845

World-Wide Web Address

oi.uchicago.edu